D1131228

WHAT
WE
LOST

This QR code will direct you to www.WhatWELost.com.

The site was established by the publisher as a place for readers to access exclusive interviews, video content, and key documents including a full Appendix.

We will notify you by email of updates if you sign up for more information.

For access to **Appendix,** please use the security code WWL!

What WE Lost is also available as an Audiobook.

361
.763
209
71
RAN

MC

OSHAWA PUBLIC LIBRARIES

39364902407423

pr06504565

Rangwala, Tawfiq S.
What WE lost : inside the attack on Cana

May 12, 2022

WHAT
WE
LOST

Inside the Attack on Canada's Largest Children's Charity

TAWFIQ S. RANGWALA

WITH A FOREWORD BY THE RIGHT HONOURABLE KIM CAMPBELL

What WE Lost
Inside the Attack on Canada's Largest Children's Charity

© Ottawa, 2022, Optimum Publishing International and Tawfiq S. Rangwala, First Edition
Published by Optimum Publishing International, a division of JF Moore Lithographers Inc.
All rights reserved. No part of this publication may be reproduced in any form or by any
means whatsoever or stored in a data base without permission in writing from the publisher,
except by a reviewer who may quote passages of customary brevity in review.

LIBRARY AND ARCHIVES CANADA CATALOGUING IN PUBLICATION

Trade Paperback
ISBN: 978-0-88890-315-0

Hardcover Edition
ISBN 978-0-88890-320-4

Digital Version of the book is also available
ISBN: 978-0-88890-321-1

Names: Rangwala, Tawfiq S. (author)
Title: What WE lost : inside the attack on canada's largest children's charity

Printed and bound in Canada
US edition printed and bound in the USA

For information on rights or any submissions please write to Optimum:

Optimum Publishing International
144 Rochester Avenue
Toronto, Ontario
M4N 1P1
Dean Baxendale, President

www.optimumpublishinginternational.com
Twitter @opibooks

Photo credits: Every effort has been made to identify copyright holders. Any oversights will
be corrected in future editions. Insert 1: 1–6, Kielburger family; 9, 10, WE Charity/Vita
Amati; 13, Dzis family; 21, 22, WE Charity/Sara Cornthwaite; 23, WE Charity/Chris
Cameron; 27, WE Charity/David Thai; 31, 33, WE Charity/Chela Crinnion. Insert 2: 4, 5, 8,
ParlVU; 9, WE Charity/Ryan Bolton; 15, 16, ParlVU.

OPTIMUM
PUBLISHING
INTERNATIONAL
MONTRÉAL | TORONTO

To my parents, who have always inspired me to act,
my son, who inspired me to recount what has been lost,
and my wife, who encouraged me when this project
seemed most daunting

CONTENTS

FOREWORD

BY THE RIGHT HONOURABLE KIM CAMPBELL, NINETEENTH PRIME MINISTER OF CANADA

The key lessons learned in our youth are irreplaceable. They are essential in developing our values and in shaping our identity. Two of my earliest lessons have come into sharp focus for me since the so-called WE Charity Scandal unfolded in 2020.

The first is the importance of answering a call to serve. This was instilled in me by my mother and father, who both enlisted in the Canadian Forces in the Second World War. My father joined the Canadian army in 1939 and would later fight and be wounded in Italy. When women became eligible to serve in the Canadian navy in 1943, my mother became a WREN. After training as a wireless operator, she tracked the transmissions of German U-boats in the North Atlantic and the Gulf of St. Lawrence. Their service—and their stories of the friends who didn't "come back" after the war—was the backdrop of my childhood.

Another lesson from my childhood is more personal. A boy attended a birthday party at our house and was convinced he had left his toy behind. My mother was falsely accused of hiding it, and I recall how much pain this caused her and how hurt she felt. The truth of her observation that there is nothing worse than being falsely accused has stayed with me and been borne out often in my observations of life.

WE Charity never hesitated to try to serve when called upon. That was certainly true with respect to the ill-fated Canada Student Service Grant (CSSG). It is sad to ponder how much could have been accomplished with the CSSG. That sadness is exacerbated by the fact that neither the government nor any private organization proved able to deliver the program when WE Charity was forced to cede administration of it, leaving young people high and dry in the middle of the COVID pandemic.

The WE Charity Scandal is a story of how disinformation can take on a life of its own. The results were tragic and the hardest hit were young people.

WE Charity became collateral damage in a partisan fight. Being the very battlefield of a struggle that has nothing to do with you is to be in a bad position. But it is even worse if more and more people jump on to seize the opportunity for publicity (their precious fifteen minutes of fame). In this case, social media, the accelerated time frame in which attacks occurred, and ultimately, the lack of sober deliberation had swift and fatal repercussions for the charity. It is quick and easy to attack, to make an accusation, true or false, and disparage someone. Answering and refuting always takes more time. There is an old saying that a lie is halfway around the world before the truth can get its pants on.

Today, integrity in our public discourse matters more than ever. So much of what happens online is designed to appeal to short attention spans and obscure the complete picture. Worse yet, lies and disinformation are often weaponized to attack one's opponents. When politicians join the fray and perpetuate lies online, disinformation can quickly gain traction in the mass media and create a narrative divorced from reality. The frightening proliferation of disinformation disempowers us all. That is why entities such as Facebook and Twitter have had to take the step of curbing political speech that is clearly designed to mislead. There are casualties when you don't follow the truth.

WE, a wonderful charity that was built in Canada by a twelve-year-old boy who called on young people to stand tall and become agents of positive change, was destroyed. WE Charity was admired the world over, and I watched with pride as even influential figures outside of Canada like Oprah Winfrey saw something special to be celebrated and a movement to be joined. That some in Canada preferred instead to pounce is a disheartening reflection of our tendency to want to cut down tall poppies. Politicians and media outlets reflexively asked: "Who are these

Kielburger brothers?" "Who do they think they are?" Tall poppy syndrome is very real.

That is why this book is so essential. It is a sober, fact-based account of how and what occurred to pulverize one of this country's foremost charities. I have an abiding faith in the ability of the Canadian people to draw fair-minded and balanced conclusions. But they must be presented with the facts to be able to do so. Not *some* facts designed to suit a particular agenda—*all* the facts. In my view, that has not been the case with respect to WE Charity.

In the chapters that follow, you will discover what the headlines and political sound bites did not convey. You will come to understand WE: what it did, how it worked, and what it stood for. And you will finally hear from the many previously unheard voices—students, teachers, volunteers, staff, donors, and those touched by WE's efforts worldwide.

If you have bought into the negative narrative about WE Charity, I challenge you to read this book.

I am not a remote observer of the values that WE Charity promoted and instilled. I watched its growth from Free the Children, with its global impact on child labour laws. When Craig and Marc Kielburger were invited to give the Lougheed College Lecture at the Peter Lougheed Leadership College at the University of Alberta in 2016, we had to relocate to a much larger hall when we were overwhelmed by the huge number of young people who had been touched by WE and wanted to hear the two young men who had inspired them to be their best.

I have seen the organization in action overseas. I stood with Margaret Kenyatta, the First Lady of Kenya, at the grand opening of WE College in rural Narok County, Kenya. The college offered the first generation of young Maasai and Kipsigis women and men the chance to complete their education without having to leave home for big cities, which for so many is not even a possibility. The pride I felt at being present for such a momentous accomplishment is immeasurable. The outpouring of gratitude from the students, teachers, and families for what Canada had helped them create in their community was tremendous.

Closer to home, I was moved to hear young people on the WE Day stage share their stories of being bullied online: how they faced it with support, and how they vowed to help other students do the same and stop it. The same is true with respect to so many pressing issues, like mental health, the environment, and gender equality.

When concerns about the charity surfaced, I refused to form a judgment without facts. I have personally listened to experts, auditors, and independent reviewers. All confirmed that WE Charity operated transparently and properly. You will learn the same in this book.

With decades of experience in public life, I have witnessed how service and the good works of charities can effect real change. WE Charity was a shining example of this. Its end in Canada should give us all great pause.

There is also a broader lesson here. I have worked around the world, and what we have in Canada is precious. It is not every country that has such a strong commitment to neighbours helping each other, volunteering, and a vibrant civil society. But that does not happen by accident; it is what we teach our children. "WE" was always a Canadian value. Teaching our children the value of service, creating volunteer clubs in schools, and celebrating hard work are all core Canadian values.

Now WE Charity has closed its doors in Canada.

Its work was uplifting at a time when we needed uplifting more than ever. Our world is diminished as a result of its loss, and our civil society is worse off. It is heartbreaking to consider, in light of how much *was* accomplished, how much more WE Charity could have done. In light of how many young Canadian lives were deeply enriched by WE, how many more will not be. In light of what we all gained, what we lost.

INTRODUCTION

This is the story of a scandal. It ran in parallel with the COVID pandemic and quickly became one of the most covered news stories in Canada. The scandal almost brought down the government of Prime Minister Justin Trudeau and caused the collapse of Canada's largest and most successful homegrown children's charity. The media gave it a name—the WE Charity Scandal. If you are a consumer of Canadian news, you've heard of it. And if you were exposed to some of the 125,000 references to the scandal in articles, podcasts, documentaries, and nightly broadcasts, you may be inclined to think you already know everything there is to know. But you would be wrong. Because there is a lot the media decided to leave out and the politicians refused to reveal. And a great deal of what happened behind the scenes has never been reported. As a result, even today, few people have a firm grip on exactly who was scandalized and who did the scandalizing.

As a member of WE Charity's board of directors, I had a front-row seat to the scandal as it unfolded. And a backstage pass. The experience was jarring and emotional, and it left me drained. That's because while many troubling accusations were levelled against the charity and its co-founders, Craig and Marc Kielburger, it didn't seem to matter to most people whether the accusations were true. Screaming headlines and political sound bites left Canadians with the impression that there was something "wrong" with the organization, even if few could explain precisely what it was. Many people—including my family, my friends, even my local barber—quickly formed strong views. The kind that are hard to dispel. My efforts to encourage people to separate fact from fiction often fell flat, so by early 2021, I had pretty much thrown in the towel on setting the record straight. I certainly wasn't looking to write this book.

That all changed at 8:38 p.m. on March 27, 2021. It was a Saturday night and I had just started watching a movie—a comedy, to lighten things up after a long week—when my phone vibrated. I probably shouldn't have checked it, but I did. It was an email from Marc Kielburger, and it quickly altered my mood because there was nothing funny about it. Attached to the email was a nine-page letter the charity had received that day from lawyers for a Las Vegas–based journalist and former donor. The letter contained a threat. If WE Charity did not pay him tens of millions of dollars, the journalist would harm the organization by saying highly negative things about it in the press. If the charity paid him off, however, he would be silent and leave everyone alone.

I was stunned. I couldn't believe what I was reading. It was not just that a journalist was trying to bankrupt a children's charity, but that the very same journalist had, only a month earlier, been rolled out as a star witness before a parliamentary ethics committee looking into WE. There, he offered incendiary testimony that was in equal parts emotional, heartbreaking, and false. And it fuelled misperceptions that linger to this day.

Naturally, the charity refused to pay and made the letter public. I assumed that at last, an uproar would follow. Newspapers that had reported the journalist's testimony on their front pages would walk it all back and focus, finally, on telling the complete story about WE. And politicians who had made strident speeches based on what he'd said would now express regret or be called out for failing to do so.

None of that happened. There was only silence. And it spoke loudly to me.

But I've already gotten ahead of myself. As a lawyer, I feel compelled to start with disclosures, so let me begin by saying that I have known the co-founders of WE Charity since they were young. I went to high school in Toronto with Marc Kielburger and met his younger brother, Craig, long before he became a household name. Although I have known them since the mid-1990s, when they founded Free the Children—the predecessor to WE Charity—I moved to New York in 2002 to start my law career and thus watched their meteoric rise from a distance. But I knew that they were busily saving the world, building schools in Africa and South America, hosting star-studded events that celebrated youth empowerment, and promoting volunteerism through "service learning" programs in schools. I also knew that people were flocking to their cause, and that the charity was being praised far and wide. So when they asked if I would be interested in joining the board in 2017, I was deeply honoured and didn't hesitate to say yes.

My first few years as a director were a whirlwind. The Kielburgers and the entire WE management team brought a disruptive energy to the charitable world. They moved and grew in a manner that left me breathless. Every board meeting was a flurry of ideas, innovations, and out-of-the-box plans. It was daunting, but I loved it. When attending WE Day celebrations, educator meetings, and lectures at the WE Global Learning Centre in downtown Toronto, I had the opportunity to talk to scores of young people who were using WE Charity as a springboard for social activism. I also travelled to the charity's international development projects in Kenya, where I witnessed first-hand how education, clean water, and income-generation programs were changing lives.

Those years were awe-inspiring and made me feel incredibly proud.

Then things went south—really far south.

The roots of the WE Charity Scandal lie in the Liberal government's fateful decision to task the organization with administering a program called the Canada Student Service Grant (CSSG). As envisioned, the CSSG was to pay post-secondary students to work at non-profits during the summer of 2020. In those early days of pandemic fear and economic uncertainty, when summer job options were scarce, the program was intended to help up to one hundred thousand students—many from diverse or marginalized backgrounds—pay for university and get through a tough time. In the end, though, the CSSG never happened, and no one got a dime. It imploded within weeks because opposition politicians alleged cronyism.

This ignited a political and media firestorm, with WE Charity unwittingly taking centre stage. The frenzy initially focused on whether some quid pro quo was in play. But for politicians looking to bring down a government, a story about awarding a contract to a trustworthy non-profit was not sufficiently scandalous. A compelling story required WE

Charity to be a bad actor. The worse WE looked, the worse the Trudeau government's judgment in choosing WE.

And so it went. In the weeks and months that followed, every aspect of the charity's mission, work, partnerships, and governance was placed under a microscope. Everything the organization had ever done became fodder for scrutiny, and eventually, suspicion and scorn. Politicians, pundits, and journalists piled on with a barrage of criticisms that left the charity reeling and its supporters ducking for cover. I watched it all from the inside and have never seen anything quite like it.

The Kielburgers—who had for decades been placed on a pedestal by Canadian society and the media—were knocked back down to earth in a ferocious fashion. They went from collecting accolades to receiving death threats. And WE Charity went from national treasure to toxic brand, seemingly overnight.

In the end, Trudeau and his government survived. WE Charity in Canada did not.

And yet, even after the charity announced it was shutting its doors, the scrutiny continued and even intensified, transitioning to an ever-broadening range of concerns. Issues sprang up at a relentless pace, and opposition politicians called for investigations by eight government agencies or committees. Quarterly board meetings became weekly and then daily. Questions were raised about the charity's real estate holdings, its relationship with its ME to WE social enterprise partner, its governance and workplace culture, its corporate partnerships, and its international development projects. And it all came to a head in accusations that the charity had engaged in a pattern of deceiving donors about how their money was spent.

I've heard others refer to it as a deluge or a perfect storm. For me, the whole experience brought back childhood memories of the carnival game Whac-a-Mole. That's the one where as soon as you hit one mole over the head, another one pops up. Quickly smash it down, and two more pop up. Pretty soon, it becomes a frantic effort to keep hitting moles, knowing full well that they are going to pop up more quickly than you can react. In this case, with every new mole that emerged, the public discourse became more convoluted and confused. And no one was prepared to give WE Charity the benefit of the doubt.

To this day, everything about WE Charity remains a thorny subject of debate. But what do people *really* know? Not a lot, it turns out. Journalists raised loads of questions, often in partnership with politicians and fringe social media players, but almost no effort was made to provide the public with answers. Most people just assumed that where there was smoke, there was fire. But in the hundreds of conversations I've had with Canadians from all walks of life, very few have been able to articulate what they think WE Charity or the Kielburgers actually did wrong.

I don't fault anyone for being confused. I was puzzled too. With every unexpected twist and turn, I experienced a wide range of emotions: frustration, shock, anger, embarrassment, and helplessness. Some news made me bury my head in my hands, some made me throw my hands in the air, and some just made me shake my head in disbelief. It was overwhelming but also cause for introspection. Was I part of an innovative and transformative organization that I had come to cherish? Or had I drunk the Kool-Aid and unknowingly become part of something sinister and deceitful? If WE Charity and the Kielburgers were not above board, they did not deserve my service or respect and were not going to get either one. But if there was nothing nefarious going on, I could not stand by and watch an organization that had been an important part of the Canadian social fabric for twenty-five years unravel based on innuendo and misinformation.

So I looked under every rock to get to the truth. I interviewed students, teachers, WE employees and board members, donors, community members served by the organization in developing countries, journalists, corporate partners, celebrity ambassadors, lawyers, and experts on topics such as charity law, corporate governance, accounting, lobbying, media and culture, international development, philanthropy, and parliamentary process. Interviews no one else has done. I watched all of the parliamentary testimony and every television broadcast and documentary, often multiple times, and read thousands of articles and social media posts. I also studied audit reports and interviewed forensic accountants who had mined the Kielburgers' personal finances and real estate transactions—even imaging their phones and laptops and examining their bank accounts. And I reviewed countless studies on WE's impact domestically and internationally, its workplace culture, its real estate holdings and strategy, and its financials. Most importantly, I asked plenty of hard questions of the Kielburgers and WE management. I insisted on complete access to any internal WE Charity or ME to WE document I wanted to see, including thousands of emails and financial records. Nothing was off limits. And I was never refused anything.

This book is an invitation to see what my investigation revealed. My goal is to cut through the noise and fog and address common misconceptions by offering up facts and context. I take you inside the rooms where it happened and reveal what went on behind the scenes, including the stories the media and politicians refused to tell and the voices they refused to hear. In many ways, this is *the story of the storytellers*. Of whether it was fair for members of Parliament to use their pulpits to attack WE Charity for political gain. Of whether trusted media outlets acted with integrity and professionalism. Of whether we were told the truth or led astray.

Let me also be clear about what this book is not. It is not a blind defence of WE Charity or the Kielburgers. They made mistakes, there is blame to be shared, and I do not shy away from revealing the missteps and taking stock. I also spend time unpacking the brothers' personal story, to try to explain why, in my view, so many Canadians found it easy to regard them with suspicion. I will be the first to admit that they are hard to relate to. They started a global non-profit as kids, act like entrepreneurs rather than charity workers, project a level of sincerity and do-gooderism that can feel performative to some, and enjoyed a celebrity status that did not fit with traditional notions of Canadian volunteerism. This lack of relatability, in my estimation, has a lot to do with how quickly negative perceptions of them took hold.

Even though I am no longer on the WE Charity board, I am still an insider and this is an inside perspective. I have also donated to WE, and at one point, my law firm represented the charity in a potential trademark dispute. That insider status may tempt you to discount the credibility of this work. I urge you, however, to refrain from rushing to judgment. My agenda is not to redeem WE or the Kielburgers in anyone's eyes. I ask only that you examine the evidence, hear the perspectives of those who were excluded, and be a proverbial "fly on the wall" in rooms to which you did not previously have access.

I think what you will learn will surprise you. It certainly did me. And I suspect that a fresh look will cause you to view politics, the media, and the ways in which these institutions interact to shape narratives and public perceptions with concern.

As I wrote this book, I was frequently reminded of an adage commonly attributed to Dr. Seuss: "Sometimes the answers are simple and the questions are complicated." In the chapters ahead, you will find previously untold answers to the key questions at the heart of the WE Charity Scandal. And I think you will find the adage holds true.

Were the Kielburgers really "buddies" with Trudeau and the Liberal government, and even if they were, did those relationships have anything to do with the CSSG? Is there any truth to claims that WE engaged in suspect real estate transactions, or that the Kielburgers somehow lined their pockets through the charity? Is there any reason to believe that children, teachers, volunteers, donors, or staff were manipulated or used for some ignoble purpose? Is there any proof that donors to international programs were deceived by the charity (and what do the donors themselves actually think)? And perhaps most significantly, did WE Charity ever break any laws or harm anyone?

What if I told you the answer to all these questions is no?

And yet, as bad as the misinformation and political gamesmanship was, the most disturbing part of this whole affair for me is that no politicians or journalists ever reflected on what has been lost as result of the attack on WE Charity. Nothing has been said about the millions of Canadian young people who will no longer benefit from the charity's programming in over seven thousand schools across the country. Nothing about the loss of initiatives relating to mental health, suicide prevention, and cyberbullying. Nothing about the thousands of teachers who relied on WE Schools resources to inspire their students to be engaged citizens. Nothing about all the entrepreneurs who were going to change the world by starting socially conscious businesses with the support of WE. And most upsetting of all, barely a mention anywhere of the hundreds of thousands in the developing world—particularly women and children—who will now go without access to education, clean water, and small business initiatives.

It has been easy for many people to fall into the trap of thinking the attack on WE Charity impacted just an amorphous entity or two individuals. Seen that way, the losses, even if unjustified, do not seem profound. But WE is not just a name on a building or a school. Nor is it simply two brothers named Kielburger. It is a collection of people who have devoted their lives to helping children and those in need, and millions more who have been impacted around the world.

You can't talk about what has been lost, however, if you don't appreciate what you had. Of all the phrases that became part of our common vocabulary during the COVID pandemic, perhaps none was more ubiquitous than "you're on mute." That, in essence, was the experience of most supporters and beneficiaries of WE Charity throughout this scandal. Their voices were silenced or ignored because they did not fit the narrative the politicians and reporters wanted to tell. In what is perhaps the most salient example, the CBC's *Fifth Estate* aired two highly critical documentaries about the charity that didn't include the perspectives of teachers or students who had participated in WE Charity programs— the two key groups the organization served for a quarter-century. It still boggles my mind that the country's national public broadcaster, in the middle of a pandemic that created profound strain and dislocation for teachers and students, could simply disregard them. And then, to compound that error, the *Fifth Estate* team went all the way to Kenya to visit the charity's projects and failed to feature even a single community member or beneficiary of WE's work in their shows.

In this book, I do what the CBC—and the Canadian media as a whole—never did: give space to the voices that have not been heard. You will hear the perspectives of current and former staff, youth volunteers, students, teachers, parents, donors large and small, and Kenyan women educated in international WE schools and trained in empowerment centres. Hearing them now is necessary, in my view, to determine whether the collateral damage of this political scandal was justified. And whether we should be satisfied with how things turned out.

But I want to do more than simply set the record straight about WE Charity or the scandal itself because I believe this story is about much more than that. It is representative of broader societal currents that should be of great relevance and concern to us all. These currents matter to Canadians, to be sure, but they also matter to people everywhere. And they should matter to you, even if you never donated a dollar to the charity or participated in any of its programming.

To me, the downfall of WE Charity in Canada drove home the realization that it's not easy to be different. There's a lot packed into that sentence. WE was always different. So were the brothers who founded it and the young people who benefited most from it. When you are on the upswing, difference is often celebrated and uncommon ways of doing things are regarded as fresh or innovative. But when you are down on your luck or are seen as flying too close to the sun, difference invites suspicion. It makes you a target. And whether it's on playgrounds, in newsrooms, or on the steps of Parliament Hill, bullies love to prey on difference.

As an organization, WE Charity was different because it fused charitable work with entrepreneurship. It saw socially minded enterprise as part of the solution to the world's problems, and it thought a charity should be run with the same intensity as a business. That impressed a lot of people, but it was also easy to label it as confusing or suggest there was something shady about mixing commerce and charity. WE did not behave the way some people thought a charity should. To those who didn't understand the organization (or didn't want to), it was convenient to call it a sham.

The Kielburgers are different too. The brothers built their charity from a cottage industry into a global movement with millions of followers by working non-stop and doing little else. They are not guys you relax and have a beer with. It was easy for admirers to see them as visionaries, and just as easy for detractors to portray them as not being on the level. Because they are not like you and me, they must be up to something.

Many of the young people who embraced the message of WE were different too. They were not usually the captain of the football team or the prom queen. They were not the cool kids. But they found a way to be cool through WE, because the organization celebrated being different and made that something to be proud of.

As a board member, I believed that the differences embodied in, and championed by, WE Charity and the Kielburgers were always cause for celebration. Those differences were in sync, I thought, with the ethos of diversity that is a core part of Canadian identity. And they allowed a homegrown charity to expand across the globe and serve as an inspiration to countless other non-profits and social enterprises. It was innovation and exceptionalism of a variety not often seen in Canada. As you read this book, it is worth reflecting on whether our elected representatives and media nurtured these differences, as we might have hoped, or exploited them to serve their purposes.

The demise of WE Charity in Canada also serves as a cautionary tale about the consequences of increased political polarization and hyper-partisanship. I see more clearly now that Canadian politics has become "Americanized" to a far greater extent than I realized. Having lived and practised law in the US for two decades, I am no stranger to partisan politics and the reality that some people just end up as road-kill in the age of social media and the twenty-four-hour news cycle. As Canadians, however, we have long been fond of trumpeting how our public discourse is more civilized and contemplative than that of our southern neighbours. We have to ask ourselves if that is really true any-more. Throughout this affair, the impunity with which legislators on all sides of the spectrum trafficked in lies and stoked public outrage to serve their own short-term goals suggests that many have now firmly embraced the politics of anything goes.

And far from being a check on the worst instincts of politicians, the media instead proved to be a willing accomplice. The speed and ferocity with which the press shredded WE Charity and the Kielburgers was shocking. So was the degree to which certain reporters I had previously held in high regard seemed willing to abandon their integrity and jour-nalistic standards to create stories where there really were none to tell. Mainstream news outlets blasted out whatever negative narrative critics chose to offer, without much in the way of independent fact-checking or investigation, even when information was readily available. One day's tweet became the next day's headline, and back and forth it went, in a vicious cycle that became an echo chamber. Instead of critically challenging narratives and assumptions, media outlets simply piled on in the attack. It didn't surprise me that certain journalists lit the fuse, but I *was* surprised that no one else attempted to stamp it out. I try to unpack how and why this occurred, and what it means for all of us.

The avalanche of negative media coverage and political hysteria that engulfed WE Charity also brought with it a climate of fear. Supporters were reluctant to speak out, and those who did were subjected to harassment or ridicule. It is telling that even after all this time, so many people were willing to talk to me about all that WE has meant to them but were hesitant to do so on the record. Many donors and educators eventually felt compelled to speak out loudly to oppose what they saw as unethical and irresponsible journalism. But I still feel deeply for those who gave so much to WE, or got so much out of it, and yet remain apprehensive about airing their feelings. I hope this book helps them turn the page.

In the end, I leave it to you, the reader, to assess whether the story the public was told about the WE Charity Scandal truthfully identified the real victims and the real villains. Whether what has been lost is justifiable. And whether the real scandal is the one perpetrated on us all.

CHAPTER 1

BAD OMENS

As the first cases of COVID began to appear outside China in January 2020, Craig Kielburger received ominous advice from eBay's founding president, Jeff Skoll, a long-time mentor. Like Craig and his older brother, Marc, Skoll grew up in Thornhill, Ontario, a suburban community just outside Toronto. He became a wildly successful social entrepreneur—and something of an expert on pandemics.

In 2011, Skoll's film studio, Participant Media, released the Steven Soderbergh movie *Contagion*, an eerily accurate picture of what a global pandemic would look like. After the film's release, Skoll poured millions into pandemic research and prevention and funded the launch of Ending Pandemics, a non-profit dedicated to preparing countries to better track and manage disease spread. During a hike with Craig in California in early January, Skoll predicted that COVID might be a game changer. As Craig recounted to me, Jeff noted that predicting contagions was an uncertain line of work. Still, he was already making shifts within his own organizations and investments to brace for the impact of COVID.

It was not surprising that Craig had sought out Skoll's advice. The Kielburgers have a long-standing practice of quickly identifying the smartest people in a space, hitting them up for wisdom, and reacting swiftly to what they believe is solid information. With Skoll's warning top of mind, the Kielburger brothers and the WE executive team decided the prudent course when it came to COVID was to hope for the best but plan for the worst, even as WE was riding high and calamity seemed an unlikely possibility.

As a former WE Charity board member, I look back on the success the organization was enjoying in early 2020 with a mix of pride and gloom. In February of that year, Marc sent staff an email that makes me want to both laugh and cry. "I just wanted to be in touch to say a BIG THANK YOU for helping us kick off 2020 in such an awesome way," he wrote. "Although it's still early in the year, our teams have already accomplished so much . . . I'm really looking forward to what the next few months will hold." WE was firing on all cylinders, in Canada and around the world.

No one saw what was coming—the end of WE Charity as we knew it.

In those early months of 2020, staff were planning special events to mark the organization's silver anniversary. April 19 would be twenty-five years to the day that Craig asked his grade seven classmates to raise their hands if they wanted to join him in the fight to end child labour. Eleven did, marking the early beginnings of what eventually became WE Charity. "We were on the cusp of something truly amazing after twenty-five years of building and then proving this model," Craig said. "We joked that it was the longest, hardest overnight success to scale globally."

Meanwhile, teachers involved in WE Schools programming across Canada were busy integrating new social and emotional learning curricula into lesson plans to support their students' well-being. While kids were out on March Break—an escape from the classroom that would last far longer than anyone could have imagined—many teachers were reflecting on how they could use WE resources to keep students focused on taking action and being good citizens if virtual learning became the new reality.

At the WE Global Learning Centre (WE GLC) in the Moss Park area of downtown Toronto, young entrepreneurs were developing ideas for new social enterprises and getting coached on how to bring those ideas to fruition. The WE GLC, funded through targeted donations from Canadian philanthropists like Hartley Richardson and David Aisenstat, was WE Charity's global headquarters. The building—completed in

2017 and opened with great fanfare in a ceremony with former UN secretary-general Ban-Ki Moon—helped revitalize a neighbourhood and was a place of both refuge and renewal for many young people.

Marc explained that he and Craig had seen the WE GLC as finally offering a physical space, rooted in technology, that they had never had when they were pioneering their unique brand of social innovation as teenagers. The next generation, he told me, would have an easier time making change happen. At least, that was the plan. "That building was so much more than bricks and cement," he told me. "To me, the value was in what it represented—helping the next generation of young Canadians create their own non-profit or social enterprise. Their own version of WE Charity or whatever social-purpose group they would dream up."

I recall feeling an enormous sense of possibility when I donned a hard hat and dodged nails and exposed beams during a construction phase tour. I later marvelled at the technology—donated by companies like Microsoft and Siemens—which allowed students and educators around the world to connect and swap stories and ideas. I appreciated that every piece of the WE GLC, from the locally built furniture to the recording studios soundproofed with recycled tires, was socially thoughtful. Even the carpeting was made from reclaimed fishing nets that had once trawled the bottom of the ocean, doing considerable environmental damage. And I was thrilled by the infectious buzz from the hundreds of WE staff working under one roof on everything from school programming (WE Schools), the organization's signature celebration events (WE Days), mental health initiatives (WE Well-being), and international development efforts (WE Villages). And of course, there was the vibrancy of all those visiting schoolkids filling the digital classrooms, Skype pods, and breakout rooms that took up the entire first floor.

As part of its twenty-fifth anniversary celebrations, the charity intended to expand the WE GLC by using neighbouring real estate already owned by the organization to create a broader Campus for Good, which would provide mentorship, free or discounted space, and an extensive suite of business services to youth-led social enterprises and charities. ME to WE, the social enterprise partner of WE Charity, served as the inspiration for the Campus for Good. ME to WE is a for-profit business that sells socially conscious products, creating employment for at-risk people in WE Charity partner communities around the world. Each product sold includes a barcode that lets you see how your money is used and track the impact of your spending decisions. ME to WE also offers young people, families, and donor groups trips to WE Charity's partner communities so they can meet the people WE supports and better understand the organization's impact on the ground.

Although the relationship between ME to WE and WE Charity—business and non-profit operating side by side—became a source of many misperceptions, the creation of ME to WE was a seismic event for WE Charity because it helped ensure access to a steady stream of financing that was not dependent on the whims of philanthropists and corporate partners. ME to WE was required by its by-laws to contribute at least 50 percent of its profits to the charity—in most years, the figure was closer to 90 percent. Any remaining profits were re-invested in ME to WE to advance its mission. In other words, 100 percent of the profits were either donated or invested to grow the social mission. Through this "self-financing" model, WE Charity was able to dramatically reduce its administrative costs and ensure that more donor dollars went to charitable pursuits. By 2020, the value of ME to WE's contributions to WE Charity over a twelve-year period was estimated at $24 million. Those funds were used to support WE Charity's work and were generated through creation of fair trade jobs for women in the charity's partner communities around the world.

As part of its vision for the next twenty-five years, WE wanted to help other charities and young people create their own enterprises with a mandate of fostering social good. Inspired by Toronto's MaRS, a non-profit that helps innovative science and tech companies get off the ground, the organization hoped to build a WE Social Entrepreneur Centre that would provide physical space to young changemakers, as well as skills-building resources and financial support to early stage micro social enterprises looking to bring new products or services to market.

By March 2020, the building blocks of this dream were already in place. In September 2019, the Canadian government had committed

$3 million over twenty-four months to the organization to support youth-led social enterprises in the early and growth stages of their development—particularly those from underserved communities and under-represented groups. The goal was to foster the creation of two hundred businesses focused on social good and help grow another thirty that were already in existence. To accomplish this, WE built two unique programs: WE Incubate for people under twenty-five and WE ScaleUp for aspiring social entrepreneurs under thirty-five. The goal of both programs was to ensure that young entrepreneurs were equipped with solid business plans and impact models so they could give back to their communities while also expanding globally and creating an underlying culture of social good.

While these socially minded ideas were percolating in Canada, WE Charity's development teams in countries such as Kenya, Tanzania, and Ecuador were busily implementing the charity's five-pillar model of sustainable development—education, clean water, healthcare, food security, and income opportunity. In January 2020, WE had kicked off the new year with Craig hosting a group of guests in Kenya. There was always something to celebrate on visits to partner communities on the edge of the Maasai Mara wildlife reserve, whether it was the opening of a schoolhouse or the birth of a new child at Baraka Hospital, a healthcare facility built by WE. Guests visited the charity's partner villages, where they took part in traditional water walks, trudging a few kilometres from a muddy river with heavy jugs hoisted on their backs and strapped to their heads—a glimpse of life before WE Charity established local clean water programs. Later, they bumped along the unpaved roads to the Baraka Hospital to hear personal stories from mothers awaiting inoculations for their babies, then were swarmed at the Kisaruni Girls Boarding High School by ambitious teens eager to share their dreams.

This school was also where CNN did a live broadcast on March 11, as part of its reporting on #MyFreedomDay, a student-driven initiative to raise awareness of modern-day slavery.[1] During that broadcast, CNN shared the story of Faith Cherop from the small community of Salabwek. Faith, who had eight brothers, six sisters, and no mother, convinced her father to let her complete her education instead of sending her off into an early marriage. She eventually graduated from Kisaruni and was the school's valedictorian. She went on to study tourism management at WE College, a post-secondary institution built by the charity in 2017. CNN's broadcast brought the story of WE Charity's work in Kenya to more than 384 million households across two hundred countries.

It seemed like everywhere WE operated, there was excitement and hope in the air. No one sensed how much the world would change in the days, weeks, and months ahead. But in short order, all WE Days everywhere would be cancelled, ME to WE Trips would be grounded, schools in countries around the world would be closed, and most people's lives would be turned upside down. WE Charity's twenty-fifth anniversary would be all but forgotten, the life's work of countless employees would be in ruins, and hundreds of thousands of children who benefited from the charity's efforts in Canada and developing countries around the world would have to go without.

COVID TAKES FLIGHT

Prompted by Jeff Skoll's advice, Craig and Marc directed both WE Charity and ME to WE to prepare for the possibility of a trip participant contracting COVID or the virus spreading rapidly through a partner community overseas. The charity established sanitation requirements for WE country offices and facilities, and began to hunt for a supplier of personal protective equipment. By mid-February, two task force groups had been formed at WE's headquarters in Toronto, and both were meeting daily. The risk management team—composed of executives, country directors, and other key operational staff—was tracking events and preparing strategies and contingencies. And a stakeholder service team was tasked with keeping the organization's donors, educators, school groups, and trip participants abreast of developments.

At the time, COVID seemed like a real but distant problem—until it began spreading across Italy and appearing in numerous other European countries. By February, it had already jumped the English Channel to the United Kingdom and was moving, albeit relatively slowly. There were concerns about proceeding with WE Day UK in early March, but after the National Health Service said live events were safe, the decision was made to go ahead. As the day approached, though, some members of the WE team felt a Damoclean sword hanging overhead.

"I had this feeling that something bad was coming around the corner," Marc told me. "I'm not really a guy who relies on vibes—I like facts and data—but there was just this feeling. I can't describe it, although it was impossible to ignore. But I never thought WE Day UK would be our last."

That year's event garnered attention because of its A-list attendees—including actor Idris Elba, race car driver Lewis Hamilton, the cast of *Game of Thrones*, and the wife and mother of Prime Minister Justin Trudeau—and because it was a stadium-sized gathering held while the scope and gravity of COVID was slowly becoming clear. Ahead of the event, ITV News, one of the largest broadcasters in the UK, filmed at ten different schools in ten different regions across England, interviewing teachers and students about their involvement in WE Schools and what volunteer work they had done to earn their way to WE Day.

The event marked the first time that the Canadian prime minister's daughter, Ella-Grace, would take the stage, but the Trudeaus had a long history with WE. Margaret Trudeau, the prime minister's mother, is a professional public speaker who was a regular on the WE Day stage as an advocate for clean water and mental health. She was also paid an honorarium to speak at WE fundraising events (an inconsequential fact that eventually became rather consequential). His wife, Sophie Grégoire Trudeau, was an ambassador for WE Well-being and hosted a podcast on mental health and wellness for the organization. Even before Trudeau was elected prime minister, he and his wife co-hosted WE Day Montreal in 2012, and his first public appearance after being sworn into office was at WE Day Ottawa in 2015. Suffice it to say that the Trudeaus liked WE and seemed to think highly of the organization and the Kielburgers.

WE had covered the costs for Grégoire Trudeau, Ella-Grace, and Margaret Trudeau to travel to the UK, as it had for other speakers. The prime minister's wife also made other public appearances while she was there, including at the Canadian High Commission and an International

Women's Day event. In a matter of days, her whereabouts and interactions would become the subject of international media scrutiny.

Grégoire Trudeau returned to Canada on March 6, and soon after, she began to experience flu-like symptoms. She was tested for COVID on March 11, and the next day, she was confirmed to be the 158th—and most famous—Canadian to have the virus. The Prime Minister's Office released a press statement that sparked media speculation and unleashed criticism of the charity. Even though Grégoire Trudeau had been back in Canada for several days before experiencing a fever, the statement implied that she had caught the virus at WE Day. It read: "Having recently returned from a speaking engagement in London, UK, the Prime Minister's wife Sophie Grégoire Trudeau began exhibiting mild flu-like symptoms including a low fever late last night."[2] This statement put WE Day in the crosshairs of media outlets around the globe. Even though there were no reports of young people or teachers contracting COVID, and no WE staff, including those who had interacted with Grégoire Trudeau, tested positive, many people quickly assumed that WE Day was some kind of super-spreader event.

The *Daily Mail*, the *Guardian*, and dozens of other UK and Canadian newspapers and magazines began calling and emailing WE's public relations and UK teams, asking for comment on Grégoire Trudeau. Who was she in contact with at the event? Did anyone else test positive? WE's PR team was inundated.

The Canadian press took a decidedly alarmist tone, pondering who else had been tested and might be at risk. "But what about their children?" asked reporter Michael Fraiman in an article on macleans.ca. "What about Trudeau's mother, who attended the conference with her? What about everyone who took a selfie with Sophie, who may pose a risk?[3] A columnist for the *Journal de Montréal* dedicated nearly eight hundred words to questioning Grégoire Trudeau's fitness as a mother. "I'm sure you're very happy to know," wrote Sophie Durocher, "that it was to spout this kind of new age gibberish that Mrs. Grégoire Trudeau risked her health, that of her daughter, her mother-in-law, her sister-in-law . . . and that of our Prime Minister."[4]

Four days later, there was another uptick in media coverage when

Idris Elba also tested positive for the virus. Rumours began to swirl that Grégoire Trudeau had passed on COVID to others. The lifestyle and beauty website *The Kit* went so far as to track the deadly virus from Grégoire Trudeau to Lewis Hamilton (who had not contracted it at that time), to Prince Harry (who had been in contact with Hamilton on March 6), to the Queen. "It just occurred to me that Harry was hanging out with the Queen while he was in the UK," Sarah Laing wrote on the site on March 18. "Is there any chance that he might have passed it on to his 93-year-old grandmother?"[5] On social media, Internet trolls and journalists alike speculated that WE had put thousands in harm's way. Chris Selley, a columnist for the *National Post* who would later hop on the anti-WE media bandwagon, tweeted, "On the bright side, maybe coronavirus will kill WE Day."[6]

In fact, the coronavirus *did* kill WE Day.

The potential threat posed by the pandemic had been top of mind for WE executives for two months. Throughout the first week and a half of March, the risk management task force closely watched how other major large-scale events, such as conferences and music festivals, were reacting to the growing crisis. WE executives were also worried about staff members who had gone to the UK—all were told to stay home and get tested for COVID if symptoms emerged. The climate at WE, where there were so many people returning from international travel, became one of uneasiness and uncertainty.

Dr. David Fisman, an epidemiologist from the University of Toronto, was hired to help the organization understand what it needed to do to respond to the medical needs of its communities around the world. He was also asked for guidance on how the organization's domestic programs would be impacted and when things might be expected to return to normal. WE could not have had a more qualified adviser. Dr. Fisman's research interests fall at the intersection of applied epidemiology, mathematical modelling, and applied health economics. He is focused on developing and applying methodological tools that allow physicians and public health experts to make the best possible decisions around communicable diseases. He has a master's degree from the Harvard School of Public Health and was part of the Ontario COVID Science Advisory

Table. Over the course of the pandemic, his advice has been sought by foreign governments, financial institutions like JPMorgan Chase and Farallon Capital Management, and organizations like the Ontario Teachers' Federation and the Ontario Nurses' Association.

Dr. Fisman was in regular contact with WE Charity to try to help the organization make prudent decisions. He had a simple warning: this is going to be bad, and things will not get back to normal for a long time.

Looking back on those early days of the pandemic, Fisman, an over-worked but good-humoured man who peppers scientific explanations with humanistic references to Franklin Roosevelt and Laozi, told me that Craig kept "drilling down" on every detail in the hope of uncovering some prospect of better times. But Fisman—the "bearer of bad news"—explained that the pandemic would likely come in waves, with government policy decisions influencing the trajectory more than the virus itself. "It was," he acknowledged to me in an interview, "a very tough card for WE to be dealt," because so many of its activities would likely be shuttered for an indefinite period.

The doom that Marc had felt just a few weeks earlier proved pre-scient. And that feeling was building. Every part of WE—which was in the business of live events, school programs, international travel, and retail—would be impacted by COVID, starting with WE Day.

Based on Fisman's advice, the WE executive team decided the organization needed to be proactive. On March 10, all stakeholders—educators, vendors, donors, staffers—were informed that the live WE Day events would be cancelled for the spring 2020 season. When schools began closing across North America later that month, the full WE Day 2020–21 season was terminated. In an email to partners and donors announcing the initial spring cancellation, Marc wrote: "I know it will be heartbreaking for the hundreds of thousands of students, educators, speakers and partners who participate every year. It was a heartbreaking decision for all of us at WE." He added that "the safety and peace of mind of participants and their families, and our staff, is our highest priority." Similar emails were sent to students, educators, and speakers. The next day, March 11, the World Health Organization officially declared COVID a global pandemic. Two days later, Canada issued an advisory recommending against travel abroad and called on all Canadians outside the country to come home.

As travel warnings went into effect, WE went from worrying about the fallout of WE Day UK to grappling with how to repatriate more than one hundred travellers from Kenya, Tanzania, and Ecuador. And what of the WE employees who lived and worked in other countries? So much was at stake, and the organization had to act quickly.

THE MAD SCRAMBLE TO SAFETY

Russ McLeod, then the executive director of ME to WE, was in his office for a weekly status check with Nora Griffiths, head of ME to WE Trips, when she heard the ping of an incoming email and glanced at her laptop. The normally unflappable Nora, a former elite rower who had competed around the world under immense pressure, turned to Russ, wide-eyed with alarm.

"I just got an alert that a global pandemic has been declared."

Though shaken, Russ headed instantly for the office whiteboard. "Okay, let's go through our strategy."

The risk management team had been planning for the worst, mapping out different scenarios and establishing protocols to ensure that all travellers got home safely. All that planning would now be put to the test.

In 2004, Russ had arrived for his first day at WE Charity armed with a business degree and wearing a suit, which was a bit stiff for a crowd who had got their start protesting child labour and sex trafficking and collecting signatures on petitions. Russ quickly dispensed with the suit, and some days even his shoes. To save money, he lived on the top floor of WE Charity's first downtown headquarters, in Toronto's Cabbagetown neighbourhood, sleeping on a mattress on the floor.

Russ was the guy you turned to in order to get things done. He pitched in wherever he was needed—writing grant proposals, schlepping boxes, and organizing promotional tours and book sales. He quickly became invaluable to the organization and moved up the ranks, eventually launching WE Day, first in Toronto in 2007 and later across North America and in the UK. He'd juggled WE Day schedules, celebrity timetables, and trips on many continents. He was just the person you wanted in a crisis.

March 11 was the beginning of what Russ described as "a mad scramble" to get WE Charity and ME to WE staff and trip participants back home from sometimes remote communities across the globe. He knew he had to move at lightning speed—borders were closing, countries were enacting travel restrictions, and flights were being cancelled by the minute. The window to repatriate people was closing fast.

For many overseas employees, the decision to leave was one of the toughest of their lives. Robin Wiszowaty, the head of Kenyan operations, is an American who had lived and worked in Kenya for over a decade. She'd learned Swahili through immersive living with a rural Maasai family and had even published a book about her experiences called *My Maasai Life*. Kenya was her home, and she was based there with her husband and children.

On March 14, Marc arrived in the country to consult directly with Robin and other senior staffers on the pandemic response. In this whirlwind, twenty-four-hour stopover, he wanted to learn what he could about what was needed to get people out of the country and to prepare Baraka Hospital for an expected deluge of patients. Six days later, he called Robin to pass on a warning—international flights would likely be shut down in a matter of days. There was no more time to waste. Robin called the rest of the expatriate staff to relay Marc's message. Then she called her husband: "Mike, we gotta go."

Robin was reluctant to leave the Kenya team behind. There was so much work to be done to stave off the spread of COVID in the community. "A part of me felt like I was leaving them when they needed me most," she said. But a few months earlier, her father had passed away in the US. With the pandemic escalating, she decided that she wanted to be near her family and should go in case it soon became impossible to leave Kenya for months, if not years. Forty-eight hours later, she boarded a flight to Michigan with her husband and kids.

At the same time, Scott Baker, then serving as head of programs in Ecuador and now the chief operations officer for WE Charity international programs, was deciding whether to remain in the capital, Quito.

Like Robin and Russ, he had worked with the organization for almost twenty years in a variety of roles. While he was volunteering at Mother Teresa's orphanages in Calcutta, another Canadian gave him a copy of Craig's first book, *Free the Children*. Scott read it, returned to Canada, and lived for a time in a tent in the backyard of the Kielburger family home while he took on responsibility for building and growing a youth volunteer leadership program for the Toronto Catholic District School Board. Before moving to Quito with his Ecuadorian wife and their two children to spearhead WE Charity's sustainable development programming in the Amazon, he did a long stint as executive director of the charity, from 2010 to 2018.

As Ecuador closed its borders on March 14, Scott scrambled to get trip participants out on the last scheduled commercial flights. COVID restrictions had caused turmoil in the country, with civil unrest and looting. He realized that once those flights ended, he would likely have no chance to leave with his family until the pandemic was over. "We were living day to day," he recalled. "It was this crazy, uncertain world." Once he'd made arrangements for all staff and trip participants to return home, he came to the difficult decision to leave as well—but by that point, the airport was closed and there were no commercial flights out. Scott's plight was one of several stories featured in a March 21 CTV News report on the travel challenges facing Canadians abroad.[7] He says the news coverage helped him and his family secure space on one of the very first charter flights, but "we left our house, furniture, car, and dog to make it out." (I made inquiries about the dog—her name is Luna, and she was taken in by Scott's in-laws.)

Back in Toronto, Russ and other WE employees were feeling the toll of trying to manage a coordinated exodus on a global scale. Red tape was shredded to ensure maximum efficiency. If staffers found a flight that could accommodate someone, they were instructed to grab it without going through the standard internal approvals. "We didn't want to give up a seat on a plane because we would have to chase someone for approval to spend that amount," Nora recalled.

Meanwhile, Marc and the travel team worked the phones for hours each day, talking to airlines, Global Affairs Canada, and numerous foreign consulates and Canadian embassies as they tried to bring more people home. Despite the hurdles, all trip participants were repatriated in under a week, and by March 21, just ten days after the pandemic was declared, the last of the WE staff members had returned—except for one.

In Udaipur, India, in the northwestern province of Rajasthan, program head Lloyd Hanoman was still working to close the office, secure all WE properties, and ensure that the needs of national staff were addressed. Originally from Guyana, with degrees in conflict studies and political science, Lloyd had worked for UNICEF and Global Affairs Canada before turning up at WE's Toronto headquarters one day to pack school and health kits to ship to children overseas. He quickly became a key team member and went on to lead the organization's international development work around the globe. Before moving to India, he had lived and worked for WE Charity in Sierra Leone and Sri Lanka. "What I thought would be a few hours of volunteering turned into a twenty-year career," he said.

Like Robin and Scott, Lloyd was reluctant to leave the country he had come to think of as home. He also didn't want to leave his team members, who were supporting dozens of projects and thousands of impoverished community members. Marc was worried time was running out, and he phoned to urge haste. But it was too late. On March 24, the Indian government locked down the entire country. All forms of transportation were halted, and people were told not to leave their homes except to get food or seek medical attention. The WE Charity team had to make multiple calls to Global Affairs Canada in Ottawa and send repeated electronic requests through a web portal set up by the Canadian consulate in India before they were able to get Lloyd a seat on a government flight out of the country. With the airport in Udaipur shuttered and no inter-regional flights allowed, he had to get special permission from Indian authorities to break the lockdown and make the eleven-hour drive to Delhi to catch his plane.

As March drew to a close, most Canadian journalists, politicians, and pundits were still suggesting that the pandemic would have a relatively small impact on daily life, with everything returning to normal as soon as the summer or fall of 2020. But the information coming into WE told an entirely different story.

SAD GOODBYES

Marc and Craig continued to get advice and data on the short- and long-term consequences of the pandemic from Dr. Fisman and others. It was all bad news. For example, a briefing from the Wellcome Trust, the world's largest non-governmental funding source for health research, predicted significant and long-lasting societal changes, such as shuttered schools and supply chain disruptions. Its experts also foresaw the high death toll that became a reality around the world.

Similarly, Chris Hansen of Valiant Capital Management, a long-time WE Charity donor, told leadership that he expected the financial impact of COVID to be heavy and advised the charity to prepare for what was coming. His fund would famously short key industries such as travel and tourism, accurately predicting the market consequences of the pandemic. Bill Thomas, the global chairman of KPMG International, called to say that based on what his company was seeing in China, he thought COVID could ultimately make the 2008 Great Recession look like a picnic. And the Bill and Melinda Gates Foundation was projecting that millions of lives would be lost in developing countries like India and parts of Africa. "One after another, some of the smartest people around the globe, experts in these areas, were telling us that we needed to prepare for the worst-case scenario," Marc recalled. "There were some industry leaders who were slightly more optimistic, but the information we were getting was that we needed to act and act quickly."

It became clear that COVID would be around for a long time—even if a vaccine was developed at a record pace. And the logistics of distributing a vaccine to billions of people in countries across the globe were staggering. The last regions to receive it would likely be rural areas of Africa and the Amazon basin, the very places where WE was most active. It would be irresponsible to expose local communities in these high-risk areas to international volunteers and guests. The most optimistic estimate suggested it would be two years before ME to WE was able to resume offering travel experiences. Two years! Retail sales for the ME to WE Artisans line of handcrafted accessories would also evaporate as malls and stores shut down. With no retail and no trips, WE Charity, which relied on donations from ME to WE to operate, would struggle.

The forecast was the same for WE Days. It became apparent that even in the best-case scenario, students and teachers would be reluctant to crowd into large arenas well into 2021 and beyond. And even if schools themselves reopened, the pandemic would almost certainly preclude motivational speakers and those who delivered WE Schools programs from visiting classrooms. What, then, should be done about the teams that produced these programs?

One bright light was that WE Days and WE Schools resources could be moved to an online format. But that would require nowhere near the previous level of staffing. An online broadcast is very different from a live event because the latter requires actual bodies to build stages, operate concourse booths, seat attendees, manage talent, and much more.

At the same time, WE Charity was thinking about shifting into disaster-relief mode and diverting time and resources to securing much-needed medical supplies, including PPE, for vulnerable partner communities. WE had already learned from its experience in the Haiti earthquake of 2010 that the costs of shipping medical supplies abroad were significant. Similarly, in 2014, the organization had helped fight the Ebola epidemic in West Africa, delivering medical supplies through partner organizations on the ground, particularly in Sierra Leone, where WE maintained an active presence for two decades. That relief effort had a ripple effect on the financial feasibility of other operations, and the experience taught the charity some difficult lessons. "Ebola had a pretty significant impact," Russ explained. "We learned the hard way to get ahead of crises."

Since no one had ever faced a pandemic of a scale that the experts were predicting with COVID, it was impossible to know what expenditures would be necessary in the long term. But WE Charity's early estimates were that a minimum of $10 million would be needed to supply medical aid and combat food insecurity in communities where WE was the most active non-profit. In Kenya, for example, a field hospital was needed. This was the best way to prevent an ailing patient from entering Baraka

Hospital and infecting everyone inside. Robin Wiszowaty was already working on a plan to repurpose the buildings of WE College, which had been sitting empty ever since the pandemic had shut down schools.

No one liked the idea of laying off team members who had given so much of themselves to WE, but there were difficult choices to be made. Could the organization really continue to carry hundreds of people whose programs were on indefinite hold? Or was the prudent course to reallocate funds to support medical shipments, healthcare, and food security in vulnerable communities around the world? Ultimately, the path was clear—the priority had to be the communities overseas. The writing was on the wall: WE was going to have to slim down very quickly.

And so layoffs, which would be emotionally devastating for the organization, began the week of March 16. WE Charity and ME to WE announced to staff, in a videoconference town hall, that they were downsizing. Each departing staff member received a minimum of twelve weeks in severance pay, and all those affected were contacted personally by their direct managers—no impersonal email terminations.

It was an agonizing process for those making the calls and those receiving them. When I talked to current and former staff members who were part of this sad moment, the words that came up most frequently were "pain" and "loss." A consistent theme was that working for WE was more than just a job. Most employees felt that they were part of something bigger. That's why almost one hundred people had worked at the organization for a decade or longer—and some of these people were among those slated to be let go. Russ said it was gut-wrenching. "I couldn't help shedding many tears."

Dalal Al-Waheidi, executive director of WE Charity, said the experience was a tragic coda to her eighteen years at the organization. She started as an intern after graduating from university and rose through the ranks, eventually running the organization's WE Day programs for many years. Like most staff, she had toiled across late nights and weekends on a modest salary, putting life plans on hold to advance the mission of the organization. Employees often started at WE when they were young, right out of college, and the organization purposely hired people with passion even if they lacked practical experience. Reflecting on the sadness of making the difficult decision to let old friends go, Dalal recalled, "I was directly involved in shaping and growing the organization, alongside passionate and dedicated team members. It was our dream to make it cool for kids to care about social issues and to contribute to positive change. Having to say goodbye made me realize just how much I cared for these people who had shared my dreams and mission."

She noted that WE's focus was on "doing this in an honourable way, in the best way we knew how." But behind the administrative process was a real sense of tragedy. Among the people let go was Viki Alincy, who came to WE after decades working in media, marketing, and communications. She thought she'd found her perfect fit, a way of connecting her professional expertise with her personal passion, but she was laid off just one month after she started. "I didn't feel any ill will," she noted. "I've been around business and understand why that decision had to be made." That said, she was personally upset. "I felt numbness, then a sadness about the fact that I thought I'd found my dream job after thirty years. Imagine finally finding your dream job and then losing it."

Unfortunately, even these initial cuts did not prove sufficient. As March dragged on, it became increasingly clear that the impact of COVID would be heavier than anticipated. As fears of a pandemic recession grew, it was also unclear what economic uncertainty might mean for donor funding commitments. The WE executive team saw no option but to expand the layoffs. Additional staff were let go the week of March 23, with the same termination package as those who had been laid off in the first round. Of the permanent full-time staff who remained, many were switched to short-term renewable contracts, some at reduced pay. To try to preserve jobs and funds for emergency programs, WE's senior management took a 20 percent cut, while the executive team cut their own salaries by a quarter. Marc's and Craig's salaries—paid by ME to WE, not WE Charity—were cut in half.

Dan Kuzmicki, head of enterprise services, laid off more than half of his team in March. From his vantage point at the WE GLC, where he was helping the remaining staff members transition to at-home work, he had a front-row seat to the painful decisions the founders and executive team were making. "Our executive team is just weeping in the hallways and sitting around in a room for twenty-four hours at a time. They were people at the absolute worst time in their lives," recalled Dan. Although it was a distressing period, he appreciated the personal care and thought that went into the process. "A lot of my friends have been laid off over the years, and their experience was just shockingly abrupt, like this location is now closed and sorry for the inconvenience." In contrast, WE's leadership team had one-on-one calls with each person being let go. Dan couldn't envision what was to come—no one could—but he felt confident that "we'd make it through to the other side somehow."

By the end of March, total staffing levels in North America and the UK had been reduced from 568 to 320 across both WE Charity and ME to WE. With these painful cuts, the internal upheaval appeared to be subsiding. On March 27, Marc held an emotional town hall with remaining staff. To help employees cope with the pandemic and the emotional toll of the layoffs, he announced an increase in holidays and more scheduling flexibility. Marc then spoke about how the organization's local and global programs were more important than ever, as the most vulnerable are always hit the hardest in times of crisis. He thanked the hundreds of remaining team members for persevering through the past few difficult weeks and said that the organization was well positioned to face the pandemic and deliver on its mission to help children.

But mostly, he tried to reassure. "Please allow me to separately put your minds at ease about the financial solvency of the organization," he said. "We acted quickly, and as a result, we will be okay. We will be okay."

When I later heard Marc's message, I fervently hoped he was right. He was, of course, very wrong.

But not because of COVID.

CHAPTER 2

GOOD ENOUGH IS NOT GOOD ENOUGH

As the pandemic firmly took hold, WE Charity was unexpectedly presented with what seemed like a one-of-a-kind opportunity to help when the government came calling with the Canada Student Services Grant (CSSG) program. The CSSG was supposed to provide grants to tens of thousands of students to work at non-profits during the summer of 2020. The goal of the program was to help students who couldn't find work and struggling non-profits trying to address the needs of Canadians during COVID.

The CSSG unfortunately came to an abrupt end before anyone was helped, and the government never managed to get it off the ground. Its demise, however, turned out to be just the beginning of a firestorm that decimated WE Charity.

Once heralded as a homegrown success story, WE Charity suddenly became the subject of a lot of negative attention across 2020 and 2021. At the kinder end of the spectrum, critics labelled the organization "convoluted," "complicated," and "superficial." Some went further, calling it a cult and wishing its downfall. Others found its complexity inherently suspect, particularly for a charity, and decided there had to be some funny business going on. Whatever the criticism, one thing is clear: the attack on WE was really, in many ways, an attack on the character and credibility of its co-founders, Craig and Marc Kielburger.

The story of WE and the story of the Kielburgers are inextricably linked. I have a unique perspective on both because I have known the Kielburgers since they were young, and I was a WE Charity board member. I went to high school with Marc, stayed in touch with the brothers over the years, and have watched with interest, and often amazement, as they disrupted—and more recently, upended—the charitable sector. From the beginning, Craig and Marc were young men in a hurry. They brought the zeal and ambition of a Silicon Valley start-up to the charity sector. They wanted to generate impact through innovation and push for systemic change, and they wanted to do it at breakneck speed with as little interference as possible. Over twenty-five years, this approach led to breathtaking results, but it could also be nerve-racking. I came to understand—through the events of the past two years—that their drive to always do and deliver more is both their best asset and their Achilles heel.

Looking back, I can see that "perfectionism to a fault" was in their DNA from day one. It is perhaps best captured for me in an experience I had working with Marc on a school project more than thirty years ago. It was a ninth-grade class presentation, and we got together one Saturday to do the research, fill a poster board with cut-out images, and prepare talking points. We had been at it all day. Fourteen-year-old me thought we were done and proposed (as I probably still would today) that we head out to get pizza. Marc looked at me, puzzled, and said he thought we were just getting started.

"Marc," I said, "it's totally good enough."

Without skipping a beat, he responded, "You go ahead, then. For me, good enough is not good enough."

Something Marc and I had in common is that we each had only one sibling, a kid brother approximately six years younger. At first, the relationships seemed comparable—deep affection with a healthy dose of annoyance. I tried to dodge my pesky brother whenever I could, and Marc might have occasionally thrown Craig into the pool against his will. The comparisons probably end there. (The Kielburger brothers have outperformed the Rangwala brothers based on most metrics, other than knowing how to relax. There, we are more talented, and they fail miserably.)

Today, Marc and especially Craig are undeniably famous. They have been granted many honorary doctorates (twenty-five between the two of them), shared stages with international luminaries, appeared on *The Oprah Winfrey Show*, received the Order of Canada, and been nominated multiple times for the Nobel Peace Prize. But I can still easily call to mind my overachieving high school classmate and his shy younger brother, who had a noticeable speech impediment and trouble looking me in the eye. In my wildest dreams, I never would have imagined that boy would become the standard-bearer of a global empowerment movement.

In 2017, the Kielburgers asked me to join WE Charity's US board of directors because they felt it would be useful to have a lawyer experienced in litigation and crisis management as the charity continued to grow rapidly. I was honoured and said yes. I did not, of course, expect my skill set to come in quite so handy. My tenure on the board—which ended when I stepped down to write this book in the summer of 2021—always felt like an adrenaline rush.

I never knew what I would get when I showed up for board meetings. Things happened fast in the WE world. Board members might arrive expecting to hear about progress on an elementary school being built in Kenya, only to be briefed instead on a proposal to start a university called WE College. ("We figured out that the communities were only going to allow young people, especially girls, to go to university if there was one available locally, so there's no point stopping at high schools," Craig explained, as though he were proposing something as simple as changing a light bulb.) Talk of a medical clinic would quickly morph into an idea for a hospital. A proposal to add a subject to WE Schools programming in North America and the UK would become a vision for a whole new online curriculum. A brainstorming session about using technology to advance service learning would result in a partnership with Microsoft to broadcast communal learning to communities around the world. And even as all this was happening, creative social business ideas—whether in the form of fair trade chocolate and coffee or handmade artisan jewellery—were designed, developed, and implemented at a pace that left me amazed.

The Kielburgers' work ethic—around-the-clock action with an emphasis on world-class content and performance at every turn—set the tone across the organization. For more than two decades, Marc and Craig logged hundreds of days per year travelling the globe to build partnerships and launch bold initiatives. They appeared in small-town Canadian classrooms, mud huts in Ethiopia, boardrooms in New York and London, conference halls in Davos, a lodge in the Amazon rainforest, and everywhere in between. The brothers never stopped running and had limited patience for those who wanted to walk.

Members of WE's senior leadership team—many of whom had been involved with the charity for almost two decades—were just as fast-moving and were the hardest-working group of people I have ever encountered. Coming from a partner at a large corporate law firm in New York, that is saying something. Many WE Charity employees were prepared to give everything, in terms of both inspiration and perspiration, because they believed that was the recipe for changing the world for the better. WE was more than just a place where they worked. The organization was the product of decades of sleepless nights and sacrifices. The leadership team—and most WE staff generally—felt a sense of responsibility to their colleagues, who had become like a second family. That core group would stand by WE, and the Kielburgers, throughout the trials to come.

When Dan Kuzmicki, the head of enterprise services, started with WE in 2005, he was one of only about twenty employees. "I met Craig my second day on the job, and his laptop was physically on fire," Dan recalled. He had graduated just three days earlier from a database administration program and applied to an online posting. He had no idea who Craig was when he heard his voice calling out from a nearby meeting room. Craig's laptop power brick was sparking. "That started our friendship. Very little has changed—there is something always on fire."

Dan described himself as a problem-solver and Craig as a visionary. "I'm very focused on what's going to be delivered in the next day, week, month, or year, while Craig is on another plane of existence. He's thinking, you know, 'How does this action or product change the world?'"

Countless staff have told me that working at WE was the most fun they ever had, and that they relished being part of what we all viewed as a transformative movement. For others, however, the ceaseless demands resulted in quick burnout and the drive for excellence felt overbearing. Dan acknowledged the drawbacks, which included "not being compensated for all that extra time and stress," but he noted that friends in other industries did not have "quality of life in their work anywhere close to what I have." Those friends, he said, were doing "mind-numbing work, with significantly more money but just not happy at all."

Employees often joked that working at WE in the early days offered "less sleep and less pay" than other available options, but if you were the right fit for the organization, you could find benefits that went well beyond the biweekly paycheque. Dan described it as an adventure that tests your limits. "We're always doing something so crazy and innovative and just shit that you don't get to work on anywhere else. What I love about the organization is that we're always doing something just beyond what we're capable of."

My former fellow board member David Stillman knows this all too well. Before he joined the board, he was a WE employee and was responsible for much of the charity's expansion into the US. He was integral in introducing WE Schools programming into American schools and in helping stage WE Days in Seattle, Chicago, and his native Minnesota. He is the type of person who likes taking on huge challenges. He is also never short on opinions, which he tends to share openly—and sharply. "Working at WE was the most fun you could have," David said. "But working with Marc and Craig is hard, if not at times impossible."

When I relayed this to Marc and Craig, they both nodded. "That's fair," Craig conceded. "Marc and I are driven and have devoted much of our lives to building WE from the ground up. So we can be exacting and intense, and that can sometimes make us difficult people to work with."

I've often thought that the brothers had the confidence, charisma, and driving leadership of Apple founder Steve Jobs. And I mean that comparison as it is intended—the Kielburgers are impatient visionaries always pushing for change and striving to generate impact through innovation, but they can also alienate people, just as Jobs did at Apple.

Like Craig and Marc, Steve Jobs inspired a kind of messianic devotion in some and a deep suspicion in others. He was persuasive and brilliant, but not very open to criticism. One huge difference, though, is that Jobs learned how to get out of the way and let his team design iPhones. The Kielburgers, by contrast, constantly remained immersed in all aspects of the organization, no matter how big it got.

TALL POPPIES

There is no question that what the brothers built is impressive—and rare in Canada. They pioneered service-learning curricula, educational campaigns, and a celebration of service to inspire a generation of young people to become active and engaged citizens. Truly a Canadian success story, by any measure. At the same time, their need for speed and their resolute faith in their own judgment has occasionally, in my estimation, come at the expense of sober second thought. Whether they're dealing with layoffs, demands for information, or media misstatements, they sometimes react with a fervour that seems out of proportion. The same intensity that lifted WE Charity to great heights also made the landing much bumpier.

The Kielburgers' foibles, however, don't satisfactorily explain the speed and ferocity with which they were attacked in the wake of the CSSG controversy. Instead, I believe the explanation lies in the fact that the brothers have always aroused a certain degree of suspicion and wariness. When they got caught in the crosshairs of a political scandal, that suspicion morphed into outright mistrust in many quarters.

I have never had any reason to doubt the Kielburgers' sincerity, but in writing this book, I have tried to put my finger on why so many Canadians seemed quick to accept efforts to call their integrity into question. I think in large part it's because the brothers sometimes come off as almost *too* sincere and devoted to their cause, projecting a pureness so excessive that it invites skepticism. People are comfortable with go-getters who "work hard, play hard," but the Kielburgers only "work hard." We expect everyone to have at least a few indulgences or guilty pleasures, but as best as I can tell, the Kielburgers have no discernible vices—they don't drink, smoke, gamble, overeat, or get noise complaints from the neighbours. And trying to get Craig to utter a curse word is a game you will lose—I have tried, for my own amusement, many times. (Marc can be persuaded to swear if sufficiently provoked.) Add to that their somewhat evangelical speaking style, reminiscent of preachers calling the flock to a cause, and it is understandable that some people who don't really know them might wonder if they are on the level.

And then there's the impression that the Kielburgers never turn off. Yes, they do go to bed at some point. But every waking hour is spent promoting the work of WE. I say this without derision—I admire them for it. As the founders of a charity, Craig and Marc have always felt they bore the responsibility for building and growing the organization, for generating ideas and coming up with the next big thing, and of course for bringing in the resources and supporters. You cannot grow a charity from your parents' basement into a national and even global force without staying on message, making requests, and working every angle to secure the support necessary to change the world. Still, it is very hard to have a conversation with them about any aspect of their lives without them bringing it back to WE. Whether seen as a single-minded focus or a form of perennial salesmanship, this trait is clearly off-putting to some and has caused those people to question the brothers' authenticity.

All the above qualities were at times on display during the Kielburgers' two rounds of testimony before parliamentary committees into the CSSG debacle. As an insider, I felt they answered questions thoughtfully, mixing a sincere desire to speak the truth with a measured degree of combativeness when presented with false statements and loaded questions. But to many, they came off as wooden, overly rehearsed, and defensive. And let's face it—Craig and Marc are no longer wide-eyed teenagers encouraging fellow young people to take action. They are now two relatively privileged middle-aged white men defending a charity that had been treated unfairly at a time when many people are unsympathetic to hearing about unfairness from middle-aged white men.

On the other hand, a significant number of people I interviewed for this book described the criticism of the Kielburgers and the attack on WE Charity more generally as a classic example of tall poppy syndrome. This is the tendency to disparage or cut down those whose achievements make them stand out from the crowd, on the theory that their success feeds their egotism or vanity. In a July 2020 article in *Maclean's* magazine, Scott Gilmore, the conservative-leaning founder and CEO of the charity Building Markets, noted, "Canadians dislike tall poppies, and there are no more conspicuous targets than Marc and Craig Kielburger." Gilmore posited that it is their "relentless cheerfulness, and the way they whip up a cloying meringue of empathy with an almost religious fervor, that has turned the public mood against them."[1]

Former prime minister Kim Campbell also told me that she thought the way Craig and Marc were treated was emblematic of tall poppy syndrome and a "willingness to turn on people if they are getting too big." This was also the opinion of Mark Bourrie, a former journalist with the *Toronto Star* and *Globe and Mail* and the author of a self-published article titled "The Attempted Murder of the Kielburgers."[2] In Bourrie's view, there is a lot of resentment in Canada about success. He believes that the Kielburgers' habit of hobnobbing with international celebrities while paying little attention to local reporters or the Toronto elite fuelled a desire to take them down a peg. "I think Canadians really do have tall poppy syndrome," he told me.

I get it. If you are a Canadian charity struggling to arrange meetings with low-level government officials or raise enough money to keep the doors open, it must be irksome to see pictures of the Kielburgers hanging out with Oprah Winfrey, sharing yak butter tea with the Dalai Lama, dining with Richard Branson, visiting the home of Sheryl Sandberg, and traipsing the Great Rift Valley with likes of Demi Lovato, Selena Gomez, and Natalie Portman. The news that Finance Minister Bill Morneau visited WE Charity's international projects with his family or that the prime minister's wife recorded podcasts for the organization's mental health initiatives might lead a cynic to assume that the Kielburgers were tugging on some cleverly hidden strings.

The bottom line is that for a subset of Canadians who had watched the Kielburgers with a mix of amazement and jealousy, the CSSG controversy and ensuing avalanche of criticism provided the aha moment they had long hoped for: "Just as I suspected—too good to be true." Then schadenfreude kicked in.

THE REAL BROTHERS

From my vantage point, it has been painful to watch the Kielburgers go from media darlings to pariahs attacked by the same pundits and politicians who once sought their company and praised their achievements. Not just because much of the criticism is wrong or unfair, but because it glosses over the fact that they have given *everything* to try to empower young people and improve lives. To use a sports analogy, they leave it all on the field, every time. Even if you disagree with them or dislike them, it is hard to miss the nobility in that.

And there is another side to the Kielburgers that I think many Canadians do not see. In an effort to help explain them—and less so to try to redeem them in anyone's eyes—I hope to paint a picture of who Craig and Marc really are and describe some of the factors that have shaped them.

The Kielburgers I know are polite and deferential, good listeners, and generous almost to a fault. They are quick to send birthday presents to children and to offer invites to WE Day. They take a genuine interest in the good deeds of the young people who look up to them. As one example, fifteen-year-old twins Ashleigh and Emma Dzis fondly remembered meeting Marc several years ago at the now-closed ME to WE store in Toronto's Eaton Centre. They were in grade five at the time, and their mom had heard he would be there signing books. "We were just, like, totally kind of fangirls," Ashleigh recalled. When it was their turn to get their book signed, they wanted to tell Marc all about their involvement with WE, but he had a line of people waiting and asked them to come back later. They did, and he spent the next two hours with them as they excitedly described all the things they had been doing to make change happen, from collecting canned goods for the food bank to raising awareness about the dwindling bee population. At the end of the conversation, Marc extended an invitation. "I remember him saying, 'Oh my gosh, you guys are so inspirational. You're my favourite pair of twins.' We're probably the only ones he knew!" Ashleigh said. "And then he's like, 'Hey, I have this staff meeting coming up, and you guys are, like, so amazing, would you like to speak at it?' And we're, like, 'Um, YEAH!'"

WE Charity got its start as Free the Children in 1995. Craig, like any ordinary twelve-year-old, was flipping through the local paper look-ing for the comics when he noticed the story of Iqbal Masih, a Pakistani labourer of the same age who was murdered for advocating for children's rights. Craig remembers feeling shocked. "In school, I had learned about the American Civil War and the Underground Railroad," he told a mag-azine in 1999, "but I thought slavery was something out of the past, that it had been abolished."[3] Inspired to do something about it, he photo-copied the article, researched child labour around the world, and gave a talk to his seventh-grade class. His passion convinced several classmates and his brother to join his cause. Free the Children was focused on erad-icating child labour and helping children in the developing world, but it also had a broader underlying mandate to tell kids that they didn't need to wait to grow up before making a difference: they could be catalysts for change right now.

"What I remember most from those days was how many people—non-profits and community leaders—told me, often in so many words, that kids can't make a difference. When I was twelve, I called one charity and asked how I could help support their mission, and they told me to get my parents' credit card!" Craig said. "I wanted to prove to all of them, and to all the other young people, that they were wrong. Kids could make a difference."

The organization had lofty goals but humble roots. Free the Children was initially run out of Craig and Marc's parents' living room. There was pizza, pop, and a fax machine that got a lot of mileage. And when they needed all hands on deck, kids would camp out in the yard overnight. But even this modest start would not have been possible without the consid-erable support of their parents, who encouraged the boys' convictions and instilled in them the importance of helping people who had less.

"Good teachers have to have a strong work ethic. They work much harder than most people realize," Craig told me. "My parents were no different. They pushed to instill that work ethic in us. And while they were always supportive, they also believe that facing challenges is an essential part of learning and growing up. They'd say 'The only failure in life is not trying' so often that I think it should have been painted on our walls."

Fred and Theresa Kielburger are atypical Canadian success stories who passed on their values to their children. They also passed along considerable wealth, which afforded the brothers the privilege of focusing on their philanthropic interests rather than trying to earn top dollars in the private sector. But they are not old money. Fred and Theresa both came from humble backgrounds and had experienced first-hand what it means to do without.

Born in Windsor, Ontario, Theresa was the second youngest of four children. When she was only nine, her father died, leaving her mother, Mimi, to provide for the family. Having just an eighth-grade education, Mimi cleaned houses to pay the bills, but work was sometimes hard to come by, and for a period of time, the whole family lived in a tent. Theresa's mother was a force of nature, though, and she was determined to give her kids a better life.

One day, Mimi read about a fire that had destroyed all the academic records at a local high school. According to family lore, she saw in this brief news article an opportunity to change her family's fortunes. She bought a typewriter and taught herself to touch-type late at night and on weekends. Then she applied for a secretarial job at one of Windsor's biggest employers, the Chrysler Corporation. Only high school graduates were eligible to be hired, but Mimi had a plan—she claimed her records had been lost in that school fire. Because her typing skills were so good, no one ever guessed that she had not started high school, let alone finished it. She became a valued employee at Chrysler and was eventually made the head of the secretarial department.

Mimi's example taught Theresa that determination and hard work could improve her life, but she also learned that people sometimes get knocked down and need compassion and a helping hand. As an adult, she became a teacher, but she left the profession for a few years to run an outreach centre helping homeless youth escape drugs, alcoholism, and prostitution. When she went back to teaching, she focused her efforts on students with special needs. "That was another value Mom drilled into us: every single person is worthy and has potential, even if the world may not see it at first," Marc said. "During her childhood, my mother knew too well what it was like to worry about your next meal. She grew up a person of deep faith, and always said that it was incumbent on us to share and to help others achieve their potential."

Theresa's concern for others remains strong today. In speaking with her for this book, it was hard to get her to focus on how the events of the last year had affected her and Fred. In the two-hour conversation, she never spoke about her own pain; instead, she focused on how disappointed she was that no one seemed to be thinking about how the "scandal" was affecting the lives of WE Charity's beneficiaries. Her constant refrain was "The biggest loss was to the children."

And yet, unsurprisingly for an eighty-year-old mother and grandmother who has watched her children pilloried in the press, she was angry. Partway through the conversation, Theresa pulled out a box filled with newspaper clippings—articles, op-eds, and letters to the editor—as well as copies of emails and letters of support she had received, all from the last year. "I have three more boxes upstairs," she said. One article she referred to several times in the conversation profiled a thirteen-year-old boy in Pemberton, BC.[4] Sam had become so stressed about climate change that he couldn't sleep at night, but he found opportunities to take action through his school's WE Club, and in the process, he also found his purpose. "He saw that he could make a difference, that he had something to contribute," Theresa explained. "And he is, of course, only one example. It breaks my heart that other children will not be able to access those opportunities."

In her own act of defiance, she has created a library of photo albums to showcase twenty-five years of hard work. "I want to give one to all the families of the staff to remind parents how proud they should be of what their sons or daughters have done," she said. "They should all be proud of their children, like I'm proud of my sons."

Like Theresa, Fred Kielburger grew up in a family that struggled financially. His father, Peter, was a German-Romanian immigrant who had come to Canada during the Great Depression. Although he was a skilled cook and a talented musician who played eight instruments, he arrived with nothing and knew only a few words of English. He boxed to survive, then pooled his winnings with earnings he made working as a servant in Toronto's upscale Rosedale neighbourhood. Eventually, he was able to save enough to open a corner store in the bustling St. James Town area. In twenty years, that store closed exactly one day—so the family could visit Niagara Falls.

Fred's childhood and a religious upbringing taught him the importance of giving back. Like Theresa, he took those lessons of service, resiliency, and hard work and became a teacher. In his spare time, he volunteered with the Big Brother program, and one summer he even went to France to work at a home for adults with developmental disabilities.

Fred and Theresa shared many values, and they passed these on to their boys. Their own childhood struggles heightened their parental instincts, making them want more for their children—a better education and more security. They were determined to do whatever they could to give Marc and Craig every advantage and opportunity. "We didn't make much money back then as teachers," Theresa told *Canadian Living* magazine in 2019. "But we valued the importance of having a home. So, instead of choosing to have a large wedding, we put the money we'd saved towards a down payment on our first home."[5] That home cost them $40,000 in 1975. Two years later, after renovations, they sold it for twice what they'd paid. This, they quickly realized, was their path to financial freedom.

Because they were teachers, Fred and Theresa had summers off, so they devoted that time to building their new real estate hobby into an investment opportunity. Over the years, they bought, fixed up, and resold almost twenty houses—creating sizable wealth along the way. It was a true family affair. "While other kids were picking out their camps for the summer or planning vacations, our family would drive around in our station wagon looking at homes for sale," Craig said in one interview.[6] When the boys were old enough, they learned to paint and hang wallpaper, and as they grew into young men, they acquired more complex skills, such as how to install tile or put up drywall. Some of these skills came in handy when WE began to build schools in countries around the world.

Toronto's booming real estate market also allowed Theresa and Fred to help the charity take flight. Eventually, they even moved out of the family home in Thornhill to let Free the Children take it over as a makeshift office. Later, proceeds from the sale of that home were used to buy a building in Cabbagetown that became the charity's first true headquarters. The charity used the building rent-free for over a decade,[7] until it outgrew the location and moved into the WE Global Learning Centre a few blocks away. Sotheby's estimated that over the years, Fred and Theresa could have rented the Cabbagetown property and a second building they also provided to WE for about $5.4 million. The couple even refused to accept a tax receipt for their support, to avoid the appearance of impropriety. (This must have been a particularly bitter pill amid the swirling accusations about their private real estate transactions and how these transactions might somehow have benefited the family at the expense of the charity.)

Fred and Theresa's savvy investments also allowed them to support their sons even more directly. They bought Marc's and Craig's Toronto-area homes, and they continue to supplement their sons' relatively modest salaries to this day. There's no question this is a privilege that made it possible for Marc and Craig to accomplish a great deal—few people have such a head start in life. But in my view, it was a privilege that indirectly benefited millions of young people in Canada and around the world through WE Charity's programming and support. I think this fact is too often forgotten by critics who, for their own purposes, seek to paint the Kielburgers and WE as one and the same.

CARRYING STORIES HOME

It did not take long for Free the Children to grow from those pizza parties to a force to be reckoned with. At one early speech to a large crowd of labour union supporters, Craig surprised even himself by raising $150,000 on the spot. Not a bad day's work for a twelve-year-old. Recognizing that his passion could translate into real results, he embarked on a fact-finding mission to South Asia—without his parents, but with their blessing—to better understand child labour. It was an epic trip that caught the imagination of children everywhere who wanted a say in solving the world's problems. But more than twenty-five years later, critics derisively reframed this trip as white saviourism.

Back at home, Craig began to tell the harrowing stories of children he had met who were working in sweatshops or the sex trade. One eight-year-old girl in India had a job sorting used syringes from a local hospital. She squatted barefoot among the needles as they talked through an interpreter and said that nothing was done to protect her from contracting HIV or other diseases.[8]

Many people would have been ground down by the grim scenes Craig encountered on this trip, but he found hope and inspiration instead. "They don't want to be seen as little creatures who need help," he told YES! magazine, referring to the kids he met. "The only gift you can give them in return for the time they spend with you is to carry their stories home."[9] It was during that trip that Craig decided to devote his life to helping children from around the world tell their stories, as well as giving a voice to kids like him. This mission would grow into schools, water projects, farms and food security, income opportunity and healthcare.

In 1996, just a year into the life of Free the Children, Craig told his story to Ed Bradley on *60 Minutes*, and things changed literally overnight. Strangers started showing up at the house in Thornhill asking how they could help. Clubs sprouted up at schools everywhere. And the volume of mail, media interest, and financial contributions was overwhelming. Free the Children was an organization that believed kids could help other kids, but it was still run by tweens. It's ironic that at a young age, Craig started a charity to end child labour, and in the process he quickly became a workaholic child who took on tremendous responsibility.

I don't know how much young Craig realized it then, but his life really would never be normal again. His school principal threatened to keep him behind in grade eight because of poor attendance. Fortunately, Craig found a high school that had an alternative program for students who needed to miss class, mostly for elite sports. During his second week there, a *60 Minutes* television crew followed him into the cafeteria. Maybe that won him some friends, but it certainly led others to think he was full of himself.

Later in life, Craig reflected on what he called the "negative correlation" between his charity's success and his own sense of normalcy. "I remember other kids in my class talking about *Dawson's Creek*. They could all relate to the characters and plots," he remembered, "but I had no idea what it was. Until Netflix came around, there were all these series I had never heard of. I could tell you what the UN secretary-general had said at the latest global development conference about establishing the Millennium Development Goals, but I couldn't name a single top-forty song." (He still can't.) And he was and still is a straight arrow. "I never wanted to bring any disrespect to the organization, so I have never been drunk in my life, never done drugs, never partied hard in the traditional sense. But that's the life you choose, and really, I didn't know any different."

Craig's new high-profile life also stripped away other elements of childhood. Like so many kids, he'd had to deal with bullies in the playground. But now, he had to face bigger and more powerful bullies. In 1996, the now-defunct *Saturday Night* magazine ran a profile of him titled "The Most Powerful 13-Year-Old in the World." It falsely alleged that his family was benefiting financially from his not-yet-registered charity, Free the Children. It also described Craig as a "precocious pubescent" who had learned to speak in almost perfect sound bites and noted that some "cynical journalists" had referred to him as Damien, the name of the evil child in the horror film *The Omen*. The article made no mention of Craig's speech impediment and the impact it might have had on his speaking style.

While the personal criticism may have stung, the allegation of financial impropriety was something the Kielburgers took a stand on. Craig sued the magazine, editor Kenneth Whyte, and author Isabel Vincent for libel. Eventually, they consented to a judgment against them and paid a $319,000 settlement, which Craig invested in the growth of the nascent charity. But that money came at a price. This one suit, launched in 1996 and settled in 2000, created a perception that the Kielburgers are litigious, which may explain some of the problems they encountered in dealing with the media during the CSSG controversy.

Marc, meanwhile, always played more of an operational role and claimed less of the limelight. In many ways, he was the polar opposite of his brother. "He was the quintessential guy who excelled at everything,"

Craig recalled. "He was on the rugby team, student council, editor of the school newspaper. He was popular and had a lot of friends."

Some of Marc's early successes paved the way for Craig. For example, he won a Canada-wide science fair for creating recipes for eco-friendly cleaning products, earning himself accolades and media coverage across the country. In his late teens, he was selected to be a page in the House of Commons, then he headed to Thailand to volunteer at a hospice for AIDS patients. Harvard University was next for him, studying international development. The university frothed with ideas and energy. And privilege. But while his roommate used to fly off on a private jet for weekends in New York or the Caribbean, Marc took a weekly flight (economy, of course) back to Toronto.

Craig was still at home, working his tail off on Free the Children, but he couldn't continue to build the charity alone, no matter how many high school classes he skipped. So Marc began to commute, attending classes at Harvard on Monday through Wednesday, then flying home to work at Free the Children for the next four days. Even when he was at school, he would study until 7 or 8 p.m., then work on grant proposals and other paperwork until the wee hours of the morning. To a very real extent, he was squandering his chance at an Ivy League education to support a homegrown charity. "I couldn't let go of either scenario: a vocation via Harvard or making the world better with my brother at my side," Marc later recalled. "It was a lot, but I don't think I would have done it differently. It's not lost on me how privileged I am to do all of it."

Despite his punishing schedule, he made it through Harvard and didn't just scrape by—he did well enough to earn a Rhodes Scholarship, which affords foreign students the chance to study at Oxford University in the UK. He chose to study law. At Oxford, it's possible to condense your academic year into three eight-week terms. This gave Marc the flexibility to continue working with Craig despite the ocean between them. Each term, he studied intensely for two months, then flew home to work at Free the Children for six weeks. In the end, he even managed to complete his three-year degree in two years by working sixteen-hour days.

With his Oxford law degree in hand and a Rhodes Scholarship on his résumé, he was bombarded with job offers with great starting salaries, signing bonuses, and relocation expenses. He chose Free the Children, in part so Craig—who had already turned down the chance to go to an Ivy League school to keep the charity going—could attend university too. Their parents were worried they were gambling too heavily on Free the Children. The brothers were doubling down on a small charity that held little prospect of ever paying them a decent salary.

Even if everything went right, it was hard to imagine that they would work there forever.

SIMPLE COMPLEXITY

As a board member, I was frustrated by politicians, journalists, and pundits who insinuated—and sometimes outright charged—that the Kielburgers were engaged in various forms of self-dealing by supposedly using WE Charity to further their own private financial interests. The theory was that the Kielburgers were using the charity to get rich through ME to WE (which is a business they control), or that the purchase or sale of real estate assets by WE Charity or ME to WE conferred some direct or indirect financial benefit on them.

On its face, the notion that Marc and Craig developed a byzantine set of complex entities as a means to profit off the back of WE Charity makes little sense. The Kielburgers are extremely accomplished and educated people who have demonstrated that they know how to build an organization, sell a vision, and court powerful people. If they had wanted to make loads of money and eat caviar on a private yacht, they could have taken lucrative private-sector jobs and done just that. It is absurd to think that they instead decided to work sixteen-hour days for twenty-five years, spend hundreds of days per year apart from their families, and invest everything they had in building a global charity—all as a means to funnel money back to themselves. The concept becomes even more preposterous when you realize that the Kielburger family was wealthy to begin with and Fred and Theresa provided millions of dollars of support to the charity.

TESTIMONIAL: GERRY CONNELLY

Gerry Connelly is the former director of education for the Toronto District School Board and the former director of the curriculum and assessment policy branch of the Ontario Ministry of Education. She served on the board of directors of WE Charity Canada for over eight years and is currently the co-chair of WE Charity Foundation.

For almost five decades, I've worked in education as a teacher and administrator across Canada and the United States, and I have also advised on teaching and learning in the US, China, South Africa, and Estonia. I have had responsibility for ensuring that thousands of young people are inspired to learn and to become responsible and caring citizens, both locally and globally, with a commitment to equity and social justice. It was an amazing and humbling journey and a responsibility that I never took lightly.

A highlight of my career has been my service—since 2013—on WE Charity's Canadian board of directors. During my time in education, I listened to the stories of students, teachers, and parents and visited schools in Canada and other countries. I saw and heard first-hand the tremendous and positive impact WE Charity had on teaching and learning and the education system as a whole.

Nothing about the so-called WE Charity Scandal has shaken my faith in the charity and its co-founders. I know that as a board, we carefully vetted the operations, finances, and partnerships of the charity to make sure funds were directed to the right places, people, and causes. We asked hard questions about things like ME to WE and the charity's real estate acquisitions and decided that all of it was in the best interests of the charity and its beneficiaries. And I have travelled to the charity's international projects and witnessed the positive impact.

Discrediting WE Charity may have been the short-term goal of some politicians and journalists, but the long-term consequences will be a devasting loss for our children and those in the developing world. That is a tragedy. At the same time, I am confident that the charity's work internationally will be carried forward through WE Charity Foundation and will positively impact generations to come.

I have stood with WE Charity through it all. And I am proud to still do so.

Still, WE Charity's partnership with ME to WE and its real estate acquisition strategy (which I'll come back to later in the book) are subjects that were analyzed and dissected long before the CSSG scandal erupted. For almost a decade, WE Charity's board understood that these topics warranted significant scrutiny, and that potential conflicts of interest existed. With innovation comes questions. They should be asked, and they were asked—and answered definitively. Repeatedly. It is hard to think of anything relating to WE that has received more governance attention than these two issues.

Nevertheless, much has been made of the confusion surrounding the charity the Kielburgers initially founded and the sprawling enterprise it became. I see the point, as I too have found it confusing at times and have struggled to come up with an elevator pitch that describes WE. I will try to break it all down here and clear up any lingering misperceptions.

Under the WE umbrella, there were only two entities that mattered: WE Charity and ME to WE. WE Charity made no money because it was a non-profit; references to it being "paid" for anything meant only that the charity received donations to fund its activities or cover reimbursements of expenses generated in connection with those activities. That was true for the agreement governing the CSSG and for every other contract that WE Charity ever entered into with any private or public entity. ME to WE, meanwhile, was a social enterprise (i.e., a business with a social mission) focused on advancing the work of WE Charity through commercial initiatives. The two entities worked in harmony and operated under common branding. They were separate for legal reasons that I will explain in a moment.

Like other global organizations, WE Charity and ME to WE also had affiliated entities in multiple countries to assist with operational controls, ensure compliance with local laws and customs, and meet requirements imposed by donors. But those entities were all part of either WE Charity or ME to WE. Their governance and financials were all consolidated into either the charity or the social enterprise. And every entity was created and operated with advice from WE Charity's lawyers, including those at Miller Thomson LLP.

WE Charity had two streams: domestic programs focused on youth service learning and volunteerism, and international development programs focused on helping to end poverty. These two streams were designed to support and complement each other. More youth engagement in North America, for example, created greater awareness of and support for issues in developing countries. Youth trips to WE Villages sites helped bring international issues back to family dinner tables in North American homes.

The volume of negative commentary directed at WE Charity might lead people to think it was a fringe enterprise that had never been scrutinized until the CSSG brought its activities into the limelight. Nothing could be further from the truth. The charity was recognized for its work by various international bodies, including the United Nations and the World Economic Forum. It received funding from, among many others, the Bill and Melinda Gates Foundation, the Queen Elizabeth Diamond Jubilee Trust, and the global accounting firm KPMG—all of which subjected the charity to a rigorous diligence process and significant reporting requirements. It received the Roosevelt Freedom Medal, the Nelson Mandela Human Rights Award, and the World's Children's Prize for the Rights of the Child, to name just a few. In 2017, *Good Housekeeping* magazine chose WE Charity as the very first recipient of its new Good Housekeeping Humanitarian Seal. It also got a four-star rating from Charity Navigator, with a total score of 94.74 out of 100.[10] Furthermore, independent third-party firms conducted annual audits of WE Charity in Canada, the US, and the UK. The organization always received an "unqualified audit" rating, meaning the auditors identified no concerns about financial accountability and transparency.

But, some people ask, didn't ME to WE benefit from its co-branded relationship with WE Charity? Yes! And as a result, the charity benefited even more. This is because ME to WE was required to contribute at least 50 percent of its profits to WE Charity. In reality, over the past five years, ME to WE voluntarily passed on approximately 90 percent of its profits. So prior to COVID, when ME to WE did well and was profitable, the charity was the beneficiary. Any additional profits were reinvested in the business so it could continue to grow and help advance the communal mission of both organizations. In essence, ME to WE existed to help finance the activities of WE Charity and to create jobs in overseas communities where the charity operated. ME to WE made money by engaging in business activities—providing international travel experiences and selling handcrafted jewellery and other fair trade products—that supported WE Charity's mission.

The negative—and as we'll get to, politically motivated—media coverage of this "shady" organization has also caused some to ask, "Hey, wait a minute! Isn't this ME to WE entity controlled by the Kielburgers and others? And isn't it possible for the Kielburgers to make money from it?" Yes, the Kielburgers and other social impact investors, including Jeff Skoll, have an equity stake in ME to WE. There is nothing sinister or secret about this. Their financial stake gives them control over the social enterprise because they devote time and resources to running it. But in practice—and this is the most important part—the Kielburgers and other investors never took a dollar out of ME to WE (other than the brothers' relatively modest salaries). They chose not to benefit from owning ME to WE and declined to receive dividends or distributions, choosing instead to donate the profits to WE Charity or reinvest them in the social enterprise.

The fact is, ME to WE was born of legal necessity. Given their own formative experiences as teenagers, the Kielburgers saw volunteering in the developing world as an invitation to activism. In 1998, they wanted to start offering what they called service trips to young people who could learn about sustainable development and spend time working in international villages that were being supported by Free the Children. Fees from these trips would also provide a stable funding base for the charity's development work.

This simple idea was not simple to execute. While social enterprise is a growing concept, Canada still draws sharp lines between traditional non-profits and businesses, even when a business is really an enterprise with the same underlying mission as a charity.[11] As a result, Canada has strict laws governing how charities can earn income. The federal Income Tax Act, for example, restricts a charity's ability to sell products and services deemed an "unrelated business." To be related, business activities must be both linked to the work of the charity and subordinate to that work.[12] If a business gives its profits to the charity, that by itself is not a sufficient link. And if a business receives anything more than minor attention from the charity's staff, then it is not sufficiently subordinate. On top of these federal restrictions, in 1999 (when ME to WE's predecessor business, Leaders Today, was established), Ontario law barred any charity incorporated in the province from owning a business.

So in sum, legal restrictions prevented WE Charity from selling volunteer trips or owning a business selling such trips. If WE Charity tried to do these things, the Canada Revenue Agency could potentially deem such business "unrelated" to the work of the charity.[13] That could result in the organization losing its charitable status—an unacceptable risk. But in other countries, the idea of using a for-profit business to fund charitable work is not unusual. Oxfam's storefronts have been a common sight across Europe for decades, and the housing non-profit Habitat for Humanity opened its first ReStore in Georgia in 1976. The UK and a significant number of US states have modified their laws to make room for businesses with a mandate to produce returns in terms of social good rather than financial dividends. In the UK, these are called community interest companies, while Americans know them as beneficial corporations, or B corps. ME to WE is a certified B corp in the United States.

When ME to WE's predecessor was launched in 1999, the idea of social enterprise was still relatively new in Canada. The business was created under the supervision and vetting of an army of legal experts, including representatives from the Office of the Public Guardian and Trustee and the Ontario Ministry of the Attorney General. WE wanted its new enterprise to be entirely above reproach. To fulfil the required laws, management and the board of directors decided that WE Charity and ME to WE would be separate entities operating under distinct and independent governance. To avoid brand confusion, the word "charity" was specifically baked into the name of the non-profit entity. WE Charity accepted donations and issued tax receipts. ME to WE sold products and services.

ME to WE provided both cash and in-kind contributions to the charity, helping to cover the cost of things like administrative support, rent, and shared staff. As a result, WE Charity achieved a remarkable level of efficiency for the non-profit sector, with only 10 percent of its general donations spent on administration costs. (The average among US charities of a similar size is 25 percent.)[14] But ME to WE offered an even greater benefit: it created employment for thousands of people in partner communities through its retail sales of fair trade chocolate and coffee and its ME to WE Artisans line of handmade jewellery and other products. ME to WE also invested its capital to build eco-lodges near WE Charity projects in rural India, Kenya, and Ecuador. These lodges hosted international visitors, allowing guests to see first-hand the development programs their donations were funding, which inspired even more donations to the charity. "When guests see the projects and meet the people who are being supported," Robin Wiszowaty explained, "they are more willing to contribute and become part of the incredible impact."

ASK THE EXPERTS

To gain a further understanding of the interplay between charities and charity-driven businesses, I spoke with Bill Young, who, according to some, is the granddaddy of social enterprise in Canada (although I doubt he likes the honorific). For over twenty years, Young has been plugged into entrepreneurship within the non-profit sector, and it shows in how passionate he is about the work he does. I had planned to have an hour-long conversation with him, but at around the forty-five-minute mark, it became apparent to me that we had barely scratched the surface.

In 2001, Young founded Social Capital Partners, an enterprise that provides financing and advisory services to businesses with social missions built into their operations. Young also sits on the boards of a variety of social enterprises and has received the Order of Canada for his achievements as an entrepreneur. And he has served on social finance task forces for the Canadian government. He explained to me that Canada makes it very hard to run a business that has an underlying charitable mission—this is a problem, and Young has been leading the movement for reform for years. The core issue, he told me, is that CRA requirements make it difficult to be innovative in this field when it comes to charitable work. "Our regulatory environment doesn't understand hybrid organizations when you're trying to figure out how to generate revenue in a way that allows you to have more impact," he explained "Any combination of market forces and doing good has forced a bunch of us in this space to . . . end up organized in a far more complicated way than we would ever, ever have wanted."

Young's comments invite the broader question of whether Canadians view exceptionalism in business or the charitable sector as a virtue or a vice. In the US, exceptionalism is a valued part of self-identity—Americans see themselves as entrepreneurial by nature and have always held business visionaries in high esteem. In Canada, by contrast, exceptionalism is most frequently lauded when it involves being better than other countries at handling social problems. Think climate change, universal healthcare, or the cultural mosaic. But there is limited dialogue regarding the value of exceptionalism in business—for example, pride in making more things, building smarter and more creative companies, and adopting innovative approaches to solving problems. At some level, I believe the disconnect between WE's approach of using innovation to achieve social impact and the traditional ways in which many Canadians think about exceptionalism is partly to blame for how readily the public assumed, without any evidence, that WE and the Kielburgers were up to no good.

Despite the efforts WE Charity and ME to WE made to be transparent and comply with the law, novelty is sometimes misunderstood. Donors and corporate partners expected and deserved to have confidence that their contributions were being put to appropriate use. And WE Charity's directors wanted to make sure that everything about the relationship between the charity and the social enterprise was above board and consistent with the mission of the charity. To accomplish this, the organization periodically retained independent experts to review its structure and accounting operations, as well as the board's oversight.

In 2011, for example, the Honourable Peter Cory, a former Supreme Court justice, conducted two independent reviews. One pertained to the relationship between the charity and the social enterprise and their governance structures. In that case, Justice Cory concluded that the entities were "conducting their affairs openly and in compliance with their respective organizational structures and mandates."[15] The second was a review of the charity's real estate acquisitions between 2006 and 2011 and the board's governance practices during this period. His conclusions were that purchasing real estate "has greatly helped to forward the mission and effectiveness of the work of the organization," and that the board "provided sufficient oversight of the purchases."[16]

In 2018 and 2019, the Honourable Stephen Goudge, who had served on the Ontario Court of Appeal for over fifteen years, was retained to conduct a number of independent assessments, including one focused on the co-founders' compensation, the charity's reporting protocols, and the relationship between the charity and Theresa and Fred Kielburger. The report confirmed that no improper transactions took place. Goudge also noted that "ME to WE's accountants state that ME to WE has never distributed dividends," and that "neither Marc nor Craig Kielburger [has] received any form of salary from WE Charity or its predecessor, Free The Children." He even reviewed Marc and Craig's T4 filings and reported that they were both paid $113,461 in 2017 and $125,173 in 2018.[17] The salaries of both brothers were paid by ME to WE.[18]

I had the opportunity to speak with Goudge and discuss his experience working with WE Charity and its co-founders in preparing his reports. He stands squarely behind the conclusions he reached and said he has no reason to doubt the co-founders' integrity. "Was I ever constrained in the information that I thought I needed to prepare the reports? The answer is no. I have never had any impression of the Kielburgers other than [that] these are highly ethical people who just want to help the world."

As the organization expanded more heavily into the US, it commissioned a similar independent review in 2018 by Scott McCallum, a university professor, the CEO of a global technology non-profit, and the former governor of Wisconsin. McCallum was not involved with WE Charity or ME to WE and had never met the Kielburgers. He was asked to examine the impact of ME to WE's social enterprise model and assess whether the co-founders of WE Charity received "any undue benefit." He concluded that "neither Marc Kielburger nor Craig Kielburger receives any undue financial benefit from WE Charity or ME to WE Social Enterprise."[19]

As if all this wasn't enough, in the wake of the WE Charity Scandal and the tsunami of negative mainstream and social media coverage, the Kielburgers voluntarily subjected their personal and business financial information, and that of their spouses, to a comprehensive forensic review by Ken Froese and his team at Froese Forensic Partners, one of Canada's largest independent financial investigation firms. Froese is an expert in forensic accounting and has been hired by police forces, governments, media outlets, and companies of all sizes.

Because I conduct internal investigations concerning alleged financial fraud and litigate related disputes for a living, I often work with forensic accountants. Froese and I speak the same language. Although I have never previously dealt with him, I consulted with many lawyers who praised his work and reputation. After interviewing him twice for this book, I can tell you that he is serious-minded, careful, and a straight shooter. He agreed to go on the record only on the condition that no topic would be off limits. It was important to him—and to me—that he be able speak openly about both his investigative process and his findings. The Kielburgers were required to consent to this and did.

Froese explained to me that he and a team of six investigators spent over a thousand hours across a two-month period reviewing financial records for all WE entities in Canada, including WE Charity, WE Charity Foundation, and ME to WE, as well as the records of the Kielburgers and their spouses. The mission was to uncover any evidence of self-dealing by the Kielburgers or their family members. The process included "investigative research into corporations and properties potentially owned by the Kielburgers," and a search for any potential benefits to the brothers, their families, or the companies they control based on "property improvements, operating costs such as property taxes, insurance and utility payments, personal expenses or benefits such as concierge services, nanny services, food and clothing, entertainment, travel, and similar potential benefits."

Froese's people had unrestricted access to WE's accounting systems, corporate credit cards, and real estate transaction files for all properties held by WE Charity, ME to WE, and any other WE entities. They had the same unrestricted access to the personal bank accounts, credit card statements, and real estate transactions of the Kielburgers and their spouses, including the prices at which properties were bought and sold. The investigators also imaged the full contents of the brothers' computers, cellphones, and communication apps, and ran keyword searches to test the veracity and completeness of the information provided. And for good measure, they imaged the devices of WE's CFO, Victor Li, and investigated all of his personal transactions, real estate holdings, private companies and investments, and even a company operated by his wife. The investigation team included an accountant who had worked with the Ontario Provincial Police, a criminologist, and a bank fraud expert. They determined what information had to be reviewed—not the Kielburgers or anyone associated with WE.

The hope was that this investigation could set the record straight once and for all. Froese told me that he came to the project with some suspicion and wanted to make sure he covered every angle. He'd had no prior dealings with WE or the Kielburgers and knew little about the organization, other than it was a hot topic in the press. Where do the Kielburgers bank? Where do they spend money? What do real estate transaction files obtained directly from law firms show? Froese and team dove into each of these questions. I asked him if there was any information he had asked for that he did not receive. He said no. He'd received full cooperation and transparency.

In the end, his report was clear and unequivocal in its conclusions: "We found no evidence of improper financial benefits to the Kielburgers from WE Charity, M2WSE [ME to WE Social Enterprise] or any WE Canada entity," the report read. "We found no evidence of improper transactions which benefited the Kielburgers personally." Froese told me the same was true for Victor Li. Froese also found that the salaries "paid to the Kielburgers from WE entities"—at its high point, approximately $140,000 to each of Marc and Craig from ME to WE—were "not inconsistent with their positions or qualifications."

Closed book, right? Unfortunately, not. In the months that followed, politicians and journalists advanced narratives filled with so many falsehoods that a lot of Canadians came to believe something underhanded was going on.

CHAPTER 3

A CALL TO SERVE

On April 19, 2020, a cool and breezy spring day in Toronto, WE Charity's twenty-fifth anniversary finally rolled around. But it was marked with no fanfare. Ambitious plans to celebrate had been shelved amid tearful goodbyes to long-serving employees, dramatic repatriations, and open questions about when the world would return to anything resembling normal. Craig had little time to reminisce, but on that day, his thoughts turned to how far things had come—from a classroom plea to seventh-graders to a charity and social enterprise known around the world.

Just then, an early morning email chimed on his phone. As it turned out, that message was the beginning of the end.

Now, Craig is not the kind of person who can ignore an email on a Sunday. Things might have turned out differently if he knew how to shut off, but as anyone who knows him will tell you, that is not one of his many strengths. So he picked up the phone and checked.

The message was from Rachel Wernick, senior assistant deputy minister with Employment and Social Development Canada (ESDC). "I am sorry for the 'out-of-the-blue' email on a Sunday morning," she wrote. "As you know there is a lot of quick work going on to support emergency and special measures in the current [COVID] context. I wondered if you would have a bit of time today to indulge me [in] a quick conversation on something we are working on that might be of interest to WE. There is a window of opportunity today to influence thinking and I would greatly benefit from your insights."[1]

After a brief email exchange, a phone call was scheduled for 12:30 that afternoon. When she and Craig connected, Wernick explained that the federal government was looking to create a youth service program as part of its pandemic social support efforts. Put simply, the government wanted to encourage students who were unable to find summer jobs during COVID to volunteer for non-profits instead, and they planned to offer grant money to sweeten the pot. It made sense. Jobs were hard to come by, and even volunteer opportunities would be scarce in the virtual/ COVID world. At the same time, many non-profits had positions available but struggled to connect with young people who could fill them.[2]

Although Wernick described the email as "out-of-the-blue," it wasn't unusual for her to contact WE Charity. She had consulted with the organization on several occasions over the years. In the 2015 federal election, Justin Trudeau's platform included a plan to develop a youth service program akin to the US Peace Corps. When he became prime minister, government bureaucrats made several attempts to get the program off the ground, with no real success. Wernick often called on WE Charity throughout this period to learn from the organization's past successes in this area. The first time came in October 2017, when she visited the charity's offices in Toronto and briefed senior staff on what was happening with the program. By 2018, the government had launched the "design phase" of something called the Canada Service Corps, which was a precursor to the CSSG on a smaller scale. As part of this effort, WE Charity received an $887,155 grant to beta-test different approaches that would inform how the government designed its program. Those test approaches exceeded benchmarks, so a year later, ESDC asked for a concept paper on how the government could create a national framework engaging diverse youth in service activities. WE Charity delivered the paper, but nothing came of it.

Fast-forward to April 2020. Wernick presented a concept with the lofty goals and catchy buzzwords that both governments and charities have a fondness for. It was a program intended to generate skills-development opportunities in an anemic job market, subsidize students in a time of social disruption, bolster communities through volunteer work, and support non-profits suffering badly in the harsh economic climate. It ultimately became the CSSG.

The vision was a government-led initiative implemented through partnerships with multiple non-profits. As it was explained to Craig, different organizations would handle different aspects of the program— one would manage a digital platform, another would facilitate payments to participants, yet another would recruit volunteers, and so forth. But Wernick said that in her view, WE Charity had to take a lead role to get the program off the ground. The government, she said, could not run an initiative of this scale on its own.

The aim was to launch the program in late May. This was the first red flag—it was already late April! After two elections and five years of talk of a large-scale national youth service program, Wernick's department was being asked to pull together a massive program in just weeks. She made clear to Craig that she didn't know how to accomplish that Herculean task. She invited him to submit a proposal with the organization's best thinking on how such a program might work, and how WE Charity could contribute.

Many people would have said no. But as I had learned in my years as a board member, the Kielburger brothers seem to revel (annoyingly so) in impossible deadlines. Sometimes, though, the race does not go to the swift.

Ironically, this potential lifeline for thousands of young people in a time of crisis became a death sentence for a charity whose raison d'être was helping those very same people become their best selves. As Craig would later tell the House of Commons Standing Committee on Finance (commonly known as FINA), "There are days when we wish we had never answered the phone on April 19."[3]

WHY WE? WHY NOT WE?

Over the course of the so-called WE Charity Scandal, many people have asked me why the government approached the organization to administer the CSSG in the first place. To those of us familiar with the work of WE Charity, it is a baffling question because the organization's core mission involved doing just what the government hoped to do here: facilitating volunteerism by young people. This mandate was even at the heart of the organization's slogan: "WE makes doing good doable."

The slogan seems not to have worked as well as the branding experts hoped. Despite WE Charity's long history and trustworthy reputation, many Canadians really don't know what it did and why it was only natural for the government to come knocking. This lack of understanding has led some to assume that the charity was trying to build a name off the back of the CSSG. Even a documentary on CBC's *Fifth Estate* in February 2021 invited viewers to ask, "Why did WE Charity get that contract?"

In reality, WE Charity wasn't using the CSSG as a stepping stone to anything. The organization was called upon by the government because of its expertise in implementing large-scale initiatives designed to encourage young people to volunteer. It had been doing this for more than two decades.

Back in 1999, the Ontario government of Conservative premier Mike Harris decided that every high school student in the province had to complete a minimum of forty hours of volunteer activity to graduate. The Conservatives changed the diploma requirements to this effect but failed to put in place any systems or programs to facilitate volunteerism, creating chaos for students, teachers, schools, and non-profits. Students had no idea how to find placements. Schools and school boards were ill-equipped to assist. And teachers were expected to define what volunteerism looked like and how it would be implemented and tracked. Meanwhile, charities were overwhelmed with young people showing up without the skills to do more than stack boxes. These volunteers were more often a burden than a blessing for non-profits, which had to come up with things for them to do and divert staff to train and supervise them.

I talked about those days with Donna Cansfield, a former Ontario Liberal cabinet minister and member of the provincial Parliament who was chair of the Toronto District School Board (TDSB) at the time. She vividly recalled the confusion. "What does that mean? How do you do it? What should you be engaged in? What kind of charity? What kind of work? I mean, there was no program that went with it. It was just: 'You're going to do it.'"

Though still a young and relatively small organization, Free the Children approached Cansfield and David Reid, then director of education for the TDSB, offering to help. They had a proposal for a program that could be included in the grade ten civics curriculum. It would guide students on how to design their own service opportunities. "Marc and Craig came in with their handbook [*Take Action: A Guide to Active Citizenship*], just teenagers at the time," Cansfield remembered. "And David and I looked at it and said, 'Wow! This is awesome.' We thought the approach Craig and Marc pitched was perfect. And away we went, putting it in every grade ten class in the Toronto District school [system]."

At the time, Erin Barton was a part-time student also working as one of the first employees at Free the Children. She went on to have a decades-long career at WE. Her journey began in high school, where she was deeply involved in student council and leadership. When she was seventeen, her school's chaplain handed her a Free the Children brochure and suggested that she start a chapter, so she reached out to Marc and Craig and began attending weekly meetings with the organization before starting her own group within the Dufferin-Peel Catholic school district.

Her early involvement would change the course of her life. Following the devastating 2010 earthquake in Haiti, she moved to the country and oversaw WE Charity's sustainable development projects, which served more than twenty thousand people. She also adopted two children while there. Fast-forward a decade, and Barton was voted one of Canada's Top 100 Most Powerful Women by the Women's Executive Network. She was one of the unstoppable forces behind the success of WE Charity.

Back in 1999, though, she was just starting her journey. "We were called on by Ontario school boards asking for help. 'There's not enough volunteer placements for kids,'" Erin recalled. "We were being called on to offer support because the government hadn't consulted with non-profit organizations to understand whether or not there were sufficient opportunities for those under sixteen to do volunteer work. And we were going to face a whole cohort of youth who were not going to graduate high school because they [hadn't] fulfilled this forty-hour requirement."

Working with the TDSB and Nelson Education, Canada's top educational publisher, Free the Children developed a program called Take Action. It included a textbook on service for use in the classroom, school speaking tours to educate kids about service opportunities, mentorship and coaches to help students build and launch their own volunteer activities, and a system that allowed teachers to track volunteer hours.

Mary-Eileen Donovan, a former WE Charity board member and one-time superintendent with the Toronto Catholic District School Board, remembered her introduction to Take Action. "I listened to the idea and arranged for Marc to come in to present to the education council, which is a group of superintendents, the director, and the deputy director. It was a group of about twenty of us—all in charge of schools, and all knowing full well that we were going to have to help schools implement and encourage these forty volunteer hours. He came in and explained that Take Action could go into schools, working through the civics program. I always felt WE's brilliance was understanding where the gaps were. It knew how to help the teachers and was a tremendous help to the kids. And when the program took off, it was a great success in our schools—for the principals, the teachers, and most importantly, the students."

This programming and the educational support system around it came to be known as WE Schools, and it spread like wildfire. "WE Charity lit a spark in young people's minds that said, 'I can do this.' And that lit a spark across school systems around the country and beyond. The charity engaged so many young people in civic action and into making a difference through its programming in schools. It has also done extraordinary things around the world. I know this because as a school board trustee, I witnessed it," Cansfield told me. By 2020, more than eighteen thousand schools in Canada, the US, the UK, and the Caribbean had adopted the WE Schools service-learning approach, including its youth mental health programs and Indigenous youth leadership training programs.

The service-learning model at the heart of WE Schools became so popular that it eventually came to the attention of the College Board. A mainstay of US post-secondary education, the College Board is made up of over six thousand universities, colleges, and other educational institutions. Each year, the College Board helps more than seven million students prepare for a successful transition to college and oversees the SAT exam system. It also created the Advanced Placement (AP) program—a national initiative that allows American high school students to take courses for post-secondary credit and enhances qualification for entry into college and university programs.

The College Board was interested in building a service-learning component into its AP courses. It vetted organizations from around the world to assist, and eventually selected WE Charity. The AP with WE Service was born. The program weaves volunteerism and community service into the core curriculum of all AP courses. A science student could learn about biology by testing water quality in her community. A Spanish course might include helping new immigrants fill out government forms. Computer science students might supplement their coursework by coding apps for charities. The AP with WE Service became the first on-transcript recognition of service for American students applying to US colleges. In the 2018–19 academic year, it reached all fifty states.

But WE Charity's experience with large-scale initiatives went well beyond schools and college readiness. In 2017, for example, long before the CSSG, the charity partnered with Heritage Canada to celebrate the country's 150th birthday. WE Day Canada took place on Parliament Hill on Canada Day weekend. While most other Canada Day events focused on the past 150 years, WE Day Canada looked to the future and celebrated the next generation.

WE Day began in 2007 as a way to acknowledge the contribution of young people who were taking action through WE Schools programming—and encourage them to do even more. In a culture increasingly focused on material wealth, it was an event that honoured acts of kindness and giving. It wanted to bring young people together to celebrate their altruism and reward them in a unique and fun way for the work they had done over the school year.

From its modest debut at the Ricoh Coliseum in Toronto, WE Day—one part pep rally, one part motivational speech, and one part rock concert—grew into a Canadian export success story. By 2020, WE Day events were taking place annually in eighteen cities in Canada, the US, and the UK. In total, there have been more than 130 WE Days, and they have welcomed approximately 1.5 million young people. To transmit that energy and message even further, WE Day primetime specials aired regularly in both Canada and the US, garnering millions of viewers. And the best part was the catchline: "You can't buy a ticket to WE Day." Instead, the only way young people could earn the right to attend was by performing one local and one global act of service. According to WE Charity records, students completed over forty million hours of service, as verified by their teachers.[4]

Unlike almost every other charity-hosted event, WE Day was cause-inclusive, meaning attendees were under no pressure to volunteer for or give money to WE Charity. On stage, presenters and performers touted hundreds of other causes that had nothing to do with the work of WE. This kind of lateral co-promotion is all but unheard of in a sector where every non-profit is in competition for a finite pool of government grants and donor dollars.

The event's high-profile speakers and A-list celebrities spoke about their own passions in a way that motivated students. For example, comedian and actor Seth Rogen talked about raising awareness for Alzheimer's through his non-profit, HFC. Actor Charlize Theron promoted UNAIDS and shared her painful childhood experiences seeing HIV affect people she knew growing up in South Africa. These A-listers also championed the service of young people in a way that made it "cool" to give back. The implicit message was that you did not need to be a star athlete or the best-looking kid in class to be popular—instead, some of the most exciting people in the world said *they* were inspired by *you*. As Prince Harry put it during a speech at WE Day UK in Wembley Arena several years ago, "Some people don't think it's cool to help others; personally, I think it's the coolest thing in the world!"[5]

In between the stars, musical acts, and renowned activists like Malala Yousafzai and David Suzuki were ordinary—or more accurately, extraordinary—young speakers. Transgender youth, young people with physical challenges or living with HIV, First Nations people—these were speakers the student audience could relate to, be inspired by, and hope to emulate.

TESTIMONIAL: AIZA ABID

Aiza Abid is the founder of Aiza's Teddybear Foundation, a non-profit organization that serves local and global communities. She has been a lifelong advocate for children's rights and has received the Sovereign's Medal for Volunteers.

I found my voice through volunteering when I was seven years old. It was around this time that I took a trip to Pakistan with my family and witnessed the intergenerational effects of poverty. Children around my age were cleaning houses and collecting bread that was being disposed of. I returned to a life of privilege, measured against what I had experienced overseas, and I knew that I had to make a difference. One thing that stood out to me was that up until that point, I had never volunteered alongside anyone my age.

In grade seven, that all changed. I moved to a newly opened school and helped create the first WE Club there. Every week we would brainstorm ideas, organize fundraisers, and advance our personal commitments to our community. The turnout was always really inspiring, and students from every grade came out to support the club. It was also a safe haven for many, since students knew they could drop in and sit with other people who really cared about each other and the world.

One day, when I was in the tenth grade, we were asked to take action on an initiative of our choice for a civics project. I was thrilled! I could finally create an all-encompassing project that would allow me to make service activities more meaningful for and accessible to students. I founded a grassroots non-profit that works to provide physical and emotional support to children in need. Since 2013, Aiza's Teddybear Foundation has sent hundreds of thousands of "bear hugs" in the form of teddies, warm clothing, school supplies, books, and good food to under-resourced children around the world.

Through this work, I have learned the critical importance of empathy, compassion, and understanding. Once we have the tools to help ourselves, we can help others. Teaching these skills to children during their formative years can make the world a better place. And once these values become ingrained, they can stick with you for a lifetime.

For me, WE Day was less a platform and more a springboard for activists and activism. In writing this book, I listened to many young people tell me what WE Day meant to them. Their message—almost entirely ignored by Canadian journalists and politicians in the aftermath of the CSSG scandal—is one of accomplishment and promise. For them, it was invariably the case that the activists outstripped the celebrity performers in terms of real impact.

Aiza Abid has been almost a lifelong volunteer for many causes, and she was very involved with her WE Club in high school and continued to advise them after her graduation. Now a recent graduate of McMaster University, Abid lives in Toronto and operates an international non-profit called Aiza's Teddybear Foundation, which she started while in high school.

Abid and her friends found that their WE Club offered something intangible that arrived at just the right time in their young lives—inclusiveness and empathy. And WE Day was a source of perpetual inspiration to keep doing more. "WE Day is something I think students are really going to miss out on now," she said. "WE Day was one of a kind. I just remember every time we would leave, on the bus back home or on the train back home, everyone would just be oozing with so much positivity and excitement for giving back. And I think that's the coolest thing ever."

Susanne Boyce, a former WE Charity board member and executive with both CBC and CTV, expressed similar sentiments when she spoke to me about her decision to broadcast WE Day on television. She told me that she went to bat for the event because she believed that young people would respond to its positive message about making a difference. And it was also an opportunity to "export this piece of Canada," she said, to the world. But she encountered resistance from some who thought it might not be "fun" programming that would attract young viewers. Boyce felt vindicated in her decision to push because, even with the sad news of the charity's closure in Canada, "WE has changed things and influenced a generation."

I was at WE Day Canada on Parliament Hill in 2017. I brought my then six-year-old son and my parents along as well. What we experienced with the crowd of over ten thousand people was a celebration of the possibility of a bright future. These kids were fired up, and the energy was contagious, even for those on the stage.

One particularly stirring highlight was a rare public appearance by Tragically Hip frontman Gord Downie, a true Canadian icon, just three months before he died of brain cancer. "We leave behind the first 150 years," Downie said from the stage. "The ones with one big problem—trying to wipe out our Indigenous people, to take their minds and hearts, to give them the choice: become white or get lost."[6] He spoke passionately about the need for young Canadians to learn the history of residential schools, where children suffered horrendous emotional and physical abuse. He told the story of Chanie Wenjack, a twelve-year-old Indigenous boy who died of hunger and exposure trying to flee the abuse of the residential school he was forced to attend. Chanie's sisters, Pearl and Daisy, stood side by side with Downie as they performed an Indigenous song about reconciliation.

Among the many other speakers that day were Governor General David Johnston and Lieutenant-General (ret.) Roméo Dallaire, both of whom captivated the audience. At one point, Dallaire, a Canadian hero who is revered worldwide for his efforts to prevent genocide in Rwanda in 1994, spontaneously took off his tie and jubilantly threw it into the crowd, an expression of sheer joy from an otherwise sombre figure. "You are the future," he told the younger people in the crowd. "We're setting up your future. It's in your hands now. You're the generation without borders. You're global—you're communicating real time globally. You'll Skype anybody in the world. You will influence directly every human being. And so, you can be a generation that says human rights is for all humans."[7]

For his part, Johnston seemed to feel the connection with his rapt audience. "It feels like change, it feels like hope, it feels like the Canada we desire and the one we deserve—a place of peace, respect, equality, fairness, and creativity," he told the young faces looking back at him. "How do we build that Canada? You're the answer to this question. Young people like you, who are working today for a greater country tomorrow."[8]

WE Day Canada took place on the doorstep of the federal government and left an impression. Yes, WE knew how to harness celebrity star power to full effect. Yes, WE knew how to handle large-scale and complex logistics. But more importantly, WE put its connection with young people on display. That ability—not political cronyism—is why Wernick called on WE Charity, and why WE Charity felt compelled to respond.

All this history would be largely ignored in the soon-to-unfold controversy over the CSSG.

RELUCTANT WARRIORS

Many people believe that the CSSG was the brainchild of the Kielburgers, or that they pulled on every available political string to make it happen. Pithy sound bites and media headlines fed this narrative through the summer of 2020. MP Charlie Angus of the NDP repeatedly claimed that "WE was massively overextended and in economic free fall,"[9] and that the CSSG was a "bail out package for the Kielburgers."[10] Conservative MP Pierre Poilievre joined the chorus, stating that Craig had a proposal ready for Wernick when she reached out, "almost as though he was expecting her call."[11] A *Toronto Star* headline read, "How WE Charity's Youth Pitch Worked Its Way Through Trudeau's Government."[12] The *Globe and Mail* followed with "WE Charity Pitch to Morneau's Office Prior to Trudeau Announcement Included Student Service."[13]

The program, the story goes, was a lifeline for a charity facing a diminishing platform and fading fortunes. Prime Minister Trudeau, Finance Minister Bill Morneau, and others in the Liberal Party allegedly schemed to help their supposed friends at WE Charity secure the lucrative contract as payback for appearances on the WE Day stage, speaking fees to the prime minister's mother and brother, and expenses associated with trips Morneau and his family took to WE Charity international development projects. None of this, as you will learn in this chapter and those that follow, has any relation to the facts.

Inside WE Charity, there was much debate as to whether to answer the government's call by submitting a proposal. Far from jumping at the opportunity, the organization pondered how to respond by taking a series of deep breaths—with some sighs and brow-wiping thrown in for good measure. Wernick wanted WE Charity to help launch a massive national youth service program in a matter of months—a feat the government had not managed to accomplish in four years. And during a pandemic, no less. For its part, WE Charity had just laid off scores of people and was overstretched handling a series of pressing domestic and international commitments.

Just what was everyone doing? At home, the WE Schools team was working around the clock to move the organization's service-learning curriculum online for its eighteen thousand school partners and develop new options relevant to the pandemic, such as ways for students to support frontline healthcare workers and connect with seniors and other vulnerable people. In addition, the team was developing a wide range of COVID-appropriate content, with teams of educators filming daily virtual lessons for teachers from kindergarten to grade twelve.

WE's mental health programming was also a focus. When lockdowns began, the relatively new WE Well-being program quickly released a series of mental health toolkits focused on easy at-home exercises to reduce stress and anxiety. The *WE Well-being Playbook*, which had just been published in February, was given a COVID makeover and re-released for free on Amazon. Written in collaboration with mental health professionals, the book contained tips, reflection pieces, exercises, and activities to help kids and adults enhance their own mental health and the well-being of those around them. On top of all that, the WE team was producing a series of well-being podcasts hosted by Sophie Grégoire Trudeau.

Meanwhile, the charity's international programs team was in overdrive, coordinating a logistically challenging global relief effort. Even though most expatriate staff members had returned home at the start of the pandemic, in-country national staff in the nine nations where WE Charity operated were working hard to support education outreach (teaching the benefits of social distancing and mask wearing) and deliver supplies.

The largest pandemic response took place in Kenya, where WE Charity had built significant infrastructure and community relationships over decades. Partnering with World Medical Relief, the charity dispatched shipping containers loaded with masks, gloves, medical equipment, and other necessities in mid-April. Another shipment with a ventilator and ten thousand KN95 masks was delivered in May. By the end of the summer, an estimated $8 million in health supplies had arrived at WE Charity and partner facilities in the country. Similar efforts were underway in Ecuador, where a public awareness campaign brought COVID information to remote communities deep in the Amazon. And in Haiti, WE Charity helped install solar panels at a hospital in Hinche, ensuring blackouts did not threaten the lives of COVID patients on ventilators.

On the ground in Kenya, two WE-funded regional health facilities—Baraka Hospital and Kishon Health Centre—anchored COVID health measures in the region. These two facilities already provided medical care to more than 125,000 people in Narok and Bomet counties, along the edge of the Maasai Mara reserve. Now the doctors and nurses working there prepared for a potential outbreak. At the nearby WE College, Baraka staff turned empty classrooms into makeshift wards and operating theatres. The college was essentially transformed into a backup health centre to handle non-COVID medical issues. Beside the college, a field hospital like something out of *M*A*S*H* stood ready to serve as a COVID isolation ward. The huge green tents had previously been used for groups of young volunteers participating in ME to WE Trips—a poignant reminder that the social enterprise existed to support the charity.

WE Charity was also spreading the word about COVID to remote communities. A massive education and outreach campaign provided three hundred thousand people with information about the disease and how to prevent its spread. "Our people were literally going house by house talking to people. 'Have you heard of COVID? Do you know how it's transmitted? Do you understand what it looks like if you get symptoms? And do you understand what you're supposed to do if you have that?'" Robin Wiszowaty recounted. Driver Charles Kimani even mounted loudspeakers on the roof of the Landcruiser he had once used to transport trip participants, converting it into a mobile public service announcement platform. And later in the spring, staff created a radio PSA and an SMS campaign that delivered COVID-related information to the mobile phones of nearly four thousand people.

Elsewhere, education teams drove hundreds of kilometres a day to reach remote communities scattered across thousands of square kilometres of savannah. Having travelled those bumpy makeshift roads myself—although in my case with the leisure to stop and photograph cheetahs along the way—I understood what it must have been like to try to reach the communities we all loved before the virus did. The spring rainy season made things worse, as dirt roads turned into tire-grabbing bogs. But staff persisted, distributing four thousand bars of hand soap, countless packets of vegetable seeds to address food insecurity, and thirty-five thousand dehydrated meals donated by the Unstoppable Foundation. And in the ensuing months, the organization reported delivering over 1.5 million meals to support communities in the region.[14]

This was the backdrop against which WE Charity had to decide whether to accept the invitation to submit a proposal for administering the CSSG.

Undeterred, Dalal Al-Waheidi, the executive director, was championing the opportunity. For her, it came from a sense of duty. A Palestinian born in Kuwait during the Gulf War, Dalal fled to the Gaza Strip with her family in 1991. As a child, she saw the terrible impact of conflict, political instability, and violence. She experienced marginalization and deprivation, studying through power outages and living through air strikes. In Gaza, Dalal went to a school for refugee children and eventually earned a scholarship to the United World College in Norway. In 1998, she was one of two students from the college selected for a scholarship to Trent University in Peterborough, Ontario, more than nine thousand kilometres away from her family. When she graduated from Trent, she landed at WE Charity, where an internship started a twenty-year journey to the head table, steering the organization.

Dalal's intimate familiarity with the more brutal side of life—a quintessentially Canadian immigrant story—made it impossible for her to imagine refusing to contribute in a time of need. She explained to me that despite the uncertainties about how the CSSG could be implemented in such a short period of time, she felt no confusion about the benefits it would confer on young Canadians. "Imagine how challenging it must be to deal with a pandemic and, at the same time, with the prospect of not being able to find work so you can continue to go to school. And hardest hit would be young people living in marginalized or disadvantaged communities," she said. "The CSSG was a lifeline for young Canadians in an unprecedented time. We were uniquely positioned to rapidly implement, and I was confident we could prioritize diversity and those most in need." Those were the people she wanted to help. To her mind, these were reasons to move mountains.

Like Dalal, many others within the charity believed that the beating heart of the organization had always been its ability to overcome obstacles in its mission to inspire young people to serve. With every meeting on the CSSG, the executive leadership team offered creative solutions for how the program could be achieved. If WE Charity did not step up when the government wanted to help young people make it through a crisis by volunteering, who would? And yes, the CSSG also presented a chance for the charity to rehire some laid-off colleagues and get them back to doing what the organization did best. "The CSSG came as a light of hope," Dalal recalled. "We can build something, get people motivated to do good. We're good at building programs and creating impact, and we've proven this again and again."

In Dalal's confident voice, I heard echoes of thoughts shared with me by former prime minister Kim Campbell in a series of conversations we had for this book. Campbell—the nation's first and so far only female prime minister—has an easy, welcoming manner that made me feel like I was chatting with an old friend. But as is clear in her foreword, she does not mince words, and she has been an outspoken advocate for many causes in her post-political life, particularly in support of women's rights and empowerment.

Campbell told me how she had tracked WE Charity's progress from Free the Children to the global empowerment movement it became. She has seen the organization in action overseas, having taken a ME to WE volunteer trip with her sister, during which she joined the first lady of Kenya, Margaret Kenyatta, at the grand opening of WE College in rural Narok County. And she has seen WE Charity motivate young people at home too. I could clearly sense the pride she felt when she talked about how a Canadian charity had made a big difference in the world.

Her point to me was simple: there was a time when it was commonly understood by all Canadians that if the government needed your help, you answered the call to serve. That was a lesson she received from her parents, who both served in the Second World War. In her view, WE Charity should have been applauded for taking on the ill-fated CSSG, rather than put through the political wringer.

But I have got too far ahead in the story.

Battle-weary Marc and Craig were less easily convinced about the wisdom of moving forward. You could hardly fault them. They had closely followed the government's prolonged but ultimately unsuccessful efforts to establish a major national youth service program, and they had just ended twenty-five years of non-stop work by having to lay off countless employees because of the pandemic. There were personal considerations as well. For decades, people had been telling them to slow down and make time for themselves and their families. I have seen first-hand how much they sacrificed for the sake of WE Charity, and like many others, I've often felt the demands they placed on themselves and others were unreasonable. "You don't always have to run like your hair is on fire," I said to Craig and Marc on more than one occasion. Every time, they would just shrug and laugh it off.

When Craig's first child was born in 2017, he spent just five days with him before flying off to Kenya to be at project sites for a month. The intervening years were more of the same, with in excess of three hundred days a year of travel. It was time he would never get back. Craig was determined not to miss so much of the early childhood of his second son, due in June 2020, and that was a factor in his thinking about the CSSG. He told me, "No one would have blamed us for saying, 'No, thank you. I just want to sit still and hold my son in my hands.'"

For Marc, the summer of 2020 was the first in two decades when he did not need to be overseas almost every day. With his wife and their two children, he was looking forward to a more relaxing period focused on family time. He had spent much of 2018 and 2019 grappling with everything from a tense situation in Kenya to spurious allegations from the media outlet Canadaland back at home. More on those topics later. The bottom line is that he had earned a break.

So between April 19 and 21, 2020, there was a great deal of soul-searching as the Kielburgers and WE executives considered the pros and cons of saying yes to the government. This has been described to me as a series of difficult conversations, often lasting many hours. Because the initial question was only whether to submit a proposal of interest to continue the dialogue with the civil service, the charity's board members were not involved in these deliberations. So I was not in the room (or on the Zoom) when the Kielburgers and the senior leadership team eventually got to yes. If you had asked me beforehand, though, I would have told you that yes was inevitable. Partly this is because the Kielburgers are incapable, in their bones, of shrinking from a challenge that others might view as insurmountable. And partly it's because of the ethos of the organization, a philosophy best captured in the Quechuan term *minga*.

For years, Craig and Marc have shared the story of a trip to a village in Ecuador, where they heard this term for the first time. They have featured it in books they have written, in their columns in the *Globe and Mail*, and in speeches they have delivered at universities and events. *Minga* does not have an easy English translation. It refers to a social contract in which community members gather to complete a large task in a short amount of time to fulfil a collective responsibility. A traditional chief in the village explained to Craig and Marc that in times of need, she calls for a *minga*, and everyone stops in their tracks and comes together to work for the benefit of all. A sort of barn raising in the Amazon. Whatever the task—building a hut, constructing a school, or creating an entire village—you do not say no when asked to help. The CSSG was a *minga*, and thus not something the organization could walk away from.

So after much thought, the charity dove in head first. WE did not know it was the shallow end.

CHAPTER 4

MISSION CREEP

On April 22, Craig sent WE Charity's preliminary proposal for the CSSG to Rachel Wernick at Employment and Social Development Canada and copied numerous other government officials, including Finance Minister Bill Morneau, who was also the local member of Parliament for WE Charity's riding, and Bardish Chagger, the diversity and inclusion and youth minister.[1] It was a twenty-two-page outline for a digital program that would help twenty thousand young Canadians find summer service placements during the COVID pandemic. The bilingual program would consist of a web-based portal that would match people between the ages of sixteen and twenty-nine with volunteer opportunities at non-profit organizations across the country. These placements would offer alternatives to traditional summer jobs, provide skills-development opportunities, be diverse and inclusive, and address many urgent social needs. The program would run from late May to the end of August and conclude with a virtual celebration hosted by WE and streamed live online.

WE Charity was not offering placements itself—it was simply the program administrator. Its role was to match students with non-profit organizations, track their hours, and ultimately disburse government funds based on the number of hours logged. The system would set minimum and maximum hours for each volunteer opportunity, and participants would earn $500 for every thirty hours completed, or $16.67 per hour. The maximum number of hours any one student could work was three hundred—meaning the maximum grant from the government would be $5,000.

If the program attracted a full complement of twenty thousand young people, WE Charity estimated that the total cost to Canadian taxpayers would be $44.5 million. Of that, $30 million would be grant money paid directly to students (not every student would want or be able to complete the full three hundred hours); $12 million (or $600 per student) would cover the costs of developing and administering the program, vetting and supporting non-profit partners, and so on; and $2.5 million would be to reimburse costs incurred by participating organizations. Because it would soon balloon in scope and size at the government's request, WE Charity's original proposal was less than a tenth of the eventual budget for the program.

Craig also attached to the email one additional document that was unrelated to the CSSG. It was a summary of a concept for an entrepreneurship program that had been percolating within WE as COVID took hold and concerns grew about limited summer job opportunities for students. WE Charity had previously told Wernick and other civil servants that as a general matter, it viewed a pay-for-service model for promoting volunteerism (in other words, the concept behind the CSSG) as inferior to funding young people to develop socially minded businesses. As Craig explained it to me, when you pay a student to volunteer, the program requires constant injections of government cash or it runs out of money. But if you help young people build their own social enterprises, they have a self-sustaining model. It is a twist on the old adage: instead of paying someone to fish, you help them launch their own sustainable fishing business.

As conceived, WE's suggested entrepreneurship program would encourage up to eight thousand young people to create social enterprises. Each participant who completed the program would receive a grant of around $500, and $800,000 would be set aside to support the very best idea and bring it to life. The funding request for the entrepreneurship proposal ranged from $6 million to $14 million, depending on how the program was designed. So it was far smaller than the CSSG.

Craig had already tried to interest Wernick and several others—including Mary Ng, minister of small business, export promotion, and international trade; Bardish Chagger; and Bill Morneau—in this social enterprise idea, but all were focused on the pandemic and it gained little traction. But he decided to attach the alternative proposal to his email just in case—a decision he would come to regret. Opposition politicians would later point to Craig's prior outreach regarding the social entrepreneurship program and the fact that he'd included it with the initial CSSG proposal as evidence that WE Charity had lobbied for the CSSG. In fact, the opposite was true: WE Charity was raising flags about the CSSG concept. But as this story unfolded, truth proved insufficient to stop questions, suspicions, and politically motivated efforts to sow confusion.

A WTF MOMENT

On the very day WE submitted its CSSG proposal, Prime Minister Trudeau publicly announced that his government was allocating almost $9 billion to support Canadian students during the pandemic.[2] This huge amount of money would be shared among a great many initiatives, including the Canada Emergency Student Benefit, enhanced student loan programs, and research grants, as well as the CSSG.[3] "COVID has meant that there aren't as many jobs out there for students," Trudeau said, "and without a job, it can be hard to pay for tuition or the day-to-day basics. You might normally have turned to your parents for help, but right now Mom and Dad are stretched, too." The allocated funds, he explained, would provide financial support, create good job opportunities, and promote a sustainable economic recovery. He specifically mentioned the CSSG, which he said would provide grants of up to $5,000 to give students "valuable work experience and skills while they help their communities during the COVID pandemic."[4]

This announcement was a literal WTF moment at WE Charity. Clearly the announcement had been planned for some time, and there is no way anyone in government could have digested WE's preliminary proposal, which had arrived the same day. People at WE were flummoxed. How could the government announce a program when it hadn't firmed up any details? Had it already received proposals from other organizations and was further along in the process than thought? Was it not seriously considering WE Charity as administrator? Was it intending to barrel forward even if it had not yet decided how the program would work and which organization would handle its administration? No one at WE Charity knew the answers. This made everyone very nervous—and would foreshadow the chaotic process to come. "Looking back, perhaps we should have seen this coming," Dalal later told me. "The warning sign that there were just too many fundamental questions and many constant changes, and that the government wasn't ready to be collaborative and supportive."

For two days, WE Charity heard nothing more. Then, on April 24, Craig was invited to join a conference call with Wernick and senior finance officials, including Michelle Kovacevic, the assistant deputy minister, and Amitpal Singh, a senior policy adviser to Bill Morneau.[5] Craig was briefed on the prime minister's announcement and given further information on the government's intentions and priorities for the CSSG. This was when he learned that people were now imagining a program with forty thousand or even a hundred thousand participants, instead of the twenty thousand originally discussed. The understanding was still that the program would launch by the end of May, which was just over a month away.

The Kielburgers and the WE Charity leadership team immediately had misgivings. The program was beginning to look like a greater commitment than originally envisioned, with a much larger budget and scope and on a brutal and ever-changing deadline.

During the last week of April, the charity tried to get a handle on the government's expectations. As the organization's executive director, and given the significance of the initiative, Dalal personally led the project and oversaw liaison with the government. Although WE Charity didn't know which other organizations were being considered to run part or all of the program, the civil service informed the organization on a number of occasions that it was asking other charities to submit proposals. Later, documents released to the FINA committee revealed the government was looking at the online platform Do Some Good and the governor general's office as options. And other government documents showed that Shopify and TakingITGlobal had also been contacted, and that Ceridian, Imagine Canada, Volunteer Canada, the Canadian Red Cross, and the United Way were floated as possibilities. Michelle Kovacevic confirmed this when she appeared before the Standing Committee on Access to Information, Privacy and Ethics (commonly known as ETHI) in December. "In fact," she told the committee, "we went through many potential organizations as we were trying to land both a design and the potential delivery partner."[6]

On April 28, there were multiple phone calls involving Craig; Sofia Marquez, WE Charity's director of government and stakeholder relations; Wernick; Singh; and Ritu Banerjee, the executive director of ESDC. The government officials said that they had sourced another provider to handle delivery of the program through an online platform. Banerjee asked Marquez to provide contact information for WE Charity's technology staff so government tech experts could connect and discuss. Those conversations quickly revealed that the government solution and contemplated provider would not be sufficient to meet the needs of the students. By the end of the week, Dalal had set up a separate team within WE Charity to lead administration of the program, should it ultimately become the responsibility of the organization. This team began work on an updated and more comprehensive proposal based on feedback received from the government in calls and emails.

WE's willingness to hit the ground running before the CSSG contribution agreement was even signed later came under scrutiny. Conservative MP Pierre Poilievre, for one, aggressively questioned Dalal, Marquez, and Scott Baker at the FINA hearings about who had given them permission to start working. "Somebody told you over at WE that you could go and start spending money, hiring people and implementing the program," he asserted. "Who told you that?"[7] But at the time, people at WE were only thinking about the fast-approaching deadline to launch this national program. It was clear that if the charity did not start the process to ramp up—and soon—there would be no program at all. "Many people misunderstood this early activity and made fodder of WE starting to work as if the contract was in the bag," Dalal later said to me. "Not true."

As a lawyer, I knew exactly what she meant. In my line of work, it's not uncommon to spend time engaging in a detailed analysis of a case or providing advice to a client even before you are formally retained. In fact, that's often precisely how you *get* hired. You cannot say to a potential client, "Hire me and then—and *only* then—I will offer you my advice and insights." And that's especially true if it is a significant matter or a project you really care about—and WE cared about the CSSG. This was about lending a hand to young Canadians in the midst of a once-in-a-century crisis.

In her testimony before the ETHI committee, Gina Wilson, deputy minister for diversity and inclusion and youth, explained that "with contribution agreements, a start date may be identified prior to the date of the agreement's signature."[8] Here, the start date for the CSSG contribution agreement was May 5, even though the agreement was not signed until late June. That's because "it may often take weeks for a contribution agreement to be negotiated," Wilson said, "and that is what occurred in this particular instance." Meanwhile, work needed to get done if there was any chance of launching the CSSG on schedule. So WE Charity took a risk—if the contribution agreement never got signed, the organization would not have been reimbursed for any expenses.

"We were putting a lot on the line and assuming risks," Dalal said, "but what other choice did we have? If we didn't start the work, it would have been impossible for this program to launch before summer was half over."

Because she knew that WE had to act before it was too late, Dalal began to reach out to contacts in the Canadian non-profit sector to discuss logistics. She started with Bruce MacDonald, CEO of Imagine Canada, a bilingual organization that advocates for, researches, and works with Canadian charities, non-profits, and social entrepreneurs. On the call, they discussed many issues, including the wisdom of paying young people to do volunteer work. MacDonald cautioned that many non-profit organizations did not support the idea of affixing a dollar value to volunteer hours. This warning was borne out when Dalal later contacted Paula Speevak, the president and CEO of Volunteer Canada, a non-profit association promoting volunteerism, and she declined to take part in the CSSG. "Our organization had concerns about paying an hourly rate for community service . . . and calling this 'volunteering,'" Speevak subsequently testified at the FINA hearings. "This could create the wrong message about volunteering and potentially undermine volunteer engagement in the future."[9]

As these and other concerns were beginning to reveal themselves, a flurry of activity was happening within the federal government, all of it outside the purview of WE Charity. Briefing notes, funding notes, and recommendations were flying between the Privy Council Office, the Prime Minister's Office (PMO), the finance department, ESDC, the government's COVID committee, and Minister Chagger's youth and diversity office.[10] ESDC was especially focused on pushing WE as its choice to deliver the CSSG,[11] presumably because it had seen what WE could do over the years and had historically faced challenges trying to get a government-run youth program off the ground.

Later, when questions about the program reached a flashpoint, many opposition politicians and media pundits zeroed in on the idea that WE Charity had been awarded a sole-source contract. In other words, there were no other bidders. That may be a valid criticism—*of the government*. But the people at WE Charity never knew who the government was— or was not—talking to. They were told from the start that other groups had been asked to submit proposals to administer part or all of the program. Marc and Craig told me that government contacts had even described ongoing discussions with various alternative administrators, with Wernick at one point telling Marc that another organization under consideration was not a viable option because it was "archaic." Marc assumed, incorrectly, that she had reached that conclusion based on a submitted proposal. It wasn't until well after the CSSG was announced that WE Charity learned it was the only organization that had put forward a formal proposal.

In preparing his report, Ethics Commissioner Mario Dion—an independent, non-partisan parliamentary officer responsible for policing government conflicts of interest—found that in early April, ESDC officials had reached out to the Canada Service Corps, which already had a modest micro-grant program, to ask about expanding its capacity.[12] But the agency could provide only about seven thousand micro-grants and said it would take three months to put everything in place. The government wanted something bigger and wanted it faster. Rachel Wernick told Commissioner Dion that Volunteer Canada was also approached. That organization, Wernick explained, had already received government funding to develop a platform to give young people easy access to volunteer opportunities. It had built a database of eighty thousand of these opportunities, but the uptake was limited, largely because of a lack of social media integration. The government concluded that it needed a third party with a larger network and the ability to get the word out on social media. "Specifically," Dion wrote, "WE was in a position to help provide 20,000 placement opportunities, assist in populating the portal by working with its network to seek new opportunities, perform a clearinghouse function and vet opportunities based on the criteria provided, and administer the grants to each recipient."[13]

WE Charity was not privy to any of these discussions, nor should it have been. The government's internal decision-making is opaque, and stakeholders never have access to it.

To my mind, by having what appeared to be informal conversations with multiple candidates instead of acquiring formal proposals, the government fuelled much of the public perception that the decision to put the program into WE Charity's hands was part of some backroom deal. As government officials would later testify, time pressures made a typical procurement process unfeasible. I'm not positioned to say whether that is a fair basis for a sole-source contract, but it was certainly not a fair basis for the accusations hurled at WE Charity, which had no voice in the process and no obligation to do the work of the civil servants.

Instead, the organization was wholly focused on the preparation needed to roll out a project of national scope in an accelerated time frame. To that end, WE Charity delivered to Wernick a more comprehensive proposal in the form of a fifty-eight-page slide deck. The new outline was based on two core principles: (1) the need to provide meaningful volunteer opportunities for young people and do it quickly, and (2) the need to create an easy-to-implement program to facilitate the work of non-profits in a time of extreme hardship. The new maximum budget estimate (per instructions from ESDC), for a program with a hundred thousand participants, was $543.5 million. That would be $500 million in grants to students (assuming all participants earned the maximum grant, which was very unlikely) and $8.7 million to participating non-profits. WE Charity would receive a maximum of $34.8 million to administer the program, and this was just to cover reimbursement of defined eligible expenses. The organization could not make any profit or be "paid" anything because this was not a commercial contract between the government and a private company.

On May 5, WE Charity had its only point of contact with the PMO. At the request of the civil service, Craig, Marc, and Sofia Marquez spent thirty minutes briefing policy director Rick Theis on the organization's proposal for the CSSG. Critics later tried to spin this call as some kind of back-channel dialogue between WE and the prime minister, but Dion debunked that notion in his ethics report. "I could find no evidence," he wrote, "that Mr. Trudeau provided specific instruction to Cabinet or to his ministerial staff on how to proceed in respect of the student aid package.[14]

While Dalal and senior leadership continued to liaise with the government and move the program forward, Scott Baker was working to bring on board the non-profit organizations that were essential if the program was to create the needed number of volunteer placements. Here, too, the government's increased expectations were ballooning the project. WE Charity now had to bring on board at least a hundred partner organizations—double the original number.

"We were trying to solve two challenges," Scott explained. "One was to give young people an opportunity to receive money and gain professional experience during the summer months when those opportunities no longer were available. And the second challenge was to structure this in such a way that these students could substantially contribute to the not-for-profit sector within Canada."

To get much-needed funds into the hands of students in a summer that promised a job drought was obviously a high priority. Marc and Dalal had strongly recommended that the program pay minimum wage at the very least, and preferably something closer to industry standard. The government rejected this and set the honorariums at below minimum wage. WE Charity would later shoulder the blame for this, even though it was a decision that went against its initial recommendation of $16.67 per hour (an amount above the minimum wage in every province). "I think it's important to note that this was not the WE Charity program," said Scott. "It was a government program. We were following what we were being told to do. We raised all these concerns we heard from the sector, but in the end, we had to follow whatever direction ESDC wanted to take."

Dalal was more blunt in her assessment. "We were thrown under the bus," she said. "What people fail to understand is that it was the government's decision to select WE Charity. It was the government that designed the framework and parameters of the program. We did not design the program. We were the implementing partner."

MISGIVINGS MOUNT

Despite the missteps, the organization still forged ahead because WE's executive team believed that the program would help young people and struggling non-profits. One of the first orders of business was figuring out how young volunteers with little to no work experience would be trained. WE Charity had not forgotten the lessons learned in the 1990s, when it rolled out programming to help students meet their required forty volunteer hours. For small charities, the burden of training and supervising young volunteers could be prohibitive. If the CSSG was a burden on non-profits, then it would have failed to meet one of its main objectives.

· This led to the idea of inviting teachers—who would be out on summer vacation—to act as mentors for the student volunteers, taking this task off the shoulders of the participating non-profits. The teachers could also help identify and recruit Indigenous, LGBTQ, new Canadian, and economically disadvantaged youth into the program. Inclusivity was a key component of WE Charity's proposal—it did not want these paid opportunities to go entirely to privileged kids. Also, the young people who would most benefit from this program often required training and hands-on coaching to succeed. For assisting a group of students, teachers would be paid just as if they were working a summer teaching job.

Board member Gerry Connelly, a former director of education with the Toronto District School Board and now an education adviser for the Learning Partnership, a Canadian charity that develops experiential programs to help young people continue learning outside the classroom, told me how much support she saw for the CSSG among fellow educators. "I had never seen such enthusiasm and interest," she said, "and it was going to make a great impact for students. It was a complex program to put together in such a brief period, and not only did WE do so in an efficient way but comprehensively across Canada."

Connelly described listening in on many of the teleconferences that Marc, Dalal, and other team members had initiated with teachers across Canada to get them involved. "There were hundreds of people who wanted to get rolling," she said. "WE had no problem at all getting people interested. It was overwhelming."

I heard much the same thing from Ruben Borba, an educator with the Toronto Catholic District School Board who helped WE Charity recruit students for the program. He told me the CSSG offered a holistic approach and real-world opportunities to kids who wouldn't otherwise have them. "These students have talents within them. Now they had a chance to use them. They would not just be creating an impact for themselves—they would be creating an impact for the organizations that they work[ed] for."

Unfortunately, teachers participating in the short-lived program were later cast in the media as seeking to benefit financially from their students' participation. WE Charity was even accused of paying teachers a "bounty" for recruiting participants. Pierre Poilievre told the CBC that he'd never heard of teachers "being paid for any kind of compensation or bonus for recruiting their own students to an activity," and he suggested this would somehow negatively impact the professionalism of the entire school system.[15] No one in the media seemed inclined to point out that teachers who work over the summer get paid to do so, and that these teachers would be delivering months of supervision and mentorship.

Across the board, no one was giving anyone the benefit of the doubt.

These charges should have been tackled head-on in the court of public opinion, but WE Charity was muzzled by the government, which advised Marc, Dalal, and others that it viewed the contribution agreement as requiring all program communications to come from or be approved by the government. This may sound surprising given that WE Charity's name is now forever tied to the CSSG, but this directive reflected the reality that WE Charity was supposed to be a quiet partner implementing a program created and branded by the government. As it turned out, the charity had no voice, and the government was a poor advocate. "I was shocked that nobody from the government thought about what the communication strategy and plan was going to be when questions or misunderstandings came to light," Dalal recalled. "And we kept flagging this to them and gently, directly and indirectly, flagging that there needed to be a plan and immediately."

The silencing of WE Charity would have major ramifications after the program launched, as government public and media relations offices proved ineffective in addressing misunderstandings and correcting misinformation. The arrangement also prevented some proactive outreach from WE that might have had a useful impact.

Meanwhile, the projected launch date shifted five or six times, from the end of May to the end of June. In fact, the government didn't finalize the date until two days before the launch. This, too, caused headaches for WE—if the program didn't start until well into the summer, it would be impossible for many participants to get their three hundred hours in.

And there was one more surprise in store: in the days leading up to the launch, WE Charity was told that it would have to indemnify the government against any claims resulting from injuries or other harm to students participating in the program. This came as a shock because the charity was only supposed to be the back-end administrator of a program that was entirely directed and funded by the government. And in a pandemic, the risk was about as big as it could possibly get. If a student were to contract COVID at a volunteer placement, WE Charity could be held liable. If that student inadvertently brought the disease home or to church or to a senior care facility, WE Charity could be held liable. The scale of potential lawsuits could cripple the organization's ability to continue funding its core work at home and overseas.

At that moment, Craig told the government that WE planned to withdraw from the program. The government's shifting goalposts were simply unreasonable.

Wernick called Craig to explain that the program would not happen without WE Charity at this late stage. The civil service had no backup option. WE relented. Craig told me that the only reason the organization stuck it out was because it "felt a responsibility to the young people who wouldn't receive their grants and the charitable partners who had already been identified to participate in the program and were counting on the volunteers."

This is when WE Charity Foundation, which would later become the focus of so much political vitriol, entered the story. Years before, this foundation—also a registered charity—had been set up by WE Charity's lawyers at Miller Thomson to act as a potential future repository for the organization's real estate assets. It is common among large-scale non-profits to transfer assets to a separate legal entity so they are protected from creditors if a lawsuit creates significant liability. But the plan never proceeded because several WE Charity board members, including me, wanted additional time to consider legal advice and the implications of such a transfer. There were never any concerns about WE Charity Foundation itself.

So for years, WE Charity Foundation existed only on paper, ignored, unused, and owning not so much as a pencil. But when the massive liability issues around the CSSG came up, it was determined, in consultation with Miller Thomson, that the foundation was the best way to protect the organization—and perhaps more importantly, protect the work being done in communities around the world—in case the worst happened. This would also ensure cleaner reporting lines and expense management because the sole purpose of the foundation would be administration of the CSSG. WE Charity proposed this to the government, and the government agreed. So WE formally changed the mandate of the foundation to reflect its new role as the entity managing the CSSG. And WE Charity Foundation then procured liability insurance so it could satisfy the government's request for indemnification.

In the later maelstrom surrounding the program, critics such as NDP MP Charlie Angus would frequently describe the foundation as a "real estate shell company," in a deliberate attempt to suggest that WE Charity was engaged in a shady and potentially fraudulent manoeuvre.[16] The media would jump on the bandwagon with headlines such as the *National Post*'s "Government's $912M Contract for Student Volunteer Program Was Awarded to a WE Shell Company."[17] But there was nothing suspect about WE Charity Foundation. It was a registered charity. It was never used for any real estate transaction. It was simply used to facilitate a request by the government with complete transparency on the part of WE Charity. And it became another example of how the organization's efforts to find a way to make the CSSG work came back to haunt it.

READY FOR LAUNCH

Contract negotiations dragged on until June 23, when both parties finally signed on the dotted line and closed the deal. Throughout the negotiation process, the WE Charity executive team discussed CSSG program details, including use of WE Charity Foundation, with the US and Canadian board chairs, Dr. Jacqueline Sanderlin (affectionately known as Dr. J) and Greg Rogers. They then briefed the other board members: Kate Burnett, Gerry Connelly, and Dr. Astrid Christoffersen in Canada, and Kannan Arasaratnam, David Stillman, and me in the US. Initial briefings were by email, then a full presentation and discussion took place via videoconference. Many board members had questions—specifically about program logistics and contractual terms—but there was no hesitancy. There was uniform optimism and support for the CSSG.

Greg, the recently appointed chair of the Canadian board, described it as "a win-win-win program." A long-time member of the Toronto Catholic District School Board and current instructor in York University's Faculty of Education, Greg saw the CSSG as a great opportunity for students and teachers alike, and he had already been working to help the charity identify educators and non-profit partners long before the agreement was signed.

If there's anyone who knows about empowering young people, Greg is the guy. He spent his professional life not only as a teacher and school administrator but also as a successful entrepreneur, running Adventure

Learning Experiences and Olympia Sports Camp, two organizations that support learning and leadership in young people. It also happens that Greg was my grade nine vice-principal at Toronto's Brebeuf College, where Marc and I both went to high school. Affectionately known as "Rog," he is as admired for his passion as a life-long rugby coach as he is for his teaching. He taught me a great deal about leadership and has always been an inspiring mentor, then and through our time together at WE.

In an interview for this book, he described to me some of the early prospects for the CSSG. "I have a friend who's a teacher in Newfoundland and very big into sports, and he used to work for me as a counsellor. He told me he had volunteers ready to coach little kids at soccer and rugby—he had set all of that up. They were going to run soccer clinics on Zoom for high school students," Greg said. "I also knew St. Clair Catholic Church in Waterloo was going to build homes, with the help of volunteers, for the homeless in their community. We also had programs where the students were going to work on farms and so on. Those are just a few examples. There were so many more, and the possibilities were endless. We were all so excited."

Gerry Connelly also understood the potential impact of the program. "I think the idea of wanting to have WE involved in having students do volunteer work was excellent because really that's what WE is all about," she told me. "The timelines were incredibly daunting, but WE had the network for it. And having had experienced WE, I felt, 'Well, if anybody could do it, WE could.'"

The US members of the board—including me—were almost jealous. I viewed the program as a shining example of how everything that WE Charity had worked on for decades could come together and provide relief and even hope during the pandemic. I was so enthusiastic, I thought the CSSG should be replicated in the US and elsewhere. And I wasn't the only one who felt that way.

The most vocal advocate was author and generational expert David Stillman. "I was so impressed with what the Canadian government was doing—saying kids could earn grant money by volunteering, and money would be given based on the level of their work and time committed," he said. "I just thought it was brilliant, and what excited me was the long-term prospect of taking it out of politics and doing it privately in the US."

On June 25, just two days after the contribution agreement was signed, Justin Trudeau announced the launch of the CSSG. The team had moved mountains to get everything ready for roll-out in such a short period of time—an incredible achievement, and something to celebrate. What had started as a program for twenty thousand students was now meant for a hundred thousand. A $44.5 million initial budget had ballooned to $543 million. The government had imposed massive increases, and WE Charity had to shoulder responsibility for all of it, despite retaining virtually no decision-making power. "In the end, we had to pretty much do nearly everything for a hundred thousand young people," Dalal said, "and it was this mission creep that was brutal."

"Dalal and her team worked so hard to build this program," Marc told me. "It still blows my mind. Think about it: in less than two months, they built a coast-to-coast bilingual program with hundreds of full-time staff to mentor youth, a seamless technology interface, and partnerships with non-profits ready for the youth. People were working twelve-hour days, seven days a week to make this happen."

But in the moment, it all seemed worth it. Young people flocked to register, and within days of the launch, thirty-five thousand applications had come in from every province in the country. Of those, an amazing 67 percent were from under-represented populations, including visible minorities, women, LGBTQ people, and Indigenous Canadians. On the other side of the equation, eighty-four diverse non-profit partners had signed on, including Scouts Canada and Girl Guides of Canada, Spinal Cord Injury Canada, the Canadian Arab Institute, L'Arche, Anishnawbe Health, Good Shepherd Ministries, the Toronto Zoo, and the Gord Downie and Chanie Wenjack Fund.

The hard part, it seemed, was over, and the CSSG was roaring out of the gate.

Just eight days later, the ethics commissioner announced he was opening an investigation into the process of awarding of the program.

CHAPTER 5

THE STORM AFTER
THE CALM

On the day the CSSG launched, the *Toronto Star* trumpeted: "Ottawa Outsources Student-Grant Program to a Toronto Charity That Works with Justin Trudeau's Wife."[1] The article said nothing about the scope of the project, the number of people it was designed to help, its innovative approach, or the speed with which it had been brought to fruition. The *Globe and Mail* followed suit the next day with "Trudeau Accused of Cronyism Over Giving WE Charity a Contract to Run $912-Million Student Volunteer Program."[2] It was obvious that critics saw the CSSG not as a lifeline for struggling students during a global pandemic but as an opportunity to attack and embarrass the Liberal government—and once they'd seized on it, they weren't going to let go.

WE's public relations team had anticipated that Sophie Grégoire Trudeau's history with the charity—she was a volunteer ambassador for WE Well-being and had hosted a popular podcast on mental health—might be used to imply that the student program was some kind of quid pro quo. But they thought they had this covered. Before she even started working with the organization, Grégoire Trudeau had approached the ethics commissioner to review the relationship and rule on whether it created a conflict of interest. Mario Dion said it did not.[3]

None of that seemed to matter, of course, to opposition politicians who sensed blood in the water. They needed a sustainable line of attack on the government, which in the summer of 2020 was buoyed by Canadians' generally favourable opinion of its handling of the COVID crisis. By June, the Liberals had climbed past 40 percent in the opinion polls, giving them a level of support they had not seen since 2015. Just three months earlier, they'd been behind the Conservatives by several points. "It's clear that the governing party has received a boost as a result of the COVID-19 crisis—as have most parties governing provinces across the country," noted the CBC's polling analyst, Éric Grenier, on the day after the CSSG was announced.[4] Trudeau's Liberals, he concluded, were comfortably into majority government territory. If the opposition did not act quickly, the next election would be over before the writ was even dropped.

Looking back, it is fascinating to reflect on how much the pandemic changed Justin Trudeau's political fortunes. The wartime mentality created by the COVID crisis made opposition politicians reluctant to criticize him, and for months, the only story in the news was the pandemic and the government's mostly well-regarded response to it. Trudeau also improved his own position enormously through his daily pandemic press conferences, which were seen as calm and reassuring and kept his face on TV screens from coast to coast to coast. Meanwhile, the economy was showing signs of recovery and the mitigation efforts appeared to be working to slow the spread of the virus.

But by the end of June, the media craved a new story, and opposition members of Parliament were ready to stop pulling their punches.[5] The Grégoire Trudeau issue was the starting point, but it soon gave way to a broader narrative about a sweetheart backroom deal involving the Kielburgers, Trudeau, and Finance Minister Bill Morneau—all of whom, in the media's telling of it, were close personal friends. According to this fictional narrative, Trudeau himself chose WE Charity to run the CSSG as a thank you to the Kielburgers for boosting his wife's profile. Or he did it because WE Charity was on the verge of bankruptcy, and he wanted to bail out his pals. Or maybe it was because the Kielburgers had been using WE to funnel money to Trudeau's mother and brother for years. There were half a dozen other variations on the idea that Trudeau had invented the CSSG to give half a billion dollars to WE Charity in exchange for some unspecified favour. Ultimately, the details didn't really matter—it was the idea of a cozy relationship that the opposition wanted to make stick.

STRANGE BEDFELLOWS

Certain members of Parliament played an outsized role in fuelling misperceptions about the charity and its operations—chief among them Conservative Pierre Poilievre and the NDP's Charlie Angus. They are widely viewed as two of the fiercest partisan voices in their respective parties, and they set about attacking the charity in a highly politicized, hostile manner usually reserved for government ministers and party officials. As the soon-to-be-called WE Charity Scandal unfolded, Angus and Poilievre led parliamentary committee hearings, appeared at press conferences, and booked time on political shows to make their case. And they took to social media with a flurry of tweets; over the next few months, they would each post about WE Charity seventy to eighty times. They did not act in concert, but they certainly fed off each other—strange bedfellows in relentless pursuit of a shared enemy.

Poilievre was first elected to Parliament for the Ottawa riding of Nepean-Carleton in 2004, when he was just twenty-five. A prominent and outspoken figure during the Stephen Harper years, he was minister for democratic reform and minister of employment and social development, and in opposition, he has been the finance critic and the jobs and industry critic. He views himself as a champion of the free market and an enemy of government handouts.[6] To see him in action is to know that he relishes attack and is not shy about courting controversy. Back in 2008, for example, just hours after Harper offered a formal apology to residential school survivors, Poilievre told an Ottawa talk radio show that he wasn't sure Canada was "getting value" for the compensation being paid to former students. "My view," he said, "is that we need to engender the values of hard work and independence and self-reliance."[7]

Although he's found himself in hot water multiple times throughout his career, Poilievre has also been lauded by his peers for his effectiveness at pressing the party in power. In 2021, in the *Hill Times* newspaper's annual Political Savvy Survey, he was voted the best public speaker, the most effective Conservative member during Question Period, and the best opposition MP in media scrums.[8]

It would be hard to imagine a more extreme foil for Poilievre than Charlie Angus. A punk rock musician and activist turned politician, Angus was first elected to Parliament for the Northern Ontario riding of Timmins–James Bay in 2004, the same year Poilievre became an MP. He won that first election by just 613 votes, but two years later, he was re-elected by a margin ten times that size. So he knows how to get attention and keep people focused on his message.

A self-declared defender of under-represented and marginalized communities, Angus has advocated for a host of left-leaning priorities, ranging from a higher minimum wage to more affordable housing to tighter environmental regulations.[9] During his almost two decades in office, he has served as the NDP's critic and spokesperson on a long list of files, including heritage, agriculture, public works, and Indigenous affairs. This has made him one of his party's most prominent members of Parliament. He is also one of its most profane. On Twitter, he has referred to those he disagreed with as "fuckers,"[10] "jackass,"[11] "a smug, mean, aloof ass,"[12] and "an irresponsible idiot."[13] (That last zinger was directed at Poilievre!)

To the casual eye, Angus and Poilievre couldn't be more different, but in many respects, they're cut from the same cloth. Both men are ambitious and have their eyes on leadership roles in their respective parties. Angus even jockeyed to replace Thomas Mulcair as NDP leader in 2017, only to fall short in the final few weeks of the campaign. Both he and Poilievre are career politicians who seem to believe the old adage about there being no such thing as bad publicity. They both like to fight their battles in the court of public opinion, whether that's through traditional media outlets like newspapers and TV or social media platforms like Twitter. And they both exhibit a willingness to abandon the party platform (and sometimes the truth) when it serves their purposes. Poilievre's claim that the civil service should have delivered the CSSG on its own is at odds with the long-held Conservative belief in public-private partnerships. Angus's antagonism toward the CSSG was even more off-script, given the program's emphasis on reaching at-risk populations, helping students financially, and serving the non-profit sector—exactly the kind of government intervention the progressive politician usually champions. What's more, his own children had been involved in the WE Schools service-learning program and had participated in ME to WE Trips to Nicaragua. During Craig and Marc's later appearance before the FINA committee, Angus said the program had changed his kids' lives. "My oldest said that set her on a course for human rights activism,"[14] he noted. And yet that didn't deter him from contributing to the downfall of the charity.

What seems clear is that both Poilievre and Angus saw the CSSG scandal as an opportunity to get at Justin Trudeau. WE Charity became a proxy for the prime minister. Over time, they would even jockey for who could devote the most energy attacking the program and the organization, with Angus tweeting things like "Parliament doesn't sit at this time of the year. But thanks to the NDP we have [CSSG] hearings next week with the finance committee. The Conservatives never pushed for this."[15] Poilievre later returned fire: "Charlie Angus loves to talk tough. But it's all an act. He and the NDP back down and cover up for their Liberal masters."[16]

In his role as Conservative finance critic, Poilievre took centre stage in what he would consistently refer to as the "WE scandal." On June 28, 2020, three days after the launch of the CSSG, he and two other Conservative shadow ministers sent a letter to Karen Hogan, the auditor general, calling on her to include the CSSG in a review of government COVID program spending that had been mandated by the FINA committee in June. Poilievre posted a copy of the letter to his Twitter account.[17] It was the first of over seventy tweets he made about WE Charity between June and October 2020. In the days that followed, Poilievre became the Conservative point man on WE, asking questions in the House and serving as spokesperson to the media. He was quoted in hundreds of articles, and in time, it became clear that many of his public statements were false or misleading.

Meanwhile, Charlie Angus filed the complaint that prompted Ethics Commissioner Dion to launch his investigation. (Ontario Conservative MP Michael Barrett separately lodged an additional complaint.) At issue was whether Trudeau had contravened the sections of the Conflict of Interest Act prohibiting public figures from participating in decisions that further their private interests, and whether he had afforded WE Charity preferential treatment. Dion was also asked to consider whether Trudeau should have recused himself from the CSSG decision. "The awarding of this contract and the relationship between the PMO and WE Charity requires closer scrutiny," insisted Angus in his complaint to Dion.[18] He also managed to slip in that WE was "reeling" from the effects of the pandemic.

Angus's crusade against WE Charity, like Poilievre's, was marked by mischaracterizations and false statements that served to create an aura of wrongdoing on the part of the charity. His goal seemed to be to throw lots of mud and see what stuck, and it worked.

On reflection, it was a clever strategy to focus on WE Charity and the CSSG because it allowed the Conservatives and the NDP—still nervous that a full-throated attack in the middle of a pandemic could backfire—to assail the prime minister in an indirect way. Also, Trudeau did have a long history with the organization that could be misrepresented by people trying to score political points. And he was vulnerable to ethics charges because he had run afoul of the Conflict of Interest Act in the past.

SELLING A COZY RELATIONSHIP

The prime minister's first clash with the ethics commissioner was in December 2017, over what came to be known as the Aga Khan affair. In that instance, Commissioner Mary Dawson, Mario Dion's predecessor, found Trudeau to be in conflict for accepting vacations and flights from the Aga Khan, the leader of the Ismaili Muslim sect and a billionaire philanthropist with deep ties to Canada. This was a serious conflict because the Aga Khan Foundation, an international development agency focused on alleviating poverty and hunger, often lobbied the government and had received tens of millions in federal funding in 2016. Trudeau tried to refute the allegations by saying that he was personal friends with the Aga Khan and his vacations had nothing to do with his role as prime minister, but Commissioner Dawson found this to be untrue. "There were no private interactions between Mr. Trudeau and the Aga Khan until Mr. Trudeau became leader of the Liberal Party of Canada," she wrote in her report. "This led me to conclude that their relationship cannot be described as one of friends for the purposes of the act."[19] Dawson's ruling made Trudeau the only prime minister to be found guilty of violating the Conflict of Interest Act since it came into effect in 2007.

Less than two years later, in August 2019, Trudeau found himself on the wrong side of the ethics office once again. This time, he was investigated by Mario Dion for his role in the SNC-Lavalin affair—specifically, Dion looked at whether the prime minister had improperly pressured his attorney general, Jody Wilson-Raybould, to resolve a corruption case against the Montreal-based engineering firm using a deferred prosecution agreement. Such an agreement would help SNC-Lavalin escape criminal prosecution for allegedly paying millions of dollars in bribes to Libyan government officials between 2001 and 2011. In this case, Dion concluded that Trudeau had made "flagrant attempts to influence" Wilson-Raybould, both personally and through intermediaries, and that he had once again violated the Conflict of Interest Act. "The authority of the prime minister and his office was used to circumvent, undermine and ultimately discredit the decision of the director public prosecutions," Dion wrote, "as well as the authority of Ms. Wilson-Raybould as the Crown's chief law officer."[20] After Dion's report was released, the opposition attempted to interest the RCMP in a criminal investigation, but that went nowhere. Ultimately, Trudeau got away with another slap on the wrist.

You almost have to admire the way the prime minister is able to skate free of serious ethical lapses that would sink the careers of most other politicians. In my view, that is partly because of his unflappable manner. He shrugs and smiles, admits wrongdoing—"I take responsibility for the mistakes that I made," he said in the wake of the SNC-Lavalin affair[21]—and moves on. In the face of several scandals, cabinet resignations, a worldwide pandemic, economic catastrophe, and other enormous challenges, he continues to exude a calm optimism that is appealing to many. And in Canada and around the world, he displays a charm and celebrity-like magnetism that attracts a lot of fans. Plus he loves a photo op.

All these traits made him particularly well suited to WE Charity, which benefited from his involvement on the WE Day stage. Trudeau had made WE Day appearances even before he was elected prime minister, and once in office, he spoke at WE Day Ottawa, WE Day United Nations in New York City, and WE Day Canada on Parliament Hill. This last event was part of the country's sesquicentennial celebrations, as was the "WE Are Canada" campaign, a fifteen-part video series that featured Trudeau and several other notable Canadians encouraging young people to volunteer for causes like environmentalism, science and technology, and truth and reconciliation. But after the CSSG hit the headlines, critics were quick to cast his previous WE involvement in a negative light. For example, the *National Post* called the Canada 150 video "a campaign-style production that doubles as a promo for the charity."[22] In the same article, Manitoba Conservative MP Candice Bergen was quoted as saying the video was proof that "WE works for Trudeau and Trudeau for them."

Critics can justifiably argue that it was naive of both the Kielburgers and the prime minister to think they could share a stage and engage in high-profile photo ops without it coming back to bite them. Once the WE Charity Scandal took hold, it was difficult to find a newspaper that wasn't featuring images of the Trudeaus and the Kielburgers on the WE Day stage, appearing for all the world like the best of friends. But from my perspective, it is troubling that many media outlets propagated the idea that there was something wrong with the charity's efforts to invite participation from politicians and cultivate strong working relationships with them. WE Charity relied on donations and goodwill, and it was smart to court the support of influential people who could amplify its message. Why would the charity invite the prime minster to the WE Day stage? Because he *was* the prime minister. Almost any charity in Canada would be thrilled to have the prime minister attend an event. Why did WE Charity film a video that included the prime minister encouraging young people to volunteer? Same answer. And why ask Sophie Grégoire Trudeau to host a podcast? Because like many spouses of heads of state, she had a platform that allowed the charity's messaging regarding youth mental health to reach a larger audience.[23] So the "shock" and "surprise" expressed by some critics at the fact that WE welcomed the participation of the Trudeaus and other prominent members of government has always struck me as manufactured outrage.

There is no question that the Kielburger brothers and the prime minister had a lot in common—they were close in age, interested in the same issues, shared a global perspective, and yes, enjoyed the spotlight. But it's equally true that the relationship was inflated by the media and opposition MPs for partisan reasons. The Kielburgers were not friends with the prime minister in any traditional sense of the word. They didn't have his phone number or email address, never dined or socialized with him, and didn't get invited for cottage weekends at Harrington Lake.

The relationship with Bill Morneau ran a little deeper. Morneau was the member of Parliament for Toronto Centre, the riding where WE was headquartered. One of his daughters—an extraordinary woman named Grace Acan, who was kidnapped and held captive by the Lord's Resistance Army in Uganda for eight years before escaping, moving to Canada, and joining the Morneau family—worked at ME to WE for a period of time. And in 2017, Morneau's wife and daughter visited WE Villages projects in Kenya, and later that year, Morneau travelled with his family to projects in Ecuador. Morneau's wife, Nancy McCain (yes, of the "french fry" McCains), is a well-known philanthropist. That—and not the fact that Morneau was finance minister—was what prompted WE Charity to view her as a potential donor. Because the organization thought it might benefit from having her see its international work first-hand, the family was not sent a bill for portions of these trips. It wasn't unusual for WE (like countless other charities) to comp local hosting at project sites for influential people if there was a decent chance that a visit might yield a sizable donation. It worked in this case—McCain eventually donated approximately $100,000 to WE Charity.[24]

It also isn't unusual for MPs and their constituents to have relationships. In fact, it is the role of an MP to know his or her constituents and take their views into account. Morneau called the brothers by their first names and was invited to tour the WE GLC, and he and McCain once hosted Craig and his wife for lunch at their home. Over time, a relationship of mutual admiration and respect developed, and this was the context in which Craig wrote to Morneau and his wife in April 2017 to tell them that he would soon become a father. "In his email," wrote Dion, "Mr. Kielburger wrote that Mr. Morneau and Ms. McCain were 'among the first to know' the news and expressed his gratitude for the 'many wonderful friends and family' to impart parenting advice."[25] This and other overtures led Dion to conclude that this relationship was a kind of friendship.

In hindsight, the charity should have been more wary about engaging with politicians and the optics around such interactions. I see that as a former board member. But Canadians may be surprised to hear that contrary to the impression given in the media, WE Charity never relied heavily on government funding. This is why, unlike many other charities of similar size and scope, it did not have a dedicated government relations officer. In 2019, government grants made up just 2.4 percent of WE Charity's revenues. The year before that, it was 3.7 percent. By comparison, the Canadian charity Right to Play took in $18.75 million in government grants in 2020, or 38.1 percent of its revenue.[26] And Plan International Canada received more than $43.5 million in government grants, representing 18.1 percent of its annual budget for 2020.[27] I offer this not as an excuse but to help explain why the Kielburgers and many others within the organization did not immediately see their interactions with politicians as a potential lightning rod.

In any event, Trudeau, Morneau, and the Liberals were certainly not alone in receiving warm welcomes from WE and the Kielburgers. A former staff member who worked in the charity's executive office told me how, in advance of every WE Day season, the organization would invite everyone from the governor general and the prime minister to premiers and local mayors to offer greetings at the start of the celebrations. It was completely irrelevant what party people belonged to. The same approach was typically followed for WE Days in the US, where polarization, as everyone knows, is even more pronounced.

In fact, although the whole WE Charity Scandal hinges on the idea of a "cozy" relationship between the Kielburgers and members of the Liberal Party, the reality is that the organization was applauded, approached, and accessed by politicians of all stripes, including leaders within the Conservative and NDP parties. In its dozen-year history, WE Day welcomed to the stage such diverse political figures as Alberta NDP premier Rachel Notley, Manitoba Conservative premier Brian Pallister, and Manitoba NDP opposition leader Wab Kinew. Trudeau and his wife were not the only first family to be involved with the organization. Ben Mulroney, son of former prime minister Brian Mulroney and one-time presenter on CTV's *etalk*, hosted the first WE Day in 2007. Mulroney went on to host four more WE Days, even taking up that role for the primetime WE Day broadcast on CTV. Although former prime minister Stephen Harper declined his invitation to WE Day each year he was in office, his wife, Laureen, hosted a WE Day after-party at 24 Sussex Drive in 2013.

Former Conservative leader Erin O'Toole—who headed his party during the WE Charity Scandal—was also a stalwart WE backer. In 2016, he emailed the Kielburgers to ask for tickets to WE Day for his wife and daughter. It was a favour for the MP, whose daughter had just changed schools and had not yet been able to earn her way to the event. "Our family just relocated to Ottawa a week ago and my daughter's class has already done the work and are planning to attend We Day in Ottawa this Wednesday," he wrote in his email. "Would it be possible to get two tickets for my daughter Mollie & my wife Rebecca to attend with her? Sorry for the short notice but it would not be fun for Mollie if most of her class goes and she can't get there."[28] A few days later, he wrote again to thank the brothers and report on his wife and daughter's experience. "It inspired an already thoughtful and engaged young girl," he said. "That is your specialty after all and it makes us proud."[29]

The following year, during his first bid for the Conservative Party leadership, O'Toole approached Marc for advice on a policy paper he was preparing. "I am putting together a policy paper on community engagement and the enhancement or encouragement of social enterprises," he wrote. "Your organization has been a leader on leveraging business models for social good. Any advice on policy or tax changes that would help organizations like yours that I could put out there?"[30]

In 2018, he sought permission to bring a group of young people to whom he was presenting community service awards to that year's WE Day in Toronto. "You have been great in the past but want to check before doing it," he wrote.[31] In March 2019, O'Toole asked if either Craig or Marc would like to present a keynote address at a youth mental health summit he was organizing in his constituency. He noted that he "particularly liked [their] article on social media and filter bubbles and risks to youth," and that "it would help me launch this great initiative with the participation of someone with your profile."[32] And when WE Charity teamed up with the Pinball Clemons Foundation to expand educational opportunities for children in developing countries, O'Toole joined in the fundraising campaign through his Rotary Club, which raised several thousand dollars.[33]

In my view, it is reasonable to conclude that Erin O'Toole knew what WE Charity was all about. He knew the impact the organization had on young people. He even tweeted a picture he took of Laureen Harper and Craig Kielburger at the WE reception that Harper threw at 24 Sussex Drive—tagging both of them and posting "@Laureen_Harper hosts a lovely #WeDay wrap up reception at 24 Sussex with @craigkielburger & @freethechildren."[34] Yet he stood silent while Poilievre and others in his party worked to tear the charity apart. It struck me as a classic display of politics over principle—a charge that O'Toole frequently levelled at Justin Trudeau and Liberal Party during the 2021 election, which took place as I was finishing this book.

One-time Conservative leadership hopeful Peter MacKay was no different. He had ties to WE through his wife, human rights activist Nazanin Afshin-Jam. After WE Day Ottawa in November 2018, he tweeted, "Extremely proud of Nazanin who joined Kareem Abdul-Jabbar+others 2 speak #WEDay Ottawa before 16K enthusiastic participants. She delivered a pos empowering msg for next Gen of leaders. The Kielburger bros + @WEMovement are a remarkable Cdn force for good." But by July 10, 2020, with both the CSSG scandal and the Conservative leadership race in full swing, he seemed to have had a change of heart. That tweet was deleted—not by MacKay, a spokesperson later told the *Post Millennial* website, but by an unnamed campaign worker concerned about "inappropriate attention" being paid to Afshin-Jam "from dark corners of the Web."[35] That wasn't the first or last time Afshin-Jam participated in WE events. Just before COVID shut down the world, she was at WE's headquarters for an International Women's Day event, sharing her own experiences.

In the winter of 2019, a few months before COVID and the CSSG exploded in the headlines, Saskatchewan premier Scott Moe and his wife went on a ME to WE Trip to Kenya to see the charity's work first-hand. On his return, Moe shared details of this trip with reporters. "We were happy to give what little we could," he told the *Regina Leader-Post*, "but it paled in comparison and proportion to the kindness of the people of Kenya and what they were able to give back to us in the time that we had."[36]

The list goes on and on. In Ontario, Conservative premier Doug Ford and his late brother, former Toronto mayor Rob Ford, attended several WE Days. The Conservative minister of education, Stephen Lecce, had his staff frequently reach out to ask if WE could host the minister for events at the WE GLC. "He wanted to engage in anti-bullying seminars with kids," Marc explained, "and also to help ensure that kids had access to mental health resources."

In a hot political minute, however, these people tried to distance themselves from WE Charity. For the attacks on Trudeau and Morneau to stick, the organization had to be portrayed as an extension of the Liberal Party. And more than that, the charity had to be a bad actor. An undisclosed conflict of interest is not so bad if the other party is viewed as having clean hands—in fact, this was exactly what happened in the Aga Khan affair. To create a compelling and sufficiently scandalous story with the potential to topple the Liberal government, opposition politicians needed more. Even though to this day no one has offered a shred of evidence that WE Charity broke any law or did any harm, it had to be cast as untrustworthy for anyone to care.

At times, it felt like the organization was being used as both a sword and a shield. "On one hand, opposition MPs were using us as a weapon to attack their enemy, and on the other side, the Liberals were letting WE take all the hits," Dalal said. "The end result was WE getting beat up, and badly. It felt like we were in a wrestling ring and were knocked down over and over, and there was no referee to judge fairly."

Looking back, I think the media did a great disservice to the Canadian people by failing to report on the long history of engagement between WE Charity or the Kielburgers and influential members of the Conservative and NDP parties. To have done so would have exposed as false the key myth underlying the whole scandal—that WE Charity enjoyed a singularly cozy relationship with the Liberals. The narrative doesn't work if WE and the Kielburgers also had deep ties with critics of the Liberal government. And yet that is the truth.

Of course, in politics (and life generally), where you stand often depends on where you sit. The fact of the matter is, media and opposition parties could have spun a tale of cronyism no matter who was in power. If O'Toole had been prime minister, I have little doubt the Liberals would have been just as vicious in denouncing the "cozy" relationship that allowed him to ask the Kielburgers for favours for his daughter or advice on policy regarding social enterprise. They would have painted O'Toole as having a track record of reciprocating by donating to support WE Charity's work. Instead of focusing on Grégoire Trudeau's podcast about mental health, the politicians might have cried foul about Peter McKay's wife speaking about her human-trafficking charity at WE Day. Instead of criticizing Liberal insider Bill Morneau for travelling to Ecuador, the opposition might have featured pictures of influential conservative Scott Moe building schools in Kenya. And if the NDP were in power, Liberals might have been up in arms about the fact that Charlie Angus had once said WE Charity changed the lives of his children. He must be trying to return the favour! At a minimum, Angus would presumably have refrained from telling the press that the appointment of WE "stinks of cronyism."[37]

The bottom line is that WE Charity was agnostic when it came to politics; it cared only about impact and support for the students, teachers, and international communities it served. Michelle Douglas, the former chair of WE Charity's Canadian board and a retired civil servant, later confirmed this during her testimony before the FINA committee. "It was always our view, at least on the board of directors, that we were indeed non-partisan, which had the potential of engaging any government—provincial, municipal, or federal," she said. "Certainly, I did not see [us] as multi-partisan, but rather non-partisan, as an organization."[38]

When I asked Craig why the organization had invited politicians onto the WE Day stage, he answered with an idealism that seemed out of place given everything that had happened: "The purpose of WE Day was to encourage youth to serve. We invited activists, artists, entrepreneurs, and yes, politicians on stage as role models to encourage the students. Politics is supposed to be about bettering your community."

Craig's idealism aside, we all know that at the end of the day, politics can be a dirty game. What makes this situation different, though, is that politicians—aided in part by the media—allowed the game to spiral out of control, and in the process, a lot of non-elected people got hurt. Millions of children in Canada and around the world have lost benefits and life-saving support. Teachers have been robbed of tools to help nurture a generation of active citizens. And tens of thousands of WE staff and participants in volunteer trips now may think twice before listing WE on their résumés. Our representatives have an obligation to contain the collateral damage from partisan squabbles, and they need to be held to account for their failure to even acknowledge the damage they caused.

SELF-INFLICTED WOUNDS

The narrative of a particularly tight relationship between WE and the Liberal Party was also fuelled by a series of unforced errors by the government and the charity. For example, when Bardish Chagger, the minister of diversity and inclusion and youth, was asked, at a daily COVID briefing on June 25, about Sophie Grégoire Trudeau's involvement with the charity, she offered a convoluted response that sounded evasive. "I would have confidence that the department has done all the checks and balances to ensure that everything will be successful," she said, "and will work for the young people that we are here to represent."[39] She failed to point out that Grégoire Trudeau's role had already been cleared by the ethics commissioner.

In fact, many of the issues that would soon form the basis of the WE Charity Scandal could have been easily addressed that day by

Minister Chagger as she made her media rounds in support of the announcement. Instead, she neglected to correct journalists who said the program's price tag was $912 million—it was actually a maximum of $543 million. The higher figure came from a single line in a background document provided to the media in April 2020, when the prime minister announced a suite of student support mechanisms to be rolled out in response to the pandemic.[40] This erroneous number, which came as a total shock to WE Charity, quickly stuck, with journalists and opposition politicians alike tagging the CSSG as the "billion-dollar program." Conservative MP Michael Barrett, for one, railed that "Justin Trudeau handed almost a billion-dollar contract" to WE Charity,[41] and even as late as March 2021, Charlie Angus was still using the figure: "When we end up in a situation in the middle of a pandemic, in which $900 million is awarded to a group that has deep ties to the Trudeau family, the obvious question is why that did not raise flags in the Prime Minister's Office."[42]

Chagger also let stand assumptions on how the money would be spent. She failed to explain that the vast majority—$500 million—would simply flow through WE Charity on its way into the hands of students. Most critically, she did not correct the narrative that suggested the organization was being *paid* to administer the program—in reality, any funds going to WE Charity were simply cost reimbursements.

"It was a disaster because Minister Chagger didn't seem equipped to speak to or answer questions about the program or the financials," Dalal recalled. "It was very frustrating because we had flagged these issues to them during the contract negotiations and leading up to program launch. We said, 'You need to point to the ethics commissioner's [findings] re Sophie Trudeau. You need to explain that we are only administrators of the program which was designed by you, and that we will be working with many non-profits to launch and execute the program.' We kept asking, 'Can we make this really clear?' And unfortunately, it just did not happen."

Matters were being made worse by the government's insistence that it should have a stranglehold on all public communications about the program. When bad headlines appeared, WE Charity was not permitted to address them—and soon, the bad headlines were everywhere. "Trudeau Defends Decision to Have Charity with Ties to Family Administer Student Volunteer Program," reported the CBC on June 26.[43] Two days later, the *Globe and Mail* declared, "Volunteer Canada Declined to Work for WE Charities Over Wage Concerns with Student Grant Program."[44] And on June 29, the *National Post* announced, "Records Show Charity Closely Tied to PM Received Multiple Sole-Source Contracts,"[45] while the *Toronto Sun* blared, "#WeHaveAProblem: Canadians Upset Over We Charity Controversy."[46] During those first few days of coverage, WE Charity was unable to lend its voice or its perspective to the media reports. And once a narrative is set, it is very hard to redirect.

The hits just kept on coming. On June 26, Trudeau's efforts to address his family connections to WE only exacerbated the situation. "This is one of the reasons why we leaned heavily on the public service to try and find different ways of delivering this," he told reporters, "and they came back and demonstrated that the WE organization is the only organization in Canada that has the scale and the ability to deliver volunteer opportunities for young people right across the country at all level of organizations."[47]

His insistence that WE Charity was "the only organization in Canada" capable of delivering the program became one of his talking points about the CSSG. But once again, this harmed rather than helped the situation from WE's perspective. His statement shifted the spotlight from the government procurement process—which opposition politicians and the media had every right to scrutinize—to the charity. To disprove Trudeau, it became necessary for anyone with an anti-Liberal viewpoint to malign WE Charity and find a basis to claim it was an unworthy steward of taxpayer dollars. As Scott Baker told me, "With this one line, it was as though Trudeau put a target on WE's back. All eyes were suddenly on the organization, and I felt as though we became helpless observers to our own dismantling."

This development was painfully ironic because WE Charity was supposed to be a silent administrative partner. The organization had been adamant with ESDC that it was to be a "white label" solution for the CSSG—meaning that there would be no WE branding on the website, no references to WE Charity in the press releases, and no form of public attention. It was a program designed by the government, and all the decision-making remained with the government, including media engagement. Now opposition MPs were laser-focused on discrediting the prime minister by discrediting WE Charity.

On June 26, Charlie Angus told the *Globe and Mail*, "I find it extraordinary that Canada's civil service would come to the Prime Minister and say, 'Listen, we're not equipped to deliver programs for the Canadian people. You should privatize it and give it to a group that's very close to you.' I would love to see who gave that recommendation because it just boggles the imagination."[48] Duff Conacher, the co-founder of Democracy Watch, also advanced the notion that the government could somehow administer the program itself. "There's no reason to involve a private organization," he asserted to the *Toronto Star*, "and to make a private organization—that is not subject to any of the conflict of interest rules—the gatekeeper."[49] The *Star* failed to note that the government hadn't succeeded in getting a similar large-scale youth service program off the ground in nearly five years of trying. And the Liberal government stayed quiet, making no effort to respond to such comments with answers or explanations.

But Trudeau and Chagger weren't the only ones causing self-inflicted wounds. On June 30, Marc Kielburger found himself in hot water when a recording of a four-week-old video call between him and a group of youth leaders was leaked to the Canadian Press. In it, Marc says that the Prime Minister's Office invited WE Charity to implement the CSSG the day after Trudeau announced plans for the program on April 22. "Then the next day, the Prime Minister's Office kindly called us and said: 'You know that announcement we just made? Would you be interested in helping us actually implement?'" Kielburger said in the call. "After much consideration, we put up our hand and said: 'Of course, we're happy to be of assistance.'"[50] This statement—which was incorrect—undercut the assertion that the decision to award the CSSG to WE Charity had been made by non-partisan public servants, not by the prime minister or his office. It was an unfortunate and unnecessary error, and it added fuel to the fire for MPs like Angus and Poilievre, who continued to insist that the Kielburgers had been tossed a lifeline by their good friend Justin Trudeau.

The same day, Marc moved to correct the record, releasing a statement and offering an apology. "Speaking loosely and enthusiastically, I incorrectly referred to the Prime Minister's Office," he said in his statement. "In fact, the outreach came from unelected officials at Employment and Social Development Canada."[51] He later explained to me that he got carried away in the excitement of talking about the program, and that he had simply resorted to using the shorthand "PMO" in one of dozens of similar calls he'd made that day. Whether he misspoke or was trying to make it all sound more grand—let's face it, telling young people the Prime Minister's Office called is a lot sexier than saying you were contacted by bureaucrats at ESDC—it would have been an irrelevant error in normal times. But this mistake would be brought up again and again by politicians and reporters alike.

Within days, it was clear that the negative narrative about the CSSG was only getting worse. Journalists and pundits took to the air with a barrage of criticisms, and social media was in a frenzy. The WE Charity leadership team felt that the entire program would be dragged down by the politics unless dramatic action was taken.

There appeared to be only one way to remove the pressure of the growing political and media storm. "It wasn't the decision we wanted to make, because every one of our staff put so much time into building the CSSG," said Marc, "but we knew the right thing to do for everyone was separate ourselves from this project." On Canada Day, WE Charity held multiple closed-door meetings with officials from ESDC to decide the best course of action. Everyone was concerned that other non-profits might drop out of the program because of the negative brand association, or that students would choose not to apply because of all the damaging media coverage. The charity wanted assurances from the civil servants that the program would continue even if WE wasn't involved, and it got that. So on July 3, 2020, it was officially announced that the government itself would administer the program. In a statement to the media, Chagger stated that it was a "mutually agreed upon decision," and that the government wanted to ensure that those who had already applied were not "adversely affected." "Our government's objective remains to connect the skills and abilities of young people with service opportunities to help heal their communities."[52]

WE Charity also released its own statement: "Even as CSSG take-up has been very strong, the program has also been enmeshed in controversy from the moment of its announcement. Our concern is that to continue in this way, the program itself will begin to suffer—and as a consequence, opportunities for students might be negatively affected. Not only would that be unwelcome, but it is also unnecessary. The program has now been launched with a level of operational functionality and a critical mass of engagement that permits it to be otherwise administered . . . WE Charity and ESDC have mutually agreed that the operational responsibility will be passed to the Government of Canada."[53]

In the hope that a clean slate would be in the best interests of the CSSG, the organization also waived all fees already incurred—a not insubstantial amount of money. The charity had spent approximately $5 million on hiring and training hundreds of staff to administer this program and had made payments to vendors who provided technology services and backend support. I always found the decision to waive fees particularly frustrating because the negative spin was that WE Charity had sought the CSSG for financial gain or as some type of bailout. And then WE Charity actually took a loss and *bailed out the government*. WE covered these costs using a small endowment—a rainy day fund—and with help from ME to WE. No outside donations to specific projects were used.

As soon as the announcement was made, Trudeau was peppered with questions about next steps for the CSSG. Unfortunately, his efforts to provide clarity once again only worsened the situation. He mistakenly said it was WE Charity's decision to pull out instead of one mutually agreed to. When asked by a reporter from the CBC if he would continue his work with WE, he avoided the question and made a statement that seemed to place blame upon the charity: "I think the organization is going to take some time to reflect on its next steps and how exactly it responds to this situation."[54]

But the prime minister's attempts to distance himself from the organization that he had once championed did not go as planned, and in the days ahead, new information came to light that changed the game for everyone involved.

HOUSE OF CARDS

At a press briefing on July 8, 2020, Prime Minister Trudeau was asked by Marieke Walsh of the *Globe and Mail* if he had recused himself from cabinet discussions about WE Charity and the CSSG. He said no. Then he dodged the question when asked why. "I have long worked on youth issues, both before I got into politics and since I've been in politics as a youth critic," he said. "Getting young people involved in serving their country, recognizing their desire to build a better Canada, particularly through this time of crisis, is something that I believe in deeply."[55]

Just two days later, the CBC ran a story revealing that Bill Morneau had also failed to recuse himself from conversations about the organization.[56] After some initial defiance, the finance minister backtracked and posted a written apology to Twitter.[57]

The fact that Trudeau and Morneau did not recuse themselves from the cabinet decision to appoint WE as the administrator of the CSSG came as a complete shock to the organization. This bears repeating because it is so misunderstood: WE Charity and the Kielburgers had no idea whether politicians had recused themselves or what steps they did or did not take to comply with their own ethics rules on government process. After all, from WE's perspective, nothing about the organization's involvement with the Trudeaus or Morneau was a secret. In fact, WE advertised Trudeau's involvement to the world by putting him and his wife on stage and having his mother and brother speak at dozens of public events. Similarly, WE Charity was proud that the Morneau-McCains were donors and had visited international projects. The hope was that they would tell everyone who would listen about their experiences—that was the point.

For everyone at WE, the assumption was that all government rules were followed and those who should have recused themselves did. No one asked anyone at WE for an opinion about whether Trudeau and Morneau should recuse themselves, and no one at WE offered one. And that is precisely as it should be.

In a one-two punch, WE Charity learned *from the press* at around the same time that the CSSG was a sole-source contract. This also came as a complete surprise. The organization had been told by various civil servants that they were asking other groups to submit proposals to deliver part or all of the program. In testimony before the FINA committee, Wernick and others would later explain that they had explored multiple options but finally determined that no other group had the capacity to administer the CSSG. Due to the tight time frame and the lack of viable options, the civil service asked only WE Charity to submit a formal proposal. Unlike WE—which had no idea it was entering into a sole-source contract—the cabinet members making the decision could of course have learned of this fact. Looking back, it is mind-boggling to me that in addition to failing to recuse themselves, both Trudeau and Morneau did not ask, did not care, or did not perceive how a sole-source contract might appear to the public or be exploited by opposition parties. In any event, their failure to hold up a stop sign and demand additional proposals from ESDC was catastrophic for WE Charity.

As both a board member and in the course of writing this book, I have been surprised by the number of people—including those who continue to be supportive of WE Charity—who suggest that the organization was foolish not to see a conflict-of-interest issue coming. How did WE not make sure there was no conflict when dealing with the government? Did the Kielburgers just miss this conflict because they were in a rush? Was the board asleep at the wheel? Perhaps WE should have had someone experienced in government procurement issues in the room?

As a lawyer who spends a lot of time thinking about and advising companies on conflict-of-interest issues, I find these questions both vexing and confusing. Let's be clear: entities and individuals have an obligation to monitor and, where necessary, disclose their own conflicts of interest. So I would have been concerned if someone within WE Charity had an undisclosed conflict because she was, for example, running an unrelated non-profit that would benefit from volunteer hours through the CSSG. WE Charity did not, however, have any responsibility to address conflicts of interest on the part of the government. Nor could it. How could any organization signing a contract with the government possibly know every rule that must be complied with, which employees might have conflicts, and whether internal checks and balances have been observed? Given that cabinet discussions are always confidential, outside groups have no insight into the decision-making process. If companies that engaged in activities with the government—whether selling pencils, providing healthcare, or delivering charitable services—were responsible for policing internal government compliance with its own rules, it would lead to paralysis and turn into a legal nightmare. How could any entity possibly be sure that every actor in the government had done the right thing?

This is why, with the CSSG, the obligation of recusal belonged to the ministers and other public office holders who were involved in making decisions. Period. To hold WE Charity accountable for ethics decisions by government actors is as ridiculous as holding a job applicant responsible for an employer's failure to comply with its internal hiring policies or labour laws. And yet, in peddling a scandal, this is the type of responsibility some politicians and media outlets tried to lay at the doorstep of WE Charity.

Morneau's failure to recuse was particularly thorny for the government. Things only grew worse when Brian Lilley published a story about the Morneau family's Ecuador trip in the *Toronto Sun* on July 11. "It's getting harder to tell where the Liberal Party of Canada ends and WE Charity begins,"[58] Lilley wrote, before suggesting that it might be easier to ask which top Liberals didn't have a connection to WE than which did. The article also included a quote from Morneau's spokesperson, Pierre-Olivier Herbert, insisting that "the Morneau family covered all associated costs and expenses." This statement turned out to be inaccurate. Eleven days later, Morneau told the FINA committee that while preparing for his testimony, he realized ME to WE had not charged him for some of the expenses associated with his family's stay. His office, he said, had asked ME to WE for an invoice. The costs of lodging, food, and in-country transportation were in the range of $13,000, but Morneau's team twice asked WE to raise the tally to the highest possible amount someone could pay for such a trip. The Morneau-McCain family had stayed for a shorter visit than was typical, but his office wanted a total with no deductions for the excluded days or any other discounts whatsoever. It probably seems unusual to most Canadians to dramatically overpay for a trip, but this request was likely made to avoid future issues with the ethics commissioner. The morning of his FINA appearance, Morneau wrote a cheque for $41,000, the maximum possible amount. The money was paid to WE Charity rather than ME to WE (with the social enterprise eating the costs for the benefit of the charity). And no, the minister did not receive a tax receipt.

Meanwhile, even though WE Charity had stepped away from the CSSG, the media's interest in the organization did not subside. In fact, the number of media requests grew exponentially in the aftermath of Trudeau's non-recusal admission. On a single day in July, four different CBC reporters contacted WE for comment on a variety of stories, as did dozens of other journalists from news outlets across Canada. In the days, weeks, and months that followed, the organization's small public relations team—a fraction of its usual size because of the COVID layoffs—was pushed to its limits, responding to over five thousand media requests, many with deadlines of only a few hours. "Even if we had the staff at this time, our PR team was never built to be a crisis communications department," Craig explained. "Their focus has always been to share positive news with the public, like WE Day celebrations and impacts being made in partner communities overseas."

And soon, the media had a new angle on WE's relationship with the Trudeaus. On June 26, in response to a question from CBC journalist Janyce McGregor regarding Trudeau family member appearances at WE Days, the charity stated that it had never paid honorariums to anyone in the family, although it had covered Sophie Grégoire Trudeau's travel costs. As it turned out, there were two problems with this statement. First, it was an overly technical answer. The organization should have proactively acknowledged that while the *charity* had not paid speaking fees, its social enterprise partner, ME to WE, *had* paid honorariums to Margaret Trudeau and Alexandre Trudeau for their participation at fundraising events that sometimes ran parallel to WE Days. Second, and more troublingly, it turned out that the accounting team at WE Charity had mistakenly paid certain honorarium bills instead of ME to WE. This error came to light when journalist Jesse Brown said he had an invoice showing WE Charity had paid an agency called Speakers' Spotlight $7,000 to hire Margaret Trudeau for an event on October 20, 2017.

The mere fact of hiring public speakers is not an issue. Hospitals pay honorariums for celebrity golf tournaments and universities for lecture series, and countless charities pay celebrities to speak at gala dinners. WE Charity did not typically rely on traditional fundraising vehicles like lotteries, telemarketing calls, street canvassers, or TV commercials, and instead found it more cost-effective and impactful to at times pay high-profile supporters to attend smaller fundraising events, engage with guests, and hopefully boost donations. Speakers and performers were never paid for appearing at WE Day—that was viewed as a privilege. Even big names like Selena Gomez, Jennifer Aniston, Demi Lovato, and Lilly Singh—people who could command hundreds of thousands of dollars for appearances—were not paid (other than being reimbursed in some cases for out-of-pocket expenses).

Fundraising events, however, were different because they required additional commitments that were not always easy to secure for free. Dalal, Craig, and Marc explained to me that when speakers were willing to appear at no cost, that was the preferred option. But those who typically charged for their services and were perceived as likely to boost fundraising at these ancillary events were given honorariums. It was a discretionary decision by WE executive management. Other paid speakers at WE fundraising events included well-known Canadians like astronaut Chris Hadfield, wheelchair racer and senator Chantal Petitclerc, and rapper Kardinal Offishall. If funding for speakers was available from corporate sponsors for specific initiatives run by WE Charity, the bill was footed by those sponsors or included as part of the packaged cost of sponsoring an event. When funding was not available, ME to WE would step in and pay to assist WE Charity. This was the case with Margaret Trudeau.

TESTIMONIAL: CHIP WILSON

Chip Wilson is a Canadian entrepreneur, philanthropist, and proud father to five. He has founded several apparel companies, most notably Lululemon Athletica. In 2007, Wilson and his wife, Shannon, launched imagine1day, an international charity dedicated to improving access to education in Ethiopia.

Canadian politicians have a lot to answer for.

In 2007, my wife and I started a charity called imagine1day, which focuses on building systems to ensure that Ethiopian children have access to primary school education. In 2017, we merged imagine1day with WE Charity. In deciding to partner with WE Charity, we did plenty of diligence, visited its overseas operations, and made sure that we trusted the organization and its founders. That trust remains strong, and I would do it again if I could.

But now, because of the destruction of WE Charity by politicians bent on scoring points in a partisan fight, I estimate that over the next ten years, approximately three hundred thousand Ethiopian children will lose their access to primary education. It will simply vanish because of the loss of WE Charity's work.

I'm left to reflect on the how and why of it all. Headlines bent on selling advertising instead of reporting the truth, one party's quest to win the next federal election, and the questionable ethics of opposition parties using a children's charity as a political pawn. And many Canadians who believed in WE and knew that falsehoods were being peddled seemed silent (or silenced). Sometimes their voices were drowned out or ignored. Some were scared. And in my view, some Canadians tend to confuse standing back and passively reacting with a form of politeness. Unfortunately, it is not an effective way to deal with bullies.

Justin Trudeau and Bill Morneau should have recused themselves. But those missteps do not justify the destruction of a charity that made a massive difference in the lives of so many, particularly when even today there is no evidence that the charity did anything wrong. WE Charity was tossed aside by Justin Trudeau and a Liberal government that wanted to shift blame. And it was simultaneously used by the NDP and Conservatives as a tool to attack Trudeau. The result, among many other catastrophic consequences, is that hundreds of thousands of young people in Ethiopia have lost the ability to receive a primary education.

WE Charity, its employees, and the thousands of people who have volunteered deserve an apology from all political parties. So do all Canadians.

According to WE Charity, between October 2016 and March 2020, she was hired to take part in twenty-seven events, and for each of those, she provided an average of three to five "extras" per engagement (things like meeting and greeting donors and guests before and after events). For this work, she received a total of $180,000 in fees, or an average of $6,666 per engagement. The total expenses for these appearances, which included several international trips to the US and the UK and covered things like flights, food, hotels, and car services, were just over $163,600. These are hardly astronomical numbers given her profile as a bestselling author, well-known mental health activist, and yes, mother of the current prime minister and spouse of a former prime minister. For his part, Alexandre Trudeau was hired nine times and received $36,000, or $4,333 per engagement, to speak about his documentary films and environmental work. These honorariums were in line with those received by other well-known individuals who participated in WE fundraising events over the past decades. Everything was arranged and paid through Speakers' Spotlight, a large talent and speaker agency that represents celebrities of all types, including Joe Clark, Mary Walsh, and Peter Mansbridge.

It is important to note here that Margaret Trudeau is a professional speaker. Her relationship with WE Charity is not unique. She has for decades accepted paid engagements from companies and organizations. Past clients listed on her speaking bureau website include the Economic Club of Canada, the Royal Inland Hospital Foundation, Northern Ontario Business, Pathstone Foundation, and AppDynamics, as well as many non-profits that receive government funding, such as the Canadian Mental Health Association, the University of Ontario Institute of Technology, the YWCA, and McMaster University. She has also been engaged by corporations that do business with the government, such as the Bank of Montreal.[59]

Although I don't know how much Margaret Trudeau was paid by these organizations, I think it is fair to assume it is, in total, many times greater than the amount paid to her by WE. None of these entities are, to my knowledge, prohibited from working with the government or from accepting federal funding. And I am not aware of any public or private effort to investigate the extent to which these organizations have interacted with the Liberals over the years in which Justin Trudeau has been prime minister.

The bottom line is that any scrutiny regarding Margaret Trudeau's speaking engagements for WE Charity should have focused on whether her speeches created a conflict of interest for her son, and if so, whether he managed the conflict by recusing himself from the decision to award the CSSG to WE. The charity had no say in that decision. But none of this mattered to the politicians, pundits, and journalists looking for scandal.

Coming back to the invoice, as soon as they saw it, WE officials double-checked their records and realized a billing error had occurred for a set of fundraising events. ME to WE should have paid Margaret Trudeau's speaking bureau, not WE Charity. The organization immediately contacted Janyce McGregor, the CBC reporter who had been given the incorrect information, and offered a clarification.

Reaction was swift. The media presented the news as a "revelation" with serious implications for the charity, Justin Trudeau, and the Liberal Party. Opposition politicians savoured the moment, with Charlie Angus accusing the Liberals of thinking "they could play Canadians for suckers," Conservatives calling it "scandalous," and the Bloc Québécois calling for Trudeau to step down pending an investigation.[60] Where it was possible to create the impression that even more dirt might exist, critics went for it. For example, the *National Post* questioned whether Margaret Trudeau was paid to speak at the WE Day on Parliament Hill to celebrate Canada's 150th birthday but never bothered to ferret out the answer: she was not. The *Post* just fronted the issue so that Conservative MP and ethics critic Michael Barrett could offer this nugget: "It would be entirely unacceptable for Canadian tax dollars to be used to pay a speaking fee for the mother of the prime minister at an event where she was appearing with him. It's an unbelievable revelation in a series of unbelievable revelations."[61]

WE Charity's mistake would have been a small one in ordinary times, but the moment was anything but ordinary. To me and other board members, it was clear that the organization had really stepped in it. Now it appeared as though WE Charity was part of a scheme to protect the Liberals and Trudeau, and we knew it would be easier for opposition members and the media to make WE part of the story.

It quickly became apparent that the charity was in jeopardy of losing the public's trust if it did not try to make amends and set the record straight. Staff members were anxious, sad, frustrated, and angry (often all at once). Supporters watched in stunned silence. To their credit, the Kielburgers owned it. Before the board, they acknowledged that the mistake was the product of moving too fast and trying too hard to differentiate between WE Charity and ME to WE. On this latter point, I was unhappy, but I understand why it happened. The organization had always focused on making sure there was no confusion between the work of the charity and the activities of its social enterprise partner. Everyone knew that the relationship was novel in Canada and thus attracted scrutiny. Precision, whether in accounting, donor engagement, or public relations, was expected and required. Here, though, a reflexive attempt to be precise came off as way too cute.

The bottom line is it should never have happened. In an effort to speak directly to Canadians, the Kielburgers made a public apology—through a full-page ad that appeared in the *Globe and Mail*, the *Vancouver Sun*, and the *Toronto Star*—to accept personal responsibility for the challenges facing the charity. "Once we learned that the charity did pay for their speeches, the error was identified, and the charity was reimbursed," they wrote in the ad. "Yet, the error should not have happened, and we apologize."[62]

Unfortunately, the ad did little to tamp down the media frenzy, and misleading articles continued to be published. The opposition, it seemed, had found a big juicy target in WE Charity and the Kielburgers, and in the already hot political climate, with Trudeau's history of ethics violations, no one was in a forgiving mood.

And that mood was about to get worse.

CHAPTER 6

PILING ON

The knives came out as soon as the opposition parties realized that to make their attacks on the prime minister and the Liberal Party stick, they had to cast WE and the Kielburgers in the role of villain. And the media was only too happy to join in.

Historically, vague suspicions about the Kielburgers and their success—whether based on tall poppy syndrome, jealousy, or the brothers' own foibles and shortcomings—were not reason enough for most reputable reporters to dig into every aspect of their lives or the activities of WE. A cardinal rule of journalism is that something must be in the public interest to warrant invasions of privacy and potential reputational harm. WE did not qualify. But now, with a political scandal involving taxpayer dollars, it was open season. Pundits and commentators spread myths and floated leading questions without seeking or providing answers. Politicians both fed into these narratives and fed off them. And traditional media outlets recycled it all. It became a vicious loop of innuendo and inflammatory headlines that dragged on for almost a year.

WE Charity in Canada would never be the same.

Of course, if you want to push a sensationalist narrative to fill column inches and generate clicks, one of the first tasks is to find an expert to say it for you. The more outrageous and outspoken, the better.

The media's favourite commentators throughout the CSSG controversy—apart from Charlie Angus and Pierre Poilievre—were charity analyst Kate Bahen and lawyer Mark Blumberg. Both eagerly accepted their roles as the chief critics of the WE organization, appearing in hundreds of news stories over the summer of 2020. And it appears to me that both adeptly leveraged their increased media presence for professional and financial success. Bahen and Blumberg advanced many narratives that I contend were misleading, and their commentary was seized on by politicians and journalists to become part of the larger story. A number of these misleading narratives are now assumed to be fact.

Bahen is the managing director of Charity Intelligence (Ci), a self-appointed watchdog agency that she founded in 2006. Ci analyzes charities on factors like financial transparency and social impact, then posts the results on its website. Bahen likens her approach to that of a financial analyst who researches stocks to find the best investment opportunities for clients. Ci is a small operation—based on publicly available information, it has just five permanent staff, including Bahen, and does not employ any full-time accountants or auditors.[1] Research director Greg Thomson admitted to the FINA committee that he and Bahen are "analysts, not auditors."[2] Ci has a three-member board of directors that includes Bahen and Thomson.[3]

When Ci launched its online search engine in 2011, it was the subject of a flattering profile in the *Toronto Star*, but it was met with considerable skepticism from other quarters.[4] For an article posted to its website, Charity Village, a company that recruits people to work in the charitable sector, spoke to many who criticized Ci's "naïve analysis of data and lack of understanding of CRA guidelines and how nonprofits in Canada actually work."[5] Mark Blumberg, for example, said that "to telescope the issue of transparency into disclosure of an audited financial statement on the website of a charity is a simplification of the complexity of the issues." Malcolm Burrows, the head of philanthropic advisory services for Scotia Wealth Management, concurred. "Ci seems to want to put all [charities] into a single space, and I think that does a real disservice," he said. "They need to look at that before they make these huge generalizations in public . . . You can't have a 'one-size-fits-all' standard of accountability in the sector." And Imagine Canada's then CEO, Marcel Lauzière, offered a similar observation. "They've taken a [data-gathering] model from the investment world," he noted, "where you look at inputs and then tell your investors where to put their dollars . . . It's not that simple when you're looking at charities and at their outcomes and impacts."

All this matters because when Bahen later began commenting publicly on WE Charity's involvement with the CSSG and presenting herself as an expert on the charitable industry, some of her assertions were based on exactly this kind of superficial and inaccurate analysis of the organization's financial statements and structure. For instance, she told journalist Jesse Brown, in an interview for his Canadaland website, that the charity was "in breach of its bank covenants," a situation she characterized as "a massive, massive red flag."[6] She compared it to a person who is close to maxed out on her credit cards but can't stop spending. In fact, though, this was a simple technicality arising from WE Charity's decision to shift its fiscal year from the standard calendar year to one that aligns with the academic year. That made sense because most of the expenditures for and work around the charity's domestic programs followed the educational calendar. The switch created a minor complication because WE Charity's real estate mortgage agreements required the organization to earn a minimum level of revenue each year. In the year of the change, 2018, the charity did not demonstrate the required level of revenue because its financial report covered just eight months instead of twelve. The shift also required the organization to defer some revenue to align with the year in which related program spending would occur. So the same issue came up in 2019. WE Charity's lenders understood this and waived compliance with the covenants, and its auditors noted the waiver in footnotes to the organization's financial statements without using the word "breach."[7]

It's very simple and uncontroversial stuff, but you would never know it if you listened to Bahen. Although she presented herself as an unbiased observer, her public comments were often one-sided and carried charged language. In the more than one hundred tweets she made about the charity between June and October 2020, she often used the hashtag #WEHaveAProblem, and in one, she asked sarcastically, "Does anyone think it is a good idea for WE Charity to implement this $900m government grant?"[8] Months later, as Marc and Craig were preparing to testify before the ETHI committee, she tweeted the words "Burger time!" with an image of a hamburger and a side of cauliflower alongside the brothers on a television screen.[9]

In dozens of interviews with print and TV media outlets, Bahen relentlessly pushed her "breached" bank covenant narrative, implying that before the CSSG came along, WE Charity was teetering like a house of cards. It quickly became a central plank in the opposition parties' theory that the Kielburgers asked their friends in the Liberal government for a bailout and were handed the CSSG. To this day, Bahen's claim that WE Charity was broke—which was grounded in nothing more than this bank covenant issue—remains part of Conservative and NDP talking points and is a common misperception among Canadians.

In my interviews with Marc and Craig, they cited several pivotal moments in the CSSG fiasco. This was one of them. Trudeau may have shifted the media spotlight when he said that WE Charity was the only organization capable of delivering the program, but Bahen made sure the focus remained on the charity. "One minute we're referring questions to the PMO about Sophie's speaking engagements and the prime minister's failure to recuse himself," Craig said, "and the next minute we're dealing with people questioning the integrity of the charity."

Every effort made to dispel this particular myth fell flat. This was an enormous problem, both because the myth suggested that WE Charity had somehow invented the CSSG to save itself from ruin and because it gave the charity's donors and partners pause about the stability of the organization. Eventually, the Stillman Family Foundation, led by long-time donor Andy Stillman, stepped in and commissioned a series of independent investigations to try to get to the bottom of things and eliminate any confusion. One report, issued by Dr. Al Rosen in October 2020, squarely addressed Bahen's claims.

Rosen is a specialist in investigative and forensic accounting and a certified fraud examiner and forensic certified public accountant. He is famous for having predicted the collapse of telecommunications giant Nortel Networks almost two years before its demise.[10] His work and views have been written about in the *New York Times* and many other publications, he has served as an expert witness on forensic accounting matters in hundreds of litigated cases, and he is author of *Swindlers: Cons & Cheats and How to Protect Your Investments from Them.*[11]

Rosen did a deep dive into WE Charity's books and concluded that prior to the CSSG, the charity was financially sound and not looking for a bailout.[12] "At issue seems to be whether . . . WE was in financial difficulty and was reliant on the [CSSG contribution agreement] to continue maintaining its charitable operations. Our analyses do not support such assertions of financial instability."[13] He noted that the charity had $50 million in cash and real estate, and that these assets had been acquired specifically to help the organization manage year-to-year variations in funding. He acknowledged that like many Canadian entities, WE Charity faced some economic uncertainty because of COVID but had laid off staff to better ensure the long-term health and financial viability of the organization. "The primary difference between our findings and the assertions made by the organization's critics," he noted, "is that ours were developed as a result of a detailed investigation into the organization's finances before, and since, the onset of the Pandemic. Conversely, the allegations and narrative asserted by critics often appear to be largely based on conjecture, and have not been substantiated in any convincing way by documentation or other evidence."[14] In short, he wrote, "critics' conclusions were reached without sufficient facts having been gathered and evaluated."[15]

In an interview, Rosen told me that he thought the concerns raised by commentators like Bahen and parroted by the media and politicians were ill-informed and inconsistent with the facts and numbers. He also confirmed to me that he got all the information and cooperation he needed from the charity and its co-founders.

Scott Baker, WE Charity's chief operating officer, described the hours he spent with Rosen, reviewing financial documents and answering his questions. A self-described "math geek" who holds a master's degree in mathematics from the University of Toronto, Scott enjoyed going through the charity's finances in painstaking detail with someone of Rosen's pedigree. But his face quickly clouded with frustration when he contrasted that approach to the media's "reckless" acceptance of Bahen's so-called analysis. "You cannot compare the two," he said.

"On one hand, you have Dr. Rosen, who has left no stone unturned and asked thoughtful questions when the answers were not clearly in front of him. On the other, you have Kate Bahen, who has no accountants on her team and has based her entire analysis on one document she misinterpreted. There was no effort by the media to understand. Of course it was frustrating."

The second myth Bahen launched into the mediasphere concerned the relationship between WE Charity and ME to WE. In an appearance on CBC Radio's *The Current*, she argued that there is an inherent conflict in an organization that includes a public charity and a private social enterprise.[16] "And these two," she declared, "are joined at the hip." But as we've already seen, that was exactly the point—the two entities worked together, with the for-profit social enterprise supporting the activities and mission of the non-profit charity. Even Bahen seemed to acknowledge how common this is when she said, "Many companies—big companies, public companies—have philanthropic arms."

And yet, that didn't stop her from accusing WE of improperly channelling millions of dollars from the charity to the social enterprise as part of a process she referred to as backwashing. "We've never seen the backwash before," she told host Nahlah Ayed, noting that usually the money flows solely from the social enterprise to the charitable organization. But what she was describing was the purchase by WE Charity—at or below cost—of volunteer trips and handmade artisan products that were an integral part of the charity's fundraising efforts. When WE Charity bought things from ME to WE, it paid an entity that was giving its profits back to the charity. If it had bought the same trips or products from an unrelated entity, that entity had no obligation to contribute anything to the charity. So far from being backwash, the flow of funds between the organizations was one aspect of an innovative partnership that, in my view, should serve as a model for others seeking to achieve maximum philanthropic impact.

Throughout her many media appearances, Bahen maintained that Charity Intelligence had long-standing concerns about the organization, and that she was not simply jumping on the anti-WE bandwagon. But this was belied by years of consistently good ratings for the charity from

Ci. In testimony to the FINA committee, Greg Thomson, the director of research, said, "Starting in 2014, Ci rated WE Charity with our highest four-star rating based on transparency, reporting and overhead spending. WE Charity ticked all of the boxes and performed well relative to other Canadian charities."[17] And in 2019, WE was given an A grade for transparency and reporting—the very things Bahen was now calling into question. Other rating agencies agreed with Ci's previous assessments. Charity Navigator, the largest evaluator of non-profits in North America, gave WE a perfect four-star rating in fall 2020, with an overall score of 93.98 out of 100.

No one reported any of this—and inexplicably, no one challenged Bahen on her comments.

INSIDE THE ECHO CHAMBER

If it's true that the squeaky wheel gets the grease, then it is even more true that the outraged wheel gets the microphone. This was certainly the case with Mark Blumberg, a Toronto lawyer whose practice focuses on non-profit and charity law. Among other things, Blumberg is his firm's resident blogger, penning near daily missives on law and the charitable sector.

In the CSSG scandal, Blumberg appeared to see a chance to inject himself into the story and gain attention for his long-held views about the need for expanded government funding in the charitable sector. As a vocal critic of social enterprise generally,[18] Blumberg was particularly suspicious of the partnership between WE Charity and ME to WE, and quickly became a source for negative news coverage, including on major outlets like the CBC and Global News.[19] The media's frequent amplification of his criticism contributed to the public perception that there was some kind of funny business going on at WE.

In his media appearances, Blumberg persistently raised concerns about the supposed complexity of the WE organization and expressed the opinion that giving charities more freedom to set up businesses like ME to WE could actually hurt the sector instead of helping it.[20] He eventually even took those concerns to Ottawa, telling the ETHI committee, "It's not that charities can't do business; there are charities that do lots of business. If you ever go to a hospital and you park in the parking lot, that's a related business. It could be perfectly fine. What is unusual here is that normally the charity owns the business."[21]

But as an expert in charity law, Blumberg knew well—or should have—that when ME to WE's precursor organization was founded in 1999, an Ontario-based charity could not own a for-profit business.[22] Even today, the CRA limits a charity's ability to operate an unrelated business, and a non-profit engaged in any form of innovative social enterprise risks losing its charitable status if the CRA deems the businesses to be insufficiently related.[23] Yet for some reason, Blumberg failed to offer this important context whenever he talked about WE Charity and ME to WE. And interestingly, it doesn't appear that the media ever sought comment from Torys LLP or Miller Thomson LLP, even though these well-respected firms both have large non-profit practices and advised WE Charity on its structure and operations.

Despite being the media's preferred pundits, Blumberg and Bahen, to my knowledge, had no meaningful involvement with WE Charity prior to the CSSG. They had never interviewed its board members or co-founders, had never attended any of its domestic education programs, had never visited any of the international development sites, and had never conducted any studies about the efficacy of the charity's programs. And yet, by December 2020, Bahen or Ci had appeared in 698 print and online articles, 356 television reports, and 659 radio reports—all to talk about WE Charity, ME to WE, the Kielburgers, and the CSSG. And from late June to late October, Blumberg appeared in at least ten different newspaper articles on the CSSG, doubling the number of media appearances he'd made the previous year. On social media, he posted more than sixty tweets about WE Charity in that same period, often taking the opportunity to also promote his law firm's services and online webinars.[24]

Why all the focus on Blumberg and Bahen? There were plenty of people—both within WE and externally—who could have offered insight into the way the organization really operated. Explanations were readily available, but no one in the media was interested.[25] Asking the questions, it seemed, made for better storytelling than giving the answers. "It was like one of those nightmares when you're in a room and you can see and hear everything, but no one can see or hear anything you're saying," Marc later told me. "But in this case, we could never wake up from the nightmare. We kept trying to get the facts out there, but it was like we were invisible. No one wanted to hear us."

Thanks to their numerous public statements about WE Charity, Blumberg and particularly Bahen gained the attention of opposition politicians and were eventually invited to appear before the FINA committee as witnesses. This could have been a good opportunity to educate the public on relevant issues like how non-profits work and what information they must disclose, but instead Bahen used her time to note that her organization had become "a go-to for the media," and to repeat many of her favourite claims about the relationship between WE Charity and ME to WE, the bank covenant, and the downgrade in WE's Ci rating. This was music to the ears of opposition MPs, who used her testimony as an excuse to read their own baseless allegations into the record. NDP MP Peter Julian, for example, suggested, without citing any evidence, that WE Charity could somehow divert government funds to its social enterprise partner and from there straight into the Kielburgers' pockets. "Are you concerned," he asked Bahen, "about monies being potentially redirected to one of the for-profit entities that are part of this very labyrinthine organization?"[26]

Bahen herself spun a new yarn about WE Charity possibly engaging in some kind of bait-and-switch scheme that even the government was unaware of. "Maybe people, as we're all learning," she said, "weren't aware that the contract [for the CSSG] was with the WE Charity Foundation, which is very different from WE Charity." She wondered aloud—without any evidence—if perhaps the organization had a pattern of duping partners into thinking they were entering into an agreement with the charity, only to realize later that ME to WE's name was on the contract.

Meanwhile, she was noncommittal when MPs tried to get her to acknowledge some basic holes in her theories about WE Charity and the CSSG. When Quebec MP Annie Koutrakis pointed out that Ci didn't downgrade the charity's rating until July 10, which was after the

CSSG announcement had been made, Bahen replied, "That's an excellent point. That's a point our research team will be going through."

Koutrakis's observation meant that far from raising all kinds of red flags, as Bahen and the opposition MPs kept implying, the charity was in fact in good standing when the government decided to give it the contract for the CSSG. And similarly, Bahen had no real answer for Toronto MP Adam Vaughan when he asked if she was aware that many charities most Canadians would consider highly reputable—including Habitat for Humanity, the YWCA, and the Canadian Hearing Foundation—had received lower ratings from Ci than WE Charity had.

Bahen was also questioned by Liberal MP Francesco Sorbara about previous errors in Ci's reporting. "I appreciate the work you are doing at Charity Intelligence," he said. "It's important, but it's also a double-edged sword, because when you make a wrong call, you can actually hurt a charity significantly. I don't know who's doing the due diligence on Charity Intelligence on your calls. You have had to apologize in the past when you've made that wrong call and when the damage is, I would say, done."

Sorbara was referring to disparaging comments Bahen made in 2019 about the Winnipeg Jets' youth charity, the True North Youth Foundation. Bahen claimed that among other problems, the foundation was overspending on fundraising.[27] Later, she issued a formal apology acknowledging that Ci's own report showed the foundation's fundraising and administrative costs fell within "a reasonable range." She also offered contrition for calling the foundation a "puck hog" in a CityNews interview and ended with a mea culpa for her "unfortunate mischaracterization of TNYF."[28] But when challenged on these matters by Sorbara, Bahen claimed she did nothing wrong. "Our research report stands," she said.

Pundits like Bahen and Blumberg can cause real harm by offering claims but no evidence to back those claims. When their views are amplified by news outlets that give them a platform without doing any due diligence of their own, their credibility in the eyes of the public grows. This encourages more media outlets to call, which in turn leads to even greater exposure. It's a feedback loop that can be almost impossible to stop.

It might sound like a game, but it's anything but for the people who are watching their reputations being called into question. "They were given licence to say whatever they wanted with no consequence or consideration for the outsized impact they were having," Marc said. "It was one thing to come after me and Craig, but they were attacking the integrity of the board, the staff, our donors—everyone who had put so much energy into building something meaningful."

WELCOME TO CANADALAND

The Kielburgers' relationship with the media is complicated—love-hate, you might say. That early experience with *Saturday Night* magazine was formative—the article accused the Kielburger family of bilking funds from the charity, and a painful legal battle ensued, with the magazine eventually settling the action and paying damages—and it taught the brothers to approach journalists with a degree of skepticism and to fight back hard when they or the organization they had built were being unfairly maligned.

At the same time, as Craig has frequently noted, the charity as a whole was inspired by a news article he read as a child. Had that journalist not been moved to tell the story of Iqbal Masih, the murdered Pakistani child labourer, Free the Children might never have been created. "If it wasn't for that story, I don't know where I would be right now or what my life would look like," Craig told me. "I've never met that journalist, but I've always wanted to thank them because that one article changed my life and positively impacted the lives of millions of children."

It is also true that through most of its history, WE Charity enjoyed glowing and influential media coverage—over the years, the brothers had appeared on such high-profile programs as *60 Minutes*, *The Oprah Winfrey Show*, and *The Colbert Report*. And they contributed regular columns to the *Toronto Star*, the *Globe and Mail*, and some Postmedia dailies. Editors and publishers from news outlets across Canada, including the *Vancouver Sun*, *Edmonton Journal*, and *Calgary Herald*, also appeared on the WE Day stage to speak to the young audience. In one instance, the *Globe and Mail*'s editor-in-chief, David Walmsley, took to the stage, a copy of his paper in hand, to speak about the importance of media literacy. So there's no doubt that the charity and the Kielburgers had many positive and long-standing relationships with media partners, and they relied on those relationships to bring attention to their work—as any organization would.

Then along came Canadaland and WE Charity's *bête noire*, Jesse Brown.

Brown got his start in traditional media, working for CBC Radio (where he was disciplined for fabricating content)[29] and contributing to magazines like *Maclean's* and *Toronto Life*. He has made a career out of taking on sacred cows and is perhaps most famous for partnering with *Toronto Star* reporter Kevin Donovan to break the story of the sexual assault allegations against CBC Radio host Jian Ghomeshi. That collaboration ended, however, when Brown wanted to publish before Donovan felt full due diligence had been done.[30]

Today, Brown is the founder, owner, publisher, editor, feature writer, and podcast host of Canadaland. In January 2015, the *Globe and Mail's* media critic, Simon Houpt, profiled Brown in his column, saying he views himself as "a fearless David taking on the Goliath of Canadian corporate media."[31] But Houpt also noted that Brown "has a track record of playing fast and loose with facts." He has been accused of sensationalizing stories, relying too heavily on rumour and innuendo, and making allegations without doing the hard work to substantiate them. But his small media footprint—his website had just over a million visitors in all of 2020, compared to the *Globe and Mail's* average of 4.5 million *weekly* visitors that same year[32]—is disproportionally influential because of his sensationalist commentary on the media industry. Journalists follow him for the schadenfreude of watching other media outlets get taken down, and out of dread that they themselves will be his next victims.

WE and Brown first collided in March 2015, when he published an article alleging that the CBC had pulled a documentary about voluntourism at the last minute because it was critical of ME to WE. In fact, the documentary was simply rescheduled because it included WE Day footage for which rights had not been cleared and it had to be re-edited. There was no critical coverage of ME to WE in the film, and the company was not one of the tour operators profiled. Two weeks and three articles later, that seemed to be the end of it.

But in October 2018, it became apparent that Brown had not forgotten about WE after all. That month, Canadaland published an article charging that the charity was "connected to no fewer than three companies known to use child and slave labour in their supply chain," and that the organization "promot[ed] products made in part by children, including Hershey's products that contain cocoa farmed by child labourers in West African countries, and Kellogg's products that contain palm oil farmed by child labourers in Indonesia."[33] The article and its accompanying podcast also just happened to kick off Canadaland's crowdfunding season. Brown spent more than thirteen minutes of the podcast soliciting support for his website, then followed up with the same plea on every subsequent episode for a month.

The article was written by a rookie journalist named Jaren Kerr. On the podcast, Brown explained that he had "assigned reporter after reporter" to do a story on WE before finally, in the summer of 2018, asking Kerr to take it on.[34] "He had a story in mind," Kerr said on stage at the Investigative Reporters and Editors conference in May 2019. "He sold me on the story as, you know, 'You'll have time, you'll have resources, you have legal insurance. Give it a shot.'"[35] For Kerr, it was an opportunity to make a name for himself. "I saw this as an opportunity, when my contract was ending at the [Toronto] Star, to try to make a splash before I had to consider other options," he told the reporters at the conference.

The article relied heavily on information attributed to anonymous former employees, was riddled with errors, and included digitally altered financial documents and a digital image of a non-existent Kellogg's cereal box that had ME to WE's logo on the front.[36] This was billed on the podcast as "extensive proof" that WE Charity was lying when it said it did not condone or support child labour. But the image of the cereal box was simply a mock-up someone had created to pitch ME to WE on a potential partnership that never came to fruition. (Journalist Mark Bourrie amusingly offered $10,000 to anyone who could find an actual box of Frosted Mini-Wheats with the ME to WE logo. The prize has never been claimed.)

Not sure how best to combat the Canadaland story, WE Charity retained the services of one of Canada's most respected jurists, former Ontario Court of Appeal Justice Stephen Goudge.[37] He was asked to conduct a review of Canadaland's various allegations, as well as WE Charity's responses and source documentation. In his findings, he wrote that the Canadaland claims were "without merit."

"We wanted to ignore it," Dalal recalled, "but it was hard to do. Social media today amplifies everything, especially sensational content. People like Jesse Brown can put anything they want online, and it gets retweeted and shared without any context or fact-checking. We were getting calls from all of our stakeholders—teachers, students, sponsors— and these false statements were causing real damage to the organization. We felt like we had no choice but to push for accuracy."

When WE asked for corrections, however, Canadaland refused. "We had never experienced anything like this before, and we really didn't know how to react," Marc recalled. "There was a thinking that if we provided the reporter with as much information as possible, his narrative would shift. It didn't, obviously." Lawyers got involved, with one noting that "it is sadly evident that salacious articles and podcasts increases page views and 'clicks,' and thus directly serves your financial interests as the owner of Canadaland website with revenue generated from advertisements."[38] On November 6, 2018, a notice of libel was served.

Predictably, this salvo only made Brown *more* interested in pursuing WE, and the charity became a regular feature of his weekly podcast. In the next few months, Jaren Kerr also published two more stories: "Inside the 'Cult' of Kielburger" and "How the Kielburgers Handle the Press." The latter article alleged that WE Charity's relationships with media partners for events like WE Day had given the organization an enormous platform and made journalists and editors reluctant to publish negative stories. "Nearly two dozen sources, comprising journalists and former WE employees," wrote Kerr, "have described to CANADALAND a concerted effort by WE to meticulously—and sometimes forcefully— manage their media profile to mitigate and minimize criticism."[39] In reality, WE Charity had issued only one notice of libel in over twenty years—to Canadaland. This article prompted a second notice of libel.

At this point, it's worth noting that sometimes WE took a bad situation and made it worse. The Kielburgers often felt compelled to combat any error with a full-throated defence. Over the years, many board members, including me, had questioned whether it was counterproductive to respond in such an aggressive manner. In fact, Jesse Brown later revealed just how counterproductive it could be, telling CBC's *Fifth Estate*, "My impulse, when people fight that hard, is you have to wonder why."[40] But whenever this issue was raised, the Kielburgers replied with an eloquent explanation of why this particular set of errors was particularly egregious, or why other advisers who were in favour of a more combative response were correct. In most cases, the board deferred to the co-founders. We understood that a charity's most valuable asset is its reputation. A charity operates on trust. No trust, no donations, no impact. And to be fair, it is hard to fault Marc and Craig for wanting to push back on attacks on a lifetime of work. On reflection, however, I wish we had sometimes urged restraint more strongly. Instead of putting out the fire, we occasionally poured gasoline on it.

In any event, the organization's strategy for dealing with Canadaland seemed to work, at least for a moment. Just as WE was gearing up for a legal fight, Canadaland's intensely negative coverage came to a screeching halt. In a June 2019 podcast episode titled "A Former WE Employee Speaks Out," Brown seemed to have recognized that there was no grand scheme afoot. "There is no smoking gun," he said. "There is no big scandal . . . One thing that became really clear to us is that WE is legit. This was never going to be a story about a crooked charity."[41]

Perhaps not surprisingly, though, Brown's tune changed again when the CSSG story took over the headlines and he wanted a starring role. He started regularly complaining about getting no credit for being the first to report negatively on the charity, and he churned out new anti-WE content at a furious rate. In July 2020 alone, Canadaland posted ten stories and two podcast episodes about the organization, covering everything from payments to Margaret Trudeau to trips made by Bill Morneau to the groundbreaking news that the accounting department was walled off from the rest of the office in the open-concept WE Global Learning Centre. (Even today, Brown is still at it—he recently released a five-part podcast series called *The White Saviours* that was a rehash of his previous allegations.)

While on the attack, Brown nevertheless often positioned himself as a victim of WE Charity's aggressive tactics. His most common claim was that the organization had hired private investigators to conduct research on him as an intimidation tactic. In reality, the charity's attorney, Peter Downard at Fasken LLP, one of Canada's most highly regarded defamation lawyers, indicated that he had simply done a standard background check as part of preparing a potential libel suit against Brown and Canadaland. In a private message to Brown in response to allegations that he was being improperly targeted, Downard stated, "The report you ask about is a typical example of due diligence in advance of commencing a libel action. It is typical where a client has been irresponsibly and maliciously attacked." Brown made the exchange public by posting it to Twitter.[42]

On July 20, Brown announced on Twitter that like Bahen, he had been called to testify before the opposition-dominated FINA committee.[43] On this, at least, he got a fair bit of pushback from fellow journalists. David Akin, chief political correspondent for Global News, replied, "Why? Was there something you neglected to report on that you are going to tell the committee? If not: Just tell the MPs to read what you wrote. MPs should not be summoning journalists to testify at Commons committees. Terrible precedent."[44] And James McLeod from the *Financial Post* wrote: "As with many Jesse Brown things, it's fun to imagine how Jesse Brown would react if a journalist at the CBC or a legacy media outlet did this."[45]

HUNGRY FOR CLICKS

Canadaland's sensationalist and obsessive style of reporting about WE quickly began to impact the style and tone of coverage by traditional news outlets as well. As early as July 10, the media was referring to the CSSG debacle—which, let's not forget, was about the government's approach to awarding contracts and whether cabinet ministers had or had not complied with ethics rules—as the "WE Charity Scandal." Not the CSSG Controversy or the Trudeau Scandal. Not even the WE

Charity "affair," a blander term that was attached to Trudeau's prior ethics scandals. The name stuck, and from then, it quickly became an exercise in piling on. Many reporters displayed an almost fanatical hunger for more negative WE content, and the willingness to use the charity to discredit the government began to make once-staid Canadian news outlets look more like the nakedly partisan broadcasters south of the border.

Between June 25 and the end of November 2020, WE Charity, WE Charity Foundation, ME to WE, and various other WE entities were mentioned in the press more than 129,000 times, and the Kielburger name appeared another 15,000 times. "It was like watching a car crash," Craig said. "We knew that people overseas would suffer and lives would be lost when projects couldn't be fulfilled. But no one seemed to care." Marc added: "WE Charity is far from perfect. And if someone criticizes a mistake that we've made, that's fair. But there is a difference between fair and false."

Marc recalls having to explain to his elderly parents and others that there was no truth to two *Globe and Mail* articles that implied the charity was the focus of an RCMP investigation.[46] The RCMP confirmed that it was simply "examining carefully the government's decision to award WE the contract"—something it was required to do given opposition MPs' direct requests for an inquiry. This was not by any stretch the same thing as a criminal investigation into WE. But coverage like this left a lasting impression that coloured public perceptions of the charity and the Kielburgers, and made it harder for them to be heard when trying to set the record straight. "Donors, staff, and teachers who read the articles inferred that we were under criminal investigation. That is a serious thing. For our young staff members, in particular, it was scary. For others, it was embarrassing, because they were constantly answering questions from friends and family. We all found ourselves having to defend something we cared deeply about."

The *Globe's* reporting on the organization was as varied as it was constant. Paul Waldie reported that WE Charity US had paid so-called political consultants to undermine the media using unscrupulous tactics. "WE Charity spent more than US$600,000 on political consultants in Washington last year [2019]," Waldie asserted, "including a firm co-founded by a trio of long-time Republican Party strategists."[47] In fact, those funds were paid to a psychologist to provide well-being support to WE staff and to a DC-based PR firm hired to launch two WE Days in the Baltimore/DC area—hardly a political pursuit.[48] A few days later, Waldie erred again by substantially overstating—by more than $100 million—the level of donations WE Charity had received from major US corporations such as Allstate and Microsoft.[49] This mistake appeared to stem from Waldie's misreading of the charity's US tax filings. WE Charity was not asked for comment prior to publication, and the *Globe* refused to correct the error.

When the charity requested corrections, it was rebuffed. So the organization appealed to the public editor, Sylvia Stead. "We saw her as an ombudsman, someone who would uphold the *Globe*'s journalistic standards," Craig explained to me. "We weren't getting anywhere with the journalists or their editors. But we thought, as the person responsible for journalism ethics at the *Globe*, she would at least meet us partway." She did not.

In one remarkable instance, Stead refused to address the fact that the *Globe* was misreporting the total amount of the CSSG agreement with WE Charity as $912 million rather than $543 million. This was not nitpicking. As we've already seen, the $912 million figure had been used by critics to tag the CSSG as a "billion-dollar program." The correct number was on the public record, as was the text of the contribution agreement, yet the *Globe* misreported this on more than one hundred occasions. Still, Stead remarkably argued that because Google searches yielded more results for the higher figure, the error did not require correction. She wrote: "Google: WE Charity + $912 million or $900 million = 188,000 results. WE Charity + $543 million = 24,400 results."[50]

Things were no better over at the *Toronto Sun*, where Brian Lilley, the paper's political columnist, had hopped gleefully on the anti-WE bandwagon. Starting with an article titled "Maybe We Should Have Been Looking at WE Charity Earlier,"[51] published on July 7, 2020, Lilley spent the entire month seemingly writing only about WE—an astonishing twenty-seven articles in all.

At one point, Lilley published Marc's home address. As a result, Marc's and Craig's families began receiving death threats by phone, email, and tweet, including several directed at their young children. The police had to be contacted on multiple occasions. "While Marc was explaining to his family what happened, I frantically called Postmedia [parent company of the *Toronto Sun*] to explain about the death threats," Craig explained. "I told them there were young children in the house and the police were giving us warnings. I was pleading with them to at a minimum remove the specific house number from the online article. I still cannot believe that they refused."

On July 20, in a piece titled "WE Flips for Real Estate," Lilley made multiple errors about WE Charity's chief financial officer, Victor Li, who he implied was selling WE real estate to family members at below-market rates. "The [property] was purchased from Free the Children, the charity now called WE," Lilley wrote. "WE is where [buyer] Mingze Li's father, Victor, works as chief financial officer."[52] In fact, there was no family relationship between the two. When social media users pointed out his error, which was perhaps grounded in the xenophobic notion that two people named Li must be related, the online story was quietly changed, without any public correction or note for readers who had seen the earlier version.

The same article also included several mischaracterizations regarding the private real estate holdings of Fred and Theresa Kielburger. Intermixing WE Charity property and private family property, Lilley wrote that the Kielburger family "traded some pieces of real estate multiple times before transferring them to a numbered company for what is recorded as a $0 transaction." He was told by WE's media relations team multiple times that the properties in question were never owned by WE Charity or ME to WE. The transactions were part of personal inheritance planning by the eighty-year old Kielburger parents.

Other media outlets also zeroed in on WE's real estate holdings, with dozens of articles pointing to this as "evidence" of impropriety. "Real Estate Is Central to the WE/Kielburger Story," read a headline in the *Toronto Sun*.[53] The *National Post* declared, "Property Brothers:

Kielburgers Facing Scrutiny Over WE Organization's $50M Real Estate Empire."[54]

Unfortunately, many of the claims in these articles, both express and implied, were based on a misunderstanding of the charity's mission and on statements from "experts" that simply did not apply to WE. For example, the article in the *National Post* described WE Charity as "one of the largest international development organizations in the country," and then implied that there was something nefarious about these types of organizations investing in real estate. "Some of the biggest names in international development," the article said, "own either no real estate, or significantly less than WE Charity, Canada Revenue Agency filings show." The reporter noted that the paper had consulted legal experts, and they were "of the opinion that this kind of set-up is more typical for religious institutions like the Catholic Church, or large hospitals that require massive premises, rather than an international development organization."

Sounds pretty shady, unless you understand that domestic programming was a much larger part of WE Charity's budget and overseas development work was only a fraction of the activities taking place at WE Charity's Toronto headquarters (the organization's main real estate asset). The building was more than just an office space—it was also the vehicle through which WE Charity delivered much of its domestic programming, with the entire first floor dedicated to hosting visiting school groups. Instead of suggesting that WE Charity was analogous to international aid organizations that do not provide programming in Canada, the article should have compared it to other domestic charities that deliver youth programs, like the Boys & Girls Club, the YMCA, Scouts Canada, and science centers in various cities—all of which hold substantially more real estate than WE. Attempts to get the *National Post* to correct the misleading statement were ignored.

The fact is, purchasing real estate is a completely ordinary and low-risk investment strategy in the Canadian charitable sector. Even lawyer Mark Blumberg, hardly WE's biggest backer, acknowledged that real estate ownership is common, and that WE Charity owned relatively little in comparison to other Canadian charities. "While 22,000 charities own real estate of some sort," Blumberg wrote in a 2020 article in

Foundation magazine, "over 10,000 charities have real estate valued at over $1 million and over 640 charities had real estate which was worth more than the $43 million of real estate held by WE Charity."[55]

For WE Charity, real estate served as a form of reserve fund. All charities need such a fund to provide a cushion for unplanned expenditures or events (say, for example, a global pandemic or a political scandal). Some choose to invest their reserve fund in the stock market. WE Charity chose real estate instead. It's that simple.

WE Charity's board, for its part, had always weighed in on and voted to approve every real estate transaction. As part of that process, the board repeatedly sought independent advice, going back to a report prepared by former Supreme Court Justice Peter Cory in 2011. (I covered that back in chapter 2.) More recently, Justice Goudge was retained to assess the reasonableness of WE Charity's reserve fund policy. In his 2019 report on this matter, he noted that real estate provides a predictable and low-risk investment, particularly in the booming Toronto market, and that a reserve of somewhere between three months to three years of operating expenses is most appropriate for charities. WE Charity's reserve fund through real estate represented eight to nine months of its annual operating revenue.[56] Former Wisconsin governor Scott McCallum conducted a similar assessment and wrote, "Based on a thorough review and my 40 years of experience working in the non-profit sector, I can conclude that WE Charity's investments in real estate assets represent a best-in-class example for other non-profits to follow. The charity's investments have been prudent, low-risk, and carried out in close consultation with WE Charity's Board of Directors, who are well-qualified and experienced in overseeing such decisions."[57]

So real estate investment is both a common strategy and an entirely proper one. Early in its history, WE Charity looked to peers like the YMCA, Scouts Canada, and Oxfam—all of which own their operational properties to help ensure fiscal stability, maximize program delivery, and facilitate long-term impact. The organization realized that adopting the same approach was smart and fiscally prudent—it made no sense to pay rent to house a huge domestic team, particularly when the charity had donors like Hartley Richardson, David Aisenstat, Peter Gilgan, Mario

Romano, and Fred Losani, who wanted to make targeted donations for the specific purpose of helping the organization acquire real estate. (No youth fundraising or international development donations were used.) Former WE Charity board chair Michelle Douglas made exactly this point when she wrote an October 2019 testimonial in response to media inquiries. "I am pleased to speak about our real estate philosophy, which has been part of our operations over the past twelve years," she said. "WE Charity adopted an early philosophy of using real estate as a stabilizing, organizational asset. Our philosophy has proven to be a demonstrably positive approach that supports our mission."[58] Unfortunately, all this nuance was ignored by the media.

Journalists were quick to jump the gun whenever a potential story emerged. In one striking instance, Travis Dhanraj, then the Queen's Park bureau chief for Global News, tweeted speculation that WE was packing up its headquarters because he spotted eleven U-Haul trucks out front of the WE GLC. After tweeting out this false news, Dhanraj reached out to the PR team to ask if the trucks had been hired by the organization. He was told there was a U-Haul depot nearby. To his credit, Dhanraj was the rare journalist who acknowledged and corrected his error. "Deleted previous tweet re @WEMovement & Uhaul vehicles—I should not have linked the two. There's a dealer about 1.1km away and upon further investigation turns out you can drop off vehicles on Queen St! Apologies."[59] But the damage was done—the content was already circulating via social media, and many people readily assumed the organization was closing shop or carting away damning evidence.

This wasn't the most egregious mistake, but it was an example of the "shoot first" mentality of the media. "It was open season," Dalal said, "and no one seemed to care if they were correct as long as they were first."

As a board member, I felt helpless in the face of this never-ending avalanche of bad news. So did everyone at WE Charity. Efforts to set the record straight proved fruitless. Even when the WE Charity team worked through the night to present accurate facts in response to false reporting and did get corrections, they were made long after the initial story had been read and ingested by the public. Anyone who has ever tried to recall an unintended email knows the feeling. What's read can't be unread.

Meanwhile, reports by people like Dr. Rosen and former Ontario deputy solicitor general Matt Torigian—which debunked the myths relating to the CSSG long before Ethics Commissioner Mario Dion did the same in mid-2021—received scant attention. WE also created a transparency website to house information regarding reviews of its programs and operations over the years. Interested journalists and other Canadians could find, among other things, reports from auditors, HR firms, retired Supreme Court and appellate court justices, B corp and fair trade accreditors, pedagogy experts, the Treadright Foundation (relating to global sustainable travel), Plan to Protect (relating to youth safety), and years of impact studies by consulting firm Mission Measurement. Everything seemingly went unread or was ignored.

To this day, I am shocked by the speed and ferocity with which a negative narrative pushed by a small group of fringe journalists and pundits was so thoroughly embraced by the mainstream media. And I'm dismayed by the absence of meaningful coverage of the perspectives of the key beneficiaries of WE Charity. Who listened to the students who lost access to the CSSG in the middle of a pandemic? How could journalists cover this story without providing the perspective of millions of schoolkids who relied on WE Schools programming to cope with challenges like bullying and depression? What about the teachers who implemented the WE curriculum as part of the often-thankless work of educating our children? And what did the countless women, men, and children helped by WE's programs in the developing world have to say?

All these voices were almost entirely ignored.

And for those who might have wanted to support the charity and its mission, the intensity of negative press coverage created a climate of fear. In dozens of interviews, people told me about vile name calling on social media and concerns about being unflatteringly featured in the press. No one wanted to be part of the firestorm. While the media is certainly not responsible for every crazy tweet or email, it does need to be careful about the climate it creates. Otherwise, voices are stifled and important stories go untold.

TESTIMONIAL: JENNIFER TORY

Jennifer Tory is the former chief administrative officer of the Royal Bank of Canada, where she was responsible for the bank's brand, marketing, citizenship, communications, procurement, and real estate functions globally. She currently serves as a director on the boards of BCE Inc. and Allied REIT, is chair of the board of the Toronto International Film Festival, and sits on the board of the Sunnybrook Hospital Foundation. In 2019, she was appointed a member of the Order of Canada.

I've been involved with WE Charity for nearly fifteen years. I have taken trips with my family to visit the organization's international projects, attended many WE Day events, and visited classrooms to observe WE Schools programming first-hand. And I have proudly donated to the charity and helped with fundraising by introducing WE to others in my network.

I also held a senior leadership position at one of WE's biggest corporate partners. This partnership started with a focus on clean water initiatives and grew to include support for WE Days across Canada. It was far more than corporate marketing—it was an opportunity to engage employees and their families in social good and devote resources to a cause that galvanized young people to act and see themselves as agents of change. In my view, corporate engagement with WE Charity was a vehicle to make a difference and fulfil corporate social responsibility goals that companies could aspire to.

As a donor with decades of involvement supporting charities of all sizes, I can say that the reporting and stewardship I received from WE Charity on the use of my contributions were as comprehensive and transparent as I've experienced. This, combined with the visible impact that my donations had on young women being able to go to school, clean water reaching villages, and the overall development of partner communities, is why I felt like WE Charity was a good choice for my charitable giving.

It has been hard to listen to the many allegations levelled against the charity that I know are not based on facts. Along with so many supporters of WE Charity, we considered ways to assist in getting the charity's side of the story out. But the vitriol was intense and it did not seem the media wanted to listen.

Once the dust settles, I will absolutely support whatever comes next for the Kielburgers and the organization. Canadian young people, in particular, would benefit from a new beginning.

This inability to be heard affected even powerful people who are not often dismissed. For instance, Gail Asper, a well-known philanthropist, corporate lawyer, and officer of the Order of Canada, told me that she had written an opinion letter and sent it to the top ranks of the *Globe and Mail*. In it, she outlined her grave concerns about the media's coverage of WE, an organization that had supported her efforts at Winnipeg's Canadian Museum for Human Rights. "I wrote a very passionate letter that [said] the opposition was attacking the government for not moving quickly enough. And here we get them moving quickly and find one of our most trusted organizations to deliver [the CSSG]. And now there's a scandal about this? And what about all the kids who didn't get to do all this work? Is anybody upset about that?"

But the letter never got published. Despite her reputation and standing, the *Globe* had no interest in presenting her views. Looking back, Asper thinks the media was encouraging sensationalism to attract readers and viewers. "I think it was yellow journalism," she told me. "I think many journalists were gleefully indifferent to the pain they were causing, not just to the charity but to the kids. Nobody seemed to care about the tens of thousands of young people who would have benefited from the Canada Student Service Grant program."

Randall Mang, founder and president of Randall Anthony Communications, felt the same sting of rejection. His company is a leading supplier of custom marketing and graphic design content to the *Globe and Mail* and provides marketing communications services to other brands. Speaking to me from his home in Sidney, British Columbia, he teared up when describing the transformative influence WE Charity had on his daughter, Nayah, and by extension his whole family. Together, they went to many WE Days and visited WE Villages projects in Kenya and India. Disturbed by what he was reading in the media, Mang penned an op-ed describing his family's experiences and sent it to various media outlets, including the CBC, the *Globe*, the *Tyee*, and Postmedia. None bit. Eventually, he published a longer version of the article on Medium.[60]

Many staff and board members, teachers, and students also wrote op-eds that were rejected by the *Globe and Mail*, *National Post*, *Vancouver*

Sun, Winnipeg Free Press, Calgary Herald, Edmonton Journal, Ottawa Citizen, and other publications. Most submissions were never even acknowledged.

So what has happened to the Canadian media landscape? Why did the press present so many headlines that raised questions and then give short shrift to the answers? Why was so much ink spilled on creating controversy and very little on investigating whether that controversy had a factual basis? The short answer to these questions is: the same thing that has happened to news media across the globe, especially in the United States. Year after year, trust in the US media declines, largely as a result of increased political polarization, which turned supposedly unbiased news organizations into mouthpieces for whichever of the two political parties they align with. Some of this polarization can be attributed to shrinking revenues for the sector as a whole. Journalism is a business, and business is down. According to a 2018 study by the Washington-based Pew Research Center, US newspaper circulation fell to its lowest level since 1940 (the first year for which data was available), while advertising revenue declined by 62 percent in the decade between 2008 and 2018.[61] With fewer ad dollars up for grabs, media outlets are encouraged to appeal more to those on the left or right of the spectrum than those in the middle. Reinforcing a consumer's beliefs creates loyalty, and generating sensational headlines creates new consumers.

The situation in Canada has not been much better. The sector has struggled so much that in 2018, the federal government developed a bailout program that provided up to $600 million in tax credits and incentives for media organizations.[62] Even so, the industry has been forced to do more with less. Fewer reporters, less advertising revenue, and an increasingly competitive market mean that stories that generate clicks are elevated over day-to-day news. Put simply, the more clicks on an article, the more money for content owners. It's a recipe for salacious headlines and inflammatory stories, and it's antithetical to nuanced reporting that takes the time to tell all sides of a story.

Columnist Frank Bruni, in his final opinion piece for the *New York Times*, took himself and other journalists to task for what he referred to as "sw[imming] with the snide tide."[63] Looking back over his ten years with the *Times*, he lamented the "toxic tenor of American discourse" and the ease with which journalists "shove ambivalence and ambiguity aside." Nuance, he noted, doesn't make for good talking points. "There aren't as many clicks," he wrote, "in cooling tempers and complicating people's understanding of situations as there are in stoking their rage . . . Too many columns are less sober analyses than snarky stand-up acts or primal screams. The stand-up and the screams sell."

1. Marc and Craig, ages eight and two, long before WE Charity and the Nobel Peace Prize nominations and other international accolades that followed.

2. The story of Iqbal Masih, a Pakistani labourer who was murdered for advocating for children's rights, inspired Craig to start Free the Children.

3. An early fundraiser, selling ice cold pop from Coco Kielburger's repurposed doghouse.

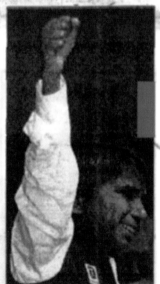

Battled child labor, boy, 12, murdered

Defied members of 'carpet mafia'

ISLAMABAD, Pakistan (AP) — When Iqbal Masih was 4 years old, his parents sold him into slavery for less than $16.

For the next six years, he remained shackled to a carpet-weaving loom most of the time, tying tiny knots hour after hour.

By age 12, he was free and travelling the world in his crusade against the horrors of child labor.

lence the young activist.

"We know his death was a conspiracy by the carpet mafia," said Ehsan Ullah Khan, chairman of the Bonded Labor Liberation Front (BLLF), a private that in Pakistan.

Iqbal, a Christian, was home from school in Lahore for the Easter holiday.

A man known only as Ashraf, a laborer in Muritke, was arrested in connection with the shooting, but has been released, Khan said.

4. On a fact-finding mission to Asia, young Craig famously confronted Prime Minister Jean Chrétien about Canada's record on child labour issues.

5. In 1996, just a year into the life of Free the Children, the organization changed forever when Craig was interviewed by Ed Bradley on *60 Minutes.*

6. In rural Pakistan, Craig met children who spent their days working in a brick kiln.

7. Free the Children staff, including Scott Baker (*first row, left*) and Russ McLeod (*second row, third from left*), pictured at the Kielburger home—also the charity's first office.

8. Craig and Marc first met Archbishop Desmond Tutu in 1998. The Arch, as he asked the brothers to call him, later contributed to two of their books.

9. In 2017, former UN secretary-general Ban-Ki Moon (*second from left*) officially opened the WE Global Learning Centre. Craig is flanked by philanthropist Hartley Richardson and actor George Takei. Mia Farrow is to the right of Takei.

10. Oprah Winfrey joined WE Charity executive director Dalal Al-Waheidi to celebrate WE Day LA in 2016. Winfrey and WE were long-time partners in the O Ambassadors program, an initiative to encourage diverse youth to volunteer.

11. The WE GLC hummed with the energy of visiting schoolkids filling its digital classrooms and breakout spaces.

12. In the Empatheatre, kids were inspired by motivational speakers who shared stories of their personal journeys.

13. Ashleigh and Emma Dzis, who participated in many WE Charity initiatives, were full of excitement when they met Marc for the first time at the ME to WE store in Toronto's Eaton Centre.

14. WE Charity Canada shipped millions of dollars of COVID relief supplies to Kenya and even created a field hospital for testing and triage.

15. The charity provided an education to former child soldiers and other children affected by war in Sierra Leone. These kids gained a chance at a peaceful, hopeful future.

16. Following the 2010 Haiti earthquake, the charity focused on building resiliency in rural areas to handle the influx of refugees from hard-hit urban regions. Healthcare, clean water, and education were at the heart of those efforts.

17. In India, WE concentrated its efforts in the northwestern province of Rajasthan. Much of the work focused on people of the lowest social castes, like the Indigenous Scheduled Tribes and the Dalits.

18. The WE Villages model recognized that it takes more than a classroom to ensure access to education. Children also need clean water, food security, and healthcare.

19. In the Chimborazo and Amazon regions of Ecuador, the organization has built or restored over one hundred school buildings. WE Charity has made a commitment to creating educational opportunities for Indigenous children.

20. Pakistani girls' education activist and Nobel laureate Malala Yousafzai helped build a schoolroom in Kenya with Craig. Over the years, the charity hosted many notable visitors.

21. In 2018, WE Charity opened the door to post-secondary opportunities in the Maasai Mara region of Kenya, providing free vocational training programs in nursing, education, tourism, and agriculture at WE College.

22. Former prime minister Kim Campbell (*left*) joined Craig and Margaret Kenyatta (*centre*), the first lady of Kenya, to celebrate this new chapter in the lives of people in Narok County. On the right is Samuel Tunai, the local governor.

23. WE Days gave young people the opportunity to hear and be inspired by some of the most prominent changemakers in the world today, including the Dalai Lama.

24. Every year, kids across North America and in the UK packed arenas in the hundreds of thousands. WE Days celebrated the work young people did over the year to create positive change.

25. Swimmer Penny Oleksiak—Canada's most decorated Olympian—brought some hometown pride to the WE Day stage in Toronto.

26. The massive events were made possible by armies of young people, parents, and educators, as well as the generous support of corporate partners.

27. Actor and activist Martin Sheen was a frequent WE Day speaker. The A-listers who appeared on stage were there not to talk about their latest movies or albums but to share the issues they cared about.

29

30

31

32

33

34

28. Prince Harry and Meghan Markle appeared at WE Day UK at Wembley Arena to thank the young audience for all they had done to help push the needle on global issues.

29. "You can do something in your own community to correct something you believe is wrong," former UN secretary-general Kofi Annan told the audience at WE Day Vancouver in 2017. "That's how you begin to lead."

30. Teachers were the linchpin of WE Charity's work with young people.

31. Prime Minister Justin Trudeau and his wife, Sophie Grégoire Trudeau, appeared at WE Day Ottawa in 2015.

32. The students who participated in WE Days earned their seats by performing at least one local and one global act of service.

33. Margaret Trudeau spoke about her struggles with mental health and showed young people that they were not alone.

34. Author and Holocaust survivor Elie Wiesel challenged young people to take action when they witness injustice.

CHAPTER 7

OPEN FLOODGATES

Because of COVID, I fled New York, where I live and practise law, and spent much of the summer of 2020 in Toronto. This gave me more exposure to Canadian news coverage. For a while, it felt refreshing to hear stories about global affairs and pandemic response strategies that did not quickly devolve into the partisan rancour I am used to hearing on US cable networks. The feeling, however, did not last long.

When it came to the so-called WE Charity Scandal, journalists seemed more interested in looking for ways to stir people's outrage than unpacking a complicated story so Canadians could understand all sides. In my view, the media tells stories in ever-expanding concentric circles. The initial story is the centre, but if the public interest is sufficiently high, a new circle is created and another one after that. Reporters and editors work to find fresh angles, and the circles continue to grow.

Here, the initial story was simply about whether proper procedures had been followed in the awarding of the CSSG program. But the circles soon expanded well beyond that to encompass virtually every aspect of the charity's operations, from its corporate partnerships to its WE Day lineups to its workplace culture. In the endless search for content, the media eagerly fed on the opinions of politicians like Charlie Angus and Pierre Poilievre or pundits like Kate Bahen and Jesse Brown, while at the same time failing to seek out the perspectives of those with first-hand experience of the organization, like students and teachers. In what seemed like the blink of an eye, the organization was being accused of horrendous acts, including manipulating children for the benefit of its corporate partners.

A scandal that came out of nowhere was suddenly *everywhere*. In sojourns out of my apartment to secure pandemic hot commodities like hand sanitizer and toilet paper, the headlines glared at me from every newsstand. COVID. WE Charity. COVID. WE Charity. When case counts mercifully—albeit briefly—started dropping and luxuries like barbers were open for business, I would lean back in the comfy leather chair and try to block out the noise of other patrons sounding off on why Justin Trudeau had handed a pile of money to those shady brothers who paid his mom. Group chat messages with friends would quickly turn from commiseration over COVID to shock when people realized I was on the board of the charity.

It seemed like Canadians were talking about little else.

Looking for respite, I suggested to my fiancée that we escape for a few days to a spa outside the city. Work at my law firm was very busy, there were calls day and night with WE Charity board members and executives, and we had not been out for so much as a dinner in months. I thought she deserved a break. She said it was a good idea because I really needed to chill out, which is code for "you have become insufferable." So off we went.

We checked in, and I was determined to relax and find solace. That didn't happen, of course. I spent most of our two-day stay on the phone with other board members and lawyers in a constant effort to put out fires for WE. It was the same all-hands-on-deck dilemma I had been immersed in for weeks. Only now I was wearing a robe and slippers.

"Go to your massage appointment," my fiancée commanded. "It's the only way you're going to get away from your phone for an hour." A professional masseuse? Tension relief? Peace and quiet? She didn't have to sell me on the idea—it sounded like the perfect tonic. I headed off and was ready to finally unwind for a few precious moments. As I stretched out on the massage table, I thought I would probably fall asleep within seconds. But regrettably, my masseuse wanted to make small talk. Her first volley? "How about that WE Charity Scandal, eh?"

CORPORATE DOLLARS

In its February 2021 documentary on WE Charity, *The Fifth Estate* zeroed in on Craig's 1999 appearance on *The Oprah Winfrey Show* as a key turning point in the trajectory of what was then still Free the Children.[1] With sixteen-year-old Craig sitting beside her on stage, Winfrey pledged to work with him to build a hundred schools in underdeveloped countries around the world. She would feature the charity on her show four more times, including once to announce the launch of O Ambassadors, a joint program to empower low-income North American students to help others. Instead of viewing these sometimes marginalized kids as problems to be solved, she wanted them to become problem-solvers.

It was undoubtedly a decisive moment—Winfrey's commitment to the charity was generous, but even more than that, the platform she gave to Craig was transformative. Free the Children was launched into the stratosphere and suddenly had the potential to change the lives of more people than Craig and Marc had ever dared to imagine.

Of course, Winfrey's gift, as extravagant as it was, had to be matched by similar gifts from other equally wealthy and influential people to keep the charity's work going. International development was one part of the equation, but even domestic programs required funding. In Canada, the US, and the UK, a key priority was to offer WE Schools resources free of charge so as not to increase the financial burden on already cash-strapped school systems. The same was true for WE Day, which was founded on the principle that it would not cost students anything to attend. And the organization also ensured that donations intended to support WE Charity's work overseas would not be used for WE Days or non-program-related costs like real estate acquisitions.

So to support its many programs and initiatives, the charity instead turned to a funding source that brought its share of criticism: corporate partnerships. In the organization's early days, most of these partnerships happened in an organic way. Inspired by the Kielburgers and their mission, young people started Free the Children clubs in their own schools and began fundraising for campaigns to fight hunger and homelessness. Parents took notice of their children's new-found activism, and sometimes those parents turned out to be people in positions of power.

"Some of those people making personal contributions were presidents of companies or senior business leaders," explained Erin Barton, WE Charity's former chief development officer for partnerships, "and they were saying, 'Hey, there's an opportunity here for my employees to get involved, for you to be our charity of choice.' And so we started to see some employee-based fundraising, employee-based giving, and early campaigns or payroll deductions. And then that started to shift to full-time partnerships when these business leaders saw that there was a halo effect with their employees. People felt good and liked to know that they had an employer that cared, that was giving back."

Jon Levy, retired CEO and co-founder of Mastermind Toys, and his wife, Karyn Levy, a Mastermind executive for decades, told me that partnering with WE provided substantial benefits to both their employees and their customers. "WE presented a platform where we could contribute financially while engaging our retail employees and customers in a meaningful way," Jon told me. "Giving to charity is one thing, but to be able to inspire our staff is a different experience. It brought camaraderie to our stores, which can be stressful places for our employees, especially during the holidays. Collaborating with WE was, in this way, a gift that kept on giving." Mastermind also appreciated that the partnership allowed for flexibility in terms of where employee contributions were directed. "We could do different things," Jon said, "from helping fund medical programs in Kenya to [supporting] education and leadership camps for Indigenous youth in Canada."

WE Charity was an early subscriber to the philosophy that global problems like poverty and climate change are best addressed by enlisting the support of private-sector partners. In addition to seeking out institutional partners like the Bill and Melinda Gates Foundation, the Skoll Foundation, and the McConnell Foundation, the organization looked for companies with the resources to enhance and expand the charity's existing programming and develop new initiatives. For instance, a strategic partnership with Microsoft provided tools like Skype pods to connect students in different communities around the world. (When the pandemic later shut down schools, that virtual infrastructure made it possible for the organization to rapidly take educational resources online.) The charity also worked with Walgreens, the US drugstore chain, on a program called WE Teachers, which gave educators grants to buy supplies for their classrooms. And through its partnership with Telus, the Canadian telecommunications company, the organization was able to develop anti-bullying and internet safety resources that helped protect many Canadian children from harm.

In the media, these types of relationships between large multinationals and charities have often been portrayed as a cynical attempt to burnish the reputations of the former through proximity to the latter. The idea is that if people see an organization they trust and admire partnering with a company they have reservations about, those reservations will diminish or even disappear. Host Mark Kelley made precisely this assertion on *The Fifth Estate*, asking Marc and Craig, "Were you concerned the corporations were trying to use you to some extent?"[2] Other journalists have also promoted this argument. In an October 2018 article for Canadaland, for example, Jaren Kerr wrote, "The Kielburgers have built a brand that is synonymous with good works, a literal virtue signal. And a brand like that is valuable to corporations."[3]

I would argue that the charity used corporations, however, and not the other way around. As Greg Rogers, chair of WE Charity's Canadian board and a retired educator and school administrator, reminded me, "WE Schools programs would not have been possible without foundations and corporate sponsors, full stop. We all know that these programs and resources cost money, and schools—some of which couldn't cover anything other than the basics—didn't have to pay a dime for any of it."

At the same time, no one ever denied that benefits accrued to corporations from their association with WE. This was not something whispered about in the shadows. The whole idea was that these partnerships could encourage businesses to become better corporate citizens.

For example, the organization worked with Hershey's to support the company in its efforts to eliminate child labour from its supply chain. WE Charity had experience in doing this and had previously built a supply chain for chocolate production in Ecuador that was without child labour and certified fair trade. And in recent years, Hershey's has made headway in addressing this serious problem, including by implementing a monitoring and remediation system that has had some success. More broadly, any corporation that donated money to support the charity's international development programs was helping to address the chronic poverty that is a root cause of child labour across the globe.

But I understand the optics here. To some people, it just looks bad for a charity founded on the idea of ridding the world of child labour to partner with a company that is part of an industry that has not yet eliminated child labour from its supply chain.[4] These are extremely complicated issues, and reasonable people can disagree on how best to persuade—or force—companies to mend their ways. WE Charity viewed business as a necessary partner in change and believed in building symbiotic relationships in the quest for greater social good. "The whole notion," Barton explained, "is that through partnership, through friendship, through allyship, you have a greater ability to advocate [and] to influence change than you do when you're organizing a boycott or standing in a protest line."

To my mind, engaging business in this way was also consistent with the United Nation's Sustainable Development Goals, which encourage partnerships with the private sector as a means of addressing social and environmental goals. This approach also takes into account the environmental, social, and governance (ESG) criteria that many investors now use to judge whether companies are committed to ethical and socially conscious business practices. And isn't it a bit rich for journalists to criticize WE Charity's corporate partnerships—which essentially involve businesses applauding the activism of young people—while their own columns appear alongside corporate ads that exist only to sell products? Or for news anchors to comment on the commercialization of WE Days before unflinchingly turning to . . . *a commercial break*?

Let's be honest: corporate partnerships are hardly unusual in the non-profit world. Almost every major charity in Canada engages with companies as both donors and partners in delivering programming. The Enbridge Ride to Conquer Cancer benefits the Princess Margaret Cancer Centre. Scouts Canada is sponsored by Hydro One, IBM Canada, Canadian National Railway, and others. Big Brothers Big Sisters of Canada is sponsored by Boston Pizza, Scotiabank, and Rogers. And for its part, WE Charity had relationships with corporations like RBC, Telus, KPMG, and Loblaws.

All this said, WE Charity's board never took any corporate partnerships lightly. During my tenure and long before, the organization's approach to these partnerships was the subject of plenty of discussion and debate. The board was full of people with diverse backgrounds who brought diverse views on the pros and cons of corporate engagement to the table. This deliberative approach translated into a rigorous vetting process for every potential corporate partnership. It involved five steps that weighed factors like a corporation's overall vision and objectives, its commitment to promoting the charity's social mission, its brand reputation, and of course its social responsibility practices (that is, environmental, community relations, and labour practices). Applying these standards, the organization declined to enter into partnerships with many corporations over the years. And if a corporate partner failed to live up to the charity's standards at any time, WE Charity reserved the right to walk away.

It's also worth noting that these corporate partners—companies like Microsoft, RBC, and KPMG—were carefully vetting WE Charity as well. Each company did substantial diligence on the charity before signing any partnership agreement. This undercuts the claim that the organization was operating without proper oversight, or that the Kielburgers were somehow enriching themselves at the charity's expense. These corporations were investing not just their money but also their brand reputations in WE, and they would not have wanted to be associated with a dodgy organization. Some of the most sophisticated and brand-conscious companies in the world trusted WE Charity and the Kielburgers (and still do)—it's not plausible that they all fell down on the job of assessing both WE Charity and ME to WE.

WE Charity also had extensive protocols in place to limit the amount of corporate marketing to which children were exposed. For example, the organization worked with local school boards and teachers to produce the WE Schools classroom resources and keep sponsor recognition to an absolute minimum—most companies got no more than a mention on the spine of a binder or a thank-you on the landing page of the website. At WE Days, corporate partners were recognized but could speak only to the social or environmental causes their companies were actively engaged on. "We never allowed WE Day to be just a place where you are trying to sell a phone or where you are trying to sell ice cream," said Barton. "It was always about telling the story of good that your company is doing."

A PLATFORM, NOT A CAUSE

Yet even WE Day came under fire as the intense media scrutiny increased. *The Fifth Estate* broadcast an interview with a former staff member who briefly held an entry-level position in 2007. He said that in his view, students who attended WE Day events were a product being sold to corporate partners. "It was a chance for the organization to say, 'Look at the access we have to all these future consumers that . . . now are going to be exposed to your brand,'" he said, likening WE to Facebook and other social media companies. But that analogy doesn't make any sense. Facebook harvests information about you and sells companies access to you through targeted advertising. The only thing being advertised by corporate partners at WE Days was their solidarity with young changemakers and their commitment to social causes. The idea that teenagers would be so moved by seeing the CEO of Allstate on stage that they would buy insurance from the company a decade later is laughable.

Some journalists went so far as to suggest that the charity used WE Days—and particularly A-list celebrity speakers—to manipulate young people. This was the theory, for example, behind a July 2020 article in *Flare* by self-proclaimed social media enthusiast June Findlay.[5] She claimed that WE targeted what she described as "the coveted, keyed-up and impressionable demographic of people aged 13 to 19," and, using communication strategies more commonly seen in politics, convinced them "to devote their time, money and, in some cases, lives to a cause or organization they likely didn't know or care about before." This brand of "charitainment," Findlay wrote, was beneficial for the celebrities (the halo effect again) and for the charity (whose profile was raised), but it used the desires of young people who wanted to make a difference "to reinforce Western views of who gets to be saved, who gets to do the saving—and most of all, who benefits from it all."

Findlay's piece frustrated me more than perhaps any other article published during the whole scandal (and that's saying something). It did not include the voice of a single teacher or student. Not one. It dismissed the volunteer work done by young people to get to WE Day as "a few acts of goodwill," treated them as inherently shallow ("you heard a pretty moving story about a girl in Kenya, and you sat through some semi-boring speeches—then you finally got to see Shawn Mendes perform live"), and called tracking the global impact of your spending a "gamification of the process." In the end, she pondered, why are WE and other charities like it even necessary when kids get everything they need "from endless access to information and inspiration via social media"?

Aside from having a somewhat different position, as a parent, on the supposed benefits of social media, I found this viewpoint insulting and condescending to everyone concerned—the celebrities, whom Findlay dismissed as opportunists who had no real interest in the causes they promoted; the young people, whom she portrayed as too suggestible and ill-informed to know their own minds; the teachers, who she seemed to think could not be trusted to know what is best for their students; and the Kielburgers, who were depicted as self-aggrandizers with a saviour complex.

Could any of this be true?

As a board member, I went to many WE Days over the years. I brought my son and my family and my friends. I didn't do so to expose them to corporations or let them be used. I brought them because I saw the redeeming value in what was happening. My fellow directors—including retired school board representatives who collectively had responsibility for educating *millions* of students in Canada and the US over decades—did the same thing. I believe that the cynical assessment offered by Findlay, the *Fifth Estate*, and other critics—who either purposely or obliviously failed to include the perspective of teachers and students—is an invitation to be misinformed. But for many Canadians already facing a deluge of negative coverage relating to WE and the CSSG, particularly those who had never attended a WE Day or looked at WE Schools curricula, it was easy for misperceptions to take hold.

I fondly recall my first WE Day as a board member—the 2017 WE Day UN in New York. Thousands of kids piled into the Theater at Madison Square Garden to listen to the likes of former Liberian president and Nobel Peace Prize winner Ellen Johnson Sirleaf, former Irish president and UN high commissioner for human rights Mary Robinson, executive director of UN Women Phumzile Mlambo-Ngcuka, Chelsea Clinton, Whoopi Goldberg, and yes, Justin Trudeau and his mother, Margaret. The high-profile speakers were interspersed with more than a dozen teachers and students who spoke with great passion about the obstacles they had overcome and the power of young people to make a difference even when the odds were tough. Much of the focus was on the empowerment of women and girls as a key to achieving international sustainable development goals. The *Globe and Mail* captured the moment: "As world leaders discussed the flight of refugees, drug trafficking and human-rights violations at the United Nations General Assembly . . . thousands of young people gathered at the Theater at Madison Square Garden with an optimistic view of the future."[6]

And those young people were not just there to listen. They screamed back, they sang, they danced, and I sensed that they went home full of purpose and a conviction that whatever their circumstances, they too could be somebody. Personally, I was very inspired but also happy to find an Advil lurking in my briefcase.

What I loved most about WE Day—and WE Schools programming too—was that it was cause-inclusive. This was a principle that meant a great deal to me and other board members. There was no need to sell WE Charity; WE Charity was selling a vision of doing good through other organizations. Former board member David Stillman summed it up well. "The ultimate objective," he said, "was always to support young people in getting involved in causes, whatever they were. If they said, 'We're really passionate about . . . the Native American population in our state,' we had a way that students could learn more through their clubs and in the classroom. Other kids might have been more passionate about battling cancer or protecting the environment. We wanted to encourage kids to engage more deeply with their causes. The charity wasn't a cause; it offered a platform."

TALENT + PASSION = CHANGE

To get some perspective on how the celebrities themselves saw things, I went straight to the president of the United States—Josiah Bartlet on TV's *The West Wing*. "Please call me Martin," said Martin Sheen as we started our interview. I was admittedly a little nervous talking to a screen legend. But he made it easy. He was humble and disarming, and he wanted to talk about systemic racism, the current state of politics, my work as a lawyer, and everything in between.

Sheen told me he first became aware of Free the Children when he saw thirteen-year-old Craig interviewed on *60 Minutes* in 1996. He said he was in awe of the teenager's passion and commitment. "I thought, 'Oh my God, who is this young man?'" Craig left an impression—so much so that when the two men finally met years later, Sheen's first thought was, "Oh my God, he's *that* guy!" They bonded, and soon the legendary actor had been invited to speak at a WE Day event in Canada. All told, Sheen appeared onstage at thirteen WE Days in both Canada and the US. He also became a regular at many events to raise funds and awareness for the organization.

When I asked Sheen what WE Day meant to him, he said it was life-changing. "It [was] very gratifying. The event itself—these huge arenas are packed to the gills, and all these kids are having a great time. And they deserve it! You can't buy a ticket; you're invited there because you've served the community on some level." He also surprised me by saying that he found public speaking nerve-racking and often felt daunted by the prospect. (Interestingly, this appears to be a family phobia—Sheen's son Emilio Estevez had told me when I met him at WE events in New York years earlier that he experienced the same butterflies.) But Sheen got over it because, he said, "it gave me a sense of keeping a commitment," and it made him aware of "how confident you must be with your principles, with what you believe." He wrote all his own speeches and enjoyed getting the chance to play himself rather than a character. And WE Day was different than other celebrity charity engagements, he told me. "WE had the insight to see the merit in using a celebrity—not to sell a product but to present an idea."

TESTIMONIAL: MARTIN SHEEN

Martin Sheen is a versatile and critically acclaimed actor, best known for his roles in films like Apocalypse Now *and* The Departed, *and for playing the American president on* The West Wing. *But he is equally passionate about his political activism and has been a tireless campaigner for nuclear disarmament, environmentalism, and youth empowerment, among many other issues.*

Acting is what I do for a living; activism is what I do to stay alive. As the child of immigrant parents, I've been involved in social justice for as long as I can remember—from trying to unionize my fellow golf course employees at the age of fourteen to getting arrested while protesting President Reagan's Strategic Defense Initiative (the first of many activism-related arrests in my lifetime). Because of this, I've always been a big believer in ordinary people coming together in movements to make a difference.

People often say we need to create a better world for our children. I think it's actually the other way around—we must raise our children to be better for the world. I first met Craig and Marc Kielburger in the late 1990s, and their mission of empowering young people to make a difference inspired me.

Over the past ten years, I've had the honour of speaking at WE Days across Canada, including in Toronto, Winnipeg, Saskatoon (which I'd never even heard of before!), Vancouver, Calgary, Edmonton, Hamilton, Montreal, and Halifax. It's given me the opportunity to see more of this beautiful country and speak to thousands of inspiring young changemakers.

This is what sets WE Day apart from other events: while most charity events with celebrities honour the stars, at WE Day, the celebrities are there to honour and thank the young people for their hard work and inspire them to keep making a difference. I always felt that WE Days were one of Canada's greatest exports, and I'm thrilled at how the WE movement took hold in America.

Nothing is more important to me than inspiring young people. The next generation will change the world for the better, which is why I've always carved out time to stay involved. Sometimes filming dates have to be pushed back or shuffled around, but it's always worth it to be part of something so life-changing.

Although this is the end of one chapter, WE Charity has sparked a passion for activism in millions of young people around the world—and that is enduring.

And that, to my mind, was the real value of having celebrities at WE Day. It's not unusual to see celebrity ambassadors supporting causes. Major charities like Oxfam, CARE, and World Vision have all used famous individuals as spokespersons.[7] Even the United Nations deploys stars like Angelina Jolie and Emma Watson as Goodwill Ambassadors. I can't comment on whether these organizations do this right (or whether most charities do it wrong), but with WE it wasn't just "charitainment."

Celebrities weren't on the WE Day stage simply to call attention to the charity or encourage people to donate or make sure the kids had a good time. It was bigger than that. They introduced young people to a wide range of causes, most of which had nothing to do with WE. They were not there to sell anything or to self-promote. They were there to inspire and to encourage doing good. You can see this is in the nostalgia of twenty-somethings like Aiza Abid (who, you will recall from earlier in the book, started Aiza's Teddybear Foundation after years of being inspired by WE). Asked for her favourite celebrity moment, she said it was seeing Marlee Matlin, the Academy Award–winning actor who lost much of her hearing as an infant. Instead of clapping at her speech, the twenty thousand young people in the arena signed back at Matlin, who had been communicating with them in American Sign Language. That does not strike me as the reflection of someone who went gaga for celebrities, was influenced by corporate partners, and missed the point of it all.

Linda Rosier, a WE board member from 2013 to 2015 and co-founder of Concept 3 Advertising Agency, told me that at every WE Day, she loved asking the young audience members who had inspired them the most. "It warmed my heart that their answers would always be the elder-heroes like Roméo Dallaire and Elie Wiesel—not their favourite rock stars who had performed. Somehow the youth at WE Day were innately drawn to the messages and sincerity of these true humanitarian heroes who had seen and been through so much, and who conveyed to them, 'We need a better world, and I'm happy to be here to speak with you and to help guide you in making that better world.'"

In fact, the celebrities were often star-struck by the young people they saw in the crowd and thus felt compelled to do more work with WE Charity. NBA star Magic Johnson, for one, pledged to donate a million dollars to the organization after speaking on the WE Day stage. So did singer Nelly Furtado. And some celebrities, like Lilly Singh, Natalie Portman, and Demi Lovato, encouraged their fans to get involved, took trips to visit the charity's international projects, and even designed products that could be made in WE Charity partner communities.

Ruben Borba, now a high school teacher with the Toronto Catholic District School Board, understands the power of WE Day well. As a grade eight student, he had the chance to go to the Toronto event with his school. It was clear from the way he spoke about the experience that it had stuck with him for all these years and even inspired him to become a teacher. Today, he brings the messages he came away with into his classroom. "Going to WE Day as a student and seeing so many other young people also feel empowered to really make a difference opened my eyes. And now, as a teacher, it has affected how I try to run my classes," he explained. "I never think of it as *my* classroom—it is *our* classroom. The students and I are a community. We're a small community within a larger community within a larger world community. And so I always try to help my students feel like they have a voice in the classroom, which is something I felt at WE Day when I was a student."

This idea of feeling empowered to make a difference—of making doing good doable—was something teacher Jo-Ann Dzis specifically mentioned to me when I asked her to talk about the impact WE Days had on her two daughters, Ashleigh and Emma, whom we met back in chapter 2. "The girls, alongside their classmates and groupmates, have really tried to take the equation of talent + passion = change and put it into action," Dzis explained. "This is consistent with the inspirational messages that they heard attending WE Days, WE Day Family, and Canada WE Day. People shared their stories of passion paired with their talents to make meaningful change. Small impacts together adding up to meaningful differences in the world, and the ability and potential that each young person brings. Through WE Charity's local initiatives, I have seen community building and connections formed that involve young people in actively impacting their community. From their global initiatives, I have seen how it has broadened Ashleigh and Emma's worldview and developed their understanding and responsibility of becoming global citizens. This is what I have seen celebrated and encouraged through WE Days and all the programming Ashleigh and Emma have been fortunate to be a part of."

To better understand how WE Days translated into the real change Jo-Ann Dzis saw in her daughters, I reached out to Noah Manduke, a management consultant who specializes in helping non-profit organizations build their brands to accelerate impact. He is the president of Durable Good and the former chief strategy officer of the Jeff Skoll Group, and he understands very well the power of celebrity. I asked him to explain the relationship between A-listers and social activism.

"When you take Bono or Elton John or other huge public figures that have used their celebrity to drive social impact, you see authenticity and relevance. Elton John takes up issues that are near and dear to his heart and then uses his relationships to galvanize others to engage in those issues . . . He influences policy and influences decision-making and behaviour."

Manduke said that in his view, WE Days were a great example of an organization leveraging celebrities for social purpose. He thought WE Days were the most innovative part of the charity's programming because they blended popular culture and good citizenship and made it cool for kids to care. "When Demi Lovato comes out on stage or when Selena Gomez comes out there, these icons are relevant to the causes they endorse. And that's what I thought was really interesting about the WE model: they brought out figures that young people could relate to."

Driving engagement isn't easy to do, but WE Charity was especially good at it, through both WE Days and its Canadian and American school programs. The organization had even hired Mission Measurement, a US consulting firm that helps non-profits analyze their social impact, to assess its results and identify avenues for improvement. The firm's founder and CEO, Jason Saul, told me that he uses data to determine if an organization is being as efficient and effective as possible. He repeatedly emphasized that the "data speaks for itself."

Saul's data showed that WE Schools alumni were twice as likely as their non-WE peers to volunteer in their communities and raise awareness about social issues. They were also more likely to be confident public speakers (2.0 times more likely), to be seen as leaders in their schools and social groups (1.8 times more likely), and to be looked at by their peers as creative problem-solvers (1.5 times more likely). They had a deeper understanding of global issues, and as young adults, they were far more likely to vote in elections. Although he leaves it to others to draw qualitative conclusions, Saul says that to his mind, this "shows that WE Schools . . . produces outcomes that can make kids better students, more likely to get into college, more likely to vote, get a better job, become a better leader, become more committed, and become passionate and effective human beings."[8]

What's most frustrating to me is that you would never learn any of this if you were getting all your information about WE Charity from what you read in the papers or on social media or saw on the TV news. The damaging allegations about the manipulation of children were made by people who likely never went to a WE Day and never fairly considered the views of teachers or students who did. But I did both, and rarely did I hear someone raving only about how much they loved Shawn Mendes's performance or how thrilled they were to see Jennifer Hudson in person. I certainly never heard a single WE Day participant gushing about buying a car from Ford or a phone from Telus. All I saw was young people inspired to make a difference in the world.

The outcomes identified by Mission Measurement were exactly the kind of meaningful change Jo-Ann Dzis saw in her own kids. But to my knowledge, no journalist ever cited that work or contacted Jason Saul to better understand the charity's impact. No one interviewed Ruben Borba. No one called Aiza Abid. No one asked Linda Rosier for her perspective. No one reached out to me. Heck, no one even called Martin Sheen!

Worse still, when journalists did talk to young people and ask for their views, any positive feedback was simply omitted from the coverage. That's exactly what happened to Ashleigh and Emma. The twins talk a mile a minute and buzz with energy. When I interviewed them, I could barely get a word in. WE Charity was a huge part of their lives, and they had a lot to say about the organization. So when the CBC's *Fifth Estate* agreed to interview them, they couldn't wait to share their perspective.

They couldn't have been more disappointed with what happened next. As Ashleigh explained, it seemed as though the reporter had a viewpoint that was "very biased and predetermined," and both sisters felt that she was searching for sound bites that "showed we were only involved with WE for the celebrities, or that we thought there were too many ads at WE Day." When they disagreed, the interviewer kept pushing. The twins had the impression that it was "almost like they were trying to catch us off guard."

The twins and their mother never heard back from the *Fifth Estate*, and they assumed that the show had gone with other young voices, which was fine. "I know a lot of young people from the WE Charity Youth Advisory Council who would have been phenomenal and could speak to all different aspects of the charity," Ashleigh told me. But they were crushed when the hour-long documentary finally aired and they realized *no students* were included at all. Nor did the show include any teachers or anyone who had participated in any of the charity's programming. They had to watch it twice to believe it. Talking over each other and in unison at times, Ashleigh and Emma said it was "quite a shock seeing the video" and realizing that "no young people's voices were shared or heard."

The saddest part of this story, in my view, was the twins' loss of faith in the media and the CBC in particular. "In school, they tell you to always learn both sides of the story, and our teachers suggest going to the CBC as a big source. So this was a real ouch moment," Ashleigh said. Emma agreed. "It was weird that they seemed to give us no voice . . . This was supposed to be a reputable program that shows both sides and be the truth. But that's not really what happened."

CHAPTER 8

BIPOC RECKONING

COVID was not the only force causing global upheaval across the spring and summer of 2020. On May 25, on a nondescript Minneapolis street, a white police officer named Derek Chauvin knelt on the neck of a handcuffed George Floyd for nine minutes and twenty-nine seconds, murdering him. It was an act of violence viewed with horror and outrage across the globe thanks to Darnella Frazier, the brave seventeen-year-old who recorded the entire incident on her smartphone. The video sparked Black Lives Matter (BLM) protests that got bigger day by day. In cities and towns across North America and in at least sixty other countries, millions of people came together to demand change.

As a partner in a large US law firm and a member of its diversity, equity, and inclusion committee, I understood that BLM and the circumstances surrounding Floyd's death required a lot of introspection and dialogue. What happened to George Floyd forced us all to take stock of systemic racism in society and examine the role we need to play in combatting it—certainly with respect to the treatment of Black people, but also with respect to discrimination faced by BIPOC people more generally. I must admit, however, that I did not expect WE Charity to face allegations of racism or racial insensitivity—even with coverage of the CSSG fiasco expanding every day. After all, equity and inclusion were central planks in the organization's programming at home and abroad, the charity was led by a BIPOC woman (executive director Dalal

Al-Waheidi), and the chair of the US board was a renowned BIPOC educator (Dr. Jacqueline Sanderlin).

Then the other shoe dropped.

SPEECHES AND TOWN HALLS

On June 16, 2020, Amanda Maitland, a former WE employee, posted a seventeen-minute video to her Instagram account, detailing her time working at WE Charity in 2018 and 2019.[1] She talked about being part of a WE Schools anti-racism tour in Alberta in 2019, when she spoke to hundreds of kids about her own experiences with discrimination. It was a heavy burden, she said, to share her personal story with honesty and transparency, and in turn to create space for the kids she was with to talk about the racism they too had experienced. She thought she was having great impact and facilitating an important conversation, but she also felt the organization didn't fully appreciate what it meant for a Black woman to bear that responsibility. For her, this lack of appreciation manifested in a particular experience where, during a brief return trip to Toronto in the middle of the tour, she was handed a revised speech to deliver. "There was no phone call. There was no email," Maitland said in the video. "There was no dialogue or heads-up that the team on the back end felt the need to change my speech." That team, she said, was made up mostly of white men and women, and she felt they had taken her lived experiences—her words—and watered them down. She described it as oppressive. "This is why it's so important," she said, "for people of colour, for people who have different lived experiences to be in the room." Maitland said she wanted to have a dialogue and wanted to see a real shift. "I'm asking you to show us what changes you are willing to implement."

Her video wasn't only about the speech. She also described a 2019 company town hall with Marc and about fifty other employees that was convened to address a negative media report about workplace culture at the organization.

"I saw the culture of fear," Maitland said in her video, describing remarks she made at the town hall. "And one thing that I said was that so many people are having siloed conversations, that they're so scared to talk to people in positions of power, where true change can get implemented. And . . . the whole room was agreeing with me." But at that moment, she said, Marc stepped forward and shut her down "in an instant." And in shutting her down, he also shut down the other fifty people in the room. "People were scared to talk. And this is what happens constantly, over and over and over again, but we need to break that fear. As people of colour, we need to break our fear."

Listening to Maitland's story was jarring for me on many levels. It was institutionally jarring because I had thought WE Charity was doing a reasonably good job on issues of equity, inclusion, and diversity. Even a hint of racism would be damaging to a youth charity that works in schools and engages in international development. And such allegations could be fatal for the organization if they were found to be true. It was also personally jarring because I am a person of colour and very active in the legal fight against systemic racism. So the allegations were unsettling to hear and, if borne out, would have been devastating to me. It was one thing to hear politicians, pundits, and journalists spin things to create a narrative around the charity and the CSSG. This was different. I had a very personal interest in seeing her charges fully and properly investigated and addressed.

A few days after Maitland posted her video, Dalal reached out to her via email. She offered to facilitate a discussion with Jacqueline Sanderlin. Dr. J was a lecturer and consultant on diversity and inclusion and the former executive director of school and community engagement in the Southern California school districts of Compton and Inglewood. In my experience and that of most who have met her, she is a person who brings wisdom and a sense of purpose to every conversation.

Maitland did not respond.

On June 18, Dr. J and Dalal posted to the charity's website an open letter outlining the organization's commitment to ending racism and empowering communities. "WE was founded on the simple but essential idea of bringing people together, of embracing and supporting one another and of overcoming barriers together," the statement began.[2] While noting that WE firmly supported inclusion and diversity, Dr. J and Dalal acknowledged that like all organizations, it had to constantly challenge itself "to confront and overcome inherent bias." To that end, they announced that the board of directors, the co-founders, and the senior leadership team had committed themselves to a series of actions, including prioritizing WE Schools programs in underserved communities, creating anti-racism educational resources, recruiting more BIPOC employees, and initiating a "listening tour" by WE Charity's management to make sure concerns were being heard. "At the heart of that effort," they said, "is the need to pay close attention to what our own team members have to say about what we're doing, how we're doing it and what we can do better."

Unfortunately, the response on social media and elsewhere was quite negative, and a number of people accused Dalal and Dr. J, both women of colour, of essentially being puppets for the Kielburgers. For example, former employee Raia Carey, who had hosted a live videocast with Maitland a few days after her initial Instagram post, replied, "Yet NO people of colour on your executive teams?" to an Instagram post from Craig Kielburger, seemingly negating the existence of Dalal, Dr. J, CFO Victor Li, and others.[3] Another commenter said, "hire a BIPOC woman to lead, not just to educate you on something you have had years to learn."

"I was really, really upset," Dalal told me. "Rest assured, I'm not a puppet, and if I didn't believe in the message that I put online, I wouldn't have put it out." It was a demoralizing experience, she said. "And I felt there was so much hypocrisy in it, because you're talking about elevating and empowering BIPOC women and then they are actually bashing another BIPOC woman . . . That's where I felt the hypocrisy, because as a BIPOC woman, they were tearing me down."

One week after Dalal and Dr. J posted the open letter, the CSSG launched. As WE became the focus of increasing public criticism, Maitland's video gained new attention, and within days, she was appearing in national news stories by CBC and CTV. These stories recounted not just what had happened with her speech but also her attempt, back in 2019, to be heard on WE's overall workplace culture at the town hall with Marc. CTV's headline was "Racialized Former WE Employees Accused Charity of Oppressive Incidents."[4] In the body of the article, Maitland is quoted as saying, "[Marc] silenced me completely, to be like . . . 'We heard you, we got your email, you tried to reach out, enough.'" She said there was a clear problem within the organization with silencing the voices of people of colour, and the article referenced another former employee who described WE's culture as "deeply oppressive."

The CBC article was almost identical. It reported that when Maitland "tried to speak up about some of the problems within the organization at a WE town hall a few months after her tour, she was 'aggressively' shut down by WE co-founder Marc Kielburger in front of a room full of her peers."[5] Maitland told the CBC, "I began to speak about the culture of fear. I began to share that what is happening in this organization is that employees are having siloed conversations . . . and Marc Kielburger immediately . . . kind of stepped forward and shut me down." The CBC reported that four former employees who were at that town hall in 2019 confirmed that Maitland spoke up and Marc abruptly ended the conversation.

ANON YIMITY

Maitland found support on social media and from a group calling itself Anon Yimity, which sent an email and petition to WE Charity's board of directors on July 1, 2020. More than a hundred former employees had signed their names to the email—and the organizers wrote that another fifty current staff had endorsed it but chose to remain anonymous for fear of retribution. The message said that the signatories had "personally witnessed actions against, or inaction against, Black, Indigenous and People of Color (BIPOC) team members that corroborate many stories of overt racism, trauma from a culture of fear, abuse of power, silencing tactics and microaggressions."[6] And it criticized the organization for engaging in "performative" acts by posting anti-racist messaging to its website and tokenizing BIPOC employees.

The email presented a list of demands, including a public apology from Craig and Marc to BIPOC staff and active engagement on this issue. It said, "You are a new Board of Directors. You are also our friends, former colleagues, or mentors to many of us who have had careers or affiliations with WE. You have an opportunity, and a responsibility, as a new board, to choose how you will show up today and every day to serve the mission of the organization you represent."

The petition was circulated openly on Change.org and garnered substantial media and social media attention during the growing CSSG controversy. It generated approximately fourteen hundred signatures as people from outside the organization viewed and then supported its contents. I was troubled by how many people were signing the original message and online petition, and many board members were surprised that the signatories included people we knew personally who had never suggested to us that there might be an issue with racism within the organization.

I was particularly interested in what Dalal, as a BIPOC woman, had to say about why the email and petition gained so much traction. "The majority of our board members were BIPOC, and the chair was a BIPOC woman," she noted. "The majority of our international staff are BIPOC. Most of our work globally for twenty-five years was about empowering BIPOC communities in Africa, Asia, Latin America, and priority communities at home. But we had an activist staff, and they are passionate about pushing the organization to do more. George Floyd was an important turning point, when all organizations firmly moved BIPOC issues to the centre of the discussion. That is a good thing. My own sense is that the petition needs to be understood with that context in mind."

I shared Dalal's perspective. In my view, the petition likely struck a chord because of the times we live in. The BLM movement and an increased focus on systemic racism have promoted a concept of allyship. It is not enough anymore to not be racist. We need to be affirmatively anti-racist.

Of course, we can't know the motives or aims of everyone who signed the petition, but a later board investigation into the allegations in the petition led me to believe that some may have signed as an act of solidarity and not because they personally had witnessed or been subject to a racially insensitive act. We also can't know whether those who signed the petition had actually heard Maitland's allegations and understood their implications. My interviews and the investigation determined that many people just thought the organization could do better and had sympathy for the concerns Maitland raised. They saw signing the petition as a way to promote better practices, encourage change, and focus attention on this issue.

Whatever the reasons, the petition elicited the hoped-for reaction—to say that the board was concerned would be a profound understatement. The allegations were serious. If WE Charity was not doing enough to promote diversity and inclusion, that was one thing. If there was merit to the allegations of racism on the part of the co-founders or anyone in executive leadership, that was quite another. I can tell you that I personally would not have stayed on the board one more minute. And Marc most certainly would have been forced to resign.

Despite what was happening with the CSSG, the racism issue became the board's top priority. Emergency meetings were called, and I drafted the response to the email, which read, in part: "The Canadian and U.S. Board members received your message and read it with great concern, empathy, and a sense of urgency to address both your demands and the issues identified. Immediate action to address racism is what is called for and nothing less will do."[7] Our response made clear that the board would work "to identify the root causes of the concerns you have raised, evaluate what has been done and not done, and then take necessary action after making informed and thoughtful decisions in the best interests of the organization and those it serves . . . Rest assured that we will be conducting an independent review of these matters without influence from members of WE management, and the co-founders and WE management are fully supportive of such independent review. Please be assured that you are heard and seen by the Board. Your voices matter enormously and will result in action."

On July 2, Craig and Marc issued a public apology to Maitland and all current and former BIPOC staff, acknowledging unconscious bias and the harm that had been done by systemic racism within the organization.[8] "You shared in your video that the words of your speech were altered," Marc also noted in a posting to his social media accounts on July 4. "It simply should not have happened. You spoke about the importance of having Black voices and having people of different lived experiences at the table. Your explanation deepened our understanding about the true power of diversity."[9]

Two days later, WE Charity released an action plan to tackle systemic racism within the organization.[10] This included hiring a BIPOC educator to assist with diversity and inclusion reform and establishing mandatory training on these issues for all staff. Amorell Saunders N'Daw, an equity expert with the respected human resources firm Knightsbridge, was contracted to lead a process that would create a safe and confidential space for staff to share their thoughts and concerns.

These were all good initiatives and a positive step forward, but they were happening at the executive level of the organization. My personal feeling was that we, as a board, had to independently take action as well. The Anon Yimity letter was addressed to us, and we had oversight responsibility.

Because I conduct sensitive internal investigations for a living, other board members turned to me for advice on how best to proceed. At their request, I took the lead and guided our strategy. The board appointed a special committee consisting of Kannan Arasaratnam, Gerry Connelly, and me to oversee an independent investigation. The actual investigative work would be handled by external professionals who were themselves people of colour—they would act at the direction of and report to the special committee. The WE management team, and more specifically, the Kielburgers, would have no say in or influence over this investigation. They agreed to cooperate fully and do whatever they were asked by the committee and its investigative team.

The board hired McCarthy Tétrault LLP, a leading national law firm whose specialities include labour and employment law, to conduct the investigation. Their team consisted of two South Asian men, an Indigenous woman, and a Black woman. To eliminate overlap, the listening tour being conducted by Saunders N'Daw was rolled into the investigation, and she was retained by McCarthy Tétrault instead of WE Charity.

While all this was being organized, the demands of the Anon Yimity group grew. In a July 6 email to the board, the group's as-yet-undisclosed spokesperson stated that "public accountability" was very important to the group and it wanted to know the board's plan for communicating what actions had been taken. The email also asked for free services, including counselling, for current and former WE Charity employees impacted by racial transgressions.[11] And it demanded the resignation of Marc Kielburger. The next day, another email from the same anonymous address advised that the group was handing over control of its affairs to three former WE Charity employees—Amanda Maitland, Raia Carey, and Talitha Tolles—and that they would handle communications with the board and the group of petitioners going forward.[12]

The investigation was announced in a public statement from the board, issued on July 23. "The Board of Directors has carefully reflected on the experiences shared by WE Charity's current and former employees and other stakeholders in recent days," the statement read.[13] "We hear you. We take your concerns seriously. That's why we have struck a Special Committee of independent directors who have retained independent professionals to conduct a review of concerns expressed about systemic and direct discrimination . . . In the coming days, we will provide employees and former employees with the opportunity to contact the review team to share their experiences . . . To ensure transparency, we will share with you our lessons learned from the review. The Board wholeheartedly agrees with the sentiment expressed by some of you— WE Are Stronger Together."

The investigation proceeded for the next several months. All current and former staff were encouraged to share their thoughts and concerns with the investigators and were assured of confidentiality in the final report. The investigators also committed to using anti-oppressive and trauma-informed best practices as they conducted their interviews. In the end, the team spoke with twenty-nine people—eight were BIPOC and eleven had signed the original letter.[14] Amanda Maitland did not respond to any of the numerous messages that were sent to her. The other two identified representatives of the Anon Yimity group declined to participate unless they were paid to do so—one of them asked for $1,500 an hour. The special committee decided that it would not be appropriate to compensate fact witnesses and refused.

SPECIAL COMMITTEE FINDINGS

On December 16, after extensive consultation with the investigative team, the special committee delivered its findings in the form of a written report. It was published on the WE website.[15] "The Review did not identify any evidence of overt acts of racism," the report stated. On a systemic level, the committee concluded that while WE Charity's policies on harassment and discrimination were adequate, its systems for ensuring equity, diversity, and inclusion (EDI) were not. There was no specific focus on EDI in WE's employment policies, and the organization did not sufficiently examine its actions through an EDI lens, leading to practices that staff felt were tokenistic or culturally insensitive. WE was also found to be lacking in training, resources, and support for addressing EDI issues and challenges.

The report also addressed the specific allegations by Amanda Maitland. The committee found that her speech had indeed been revised without her consent—something that was never in dispute. Although it was standard practice for the WE Schools senior team to review and edit all school tour speeches to ensure the content was age-appropriate and aligned with the relevant curriculum, the committee concluded that there should have been a distinct system of review for speeches about racism. The organization needed to do a better job of ensuring that BIPOC employees felt heard and empowered. Because Maitland had not raised her concerns about the edits at the time, the report highlighted that WE needed to make sure it fostered a culture in which BIPOC employees like her were comfortable raising concerns. A woman of colour should not have been told to adjust a speech about her own lived experiences by managers who did not share those experiences. The report noted, "Due to the power dynamics of her position and an insufficient awareness of how to recognize and address EDI issues at WE, the revisions to Ms. Maitland's speech became permanent even though Ms. Maitland remained uneasy about them. WE's senior management have acknowledged that, in hindsight, given the nature of Ms. Maitland's speech, comments should have been made through an EDI lens."

To consider Maitland's charge that she had been "completely shut down in an instant" by Marc at the 2019 town hall meeting, the investigation team studied the transcript. (Town hall meetings with staff were typically recorded so discussions could be shared with employees who had other commitments or worked in other time zones.) The investigators found that Maitland did not appear to have been cut off, silenced, or "aggressively" shut down. There was a dialogue between the two, and Maitland did talk about a culture of fear, as she reported. Marc replied, "I mean, fine. And I . . . look, I know you know me, and I'm happy to sit down with you and have that conversation." He stressed that he had been listening, and that he viewed the town hall as an opportunity to continue to listen. "Happy to sit down," he repeated. "And I also appreciate you. And I've worked so hard, so hard over the last twelve months to . . . protect this organization. Really important work we do . . . in, in building schools, helping kids, to leadership training . . . So I just wanted to say we are listening. If we haven't honestly done it perfectly, and I'm not claiming perfection, I just want to say thank you for your comments. And I can assure you, we're listening." Maitland thanked him but elected not to meet with him, and she left the organization soon after.

Reflecting on that town hall, Marc told me, "I am sorry that she didn't feel heard in that moment. If I came off as impatient or abrupt in any manner, it definitely had nothing to do with Amanda's race or the nature of her concerns." After this event, Marc and others agreed they needed to be more cautious and think about how tone and style could make them seem unwilling to hear other perspectives. I certainly took the lesson to heart in my own professional life.

When I read the transcript today, I have to ask myself if it's possible that Marc's tone made Maitland feel unheard. I think it is. I would not have felt that way myself, but it's not important how I feel—what matters is how she felt. Still, the transcript does not support the assertion, made in her initial Instagram post, that she was "belittled by WE's founder @marckielburger for speaking up on the incident."[16] That did not happen. Such allegations come with a level of responsibility. Because they were so concerning to me as a BIPOC member of the board, I wish Maitland had agreed to speak with me for this book so I could better understand her experiences. And I wish she had participated in the investigation that she and others demanded. Especially because her calls for "dialogue" and "accountability" were important and were acted upon.

In the end, the committee made three broad recommendations. First, WE had to make EDI an organizational priority by developing an action plan, hiring HR professionals with EDI competency, and prioritizing the hiring and retention of BIPOC employees. Second, the charity had to revamp its organizational policies to incorporate EDI principles and create a process to address employee concerns and issues. And third, WE had to commit to mandatory EDI training for all employees. The message was that it wasn't enough for WE Charity not to have overt racism. The organization had to strive to be anti-racist and push against the racism that is within all organizations and our society.

The co-founders and WE Charity executive management accepted all of the special committee's findings and pledged to implement the recommended measures. EDI training quickly became a priority. Partnering with the Canadian Centre for Diversity and Inclusion (CCDI), the charity provided all employees with EDI-related webinars and training sessions, and in spring 2021, all employees, including the co-founders, participated in a certification program with the CCDI.

Separate from the special committee review, the charity also launched, in fall 2020, a WE Teachers' Anti-racism module and a WE Embrace Anti-racism campaign. The WE Schools team worked with internal and external experts to develop the resources through a trauma-informed lens and with a focus on youth well-being. This effort was led by Dr. Kia Darling-Hammond of Stanford University. She was supported by several subject matter experts and teachers from the Los Angeles Unified School District, the University of Dayton, and the DC Arts and Humanities Education Collaborative.

At the end of the day, I found it remarkable that none of the key people who raised this issue, including Amanda Maitland and the members of the Anon Yimity group, engaged with the results. Yes, there was work to be done by the organization and the board—that much was evident. But what happened to "starting the dialogue"? What about "continuing the conversation"? Why were Maitland and other employees who raised concerns and made demands of the organization willing to take part in media interviews, asking to be heard, but not a deliberative process undertaken by the board in good faith?

I am also disappointed by how the media handled the entire affair. Given the climate at the time, I understand why they amplified Maitland's allegations, but they made no room for reaction from BIPOC leaders at the WE organization like Dalal and Dr. J. And of course, the media didn't follow the story through to the end and gave no attention to the special committee's report or the many changes the organization embraced. There were no follow-up articles or evening news reports, and not a single journalist even tweeted about the report's findings to correct the public record. Important questions were raised. They were taken seriously and deserved answers. And the answers, to my mind, were also newsworthy.

CHAPTER 9

HIGH AND DRY

All the noise created by the media frenzy over every aspect of WE Charity's activities left the organization—including its board of directors—overwhelmed and in a constant state of crisis management. Everyone was drinking from a fire hose, as the saying goes. As I noted in the introduction, it felt to me like a game of Whac-a-Mole, with events popping up with ever-increasing speed, making it harder and harder to react quickly enough to stay ahead.

Amid the chaos, however, WE remained laser-focused on exiting the CSSG in a manner that would allow the program to carry on. It bowed out only after the government agreed to take over and run the program on its own. That should have been easy, according to Charlie Angus and Pierre Poilievre. After all, they had suggested to Canadians that the civil service was more than capable of designing and implementing the CSSG. And now, the hard work of building the digital infrastructure, hiring and training staff, and enlisting non-profit partners had been done. All the government had to do was continue enrolling students, log their hours, and send them their cheques.

As part of the process of unwinding WE Charity's role in the program, ESDC issued a notice of termination of the contribution agreement on July 14. At that point, WE had already agreed to waive its right to recoup eligible expenses it had incurred, such as the costs of setting up a call centre and acquiring the technology needed to run the web portal. "A total of $30 million was sent to WE, based on the ESDC process," Marc explained to the FINA committee on July 28. "As soon as this program was put into a political nature, we immediately decided that we would not be taking any of those funds. That was a decision that the organization made. We'd be losing approximately $5 million in this process. It was a very painful, difficult decision, but we felt under the circumstances that it was the right thing to do."[1]

At the same time, WE's executive team and accountants were eager to return the $30 million—funds that were meant to pay the students and cover the program costs. But ESDC asked the charity to hold off and await further instructions. All this bureaucratic red tape once again spiralled into a Kafkaesque nightmare for the organization. On August 11—two weeks after WE returned the first $22 million—Bardish Chagger, the minister responsible for the program, told the ETHI committee that she didn't know if *any* money had come back. "We can share the details on the money that has been released: $30 million has been released to the organization through the contribution agreement," she said. "I was not aware of how much money has been returned."[2] Chagger's lack of knowledge regarding details of the CSSG once again cast WE Charity in a bad light, exactly as had happened back in June, when she failed to explain that the program didn't have a billion-dollar price tag, and that the charity wasn't being paid but would only be reimbursed for its costs. This new error was especially maddening because WE had wanted to return all the money immediately but was thwarted by the government's refusal to accept a funds transfer. "It's been exceedingly difficult to send the balance of funds back to ESDC," Marc explained to us at our September 3, 2020, board meeting. "We are constantly being told that there is a certain course to follow to send the money back. However, they are not returning to us with the details/negotiations. So we made it a non-negotiable that we are sending the money back by this Friday [September 4]."

Meanwhile, the organization was being inundated with media inquiries about the status of the funds, and social media was swirling with rumours that the Kielburgers were refusing to return the money. The day after Chagger's comment, the charity released a statement to the media to explain that it had already returned three-quarters of the funds and was simply waiting for the green light to send the rest. The *Toronto Star*, based on background provided by an unnamed official, said that the government was constrained by the complicated process of disentangling all the legal obligations associated with the program.[3]

In reality, what happened behind the scenes was not complicated at all: the government refused to accept the remaining funds until WE Charity waived its right to sue for losses it had suffered. This was a pressure tactic, plain and simple. WE believed that it might have valid claims against the government for breach of contract and even fraud. After all, the organization had been led to believe that others were competing for the CSSG (in other words, that it wasn't sole-sourced) and had relied on the government to manage its own conflicts.[4] Plus, there was a concern about the charity's exposure to potential claims from third parties down the road. Effectively, the government was forcing the charity to keep the money until the organization agreed to release it from all liability.

This was a gift to opposition politicians and pundits, who implied that Marc and Craig had stashed the money somewhere and were refusing to give it back. When WE Charity's chief operations officer, Scott Baker, appeared before FINA on August 13, the omnipresent Pierre Poilievre demanded to know where the money was and then interrupted Baker when he tried to answer. "Sorry, the question was where is the rest?" he insisted. "Where is it? In what account is it being held?"[5] Baker told him the remaining money was in a non-interest-bearing account and was not being accessed in any way. The government, however, still had not publicly confirmed receipt of the first $22 million, even though that money had been returned weeks earlier.[6] WE was left to twist in the wind.

Eventually, exasperated and feeling both unfairly pressured by the government and unjustly maligned by the press, WE threatened to make public that the charity was being asked to relinquish its legal rights. The government's lawyers then relented. In the end, the government took sixty-two days to accept WE's request to return the funds.

Also left high and dry in this process were the tens of thousands of students who had enrolled in the CSSG in the days immediately after its launch. The program appeared to be in limbo, and no one from the government was communicating with participants or explaining next steps to the media. Meanwhile, WE was flooded with complaints. "Our team kept reminding them about all these angry emails we're receiving from students saying, 'I spent all this time to apply for this program. What's going on with it?'" said Dalal. "Given that everything we do revolves around youth empowerment, it was heartbreaking and frustrating to see."

Finally, on July 28—twenty-five days after WE transferred responsibility for the program to the civil service and two full months into the summer—ESDC provided some general messaging for the organization to share on the CSSG and WE Charity Foundation websites. "The Government of Canada is currently considering options for the Canada Student Service Grant," the message read. "As such, applications for service opportunities and students are not currently being processed or accepted. The Government of Canada remains committed to supporting Canadians during this unprecedented time, including students and the not-for-profit sector. More information will be provided as soon as it is available." None of the numerous questions WE employees had been fielding from applicants were answered, and to my knowledge, no individual students were contacted directly.

In a press briefing on July 31, Trudeau was asked about the toll the CSSG had taken on WE Charity. Multiple news outlets noted that the organization's reputation had taken a nose-dive, and that several corporate sponsors had withdrawn their support—all of which could have been avoided had the prime minister simply recused himself. Trudeau expressed some regrets but stopped short of acknowledging his role in damaging the charity.[7] He also had no apology to offer the thirty thousand students who had registered for the program and now had no jobs for the summer. Or the seventy thousand others who could have participated had the program gone forward. And not a word was said to the eighty-plus non-profit organizations that had embraced the program to get much-needed volunteer support during COVID.

The agreement between WE Charity and the government was officially terminated on September 26. And the government never picked up the mantle. Nor did it find any other organization to take on the program. The CSSG was done—and it stayed that way through the summers of 2020 and 2021. Opposition party politicians and the media seemed not to care about the loss to students, and to my knowledge, none of them publicly reflected on the fact that perhaps WE *was* the only organization capable of delivering the CSSG after all.

"The CSSG was clearly a failure, and it will forever be associated with WE Charity," Marc told me. "But a failure by whom? The charity delivered exactly what was asked of it in building and launching the CSSG. The ethics commissioner would confirm that there was no undue influence by Trudeau, Morneau, or any elected official. So was the real failure the rush to judgment?"

There had to be an accounting of what happened and how things were allowed to be so horrendously misrepresented, but would that ever come? For now, a new political spectacle was about to begin—and Canadians had a front-row seat.

DISTRACTIONS AND SIDESHOWS

Back in Ottawa, parliamentary hearings got underway in mid-July. What should have been a dignified and sober-minded pursuit of the truth on behalf of the Canadian people quickly devolved into a partisan circus. Most of the facts the opposition members said they were seeking came out in about ten minutes of testimony from Bardish Chagger and were later confirmed by Rachel Wernick of ESDC and Ian Shugart, the non-partisan Clerk of the Privy Council and Canada's top civil servant.

Everything that followed—two committees spanning two parliamentary sessions and nearly ten months of testimony from a total of sixty-three witnesses—was an exercise in theatre that offered Canadians virtually nothing of value. The hearings certainly supplied fireworks and riveting drama, I'll grant that. And a great deal of ink was spilled recounting every blow. But to play the tape, as I have painfully done more than once, is to witness a lot of sound and fury with little relevance to the core question of whether there was anything improper in the decision to select WE Charity to administer the CSSG. In short, it all resembled the contentious US congressional hearings that many of us are accustomed to—lots of grandstanding and speechmaking, loaded questions and disrespect of witnesses, but no actual interest in answers or fact gathering. To my mind, a lot of this can be explained by the fact that the hearings were broadcast nationally on CBC News Network during a pandemic that required everyone to stay home. Parliamentary hearings are usually pretty obscure, but this happened to be a moment in time when Canadians were consuming a lot of news coverage. For a politician looking for a profile boost, it was a golden opportunity.

The FINA committee started its work with a session involving Chagger and Gina Wilson, her senior associate deputy minister. In her opening remarks, the minister reminded everyone of the backdrop to the CSSG and just what was at stake. "Post-secondary students and recent graduates, like all Canadians, were facing unprecedented challenges," she said. "There was economic uncertainty, and it became apparent that there would be difficulties for students to find employment over the summer months—employment that would be crucial to helping them pay for school in the fall, pay down student debt, or pay for related expenses such as housing and utilities."[8]

Young people were of course not the only intended beneficiaries of the CSSG. The program was designed to be a two-way street, and Chagger also spoke of the plight of non-profit organizations during the pandemic. "We heard from many not-for-profits that they were struggling to provide services in their communities. Almost half of not-for-profits were having trouble finding volunteers at the same time that they were seeing an increased demand for their services. With public health guidelines requiring physical distancing, many not-for-profits needed to find new ways to engage volunteers while continuing to support their local communities within the context of COVID-19." In the long story of the WE Charity Scandal, this was the first—and unfortunately, the last—time anyone would highlight the potential benefits of the CSSG for the participating non-profit organizations.

After the minister concluded her introductory remarks, Pierre Poilievre was given the floor, and he immediately assumed a combative and antagonistic stance that set the tone for almost everything that followed. In his very first question, he demanded curtly, "What is the name of the public servant who recommended that WE deliver the Canada Student Service Grant? Just the name, please." Things went downhill from there, and within minutes, Chagger was asking the chair to admonish the Conservative MP for interrupting her answers and putting words in her mouth. At one point, when the chair asked him to move on, Poilievre sniped, "Okay, she does not want to answer that question."

For the most part, though, he followed a predictable line of inquiry. Did anyone speak to the Prime Minister's Office? Did the cabinet sign off on the agreement? Whose name was on the memorandum to cabinet? How much money did WE Charity stand to make? Aside from the tone of righteous indignation, it was a worn-out recitation of opposition party talking points. We had seen the movie, but it played on anyway.

When Poilievre's time was up, there was at last a chance for some reasonable, fact-based back and forth. There was plenty of testimony establishing that civil servants had concluded, on their own, that in the middle of a pandemic, there was simply no time for a competitive bidding process. Gina Wilson explained that a standard tender approach would have taken months, effectively eliminating the possibility of having an emergency support program for the summer. "We determined at the time that a call for proposals, an open call, would take about two to three months, at a minimum, to actually get something in place," she said. "An actual call for proposals would take several months to move forward with, and we needed to get this program off the ground very quickly, because at the time of the pandemic, in the severity of the pandemic, students were graduating."

When Shugart, a figure widely praised for his lengthy service to Canada under both Conservative and Liberal governments, appeared before the committee a few days later, he confirmed that there was no time to carry out a full-scale competitive process. "I do know that early in the development of policy, meetings were held with a range of non-profit organizations, voluntary organizations, and so on," he explained. "WE Charity was one of those consulted . . . I would say, at the front end of this, it was a wide-open process. It is true there was no call for proposals. It is true there was no competitive process. I mentioned earlier that PCO [Privy Council Office] raised the question of the department [ESDC] and whether there should be or could be a competitive process. The answer was no, with reasons, and colleagues at PCO were satisfied that was the case."[9]

It may come as a surprise to many Canadians—it certainly surprised me, given the furor surrounding the CSSG—that it is not unusual for contracts of a comparable size to be awarded in the same manner. In fact, in the first few months of the pandemic, hundreds of millions of taxpayer dollars were handed out to other organizations without competitive bids—with no hint of scandal. "WE Charity was not the only third party the government turned to during the pandemic crisis to support these public objectives," Shugart told the committee. "It turned to the Canadian Red Cross, the United Way Centraide and other organizations to provide the expertise and the reach that the public service does not itself have . . . This is a normal part of doing business."

For example, through the Emergency Community Support Fund, announced in April and launched in May 2020, the government made $350 million available to eligible community organizations, including the two Shugart mentioned, to serve vulnerable Canadians during the pandemic.[10] But these sole-source contracts elicited barely a peep from the opposition parties.

On the issue of the prime minister's assertion that WE Charity was the only organization in Canada with the ability to deliver the CSSG on the scale and schedule demanded, Rachel Wernick, the senior deputy minister with ESDC and the person who first reached out to Craig back on that Sunday in April, confirmed that was the case. Testifying immediately after Chagger, Wernick said that she called WE to explore options for a student service program because of the organization's previous work with her department.

"The third party [program administrator] needed massive speed, reach and scale, [and] an ability to quickly mobilize the whole country," Wernick explained. "The third party needed a demonstrated track record of mobilizing youth for service and [needed] to be technologically strong. Some of the bodies we considered and set aside were small advocacy groups with no program delivery experience. Other organizations did not have experience with youth, nor did they have strong technological capacity. Many had never delivered a program of such complexity. I did engage WE Charity as a potential partner, letting them know the broad parameters of what the government was looking for. They were an obvious option as the largest youth service charity in Canada, with high technological capacity and a Facebook following of four million youth."[11]

Once again, this testimony was confirmed by Shugart when he appeared before the committee a few days later. "What WE was able to provide, I understand, was the full range of services that would go to the heart of this matching program that would put young people in contact with not-for-profits so they could gain the relevant experience," he explained. "WE had the ability to promote the program with a massive social media following and experience in other situations of matching young people to service opportunities. The department was not equipped to provide that."[12]

All this testimony belied the claims made by opposition politicians, the public service union, and others that just about anyone could have delivered such a massive program on an incredibly short timeline. James Cohen, the executive director of Transparency Canada International, told the *National Post* back on July 6 that he couldn't believe that "nobody met the parameters set out by the government."[13] Peter Dinsdale, the president and CEO of YMCA Canada, one of the groups the government had considered approaching before settling on WE, told CTV News his organization was absolutely up to the job. But then he immediately backpedalled and added, "It would have been tough given the state of YMCAs across the country, given the impact of COVID—really fighting for basic survival. In normal times, [this] 100 percent would have been something we could have done."[14] Of course, these weren't normal times, which was the whole reason the program was needed in the first place.

Finally, all three main witnesses—Chagger, Wernick, and Shugart—made clear that despite the opposition's claims to the contrary, there was no evidence that the prime minister or anyone in his office had put a thumb on the scale for WE Charity. Chagger testified that she had no conversations with anyone in the PMO, and Wernick confirmed that she and her colleagues at ESDC were the ones who had determined that WE's proposal "was the best available option in the time we had to work with." And when Shugart was asked about possible back-channel communications between the prime minister and the Kielburgers, he was emphatic. "There is absolutely no evidence, no suggestion, in anything that I have reviewed that would suggest that the Prime Minister had any interaction with the WE Charity in relation to this program—none whatsoever."

"As I watched Shugart testify," Craig said, "I thought that WE Charity might survive this. The most senior civil servant in the country testified how and why the civil service had selected us. He testified that it wasn't because of any political favours. He laid everything out on the table."

Shugart's assessment was confirmed by the independent ethics commissioner, Mario Dion, in the comprehensive report he issued ten months later. That report may have helped Trudeau's political fortunes, but by that time, irreparable damage had already been done to WE Charity. "Mr. Trudeau's decision to approve the CSSG proposal with WE as the administrator of the program was not, in my view, motivated by the identity of any third-party representative, given the absence of a personal relationship between Mr. Trudeau and Messrs. Marc and Craig Kielburger," Dion wrote. "The evidence also shows that Mr. Trudeau had no involvement in ESDC's recommendation that WE administer the CSSG. I am satisfied that Mr. Trudeau did not give preferential treatment to WE."[15]

DEBUNKING MYTHS

That really should have been the end of it. The members of the FINA committee could all have shut down Zoom and called it a day. Instead, they pressed on with a series of "star" witnesses who had little to offer but theatrics. It was a cavalcade of attention-seekers and puzzled non-profit representatives who seemed to recognize that they had no insights into the CSSG, even if the opposition politicians did not. Among the former group was Canadaland's Jesse Brown, who used his time to boast about his own reporting and recycle points he had been fed by Kate Bahen of Charity Intelligence, a media go-to for negative commentary on WE Charity. He was joined by Vivian Krause, a researcher, writer, and former Conservative MP staffer[16] who in the past had questioned the credibility of groups advocating for forest conservation, Indigenous rights, and action on climate change. She once gained some notoriety for alleging that foreign actors were funding Canadian environmental charities to besmirch the oil sands sector and harm the energy industry. (She has since backtracked on these allegations.)

On this day, Krause offered up a slew of generalized complaints that could have applied to any charity and were based mostly on rumour, innuendo, and her own personal feelings. WE Charity had grown too quickly, she said, and accepted money from large corporations. It advertised job opportunities, but she had only seen positions in sales and marketing. She did, however, make the stunning claim that the charity collected the personal data of children and other young people and then shared it with the Liberal Party. When asked what evidence she had of this last claim, she could only say, "I have heard that they have done so."[17] Despite the fact that this was, by Krause's own admission, unsubstantiated hearsay that would not be admissible in any court of law, Conservative MP Michael Barrett then amplified her assertion by formally complaining to the Office of the Privacy Commissioner.

"I just about fell out of my chair when I heard that statement," Craig recalled. "It was blatant political theatre. She made a claim that was completely false. A member of Parliament then repeated her claim, demanding a national investigation by the privacy commissioner. The press went wild, and it was reported in headlines across the country. It felt like we were part of some alternative reality and had no control over what was happening."

As it turned out, WE Charity never shared *any* data with *any* political party. Yet Krause's claim was reported widely in the press, including by CTV, *La Press*, and the *Toronto Sun*.[18] Even the *Globe and Mail* got in on the act with the headline "Federal Election Watchdog Looking into WE Charity, Researcher Says."[19] Months later, the non-partisan Office of the Privacy Commissioner of Canada would report that the claim was completely without merit.[20]

The contrast between Krause and the previous witnesses couldn't have been starker. Throughout their testimony, Chagger, Wernick, and Shugart were professional and fact-driven, and they clearly and dispassionately refuted most of the opposition's spurious claims about the CSSG. They explained why there was no time for a lengthy bidding process, why WE Charity was the only organization with the speed and reach to deliver the program, and who had made all these decisions in the first place. These were facts, not partisan spin.

If any journalists had been so inclined, they could have easily uncovered these and similar facts for themselves and quickly debunked the myths that were circulating on the front pages of newspapers across the country. Canadians deserved that level of scrutiny and had a right to expect the press to do more than parrot opposition talking points without determining whether they were true. In the court of public opinion, only one side of the case was ever presented, and that contributed to much of the disinformation that infected the public consciousness and turned so many Canadians against a home-grown charity they had once supported and admired.

Unfortunately, even when the facts were plainly laid out, many news outlets failed to cover them. The testimony of Chagger, Wernick, and Shugart made barely a splash in the larger narrative of the WE Charity Scandal. Journalists moved on, always in search of that next big story.

And that story would come with the very next witness.

CHAPTER 10

A QUESTION OF GOVERNANCE

Of all the charges hurled at WE Charity in the wake of the CSSG, the most disconcerting to me was the accusation that there was a governance problem at the organization, and that the Kielburgers and the executive team functioned without appropriate oversight. This was the number-one concern people raised with me, both as a board member and in interviews for this book, and it's rooted almost entirely in testimony and public statements from Michelle Douglas, the former chair of the charity's Canadian board of directors.

Everyone understands that politicians spin the facts. And people also get why the media is invested in headlines and can't always be trusted to deliver the complete story. But the former board chair taking shots at the charity and its management? That understandably raised plenty of eyebrows—even among ardent supporters of the charity. Her concerns allowed pundits and opposition politicians to falsely characterize the charity as being in disarray, with a broken governance process and a board in "shambles" at the time the CSSG was awarded.

And these characterizations fuelled public misperceptions that have never been addressed until now.

I suspect that people at WE Charity, the Kielburgers, and Michelle will all be dissatisfied with the version of events I'm about to offer and will feel it is unfair to them or incomplete in some way. But my goal is to take you inside the rooms where it happened and tell you the story to the best of my ability—including what Michelle really said, and perhaps more importantly, what she never said.

When she appeared by videoconference before the FINA committee on July 28, 2020, Michelle opened the session by offering some introductory remarks about her personal story and her fifteen years at WE Charity. She mentioned her military service and her decades-long career as a public servant, and she noted her laudable history of human rights activism, telling committee members that she viewed "volunteerism in service to others" as one of the central pillars of her life.[1] She also talked about how she came to join the board of what was then still Free the Children and spent many years "excited by the prospect of working with an organization that [inspired] young people to contribute to a more just, hopeful and loving world."

But the most important line in her opening statement was this: "Having resigned on March 27, 2020, I have no knowledge whatsoever of the Canada Student Service Grant program."

I cannot overemphasize the significance of this statement. If the committee members were looking for answers about the CSSG, they had called the wrong witness. The person testifying should have been Greg Rogers, the chair of the WE Charity Canadian board when the CSSG contribution agreement was negotiated and signed. Douglas had left WE Charity weeks before Rachel Wernick even made that first call to Craig Kielburger, and she certainly had no knowledge of the organization's interactions with the government or the process by which the charity was awarded the contract. In other words, the witness had nothing to offer, and her testimony really should have ended there. But it didn't end there, because she had advertised that she had a story to tell, and opposition politicians were hungry to hear it.

NOSES IN, FINGERS OUT

Michelle and I were friends and colleagues on the board of WE Charity—in fact, even though she declined to speak with me for this book, I still think of her as a friend to this day. I also admire her as a true Canadian hero. A highly regarded air force lieutenant who had graduated at the top of her class, she was promoted to the military's elite Special Investigation Unit (SIU) after about two years of service.[2] Ironically, one of the unit's chief tasks was to investigate suspected gay and lesbian service members—and Michelle herself was gay. Just weeks after she joined the SIU, her secret got out and she was discharged for being "not advantageously employable due to homosexuality." It was 1989, and the LGBT Purge, as it had come to be known, was in its fourth decade, having survived long after homosexual activity was removed from the Criminal Code.

After she was discharged, Michelle attended a lecture by Svend Robinson, an NDP MP and the first openly gay member of Parliament. When the talk was over, she introduced herself to him and told him her story. Robinson asked if she would consider being the face of an anti-discrimination lawsuit against the military. She agreed. On October 27, 1992, the day the trial was set to begin, the military settled the case out of court, at the direction of then attorney general Kim Campbell. "This is not simply for me," Michelle said at the time. "It's for people who are still in the Canadian Armed Forces and for those who never had the chance to take this to court. There's no question there are still people being harmed by this policy and for them it is critically important that we get it changed and now."[3] In time, Michelle went on to become director of international relations for the Department of Justice, working closely with former attorney general Jody Wilson-Raybould, and today she is executive director of the LGBT Purge Fund, a non-profit set up to manage funds recovered through the settlement of a nationwide class action suit against the Canadian government by survivors of the LGBT Purge.

Just six months before she stepped down from the board of WE Charity, Michelle wrote of her admiration for the leadership team and the co-founders and of her "great trust in their decision-making process, integrity and transparency."[4] And she frequently praised the performance of the charity's executive director, Dalal Al-Waheidi, and her predecessor, Scott Baker. So I believe that despite media narratives to the contrary, she did not think the governance of WE Charity was lacking. For almost a decade, she was the person most responsible for governance matters, and if she had seen anything that concerned her, I feel confident she wouldn't have hesitated to say so. She even touted the board's commitment to "excellent governance" in an October 2019 letter shared with media outlets, noting that the board is made up of "highly engaged experts" whose "cumulative experience allows [them] to offer informed and responsible guidance and oversight to the charity, ensuring the highest levels of integrity in [its] work."[5]

As a board member, though with nowhere near Michelle's experience and tenure, I had no concerns about governance. But I now realize that so much of WE Charity's hands-on, roll-up-your-sleeves culture—the very thing that made us feel so good about the organization—encouraged a governance philosophy that at times mixed oversight with active involvement in day-to-day affairs. We theoretically observed the governance principle of "noses in, fingers out"—meaning the board provided oversight but was not charged with operational duties—but in practice, it was often all hands on deck. This was by design. The charity, and particularly the Kielburgers, long ago eschewed the idea of a board full of celebrities and luminaries who did no real work in favour of one whose members could provide sober-minded advice and jump into the fray when needed. At the time, it seemed wise. But in hindsight, it was a recipe for problems.

When I joined the board in 2017, Michelle was one of my go-to sources of information and helped show me the ropes. This was particularly true with respect to issues that called for caution and scrutiny. For example, when I had questions about WE Charity's real estate acquisitions, most of which had occurred before I joined the board, she was able to explain why these purchases benefited the charity and supported its mission. And when it came to the relationship between WE Charity and ME to WE, Michelle understood better than most the symbiosis between the charity and the social enterprise, the legal reasons for keeping ME to WE as a distinct legal entity, and the nature and level of support that the social enterprise provided to the charity.

We were an involved board of directors—Michelle most of all. She had been volunteering with WE Charity for fifteen years and was deeply embedded in the organization. In addition to her traditional board responsibilities—which included liaising with management and other board members, attending board meetings, reviewing the financials and annual budgets, signing the audits, and offering remarks in the opening pages of the annual reports—she was immersed in the charity's actual operations. She represented WE at countless events, crafted letters in support of the Kielburgers and other senior executives, and participated in multiple trips to international projects. She was one of WE's most enthusiastic supporters and an effective and impassioned ambassador for its mission. The charity was also a family affair. Michelle's sister was employed by the organization as a fundraiser, trip host, and relationship manager, and her nephew had been hired as an overseas trip facilitator for ME to WE. Like Craig, he had become interested in humanitarian issues at a young age, raising a considerable amount of money for schools in Kenya when he was still a child.

In advance of every board meeting and on a regular basis in between, Michelle—along with Dr. Jonathan White, then US board chair—spent a great deal of time asking tough questions and getting answers from WE Charity's executives. They explained to me that they viewed their job as pushing back behind the scenes and then presenting distilled information to the board. Dalal told me that in advance of each board meeting, Michelle reviewed all pertinent documents, gave detailed feedback, and helped craft the agenda. Dalal's predecessor, Scott, said much the same. "We had great discussions in preparation for meetings and walked through any potentially sensitive issues," he explained. "Michelle was very engaged in these meetings. She was very much a governance and process-focused person."

Other board members also took on specialized roles. Educational leaders like Gerry Connelly (former director of education of the Toronto District School Board and now co-chair of WE Charity Foundation) and Mary-Eileen Donovan (a former superintendent with the Toronto Catholic District School Board) would go into the office regularly, host training sessions, and get involved in curriculum design. Jonathan White, a US-based professor, and Terry Mazany, former president and CEO of the Chicago Community Trust, spent hundreds of hours mentoring staff on strategy to expand the organizations into the US. Once I joined the board, I was often involved in looking at legal questions and engaged directly with internal and external counsel as needed.[6]

The one standing committee that was always on call was the finance committee, which oversaw finance and audit issues and risk mitigation. It consisted primarily of board members Chris Besse and Kannan Arasaratnam. (Kannan is WE Charity's current US board chair. Although the organization had legally separate Canadian and US boards, the practice for over a decade was for both boards to meet and work together as much as possible, to better coordinate the respective Canadian and US operations.) Chris and Kannan did a deep dive into the financials with the help of WE Charity staff, including the CFO, and then walked the other directors through the figures to confirm that everything was in order.

Kannan has served on the charity's board without interruption since 2011. He's a numbers guy—a CPA who worked at Deloitte and Blackrock and earned his MBA at the Kellogg School of Management and the Schulich School of Business. He advises private equity and corporate clients on accounting, finance, and corporate strategy matters. He is also humble, calm, and skeptical. He reviewed the details of WE Charity's financial position each year with a jeweller's eye. Chris Besse also boasts deep experience—he spent twenty years in educational publishing, including as CEO of Gage Learning and managing director at Nelson Education, then shifted into education technology as CEO of FreshGrade. He is currently partner and chief commercial officer at Edsby, a student engagement and learning management platform. He also completed the Advanced Management Program at Harvard Business School.

In general, there were few limits on what tasks board members would undertake to help WE Charity. They travelled to WE Days in various cities to meet young people and donors. Almost every board member visited WE Villages projects around the world. And when serious issues relating to personnel arose in Kenya in 2018—a story I'll come back to later—Michelle and fellow board member Eric Morrison, former CEO of the Canadian Press, personally flew to the country to sift through the papers and get to the bottom of things.

I think I speak for all board members when I say it was deeply satisfying for us to use our professional training to contribute directly to the charity's operations. These direct contributions seemed more tangible and impactful than simply reviewing reports and attending meetings (although of course we did those things as well). With the benefit of hindsight, I now realize that the fulfillment we got from our hands-on involvement may have given us the sense that we would and should have say in areas that are traditionally reserved for management. We did not draw sharp lines between governing and managing, and that would soon have significant repercussions.

A DRAMATIC DEPARTURE

As the pandemic loomed, WE Charity's management team tried to come to terms with its likely impacts on the organization. Things were changing day by day, and Dalal was responsible for keeping Michelle abreast of developments. Between March 2 and March 27, she or the co-founders participated in at least ten meetings or calls with Michelle and other board members. On a call with Michelle and the WE Charity executive team on March 16, Marc and Dalal first raised the need to lay off many people who would no longer have work to do. The layoffs would be in the hundreds, they said. Although every department would likely be affected to some degree, the impact would be heaviest on the WE Day and ME to WE Trips teams.

With this sobering news in hand, Michelle sent an email to the other board members, summoning us to an emergency meeting that evening. It said, in part, that the impacts of the pandemic were "serious and substantial," and that "several difficult and challenging decisions" had to be made. But she closed on an upbeat note, writing, "The values and driving principles of WE remain strong. WE all need to come together in this extraordinary time."[7]

At the board meeting, we discussed the gravity of the global situation. Craig and Marc presented the dire reports they'd received from experts like epidemiologist David Fisman, Jeff Skoll, hedge fund manager Chris Hansen, and KPMG Global chair Bill Thomas. The plan for significant layoffs triggered mixed feelings. Some directors thought it was the responsible thing to do to ensure the organization's long-term sustainability. I was among them. On a moral level, these members felt that funding for pandemic relief in vulnerable regions took precedence over continuing to pay salaries for staff in programs that would not be operational for at least two years. Others, however, balked at the speed with which decisions were being made. As a next step, Michelle convened a subcommittee with White, Morrison, and Besse to engage with management on this sensitive issue.

When I interviewed Dalal more than a year later, she maintained that the organization's approach was the right one. "I used to run WE Days and I believed in their impact," she said, "but we were told by medical experts that it would be years before schools allowed kids to fill stadiums on school trips. It just did not make sense to keep going as if nothing had changed. The math did not add up, and it was not fiscally responsible in terms of having a large amount of payroll for programs that would not receive future funding and that we would not be able to implement due to COVID restrictions."

Kannan, who was deeply immersed in the financial affairs of the charity, felt the same way. "I think WE Charity management made the case for why the layoffs were necessary," he said in an interview. "Given what was happening in the world at that stage, they weren't the only organization having to go through some type of layoff or furlough. The reality is the situation was changing daily, and they needed the leeway to be reactive." He felt he got what was needed in terms of the financials. "I think it was a very dramatic picture that they painted for us, [and] that they were doing their best to preserve the charity."

The organization's culture—that is, personal relationships built over years and the sense of belonging to one big family—made the thought of layoffs more difficult, but as board members, we had an obligation to act in the best interests of the organization. We couldn't simply choose the path that would have been easier for us on a personal level as volunteers who cared deeply about friends and colleagues whose jobs were at stake. We had to think about how best to protect and sustain the organization.

Two days after the board meeting, on March 18, Michelle asked management for a list of names of those who had been and were likely to be laid off. She also asked for access to the financial data the management team was relying on to make these choices. No one takes lightly the decision to terminate hundreds of employees, so I understand where she was coming from. But in the opinion of management and the co-founders, her request went beyond the board's governance purview. To my knowledge, they never refused to provide the information altogether. They just wanted to provide briefings in lieu of the actual names of employees and copies of real-time financial projections that were changing by the minute. And they provided those briefings to Douglas and other subcommittee members on a near daily basis.

This goes back to the things I just said about the tension between governance and management. I believe that an organization of WE Charity's size needed a board focused on oversight, policy, strategy, compliance, and overall direction. In other words, a governance board. It was the executive director's responsibility to manage the charity, although of course she had to be held accountable by the board. As directors, we needed to be satisfied that management's business case for downsizing was sound—and in my view, that was the case, given the gravity of COVID. Asking to review names on a layoff list was an example of micromanaging, and governance experts I spoke to said this is not an appropriate board function.

Kannan and I have spent much time reflecting on the fast-moving events of March 2020 and what could fairly have been expected from management. "We're there to provide strategic advice, strategic decision-making," he told me. "But we're not the operators. I don't think it was the board's position to say, 'Hey, listen, you need to lay off that person or this person,' and get into the nitty-gritty of who the individuals are. That's management's decision. There are some board members who sadly wanted to get into the details. They felt it was their right to get into the weeds. There may have been personal biases and personal stuff coming into play there."

One such personal factor was that Michelle's sister was among those on the chopping block. Now, I have no idea if anything Michelle said or did was animated by concerns over her sister's job (or the jobs of countless other people she knew and cared about). I never got to ask her, but I suspect she would say the suggestion is nonsense. And it may be. There is no doubt, however, that it created a real conflict of interest. Nobody—chair, director, officer, or manager—should be involved in a decision that could affect a family member's job. Dalal, Marc, and Craig, for their part, told me that they were concerned about providing her with that list of employee names. And Chris Besse, who was a member of the four-person subcommittee, told me in an interview for this book that he would have asked Michelle to recuse herself had he known at the time that her sister was among those slated to be let go, and that this was creating apprehension on the part of management. But it went unspoken—none of this was presented by WE management or Michelle to me or, to my knowledge, other board members. And her sister's termination did not come up in Michelle's testimony before FINA or in media coverage of her testimony and public statements.

To make matters worse, these were the stressful early days of the pandemic, when confusion reigned and people were afraid of what was to come. The team at WE Charity was no exception. Tempers were frayed and emotions raw. Michelle continued to question whether overseas travel and WE Days would truly be shut down long term, and whether the resulting loss of revenue really required such significant layoffs. Dalal and Marc, who felt they had solid information that the pandemic's consequences would be significant and lasting, became impatient with these questions and stressed that with each passing day, surplus salaries took away precious resources that could be better directed to a humanitarian pandemic response. In the middle of all this, WE was also trying to repatriate staff and trip participants and source medical shipments for global partners.

Based on communications I have reviewed and interviews I have conducted with other board members, I know that Michelle was equally frustrated with refusals to address what she viewed as non-disruptive requests that would allow for real-time oversight of a decision to lay off a large number of people. I imagine she was thinking, "Look, if you're going to let hundreds of staff go based on a projected sharp decline in revenues, provide those projections so they can be reviewed and tested." And at least some subcommittee members felt that her demands were reasonable. For Michelle, it was not a question of trust in management—it was a question of governance. To her mind, legitimate concerns were being brushed aside.

The issue came to a boil on March 23 on a phone call the subcommittee members had with Marc and Dalal. Michelle once again demanded that management provide a list of staff to be terminated and written financial justifications for the layoffs, and this time she gave a firm deadline of the next day. Marc said the deadline wasn't feasible with everything else management was trying to deal with. Terse words were exchanged. Eventually, Marc, uncharacteristically, hung up. Months later, during her FINA testimony, this is how Michelle described those events: "I would say there was one particularly dramatic or memorable meeting on or about March 23, when I had asked for the ad hoc committee . . . to be convened. I, the US board chair and two others attended that meeting by phone. I demanded that the executive team produce those records. I gave a short turnaround time, I think later that day or early the next morning. I'll simply say that the call was abruptly concluded."[8]

Two days later, Craig called Michelle to try to cool the dispute, and to stress the need to move forward with downsizing. He told her that while specific dollar figures might vary, the bigger picture would not. The organization would need to pour millions into its pandemic response around the world and would simply not be able to carry hundreds of staff who would have no real work to do.

According to Craig, the conversation bounced back and forth. He asked Michelle to allow the layoffs to proceed and noted that the entire management team felt they were absolutely a necessity. She would not acquiesce unless the executive team met her requests in full. Craig said it was a management decision, not a board decision. She disagreed. It was an impasse.

It was, I am sure, painful for all. Michelle thought of both Craig and Marc as close friends, and she had often talked of Craig especially as a personal inspiration. She once said that his example had pushed her to make a more meaningful difference in her own activism.[9] And she described Marc as "an incredibly kind and loyal leader."[10]

For his part, Craig had been mentored by Michelle and was immensely grateful that she had dedicated so much of her life to the charity he co-founded as a teenager. But now that bond was strained. According to Craig, he told her that if they could not see eye to eye on this issue—and more broadly, on the line between governance and management—then maybe after fifteen years (ten of those as chair), she had grown too close to the operation to deliver objective governance. He suggested that she consider leaving in August 2020, when other directors would also be stepping off the board as part of a prearranged transition. This was not the original plan—Michelle was supposed to exit the board in August 2021. She was offended and hurt. As she later told the FINA committee, "It was clear that there was a breakdown in trust between the founders and me as the board chair . . . As I was not going to be able to discharge my oversight duties, I opted to resign immediately."[11]

She called an emergency board meeting for the evening of March 27. Craig phoned me shortly before it started. "I don't want you to be surprised, but Michelle is going to resign. It's bad," he said. "I asked her to allow the staff layoffs to occur and then to consider transitioning off the board in six months," he explained. "But she wants to leave now."

I couldn't follow what he was saying and thought the eighteen-hour days were getting to him. I assumed he was talking about the long-term board transition plans, not something imminent. I told him I already knew that there would be a transition, and that Michelle would step away. I hadn't been part of the specific discussions and didn't know the details, but the concept was not news to me.

"No, you don't understand," Craig said. "I asked her to step off the board in August with the others, but she's resigning *today*. She's very upset. She'll tell you in the board meeting."

"What?!" I couldn't believe what I was hearing. "You need to fix this, Craig. Let me talk to her and the others," I suggested.

"It's too late," he said. "I tried without success to convince her to stay on for a six-month transition period, then asked for at least a three-month period, and she said it's a hard no."

The idea that Michelle would be leaving on bad terms sounded like a horrible development given her long service to the organization and our personal friendship. Plus, the WE Charity board—and the organization more broadly—always felt like family. Hugs were the norm at every meeting and event—handshakes would have seemed stiff and formal. Michelle had been part of that family perhaps longer than anyone, and this felt like a sudden divorce that was going to turn acrimonious.

But the board meeting was about to start and there was no time to confer with anyone else, let alone speak to Michelle. I would just have to join the meeting and see how things unfolded.

The first part of the videoconference was an in-camera session closed to members of WE Charity management. This was a common practice for our board when we wanted to discuss significant organizational issues, like the unfolding COVID-related layoffs. At first, the meeting seemed like any other. I started to think Craig was wrong and had misunderstood something Michelle had said. But then she took a deep breath and announced that she was leaving and had already submitted her resignation letter. She was visibly emotional, but she remained composed and professional, as always. She had lost the confidence of the founders, she explained, and Craig had asked her to resign in a few months' time. Because she felt like she could no longer do her job, however, she said she had no choice but to resign immediately. She briefly explained the reasons—she said she had asked for real-time information supporting layoff decisions but had not received the data she believed the board should have. For her, management's resistance to immediately providing what she'd requested was not acceptable. And that was it. She encouraged the board to continue to support the organization and the executive team, then stopped speaking.

I scanned the solemn faces on the Microsoft Teams call as people absorbed the news. Some, like me, had clearly had a bit of warning. Others appeared shocked. Board members began to pay tribute to Michelle. One by one, we thanked her for her service. One by one, we expressed sadness that she was leaving under unhappy circumstances. I think people were especially careful with their words because many of us did not fully appreciate what had happened behind the scenes.

Michelle's resignation letter was short on details. "My resignation is linked entirely to the fact that I was asked by one of the organization's co-founders to leave the board of directors over a 'disagreement over governance process' and very recent tensions between the board chairs and the co-founders," she wrote. "Otherwise, I had not intended to resign; especially during this crisis. I take the request of Craig Kielburger to mean that the co-founders lost confidence in me as the chair of the board of directors of WE Charity. I accept this and I therefore resign. I am simply unable to stay on for one to three additional months under the circumstances that led to my resignation."

Four days later, management provided the remaining directors with additional financial projections and a full list of employee layoffs—the things Michelle had been asking for all along. That day, the members of the board finance committee, Kannan and Chris Besse, as well as the other members of the subcommittee addressing layoffs (White and Morrison) received a full financial update. On April 4, the board met, without management, and received updates from the finance committee and layoff subcommittee members. Although there remained sadness at the circumstances around Michelle's departure and some questioned the way management had engaged with her, there was broad agreement that the actions taken by management were consistent with the financial picture and the organization's strategic interests. Other than Michelle, all board members remained in place at the time of this meeting.

Like Michelle and the other directors, I had wanted to understand the rationale for the layoffs and make sure they were based on a realistic assessment of the organization's prospects. Sometimes it is the job of a board to apply the brakes, and in my time with the charity, I never saw the directors fail to ask hard questions and push back when needed. In fact, I had personally been involved in situations where the board refused to proceed with initiatives that the co-founders and management team strongly supported. Having said that, I also think thorny issues arise when directors—particularly one with a conflict of interest—want to get involved in the details of employee terminations (at least where such decisions relate to non-executive positions the board is not responsible for appointing).

Even now, with much water under the bridge, I cannot tell you why Michelle didn't come to the board as a whole, explain the impasse, and ask for some collective decision on what information was needed from management. We could have debated our role, and I may well have agreed with her in the end. Nor can I explain why Michelle—ordinarily a stickler for good process—did not raise the conflict of interest involving her sister and let the board decide whether she should be part of a subcommittee assessing layoffs. At the same time, I also cannot tell you why the Kielburgers and WE Charity's executive leadership let things escalate, why they could not find a way to acquiesce, and why they thought it was reasonable to ask her to transition from the organization early without bringing the matter to the full board. All I can tell you is that cooler heads did not prevail. It was an abrupt and tragic end to Michelle's tenure with WE Charity, and one I regret.

But today, as I see it, the important takeaway is that this occurred only at a particular moment in time, and it was only with respect to the narrow issue of whether layoffs were sufficiently justified and being handled appropriately. Nothing more.

TRANSITION AND RENEWAL

Michelle did not quietly move on to bigger and better things. On June 28, three months after she resigned, she responded on Twitter to someone who was defending WE Charity's governing structure. This person had stated, incorrectly, that Michelle was the current Canadian board chair. She tweeted back: "Michelle Douglas resigned from the board of directors of WE Charity on March 27, 2020. I am no longer associated with WE."[12] Then, without providing any context, she added: "Almost all of the board of directors of WE Charity in Canada and the US resigned or was replaced in March 2020."[13]

To most people, this might have seemed an innocent effort to set the record straight. But it twisted things. The insinuation was clear— Michelle was suggesting there had been some sort of housecleaning at WE Charity. As a board member who had not resigned or been replaced, I found this statement puzzling and more than a little insulting. It seemed to erase the continuing board members, a trio of highly capable professionals. Kannan, who today is the US board chair, is a finance professional trained at some of the biggest firms in the world and had overseen the charity's financial governance for more than a decade.

Gerry, who today serves as the co-chair of WE Charity Foundation, had served on the board for almost a decade and has a deep history in education and curriculum development. And I had served on the board for three years and have been litigating and investigating matters involving financial fraud for twenty years.

"Almost all," it seems, is in the eye of the beholder.

Unfortunately, Michelle's tweets attracted attention. On July 2, the CBC posted a story titled "WE Charity Saw Resignations, Departures from Senior Ranks Before Landing Government Contract."[14] The piece linked to her tweets and said the charity had gone through a period of "organizational upheaval" over the previous few months. "The chairs of both the Canadian and U.S. boards of directors for the WE Charity resigned in the spring," the article reported. "The vast majority of the other board members in the two countries have been replaced as well. The flurry of changes began about two months before the federal government announced WE was the only organization in Canada able to administer the multi-million-dollar Canada Student Service Grant initiative. The reasons for the resignations in WE's upper ranks remain unclear."

But there was nothing unclear about it. It is true that eight members of the board transitioned off in April 2020. What Michelle's tweets and the CBC piece both failed to note, however, was that this changing of the guard was part of a renewal process that had started a year earlier and was timed to meet the changing needs of the organization as it approached its twenty-fifth anniversary. Through this process, sitting board members exited to create space for other highly capable, independent professionals who would bring new energy and fresh ideas. On April 4, the board voted to appoint new members so that those scheduled to transition could depart. It simply happened earlier than planned. But to be clear, all the existing board members remained in place and voted on the transition, and there were no other protest departures. And for this book, I spoke to several other board members who transitioned off in the weeks and months after Michelle's departure. None felt they were forced out.

Mary-Eileen Donovan, who served on the previous board for nearly thirteen years, said her transition was seamless. "My term was basically up around the time we had our annual retreat meeting. And so I had already said that this is my last term." Chris Besse similarly confirmed that he had discussed making way for renewal for some time and had no negative feelings about transitioning off the board. In fact, he quickly reappeared at a subsequent board meeting to provide the new directors with an overview of the historical decision-making process around WE Charity's real estate acquisitions. And Terry Mazany told me that he "felt no pressure and had no concerns" about transitioning off the board. "The restructuring of the board was done for strategic reasons in the best interests of WE Charity so that the organization was well positioned for growth. It made all the sense in the world," he said, "and I wished I could stay, but I realized I was not the right person as the organization grew and evolved." These are not the words or actions of people who felt they were ousted or had been silenced from expressing concerns.

The new chairs of the Canadian and US boards jointly wrote an open letter explaining that the shake-up of the board was necessary "to address renewal, sharpen the focus on future priorities and address issues such as diversity, inclusion, and range of competencies all while continuing to provide strong oversight and guidance to the organization."[15] Unfortunately, this letter received very little media attention. And deriders like Kate Bahen shot first and skipped questions altogether. "Did WE Charity *inform* the government that its board had resigned or was replaced just weeks before," she wondered aloud in a conversation with Jesse Brown at Canadaland, "and that there was a gap in governance and oversight at the charity? . . . Oh and by the way—it has no board."[16] This, of course, was not true—the organization always operated with a complete board that was composed of highly skilled people.

Kannan later reflected on how all this became a confusing political football amid the CSSG controversy. "Sadly, because all of the timing was sort of intermingled, an outsider looking in would think that somehow all of these things are related, when in reality the board restructuring was a conversation they had been having with us well before COVID and well before the CSSG."

One important advantage of the board transition was that it allowed us to prioritize greater diversity. A diverse board is more effective at oversight because diversity fosters independence, critical thinking, varied perspectives, and different opinions. Before April 2020, WE Charity's Canadian and US boards had seven men and five women, with no women of colour and only two men of colour (Kannan and me). After the transition, the board consisted of five women and four men, half of whom were people of colour. And the new US board chair was a prominent Black female educator, Dr. Jacqueline Sanderlin. So the process of renewal brought a marked improvement in diversity, something those of us on the newly constituted board were very proud of.

Of course, none of this stopped politicians and journalists from advancing the narrative that the board of directors was in disarray. In fact, this was a seed that had already been planted by Michelle prior to her July 28 appearance at FINA. On the eve of her testimony, the *Globe and Mail* ran a front-page story that featured comments from Michelle about her departure. "Former WE Charity Chair Says She Resigned Over 'Concerning Developments' at the Organization," read the headline.[17] She was quoted as saying, "My resignation as the chair of the board of directors of WE charity was as a result of concerning developments. I did not resign in the ordinary course of matters." Those two sentences were her only quotes in the thousand-word article. But it was enough to set the tone for her testimony and everything that followed.

TAKING CENTRE STAGE

Douglas's FINA appearance began with MPs paying tribute to their star witness. The committee chair, Prince Edward Islander Wayne Easter, lauded her accomplishments. "I know I speak for the committee when I say thank you for your service to the country through the military, your service as a public servant with the Department of Justice, and your human rights activism, which has been responsible for changing some of the social policy in Canada. Thank you for that."[18] Conservative Pierre Poilievre followed suit but focused only on her time in the military and did not mention LGBTQ rights.

In his opening question, Charlie Angus said that he was "very concerned" about what was happening with the board and implied that the organization was lacking in governance and oversight. Michelle effectively confirmed this when she replied, "We were pushing for information . . . just simply the information that we were told regularly was being generated on a daily basis. That information was never provided, although we asked."

"The only reason I'm asking to get into this," Angus declared, as if his own questions were beyond his control, "is that the Canadian people have given this organization close to a billion dollars and we need to know that this is an organization that has a proper structure, that it's not just the Kielburger brothers and their family, but that there is oversight." Michelle could have pushed back on Angus's deliberate inflation of the dollar value of the CSSG and his implication that all that money was going into WE's coffers, but she stayed silent. It was left to the committee chair to correct the record at the end of Angus's round of questions.

Conservative MP Michael Cooper also made several false statements during his questioning, including that there was "an upheaval in the organization in March," and that other board members had resigned, either in solidarity with Michelle or because they were being blocked from performing their oversight duties. Again, she let most of these claims stand and even validated some by saying that the pre-planned board transition did not happen "in the ordinary course," and that she had been "denied access to the chief financial officer." (The CFO said that Michelle had his email address and phone number but never reached out.)

Some MPs did try to push back on the misinformation being read into the record. For instance, Quebec MP Annie Koutrakis asked Michelle how much say she, as chair of the board, had in the overall governance and strategic direction of the organization, and had her acknowledge that the board had "power to make decisions around governance, establish a direction of oversight . . . and review financial records." (Michelle also signed off on all financial audits.) And the final questioner, Ontario MP Peter Fragiskatos, asked her point-blank if, during her fifteen years with the organization, she had ever found or seen "any irregularities, financial or otherwise, that were of concern." She responded: "I never saw anything about the integrity of the organization that caused me deep concern." He then brought the questioning back to the supposed purpose of the hearing when he mentioned the comments Michelle had made to the *Globe and Mail* about alleged "concerning developments" at the charity. "[These developments] had nothing to do with the Canada Student Service Grant," Fragiskatos said, "and nothing to do with the contribution agreement that WE eventually signed with the federal government. Is that correct?" She agreed it was.

In fact, Michelle was crystal clear in saying that her resignation was prompted by her view that "employees were being laid off and the board did not have enough information to provide oversight."

For opposition politicians with an agenda, Douglas's testimony was pure gold. Angus later translated it this way: "Our committee found out that the board of directors was fired in the middle of the pandemic for asking for financial statements."[19] Conservative MP Michael Barrett, meanwhile, declaimed, "With a deal that's this big, how was it missed that there were breached bank covenants and a board responsible for the organization in shambles, in a word, and there were all kinds of real estate transactions that are now in the public domain that are questionable at best for an organization of this type? How could, in that due diligence, something like that be missed?"[20]

In the end, here is what I think you can reasonably take away from Michelle's testimony and public statements. She had "no knowledge whatsoever" of the CSSG, and whatever issues she may have had with the way the charity was being managed, they had nothing to do with the grant program. She left the organization earlier than planned because she was unhappy with the level of information being supplied to the board with respect to pandemic-related layoffs and the way in which she was treated by the Kielburgers. Reasonable people can disagree over whether she was right or wrong in what she was demanding of management and in her decision to resign immediately when her demands were not met. And it is fair to question whether WE Charity's management and the co-founders handled the situation well.

But let's also be clear about what Michelle did *not* say and what cannot be reasonably taken away. She didn't suggest that there was a broader governance problem at WE Charity during the decade in which she was responsible for governance—in fact, she said the opposite in her testimony, in numerous written statements, and throughout her long tenure at the helm. She did not say that she did a bad job or had for some reason been keeping quiet about serious problems for years. Nor did she say that governance was lacking after she left, or that she had any basis to question the wisdom of the charity's decision to administer the CSSG. She noted that a lot of directors also transitioned off the board after she left, which is a fact. But that does not mean that other directors were pushed out or left under dubious circumstances. And it does not mean that those of us who remained in place failed to mind the shop, or that newly appointed directors—all people of exemplary character and experience—were not up to the task.

Had the media been interested in reporting her testimony fairly and accurately, that is the story they would have told. Michelle's experience and views make for an interesting—and perhaps even healthy—debate on governance. Instead, the press used her remarks to shore up the narrative they had been advancing for months. One Bloomberg headline read, "WE Charity Hearings Reveal Troubling Governance Structure."[21] *Maclean's* magazine allowed someone it identified as a charity consultant to pronounce: "Their governance structure makes no sense and is unaccountable, which we hear from the testimony of their chair. Their incorporation structure is Byzantine at best and unaccountable and needs to change."[22] Meanwhile, *National Post* columnist Chris Selley cherry-picked Michelle's words to make them fit the version of events he wanted to sell to readers. "We don't know a lot more of substance about the Kielburger Affair after the House of Commons finance committee's Tuesday meeting . . . but we do have some more details, and the details are what makes this story kind of fun as well as gross," he began. Then he asserted that "Douglas said her board was frustrated in its efforts to gain any insight into the financial condition of the organization . . . Her fruitless inquiries culminated in a meeting where Brother Marc simply hung up the phone, she testified, after which she was asked to resign."[23]

And yet, contrary to what certain MPs would have people believe, the board *did* receive financials. I know because I was one of the directors who received them. And the subcommittee charged with liaising with management also received financial information while layoffs were proceeding, just not in a form and at the depth desired by Michelle. But even had Selley's assertion been true, it was an irresponsible leap for the media to go from the board chair's complaint about documentation involving the single matter of pandemic layoffs to the claim that the board had no insight into the charity's financial condition.

It also frustrates me that journalists and politicians deliberately inflated Michelle's concerns to create a myth of widespread disorder. She herself never went that far, as we saw in her response to Peter Fragiskatos. She also told another MP that the layoffs were not triggered by financial distress, poking a hole in the popular theory that WE Charity needed a government bailout. These comments should have been the end of the partisan attacks. The supposed "whistleblower" said she had no concerns about the integrity of the organization or its finances. But in these parliamentary hearings, it was not the answers that mattered, only the questions. MPs wanted to get themselves on the evening news, so they offered up the most sensationalist statements for sound bites. This served no one's interest—least of all that of the Canadian public.

At the same time, the voices of other board members were silenced. People have often asked me why other directors didn't speak up on behalf of the charity. In fact, they did, but the media didn't allow them to be heard. Multiple board members released statements to the press, including the open letter from the two new chairs that I mentioned earlier. Board members also submitted letters to the editors of the *Globe and Mail*, the *National Post*, the *Ottawa Citizen*, the *Montreal Gazette*, and the *Vancouver Sun*—all were rejected. It seemed the media narrative had been decided and no one was interested in hearing from dissenting voices.

It is also worth noting that the charity's directors, including me, were not simply focused on defending the charity during the scandal. We were also busy discharging our governance obligations by asking hard questions of WE management in response to every allegation that surfaced. We had a duty to carefully assess whether there was merit to the headlines and political attacks. If the charity had done something wrong, we had no intention of just standing idly by—I certainly would have demanded action or resigned. But aside from the commentary I offer in this book about what could have been done better, I never learned anything that caused me to question the good faith and integrity of the charity's co-founders or leadership team.

Since the day Michelle testified in July 2020, I have heard from dozens of people that her commentary was what stuck with them most. But many of those people did not see or read her testimony in full—their understanding of what she said is based entirely on TV sound bites and social media posts by politicians. That coverage caused many to doubt the charity and convinced some corporate sponsors to withdraw their support. In fact, the charity's largest US sponsor, Walgreens, told Craig that news coverage of Michelle's testimony was the reason it decided to stop partnering with the organization on a multi-million-dollar initiative to help low-income students with free programs and to deliver global health programs at Baraka Hospital in Kenya.

With Michelle's testimony complete, it was Marc and Craig's turn in the hot seat, just eight minutes later. Postmedia columnist Licia Corbella later summed up her impact: "The Kielburgers' testimony might have been convincing and sympathetic had it not been preceded by Douglas."[24]

CHAPTER 11

POLITICAL ROADKILL

The Kielburgers' lives had become a nightmare. The organization they had built from literally nothing was clinging to survival, and they were working eighteen-hour days to keep their heads above water. To make matters so much worse, they and their families were under personal threat. Most Canadians would have been sickened to read the emails and hear the voicemails coming into WE's headquarters.

"Listen here, you bunch of corrupt motherfuckers," said one. "Get the fuck out of the country and close the building up now. We're coming for you and we're not fucking around. We are serious. We're going to fucking burn you guys out. Get the fuck out of the country."

"Hello, this is the people of Canada," said another, "and we're calling to find out when you're returning the rest of every fucking cent you were given. If we find out you haven't returned every goddamn cent for your fake satanic garbage organization, we want every fucking penny returned back to the government."

One email read, "Both of the corruptbergers need to be fucking hung, both of you are lying pieces of shit."[1]

Perhaps the most shocking was this: "WE ARE PRAYING FOR THE SAVAGE BRUTAL EXCRUCIATINGLY PAINFUL MURDERS OF THE KILBERGER BROTHERS WHO ARE FUKKIN FAGGOTS QUEERS LOSERS COWARDS COCKSUKKIN CHILD MOLESTIN HIV INFECTED DOUCHEBAG MAGGOT PIECES OF HUMAN EXCREMENT! WE PRAY THAT THEY BOTH GET COVID-19 ALONG

WITH THEIR DIRTY DISGUSTING IDIOT MORON RETARDED JERKOFF ROT-
TEN VILE EVIL FAMILIES & FUKKIN DIE ASAP!!!"[2]

And then there were the tweets—the most disturbing of which came from a notorious private investigator named Derrick Snowdy. On July 28, he tweeted, "I wonder if Craig and Marc Kielburger know that we know exactly where they live and where their families spend their time?"[3]

A week earlier, the *Toronto Sun* had run a piece by Brian Lilley that included Marc's home address.[4] Online forums were soon filled with vile commentary that referenced Lilley's coverage. Board members who were aware of the death threats insisted the brothers contact the police. Officers visited their homes, told them to make changes to their daily routines, and programmed the brothers' home phone numbers into a rapid response system. "They advised us that our kids should no longer play outside unsupervised and never play in front of the house," Craig recalled. "Trying to explain this to kids was just unreal and horrifying. We were used to criticism, but this was something different, so much worse."

Invasions of privacy and feelings of insecurity even extended to Kenya, where the Kielburger family owns a residence that was used by Craig, Marc, and various other WE staff who frequently travelled to the country. At one point, a freelance journalist working for the *Globe and Mail* posed as a potential buyer of the property to gain access to it. When the real estate agent became suspicious because most of the supposed buyer's questions were about the owners of the property and not the home itself, she revealed that she was really a reporter tasked with digging up dirt on the Kielburgers and WE.[5]

Even today, hateful messages continue to be posted online, reporters relentlessly probe the personal lives of the brothers and their families, and the Kielburgers have to worry about the safety of their loved ones.

This was the backdrop while Marc and Craig were preparing for their turn answering questions before the FINA committee. What was originally supposed to be a standard one-hour session grew to two and then four hours as opposition MPs demanded more and more of their time. Only one witness in recent history had testified before a House committee for anywhere near as long, and that was former attorney general Jody Wilson-Raybould, who'd asked to testify on the SNC-Lavalin affair.[6]

As soon as the brothers appeared onscreen to be sworn in, the toll of the past year was evident.[7] They looked tired and seemed exceedingly uncomfortable. It was difficult to watch. I have known them since high school, and they were always the epitome of self-assurance. They have met, impressed, and persuaded some of the world's most serious and accomplished people. You do not get up in front of the likes of the Dalai Lama, Mikhail Gorbachev, or Desmond Tutu unless you're confident in what you have to say. And you do not recruit captains of industry like Facebook COO Sheryl Sandberg, KPMG Global chairman Bill Thomas, and Virgin Group founder Richard Branson to champion your cause unless you are focused and on message.

Love them or hate them, the Kielburgers could stand and deliver.

This was different.

This was four hours of interruptions, hostility, and barely concealed contempt. When I thought back to Craig's previous appearances before parliamentary committees, it really brought home to me how much the tide had turned. In 2018, for example, he shared his views on social enterprise and the Canadian charitable sector with a Senate committee and was treated with respect by members of all political stripes. Conservative senator Yonah Martin was just one of many who lauded Craig's work and expertise. "Mr. Kielburger," she said, "I've been a fan of the work that you are doing with our youth, so it's really great to hear from you this evening. I have so many questions about social enterprise because I know people who are doing such good work in Canada."[8] In fact, Craig was so respected in parliamentary circles that the independent Leaders' Debates Commission appointed him to its advisory committee in 2019. This non-partisan committee was charged with reporting to Parliament on how to make future debates more equitable and accessible.

But on July 28, 2020, it was clear times had changed.

Craig and Marc were about to become political roadkill in the opposition's quest to attack the Liberals and Justin Trudeau's desire to brush past yet another scandal.

Pierre Poilievre opened the questioning and then immediately interrupted whenever Marc and Craig attempted to respond. He was rude and abrasive, and made comments like "Answer the question, then" and "I'll repeat it for the fifth time," as if he himself wasn't the reason they were unable to reply.[9] Chair Wayne Easter tried to get hold of the hearing early on by imploring Poilievre to be reasonable. "They're here for four hours, so we will allow them to answer," he chided. "We will let the witness answer the question." In Poilievre's first round of questioning, Easter had to intervene five times.

Charlie Angus was even worse. At times, he condescendingly referred to the Kielburgers as "boys," seemingly unable to muster even a sliver of respect for two accomplished men—recipients of the Order of Canada, no less. It felt as though Angus still viewed them as teenagers working out of their parents' basement and thought they deserved a scolding. Easter called him out seventeen times in his first round for being disruptive and disorderly. "Things will go a lot smoother if we allow an answer in detail, and we'll all save time," the chair patiently explained. "I want to give the witnesses an opportunity for a thorough answer. We have four hours with these witnesses. We should be able to allow them full answers."

It was embarrassing to see sitting members of Parliament behave like toddlers in the throes of a temper tantrum, and yet they carried on like this all afternoon. At one point, the chair had to threaten to end the proceedings because of Poilievre's behaviour. As Craig pleaded to be given the time to answer the question he'd been asked, Poilievre persistently interrupted to promote the false narrative that the Kielburgers stood to profit personally from the CSSG. Marc tried to explain that the program was governed by a contribution agreement that only allowed for WE to be reimbursed for expenses. But Poilievre sharply cut him off, saying, "Paid to yourself . . . you were going to pay the expenses to yourself." It was a nonsensical turn of phrase. If you've ever been reimbursed for an expense, you've had money returned to you. But no one—including the Canada Revenue Agency—thinks that you've been *paid* money that should be treated as personal income. I assume Poilievre figured that logic would be lost on those watching clips on the evening news.

Finally, even the avuncular Wayne Easter got fed up. "Mr. Poilievre," he snapped, "do I have to suspend this meeting? Now, there will be order or I'll suspend the meeting, and that's it. It's your choice."

It was clear that once again, the hearing wasn't an attempt to get to the truth or present Canadians with a fuller picture of what happened. Instead, opposition MPs were more interested in sound bites and character assassination.

"We didn't really know what to expect. We knew it wasn't going to be pleasant, but we were prepared to provide answers on the CSSG. We did not anticipate that it was going to be like standing before a firing squad for four hours," Marc recalled. "Every time we tried to pick ourselves up, there would be another round of fire."

PUNCHING BAGS

One subject that did get a lot of time and attention in this session was WE Charity Foundation. Angus was the first to raise it, and he opened with a volley of misinformation. "You moved this money into what is essentially a real estate holding company with no oversight," he alleged. "I've never heard of a real estate holding company getting upwards of $500 million of taxpayers' money to deliver a program." When Craig and Marc tried to explain that the foundation never held any real estate, that the WE Charity board was responsible for overseeing it, and that WE was to be *reimbursed* $43.5 million at the absolute most, Angus dismissed it all with a shrug of his shoulders. "There are no accountability mechanisms," he asserted. And a moment later, when Marc said they were happy to be able to set the record straight, he sneered, "I'll bet you are."

This was a gut-wrenching moment for me because I knew Angus was taking his cue from the testimony given by Michelle Douglas just before Marc and Craig's appearance. She had fanned the flames of opposition outrage by implying that the foundation was somehow dodgy. She said, for example, that when WE Charity's executive team brought forward the idea of the foundation in 2018, the board had concerns. "We simply didn't have enough information," she asserted. She testified that she had considered the matter deeply, "thinking about the interests of stakeholders and contributors to the organization, frankly, and thinking about all the youth who had done fundraising," and that no resolution on the foundation was ultimately brought to the directors because she thought the "board did not have satisfactory information at that time."

My jaw dropped. Her answer, while true, was completely misleading. I know because I was the person delegated by Michelle and the board to oversee discussions with external counsel and management on this issue. So I understood better than anyone what the foundation was and what it was not, what information was needed and had been provided, and what concerns had been raised and addressed. Let me be as clear as I can in unpacking this: WE Charity Foundation is a registered charity; it is not a company or a business. WE Charity was the founding member of the foundation, which meant that it had certain legal and governing rights over its activities.[10] The foundation was established in consultation with WE Charity's lawyers as somewhere to potentially place the charity's real estate assets to protect them in the event that the charity incurred a significant liability. In other words, it was a way for the charity to try to ensure that its real estate—which acted as a reserve fund for humanitarian projects—would not be subject to seizure by creditors if the organization was sued and owed a large amount of money. Every prudent company and non-profit thinks about this topic. It was especially important to WE Charity because the WE GLC had just been built with funds from several large donors and was worth tens of millions of dollars.

As part of this oversight process, I engaged with outside counsel, advised the board, and ultimately determined that it would take time to develop a structure whereby WE Charity could both maintain indirect control of the real estate assets and at the same time cede control of those assets to a distinct legal entity so they would be protected from creditors. There were a lot of moving parts, and the board tabled discussion on the topic for a period because of more pressing matters. So Michelle was right when she said that the board wanted more information and paused—in 2018—on the idea of using WE Charity Foundation as a repository for real estate assets. But this had absolutely nothing to do with using the foundation for the CSSG, and WE Charity's board at the time of the CSSG never had any concerns on this topic.

When WE Charity was later told by the government that it would need to assume all liability for the CSSG in the middle of a pandemic, the foundation presented a convenient solution. It was a charity that had never been used for any prior purpose. The government agreed that this would address the demand *it had made.* "We had tens of millions of dollars of insurance," Marc explained to the FINA committee, "which we added . . . to the foundation to ensure that this whole initiative was protected. Of course, in the case of liability, the government, specifically the program, and the taxpayers were well protected. We took that issue very seriously." So WE Charity Foundation formally changed its mandate to allow it to administer the CSSG, signed the contribution agreement with the government, procured the insurance, and outsourced the actual work of administering the CSSG to WE Charity. That's it.

Michelle's testimony, however, offered none of this context and left the impression that there was something improper about the foundation itself. For opposition politicians, her open-ended statement that the board had "concerns" was manna from heaven, and they took her remarks and ran with them. Angus, in particular, was uninterested in hearing about the risk involved in assuming liability for tens of thousands of young people in the midst of a global pandemic, and instead kept returning time and again to what Michelle had said. "Your board was concerned about it," he proclaimed at one point. Then a few minutes later, he said, "The board raised questions about this. The board raised questions about this." And a few minutes after that: "That's not what your former chair said. She said she didn't know why you set this up."

No matter how often and in how many ways Craig and Marc tried to explain why Angus's claims about the foundation were mistaken at best and deliberately misleading at worst, he just kept talking over them. But other MPs did seem to gain clarity as the hearing progressed. Sean Fraser, who was a lawyer himself and called it "routine" for corporations to set up new entities to limit liability, said, "What I'm hearing is that you stood to gain absolutely nothing financially, but you were asked to take on all of the liability for placing 40,000 or more students during a global pandemic."

Pierre Poilievre, though, didn't want to talk about the nuances of the charity's structure or the finer points of the contribution agreement. He just carried on interrupting and then complaining that his questions weren't being answered. "We're going to have to invite you back if you don't want to answer the question," he said at one point. "Let's bring him back for another four hours." Again and again, he demanded answers that had already been supplied, until other members of the committee began to grow weary. "Mr. Chair, have the Conservatives run out of questions?" asked Toronto MP Julie Dzerowicz. "They're starting to repeat multiple times."

Sean Fraser made a similar observation. "I'll start by just saying how frustrating it's been to be a part of this committee meeting. I am glad that we have ample time, thankfully. The inability of members to remain silent when it's not their turn to speak is deeply discouraging. I find it disrespectful. These are the kinds of things that we learned how to do in elementary school."

I thought columnist Judith Timson, commenting on the state of civility and politeness in Canadian society in an article in the *Toronto Star*, captured the tenor of the moment well. "Moving on to that volatile political sphere," she wrote, "it was painful in terms of civility to watch the elaborately, performatively polite Kielburger brothers, Marc and Craig—in the public eye since they were teens and who now run the largest youth-powered international charity in the world—be treated with aggressive disdain and rudeness during a televised parliamentary committee hearing." Reflecting on what stood out most to her, she added, "But what struck me during the Kielburgers' lengthy testimony was the savage and unnecessarily rude behaviour of lead questioner Conservative MP Pierre Poilievre, who interrupted each Kielburger many times as they sought to explain their relationship with the government and who sounded as if he was prosecuting them for murder one."[11]

From my perspective, it was hard to see how the interests of the Canadian people were being served by the whole ridiculous display.

There were important issues being raised, and they deserved a full and proper airing so Canadians could make up their own minds instead of trying to wade through the political spin. Several MPs asked about the Kielburgers' interactions with the government, for example, and whether they should have registered as lobbyists. This was a fair question that merited a thoughtful discussion, but it didn't get that. Charlie Angus used two minutes of one of his three-minute question blocks to give a speech about lobbying and conflicts of interest, with a little misinformation thrown in for good measure. "The fact is that you didn't bother to register to lobby," he declared, "and yet you're promoting a project that is going to net hundreds of millions of dollars. I don't see how guys, men as sophisticated as you, don't recognize the obligation to follow what every other charity in the country does."

Craig tried to explain that under the Lobbying Act, people are required to register only when they are paid employees (Marc and Craig were volunteers with the charity), and when a significant portion of employees' time is spent petitioning the government. (In fact, it's 20 percent of their time. Neither the Kielburgers nor any of WE Charity's paid employees ever met that threshold over the course of a year.)[12] That wasn't good enough for Angus, who then implied that any attempt to reach out for government funding made you a lobbyist. Craig, fed up, clapped back, "That's not the appropriate definition of lobbying, sir, and I believe you know that."[13]

Angus's claim that WE Charity staff should have registered as lobbyists was not surprising given the story he was trying to tell of an organization that pulled on political strings and benefited from Liberal cronyism. His narrative depended on portraying the Kielburgers as smooth political operators who knew their way around Ottawa. My impression is that many Canadians have bought into this idea.

But the opposite is true. WE Charity sought and received very little government funding and was not reliant on it to survive. In 2020, less than 1 percent of WE Charity's operating budget came from federal funds. And perhaps even more surprisingly—according to an analysis prepared by none other than ardent WE Charity critic Mark Blumberg—*over a thousand* Canadian charities received more federal money than WE Charity in 2019.[14] Non-profits that received more than ten times as much include the Canadian Red Cross Society ($62.9 million), Care Canada ($51.7 million), Plan International Canada ($48.9 million), Oxfam Quebec ($29.5 million), and Aga Khan Foundation Canada ($29.4 million). So far from being deeply plugged into the government, WE Charity was not competing for federal dollars and did not engage regularly with government officials. There was thus no perceived need to register members of the WE team as lobbyists before Rachel Wernick reached out to Craig about the CSSG in April 2020.

After the political and media firestorm, however, WE Charity chose to join the Registry of Lobbyists, voluntarily listing all government interactions by all employees—from members of the technology team who worked with counterparts in the government to staff members who joined just one phone call. Since the Kielburgers were not employees of the charity, there was no place to list their interactions. So instead, they disclosed them all on the WE Charity website.

Of course, you would never appreciate any of this based on the questions posed to the Kielburgers and other witnesses. And the media—which could have unravelled the myth of a cozy relationship between WE Charity and the government by pointing to these facts—stayed silent. It appears there was little enthusiasm for telling a story that would make *the story* go away.

As frustrating as it was to watch the smoke-and-mirrors exchanges initiated by Angus, Poilievre, and other like-minded MPs, I could only imagine what it was like to be in the line of fire. Marc told me later that he and Craig felt utterly helpless and unheard throughout the lengthy hearing. "We sat there for four hours and were maybe allowed to answer seven or eight questions in total without being interrupted," he said. "There was really no reason for us to be there—we were just backdrops for the MPs to make their speeches and score political points. They were using us as punching bags while taking shots at the Liberals."

Watching it unfold, I could not help feeling that I was witnessing an alarming display of what I see as the increasing Americanization of Canadian politics. I suspect everyone understands what I mean by that. You can call it a zero-sum game, the politics of anything goes, allegiance to party over principles, or the ends justify the means. By any name, the bitter partisanship that characterizes so much of what happens south of the border is something that Canadians have grown accustomed to seeing. Every topic—even one as straightforward as the need to wear masks during a pandemic—becomes fodder for political finger-pointing and posturing. "Alternative facts," a term that once sounded comedic, is now the norm in the US as most politicians and news outlets peddle their own version of reality. The hard work of separating fact from fiction is left to erudite publications that fewer and fewer people read. When the public space becomes so polarized, it is hard to get things done and often impossible to find common ground with those of a different political bent. Even when people have shared values and a shared history.

As a Canadian who has been living and practising law in the US for almost two decades, I confess to having become an American political junkie. But like many consumers of political drama, I recognize that my interest often comes more from its entertainment value than an appreciation of high-minded policy debates. That is in part because cable news networks and even congressional hearings typically offer only shrill speeches designed for each party's political base. The echo chamber is noisy. And middle ground is elusive, if not absent.

As Canadians—and I say this admittedly as an expat looking back in—we have always fancied ourselves above the partisanship that causes many Americans to view all issues through a red or blue lens. After all, we are too polite to succumb to the "go for the jugular" approach. Too thoughtful to form views on important issues by reading tweets. And too secure in our social contract to allow politics to inflict collateral damage on others. To my mind, the WE Charity Scandal is an invitation to reflect on the validity of these premises. My concern is perhaps best captured in the rationale offered by Jody Wilson-Raybould when she decided not to run for re-election in 2021. "Federal politics," she said, "is . . . increasingly a disgraceful triumph of harmful partisanship over substantive action."[15]

The death threats the Kielburgers received and the social media vitriol directed at WE Charity and its staff also require us to reflect on the serious consequences of extreme partisanship and misinformation peddled for the purpose of political gain. Journalist Gary Mason described these consequences in stark and sobering terms in an opinion piece in the *Globe and Mail*.[16] Having observed the growing presence of extremist elements on the campaign trail for the 2021 Canadian federal election, he wrote, "The fact is the pandemic has unleashed, or perhaps revealed, another pandemic. One of hate and extremism that is fed by a proliferation of lies and misinformation. We witnessed the danger inherent in this phenomenon when hundreds of supporters of former U.S. president Donald Trump stormed the Capitol in January. Well, there are likely thousands, maybe tens of thousands of people in Canada who pose just as much of a threat to our institutions, to our way of life, to our democracy. Far-right extremism doesn't just reside in Canada. There are many who believe it's thriving, with social media being its poisonous life blood."

Calling out "those in positions of power and influence who are contributing to the dark pool of misinformation," Mason argued that dealing in lies cannot be dismissed as "just politics." He warned against thinking this is "innocent stuff that doesn't influence those making up the toxic mobs we have seen recently . . . We are on a perilous course right now. And unless we attack this problem with vigour, horrible things are going to happen to this country."

Going back to the FINA hearing, for me the only balanced moments came when Craig and Marc got a little testy or spoke more personally about events that had affected them or issues that were of importance to them. For instance, when Edmonton Conservative MP James Cumming tried to suggest that perhaps the Kielburgers had a scheme to make up expenses and charge them back to the foundation as a way of funnelling money to themselves, Craig pushed back. "WE Charity is being raked over the coals by inaccurate statements like yours . . . The contribution agreement outlined the eligible expenses exactly," he said. "We were not making this up on the side of a napkin." And in response to a question from Quebec MP Rhéal Fortin, who repeatedly implied that Margaret Trudeau lacked the educational qualifications to speak about mental health issues, Craig said, "Sir, she has lived a life . . . I have lost a sister-in-law from mental health issues. It's a lived experience issue; it's not an academic training issue."

The brothers also engaged in a meaningful exchange with Northwest Territories MP Michael McLeod, who talked about how the charity had created platforms for Indigenous voices to be heard in classrooms through its WE Stand Together campaign, and how it had worked to promote Indigenous history in schools. Craig noted that the organization's international development sometimes overshadowed its domestic initiatives, but he spoke eloquently about the importance of WE Stand Together and a second Indigenous-focused campaign, Sacred Circle, which was "a leadership training program for indigenous youth, most often in fly-in communities in Canada, to help young people be social entrepreneurs, to identify a problem in their own communities and then to be the heroes of their problem and help to solve that issue."

This story—of what was really at stake for students and teachers and anyone else who was a supporter of the charity and believed in what it stood for—is one the media has never taken the time to tell and opposition politicians didn't seem to want people to hear. But it's the story that matters the most in all this, and I'm glad that toward the end of the gruelling hearing, there was at least some small chance to reflect on that. In his last question of the day, McLeod asked, "What we're not hearing about is what this whole initiative was focused on, and that's the youth. That's what concerns me the most. We know youth now are facing a real loss of opportunity, and there may be no replacement program. I haven't seen it yet. Could you talk about what shutting down this whole initiative, this program, is going to cost the youth?"

Craig looked like the weight of the world had lifted off his shoulders for a moment. "A question we have never been asked by any journalist or anyone here today is what was lost when it came to young people in this process," he said. "We had an extraordinary service opportunity lined up with Rotary and others to link young people to seniors to help document their lives to help overcome the reality of dementia, with so many seniors being in social isolation. We had a beautiful program lined up with hospital networks, where there would have been support for nurses and their kids at home to make sure that they had digital mentors so that the nurses could take care of us and not be afraid. We had a beautiful partnership lined up with Tim Hortons Foundation camps and others because all of the other camps had stopped over the summer, and young Canadians would have provided digital camp coaching experiences to these youth to help mentor and support them in this process.

"All of this good was lost," he lamented. "All of these extraordinary service opportunities were lost."

When the cameras switched off, Craig told me both he and Marc slumped in their chairs. "I was exhausted," he said. "My shirt was drenched. That was the most intense four hours of my life."

SCAPEGOATS

Two days later, it was Justin Trudeau's turn to testify. But while WE's employees and co-founders had together spent more than five hours fielding questions, the prime minister himself appeared for only one hour—barely longer than a regular daily session of Question Period. He offered no defence of WE Charity and mostly sought to deflect responsibility for the CSSG debacle, other than admitting that he should have recused himself from the cabinet discussions given his family's ties to WE.[17] But he stressed that he had not put his thumb on the scale for the charity. "I did not intervene to make this recommendation happen," he asserted. "When the recommendation came forward from the public service, I sent it back . . . to say that they really needed to make sure that this is indeed the only organization that can deliver this program, and that this is done exactly the right way, because there is going to be careful scrutiny on this. At that point, I should have recused myself, but I didn't. I decided to push back instead, and that I regret."

For the first time, Trudeau also addressed the future of the CSSG, acknowledging that it was essentially dead, which meant that up to a hundred thousand Canadian students who could have looked to the program for support were on their own. "It's now July 30. Our government is delivering an up-to-$9 billion aid package for students," he said. "Unfortunately, the grant for volunteer service is unlikely to be part of the package this summer, and that is something that I regret."

The next day, July 31, Trudeau attended an event with the Public Health Agency of Canada to launch the government's COVID Alert app. Afterward, he faced questions from reporters about his FINA appearance.

When asked by a CBC journalist if the CSSG was in fact no more, Trudeau replied, "That is the element that's not happening so far. We are still looking at ways that we can coordinate, oversee, and deliver grants like that to students. We're still looking for it, but at the same time, just because the grants aren't flowing doesn't mean that young people are not stepping up in a myriad of ways across the country to contribute to their communities and to support Canadians."[18] (As I write this, we've seen the end of our second COVID summer, and there has still been no government-run program to provide grants to students for serving their communities.)

At the close of the press conference, Trudeau did make one small attempt to loosely defend WE Charity. "The challenges that have followed for the WE organization and indeed the questions that have been asked of this government have been disappointing," he said, "because it gets in the way of the help that we focused on doing for young people . . . The WE organization . . . has been extremely effective in empowering young people and getting them to volunteer. Obviously, the situation that has flowed from this is deeply regrettable, and I am deeply sorry that I didn't recuse myself from the beginning. It possibly could have avoided much of this challenge. Instead, I chose to push back and ask for extra due diligence. But that wasn't the right choice, obviously."

"My first thought after that press conference was, 'Thanks for nothing,'" Dalal told me. "Our team had worked themselves to exhaustion and had pulled off miracles to help the government deliver the program on an impossible timeline during a pandemic. We had been beaten up for it. And this was the most the prime minister could offer to defend WE? The media and politicians all said that WE Charity and Trudeau were close friends. Well, with friends like that, who needs enemies?"

CHAPTER 12

CLOSING DOORS

Having finished his testimony and offered expressions of regret, Justin Trudeau promptly went on vacation. Removing himself from the centre of the storm was a clever strategy. In his absence, the feeding frenzy continued and journalists focused their attention back on WE. The charity's already beleaguered PR team was now overwhelmed with media questions. Between August 5, the day the prime minister left, and August 18, the day he reappeared publicly, there were more than twelve thousand mentions of WE in the media, focusing on everything from lobbying issues to staff reductions to real estate sales.[1] As usual, columnist Brian Lilley at the *Toronto Sun* was in high dudgeon. "Like Icarus getting too close to the sun," he wrote, "WE and the Kielburger brothers got too close to Trudeau and it burned them bad."[2] In the *Washington Post*, David Moscrop complained that the whole affair "reeks of a culture of the insider." It reminded him of the Family Compact, he said—of the bad old days of "tight-knit groups of power-wielding courtiers captured and constrained by groupthink and a self-assuredness and sense of purpose that no mere mortal ought to own."[3]

If Trudeau had imagined he could come back from his holiday and simply turn the page, he was in for a rude surprise. He must have barely had his suitcase unpacked when he and Bill Morneau sat down for a heart-to-heart on August 17. That evening, Morneau held a news conference to announce that he was resigning as both finance minister and an MP because he wanted to run for the vacant position of secretary general of the Organisation for Economic Co-operation and Development (OECD). Most people weren't buying it. Then Conservative leader Andrew Scheer immediately tweeted, "Bill Morneau's 'resignation' is further proof of a government in chaos. At a time when Canadians are worried about their health and their finances, Justin Trudeau's government is so consumed by scandal that Trudeau has amputated his right hand to try and save himself."[4] NDP leader Jagmeet Singh had much the same take. "In the middle of a financial crisis, Justin Trudeau has lost his Finance Minister," he tweeted. "Every time he gets caught breaking ethics laws, he makes someone else take the heat. That's not leadership."[5]

This whole WE Charity thing just didn't seem to want to go away. But if people were going to keep on asking questions, the prime minister at least had a way of preventing them from getting answers.

RESETTING PRIORITIES

"Today, I have asked the Governor General to prorogue Parliament, which must happen before any government can present a Throne speech,"[6] Trudeau told Canadians at a hastily convened press announcement, during which he also confirmed Morneau's resignation. Prorogation was necessary, Trudeau explained, because his government needed to "reset" its priorities, which had changed due to the pandemic. Once Parliament is prorogued, or suspended, members are released from their duties, unfinished business is dropped, and committees can no longer sit or carry on with their work. In other words, Parliament closes.

Trudeau shut things down the day before an agency called Speakers' Spotlight was to deliver to the ETHI committee the records of all speaking fees various organizations had paid to members of the Trudeau family over the years. The prime minister's timing was highly suspect, and it fuelled the perception that he had something to hide. By extension, some thought, so must WE Charity.

The political and media narrative hinged on the idea that there was something improper in an organization doing business with the government and also paying members of the prime minister's family to speak at events. But anyone could use a speaking bureau to book Margaret Trudeau or Alexandre Trudeau. And in fact, both had been hired by a long list of Canadian charities and businesses, many of which also did a considerable amount of work with the government or accepted funding from various federal departments and agencies. The speaking bureau records would have shown the many companies and non-profits that had engaged the prime minister's family members, and Canadians would have seen that there was nothing unusual about this. Perhaps the opposition and the media, so eager to knock Trudeau down, would even have shifted their attention to some of those other organizations and businesses. Instead, it was tidier and more newsworthy to portray the actions of WE as unique and questionable. The charity was hung out to dry once again, and Canadians were left with the impression that it had done something wrong, even though there was no evidence of that at all.

Marc and Craig took in the unexpected prorogation announcement in the basement of Marc's Toronto home. As they watched Trudeau shift effortlessly from English to French and back again, the words "WE Charity Scandal" scrolled by on the chyron below. They were alone, a rare occurrence, and they absorbed the news in silence. They later told me that this was the first time they'd both realized it could all be over for WE Charity in Canada. Neither one said it aloud, but they both knew that the organization they had built over twenty-five years might not survive.

"A few friends reached out to me in the days after prorogation to say that we must have been ecstatic," Marc recalled. "It was just the opposite. Proroguing Parliament made this entire situation even more political. We knew that it would enrage Trudeau's critics, and they would channel their anger toward WE Charity. And we knew that the conspiracy theorists would come out of the woodwork. It was at that moment that we saw the writing on the wall."

While Trudeau's announcement beat down the already dejected brothers, my own sense that things were permanently headed downhill came much earlier—on July 10, when Dalal informed the board of directors that the charity was planning to proactively suspend its relationships with its corporate partners. The media environment was getting increasingly toxic, and the charity believed that cutting ties with partners before they were engulfed in the tsunami of negative press coverage would improve the chances those relationships could eventually be resurrected.

"We were looking to the horizon," Craig said. "Even early on in the summer, we knew that if WE Charity were to survive in any form, we would need our partners. And if we allowed them to step aside before being dragged into the media storm, then perhaps—once the dust settled—they would be open to joining us again. We expected that the negative media cycle would pass in the weeks ahead, giving us enough time to rebuild."

This seemed like the only viable plan at the time, given that every Canadian corporate partner would face pressure to re-evaluate its relationship with the charity in light of all that was happening. But deep down, I knew it would be hard to put Humpty Dumpty back together again. What followed were many difficult but heartfelt conversations with CEOs across Canada. Craig and Marc let them know that while the organization's international COVID relief efforts would proceed as planned, most external programs would be temporarily suspended. In follow-up emails, Marc told partner companies that the main goal was to ensure that no individuals who benefited from WE's programs would be adversely affected by the reputational issues facing the charity. When presented with these proactive requests from the charity to pause partnerships, some companies opted to fulfil their financial commitments anyway. Others redirected their contributions to different WE Charity programs that would carry on or put their funding temporarily on hold. But many agreed that it made sense to part ways and check back in when things calmed down.

David Aisenstat, CEO of the Keg restaurant chain and one of the major funders behind the WE Global Learning Centre, told me that he was fully prepared to continue backing the organization in whatever way he could. He'd been a supporter of WE's mission for fifteen years, and the Keg was the title sponsor of the first WE Day in 2007. "I'm leaving my money in the organization," he affirmed. "I don't want a penny back if they can use it in their endowment." The Keg Spirit Foundation even released a statement saying that it would "wait to learn of WE's plans and . . . remain[ed] committed to evaluating their vision for continuing to inspire young people who want to make a difference."[7]

Once again, however, the media spun things differently. In their version of events, companies like RBC and GoodLife Fitness had dropped WE like a hot potato, desperate to put distance between themselves and the beleaguered charity. CTV reported that "a flood of companies announced they were dropping their support for the embattled organization."[8] In the *Globe and Mail*, Paul Waldie published a story with the headline "Virgin Suspends WE Charity Donations, Telus Drops Partnership, as Sponsors Review Ties."[9] In fact, Telus never stopped supporting WE Charity—it actually continues to help the organization to this day by providing significant in-kind support in the form of free internet and phone services. And after listing off several companies that he said had "terminated" their contracts with WE, Waldie finally got around to mentioning that Virgin had already had to slash its donations because of the pandemic. "The airline grounded all of its planes for three months," he noted, "and only recently restarted a handful of flights. That has meant that virtually no donations have been sent to WE, since most of the money Virgin contributes comes from [in-flight donations from] passengers."

But all this coverage left Canadians with the impression that WE was being abandoned in droves by leading companies. And efforts by the organization to make clear that it had proactively suspended those relationships just made WE sound like George Costanza in the pre-emptive breakup episode of *Seinfeld*. The coverage quickly had a ripple effect, and individual donors began contacting the charity to ask what had prompted the corporate partners to terminate their agreements. Was there something the corporations knew that ordinary donors did not?

Behind the scenes, executives at those same corporations were often lamenting the situation, expressing support for the charity, and indicating that they hoped to renew ties when feasible. Telus, for instance, resisted pressure to remove Craig from the board of the Friendly Future Foundation, which funds charitable programs focused on health, education, and technology. When Paul Waldie of the *Globe* called Telus to ask whether he would remain on the board, Craig offered to step down to avoid becoming a distraction. But Telus CEO Darren Entwistle called him to reiterate his support for WE and refused the offer. "I appreciated Darren's words and his moral courage," Craig told me. His term as a board member was recently renewed for 2022.

In the public square, though, other corporate supporters of WE Charity were mostly silent as they took stock of the media whirlwind and protected their brands and reputations. Today, with the benefit of hindsight, I question whether more industry leaders should have had the courage to stand by the work of the organization and try to dispel myths and misstatements that were coming from all quarters. Many of those people had big platforms and loud megaphones. But I also understand why they rushed for cover, and why businesses had to behave cautiously when serious allegations were being raised.

"All summer, the media published inaccurate information and also refused to correct or hear the facts," Craig told me. "We were constantly on the phone with stakeholders—donors, teachers, partners—correcting all the misinformation. We tried to be proactive and connect before things spiralled, but because WE was in the headlines on nearly a daily basis, it became impossible to convince some people that there was no real problem with the charity."

Many students and teachers also offered support to the charity, but the organization was reluctant to try to mobilize them, lest they become fodder for attacks by politicians and journalists. "People ask me all the time why we didn't rely on our network to fight back," Marc told me a year later. "WE has three million followers on social media—far more than any of the politicians or pundits. We have seven thousand schools with hundreds of thousands of young people in our network. We briefly—*very* briefly—talked about the idea but quickly vetoed it. Why? Because these are mostly kids. We saw the vile words being posted on social media. People who posted positive things about the charity—people we didn't even know—were immediately met with profanity, threats, and mocking. We didn't want children, educators, or even our corporate partners to be anywhere near that."

The same concerns made them wary of encouraging current and former staff members to speak out. I spoke to many who wanted to be heard, who wanted Canadians to know their own personal stories. These were people who had put life and family plans on hold to give everything they had to the charity and its mission. They had often sacrificed more lucrative opportunities because they found working at WE so redeeming. But they had seen the same online attacks Marc and Craig had, and some worried that speaking out could hurt them with new employers, now and in the future. Unfortunately, the media often made it sound as though these staff members were reluctant to speak out because they feared reprisal from WE Charity and the Kielburgers. But in my experience, it was the other way around—they were scared to say anything positive because they knew they would be castigated on social media and they couldn't bear the abuse after the turmoil they'd already been through. The climate of fear was palpable.

HARD DECISIONS

By suspending its partnership agreements, the charity hoped to be able to move forward and refocus on its WE Schools and WE Villages programs. But the media wasn't ready to let go. The phrase "WE Charity Scandal" was still everywhere, and the negative coverage about virtually every aspect of the organization's operations never ceased.

It was alarming to see that even after WE withdrew from the CSSG, the political ramifications continued to be felt. Provincial governments were quick to distance themselves from the controversy, and that started to impact the charity's domestic programs across the country. At the end of July, a spokesperson for Conservative MPP Stephen Lecce, the Ontario minister of education, told the press that the minister was "concerned and troubled" by what he was hearing about WE Charity.[10] "This is taxpayer money. Hard-working people in this province deserve to know that their money is delivering value, and these allegations raise serious questions," the spokesperson said, adding that the ministry would not be renewing its contract with the charity. Lecce himself told the *Toronto Sun* that he was "encouraging school boards across the province to halt all [new] contracts and investigate existing contracts" with WE.[11] "They cut funding for youth mental health programs in Ontario schools during the COVID pandemic because of the charity's perceived relationship with the federal Liberals," Marc said, noting that before the CSSG debacle, Lecce's staff had constantly reached out to ask if the organization could host the minister for events at the WE GLC.

In Saskatchewan, conservative-leaning premier Scott Moe—who had spent his Christmas break at a WE partner community in Kenya and had praised Craig as "dynamic" and "resilient"—also backed away from an agreement his government had been forging with the charity to deliver mental health programming to thousands of students. The provincial NDP had attacked the premier for choosing "a Trudeau-linked, Toronto-based charity to develop materials for our schools."[12]

The politicians' willingness to walk away from mental health initiatives was particularly disturbing to me because countless studies had shown that young people were experiencing a significant increase in depression and anxiety during COVID.[13] Online learning and social isolation made it more important than ever to promote mental well-being for young people. And WE Charity had a proven track record of producing high-quality resources for teachers. No one even tried to pretend that the charity's ability to deliver was in question. This was politics, pure and simple.

It felt like the lowest point in the organization's history. The Kielburgers, WE's senior leadership team, and the board of directors had many tough conversations about what could be done to salvage the charity. For the first time, people began to openly acknowledge that the Canadian operations might need to shutter permanently. Scott Baker, who had been with the organization for twenty years, said, "At this point, our daily meetings grew increasingly sombre." The guy who usually loved reviewing financial documents and looking at spreadsheets now found it hard to face the figures on the page. "There seemed to be no way to reconcile declining funding with the needs of WE Charity's beneficiaries," he explained. "It seemed that keeping the doors open in Canada was going to mean bleeding money and not preserving funds to complete existing international programs. Every meeting involved grasping at any straw, but while we were trying to find solutions, the negative news stories kept creating more problems."

Everyone recognized that it would be challenging, if not impossible, to raise money with this black cloud hanging over the charity's head. Not only had corporate and individual donations dried up, but youth fundraising had also slowed to a trickle once schools shut down due to COVID. Even ME to WE couldn't step in to help because it was also being buffeted by the pandemic. "WE Charity was primarily funded through institutional partners, such as corporations, and earned income through ME to WE," Scott explained. "We hoped to maintain more of our general donors, but the negative media was non-stop."

Through August and into September, the team worked with external financial consultants and lawyers to game out different scenarios and see if there was a way to keep going. What if WE Charity's school in Kenya boarded students for half days instead of full days? What if the local government took over Baraka Hospital? What if the organization scaled down to a very small core team of staff and let absolutely everyone else go? "We looked to our advisers and considered the scenarios," Craig told me, emotion still in his voice many months later. "It seemed too risky to keep going as we were and potentially jeopardize everything we had built." Some decisions were relatively clear. For example, they realized it was much more cost-effective to move WE Schools resources online than to keep a few school coordinators who wouldn't have the capacity to reach all of Canada's students. But other situations were more complicated. Large projects like Kenya's WE College and the Agricultural Learning Center in Ecuador were not yet self-sustainable and needed to be maintained at all costs.

The founders and executives mapped out a possible campaign to try to correct the public record and regain the trust of Canadians. But it would take lots of time and money—both in short supply. And the well might already have been too poisoned. Some well-heeled supporters of the charity's work were prepared to (and eventually did) finance an attempt to set the record straight, especially because their own reputations and philanthropic efforts were being dragged through the mud alongside WE's. Most donors, however, wanted to contribute to programming and not an effort to clear the air. And dollars spent on restoring confidence would leave even less money for the people WE served, especially in vulnerable communities around the world.

Once the precarious state of the organization's finances and its long-term ability to fundraise in Canada were fully understood, everyone agreed that the best option was to sell off the real estate holdings, valued at approximately $40 million, to pay off debt and fund an endowment. This would be enough money to finance to completion WE Charity's half-finished development projects in communities around the world and to support key programs overseas. "Every conversation was through the lens of how we protect the projects," Marc said. "Nothing else mattered. Even the organization didn't matter. When you're clear on your purpose, the answer becomes clear." But the organization needed to move quickly. "Every month the charity stayed fully open, spending money on salaries and other expenses, meant fewer funds for the endowment and fewer projects we could support globally," Scott explained.

Once the Kielburger brothers understood the full financial impact, Marc called Dalal, who had started with the organization two decades earlier and had invested her entire professional life in WE. "After a lengthy conversation and going through the numbers and different scenarios, it just led to this painful silence at the end," she said. "We knew that there was no other alternative and very hard decisions needed to be made. It was devastating to even contemplate this, saying goodbye to something this important that had been such a big part of my life—not to mention the heartbreaking impact it would have on students and teachers here and overseas."

WE Charity in Canada had to close.

THE ONLY OPTION LEFT

Shutting down the organization wasn't as easy as hanging out a For Sale sign and waiting for offers to roll in. Projections were that it would take more than a year to downsize the staff, liquidate the assets, complete outstanding development work, and shift WE Schools programs online. When it came to the WE Global Learning Centre, Marc and Craig had to make difficult calls to Hartley Richardson and David Aisenstat, the main backers, to ask their permission to put the building on the market and redirect the funds toward the planned endowment. "I apologized for letting them down," recalled Craig. "I had tears in my eyes, and they were both incredibly gracious. They said that they knew we had fought as hard as we could against the politics. And that the money was always meant to have the greatest impact on kids, and they trusted us to ensure that happened." Aisenstat told me that he was disappointed that the vision behind the WE GLC would never be realized, but he still saw the building as a sound investment in WE's ongoing mission, and he unhesitatingly gave his blessing for the charity to use the profits from the sale to support youth mental health initiatives and programs overseas.

There was some irony in the fact that the real estate holdings, which had been the target of so much outrage in the press and among politicians, was what allowed the organization to fund the completion of many essential humanitarian programs, ensuring that people had improved food security and access to clean water. Still, it was crushing for Marc and Craig to have to let go of these tangible symbols of everything they'd spent their lives building. "Starting to wind down as soon as possible was the only way . . . to save twenty-five years of project development and sustain it for generations," said Craig. But he acknowledged how much it hurt to see this happen. "Of course it was painful. Almost every decision for the past twenty-five years was made through the lens of growing the charity—choosing an alternative high school so I could keep travelling, pursuing a degree in peace and conflict studies, and spending hundreds of days every year away from home and family. I believed in the work so deeply. I still do."

When the idea of shutting down and selling off assets was first discussed with the board at a meeting on August 20, it was like a grenade went off. Many of us had questions about what these moves really meant. Was the plan to shut down WE Charity Canada temporarily or forever? What would happen in the US? What did the financial picture look like if the organization pivoted to the US only? What were the pros and cons of taking an extra month to formulate a clear plan and communication strategy? Board members compiled dozens of written questions because we wanted to be sure we had all the facts. Near daily meetings took place as we worked through scenarios, trying to ensure that every possible option had been explored.

Many board members, including me, did not want to believe that things couldn't be made to work in Canada. The Kielburgers were prepared to do anything to salvage the organization—they even told board chair Greg Rogers that they would publicly and permanently step away from the charity. But this wouldn't have solved the fundamental problem, which was that WE was running out of money. And it would have been a massive burden for the rest of the management team to lead the soul-crushing task of dismantling the organization in Canada on their own.

I eventually came to accept that if WE Charity's co-founders firmly believed the organization could not be financially sustained in Canada, there was no point in fighting that. I also took the view that there was nothing more important than meeting our commitments to the international projects, especially since WE Days and all in-person WE Schools programs were already on hold. Most of my fellow board members shared that view. Kannan Arasaratnam called it "a gut-wrenching, tough decision," but he saw it as inevitable. Others were more resistant, though, including Greg and Gerry Connelly, both of whom were lifelong educators with enduring ties to the school system and a passion for the importance of service learning as sound pedagogy. Buoyed by the behind-the-scenes encouragement they were hearing from teachers, they believed that Canadians would come back around, and that Marc and Craig would change their minds when they realized how much support they really had. Greg called me many times and expressed the hope that we could find a way through. The issue, unfortunately, was not whether teachers continued to like and use WE Schools programming but whether the organization could stop the financial bleeding.

On September 2, Craig made a presentation to the board via videoconference. The picture he painted was bleak. "The reality is such that there's been an unbelievable collapse of funding in Canada for politically motivated reasons," he said, "and we anticipate further impacts." According to the board minutes, the projected deficit for 2020–21 was US$9,147,086, based on an income of US$15,254,583 and expenses of US$24,401,669.

I was devastated as I absorbed the news. Because I was on vacation and joining the call by cellphone, I couldn't see any other faces, but

I didn't need that to know how distraught the other board members felt. I could hear it in their voices, and all the more so in the silence. A resolution had already been prepared and circulated. It was lengthy and covered topics like transferring assets to other WE entities and withdrawing the organization's charitable registration from the CRA. I asked Dalal to read it in full two times so there was no confusion, and because it was a painful event of great consequence. We were essentially voting ourselves out of existence (at least in Canada). The vote was unanimous.

For every critic of the charity—whether it was a politician on the national stage or an anonymous troll on Twitter—there were thousands of young people whose passion for change and sense of potential had been awakened by their involvement with WE. Their voices had been largely ignored, but we were all thinking of them when we voted to close WE Charity Canada.

It was the right decision, but part of me still wondered if we had made it too quickly or if there was a magic solution we had somehow overlooked. Marc and Craig wondered the same thing. "Up until the announcement, we were still making calculations to see if we could turn things around, find a way to make it work," Marc told me later. "But the math just didn't add up." Craig agreed. "Sometimes you are left with no good choice," he reflected. "The only choice is how you exit still taking care of people."

The next step was making the decision public—and therefore making it real. Craig and Marc wanted to get their message out in their own words, so they invited veteran CTV news anchor Lisa LaFlamme and her crew to the WE GLC to tape a televised interview. The building, once filled with busloads of schoolkids and hundreds of staff, now sat empty. But the Empatheatre, where the interview would take place, was stacked high with boxes filled with former employees' personal belongings. Before LaFlamme and her crew arrived, there was a mad scramble to send those boxes to their owners or get them into storage so that Marc and Craig's announcement didn't have to take place against this depressing backdrop—a potent and all-too-real symbol of how much things had fallen apart.

SAYING IT OUT LOUD

I want to pause here and explain a bit more about what the WE GLC meant to all of us. Until COVID shut down events and emptied the building, it was a gathering place for young people from across the city. It would draw in school groups to take part in workshops or hear talks from politicians, educators, and motivational speakers. In what remains one of Craig's fondest memories, Martin Luther King III spoke to a young audience about his father, racism, and other global issues.[14] "That was incredibly powerful," Craig told me. "Talking about his father and his legacy, and having schools across the country tune in and watch, with the broadcast allowing various schools to take part and ask questions. It was just amazing."

That moment, Craig said, was everything he'd envisioned for the WE GLC when he and donor Hartley Richardson first talked about the idea while trekking across the savannah of Kenya's Maasai Mara reserve several years earlier. Richardson told Craig that WE needed a headquarters to reflect the next phase in the organization's journey. Craig imagined a space where young people could come to learn and share experiences and even find support to launch their own social ventures. The kind of place he wished he'd had when he founded WE Charity with his brother all those years ago.

Thanks to targeted donations from Richardson and David Aisenstat, the organization was able to buy a heritage building in Toronto's downtown Moss Park neighbourhood, and renovations began in the spring of 2016. It was both a model of green building practices and a showcase for cutting-edge technology. Through its Skype-enabled classrooms and state-of-the-art broadcast facilities, the WE GLC made it possible to connect Canadian schools with communities around the globe. The organization was able to provide leadership training to young people in the most remote Indigenous communities and bring together schools from as far away as Australia and Egypt in a celebration of social good. Schools, youth groups, and families could take part in training and workshops, educators could engage in professional development opportunities, and young social entrepreneurs could network, hone their skills, and create new social impact plans. And employees were excited to come to work each day in a building that buzzed with energy and hope for the future.

The WE GLC opened its doors in September 2017. Dan Kuzmicki, WE's head of enterprise services, called it a privilege to be one of the few people given a "hardhat tour" while the centre was still under renovation. "We'd no longer have to have a server room that floods because someone's using the toilet upstairs," he realized. "No more raccoons chewing our Wi-Fi." He called it the crowning achievement of his career at WE. But the building also represented something highly personal for Dan. Soon after the property was acquired and the technological vision was developed, he suffered a life-threatening illness. "My pancreas exploded, and I was borderline dead," he explained. "In a coma, several surgeries, the ICU. I was hospitalized for four months." When he eventually returned to work, it was with a renewed sense of purpose and a desire to make a lasting change. "I wanted to build something extraordinary—a once-in-a-lifetime project for generations of young people in Canada." The news that the building would have to be sold was "the worst thing," he said. "It's just an absolute shame—it was my absolute pride and joy."

Dalal also felt the loss personally. "So many special events, leadership workshops, and community activities happened in that building in such a few short years," she said. One of the most meaningful events for her took place in early 2020, when she had the privilege of hosting a citizenship ceremony featuring sixty-five new Canadians. "It was so special for me because I was part of a ceremony like that many years ago. These sixty-five people represented sixty-five different stories of triumph, struggle, and ambition in one room."

Unfortunately, on Lisa LaFlamme's tour of the WE GLC, there was none of the dynamism and energy and hope that had once filled the halls and offices. It was like a ghost town. "They say that when you die, your life flashes before your eyes," Craig noted, thinking back almost a year later. "Well, that tour was all our dreams and aspirations flashing before our eyes. And every unoccupied meeting room and unused Skype pod we pointed out to Lisa made the building feel that much emptier and more forlorn." Marc agreed. "It was a difficult six months leading up to that interview, but it forced us to confront everything that had been lost," he said. "This place was supposed to be a free space for youth to launch their own charities and social enterprises. A safe space that would make it easier for young people who wanted to make a difference than it had been for us in our youth, in the days when caring about the world's problems got you taunted and shoved into lockers. It was distressing."

Marc even made this point during the interview. "We wish you could have seen it in its prime," he told LaFlamme as he led her past a wall of photographs of early petition drives, fundraisers, and other milestones of WE's history, "with students running in and having conversations. Kind of like a science centre for kids who want to change the world." But that nostalgic mood would be overshadowed by the sombre message that he and Craig were about to deliver.

Later, seated in the Empatheatre, an emotional Marc told LaFlamme: "We're going to be announcing today that we will be winding down WE Charity here in Canada. We started the organization back in 1995, when we were kids in Thornhill, in our parents' basement. And this is our twenty-fifth anniversary as an organization. So this is an incredibly sad day for us as an organization, but an important one as well in terms of what we hope to achieve with the organizational resources for the future."[15]

Dalal was watching the taping from the sidelines and said she almost broke down when Marc uttered those words. "It obviously was not a surprise to me—I had been part of the decision-making process alongside the board. But to hear it spoken aloud, there in front of a TV camera, made it somehow more real. It was really happening. It was over."

I asked Marc and Craig what they were thinking in that moment, and they echoed Dalal's reaction, but with the added weight of feeling like they had let people down. "The more I talked to Lisa, the more the thoughts were piling up in my own head," Marc said. "The things lost and the people hurt. The WE Days and school programs that my own kids and Craig's would never be able to be a part of. The staff, who were our family—literally. We attended their weddings and family funerals, and now they were struggling. They needed counselling because of everything the past year had put them through. It became a minute-by-minute effort to keep a calm presence and not let all the grief and despair and rage come pouring out there on the camera. I'm not sure I succeeded."

At one point, LaFlamme asked Marc if he was angry, and that despair was on full display.

"Of course," he replied, fighting back tears.

"You're obviously upset," LaFlamme noted.

"Of course," he said again.

"Who are you angry at?" she pressed.

"Not angry at anything," Marc answered. "I'm angry at the situation. You know, twenty-five years of incredible passion, incredible impact. The opportunity to change lives. An amazing team, who have been there throughout that process. And then politics took over."

In hindsight, Marc told LaFlamme, he and Craig should have asked more questions of the government, but they still viewed it as the right decision to say yes to the CSSG, and even knowing the outcome, they said they would make the same choice today. "If you ask us if we had the opportunity to answer that phone call again," he said, "I would say yes, we would. As crazy as that is, during a pandemic, when [given] an opportunity to help a hundred thousand young people in this country, an opportunity to put up your hand, I'd do it all over again."

A SURREAL END

At 4 p.m. on September 9, seventy-nine days after the CSSG launched and quickly imploded into a political nightmare, twenty-two days after Trudeau prorogued Parliament and left WE Charity to twist in the wind, and just an hour before Lisa LaFlamme promoted her exclusive interview on supper-hour CTV newscasts across the country, Dalal, Marc, and Craig held a virtual town hall with all staff to share the news that WE Charity Canada was closing. Most of the senior leadership team knew what was coming, but it was something else to hear the words said aloud and with such finality.

Marc and Craig were together and looked even more forlorn and haggard than they had in their appearance before the FINA committee weeks earlier. With Craig looking on and trying not to break down, Marc took a deep breath and broke the news. "We are so grateful for each and every person's contribution," he said. "Today's news is incredibly difficult. I recognize this is a lot to take in, and we all need time to process this. I'm still trying to process it all. That said, I can't underscore enough that this decision does not negate the good work we have all done."

Craig picked up the baton to remind everyone of what had been accomplished in the past twenty-five years. "I'm so proud of all that we have achieved together," he said before recalling some of his fondest memories and the impossible goals that had been reached. "None of this could have happened without all of you."

Dalal, who had been with the organization for nearly every milestone, was overcome with emotion as she also shared her gratitude to the team. "Although this news is heartbreaking, I take comfort in the fact that we will continue to do good by protecting the youth and communities we serve. The projects will be sustained for generations to come. This was always our 'why,' and even in such difficult circumstances, our compass remains the well-being and protection of the future of young people."

It was a surreal end to what was for many people years and even decades of work. Some staff members, muted on the videoconference, cried silently. Others typed their sentiments in the live chat. Several of their comments were later shared with me. "I am a better person because of WE," wrote one team member. "I am rooted in the pride of what we have accomplished together, and what is now protected in our global partner communities." Another typed, "It's been the greatest honour of my life . . . I have met the best of friends, experienced the joy of mission-based work, and remain so proud of all that we have done." A third said, "[These] past 2 years have been some of the best in my life, seeing the impact we have on youth firsthand in schools across North America and from around the world at camp. I look forward to working hard to end our story strong!"

I spoke with two long-serving staff members who were on the call and asked them what went through their minds as they took in the news. "It was a hurricane of emotions," one told me, "but the most overwhelming was guilt. Guilt that we had failed to protect our staff, our beneficiaries, and the young people for whom we do this work in both

Canada and abroad. In what was an already emotional and difficult year compounded by a summer from hell, it felt like we'd worked so hard only to let everyone down. It was an emotional journey to get to that announcement, but the light at the end of the tunnel was the promise to support and protect what was built."

"I knew what was coming," said the second, "because I had been part of some of the discussions leading up to the meeting. But knowing it was coming did not make it any easier to hear the words said out loud. It was suddenly very real. And when my colleagues started writing in the chat about what the organization meant to them, that's what really made me break down." She told me she started replaying all her happy memories—from her first WE Day to her first trip to Kenya—but then felt overwhelmed thinking about a future that would never be realized. "By now, I have gone through every stage of grief—sometimes all seven in one day," she admitted. "Anger, guilt, and depression are most prominent, but hope is starting to make a comeback."

Not surprisingly, politicians and journalists showed little sympathy. NDP MP Charlie Angus told CTV News that same night that the closure was proof of his earlier statements about WE Charity's need for a government bailout because "this was a group that was in free fall economically."[16] Conservative MP Pierre Poilievre tweeted, "WE closure changes nothing. Finance Committee will resume investigations once Parliament opens. You can run but you can't hide."[17]

As soon as LaFlamme's interview aired, a throng of reporters and TV crews surrounded the WE GLC, blocking every exit so no one inside could leave without first providing a quote. Photographers pressed their cameras against the windows to take pictures of staff members. Even an Uber Eats food delivery for employees was hijacked by the apparently hungry press brigade outside.

While Craig was stuck in the office, someone drove onto the front lawn of his home, bringing their vehicle within feet of the living room window and repeatedly flashing their high beams and blasting the horn, terrifying Craig's wife and sons inside. The police were called once again, as they had been when Marc's home address was printed in the *Toronto Sun*.

The next morning, the headlines were no better. The *Toronto Star* blared, "Keep Watching the Money as WE Charity Shuts Its Canadian Operations, Observers Say."[18] The accompanying article carried a photo of a masked man wheeling boxes out of the WE GLC. Further down the page, Mark Blumberg opined that the closure was "more of a PR initiative to quell criticism" than an attempt to resolve issues and move forward. And Kate Bahen was back to declare that she was "having a difficult time with the math." She continued to insist, without a shred of evidence, that something fishy was going on. "With everything about WE sometimes," she said, "it looks lovely on the outside and you really need to read the fine print."

A TRAIL OF LOSS

Remarkably, in this moment and in the months that followed, virtually no politicians, pundits, or journalists reflected on what the closure of WE Charity really meant. No one sought out those who stood to lose the most—the millions of students, educators, children in developing countries, social entrepreneurs, volunteers, and staff—to hear their stories and share them with others. Certainly, no one called me or any other board members to ask what we thought. No one in politics or the media even asked publicly whether this was the right outcome, or whether Canadians were better or worse off without WE.

The failure to make space for—and to listen to—those who'd lost the most is, in my view, the saddest and most frustrating part of this story. These were the voices of thousands of WE staff who gave their hearts and souls to the mission. Of thousands of young volunteers who had travelled to WE partner communities abroad and been transformed by what they saw. Of hundreds of thousands of students who had benefited from programming in WE Schools across the country. And of those most in need—people in developing countries who relied on and partnered with WE Charity (whose profound losses I will come back to in later chapters).

It is long past time to let those voices be heard.

One of the most poignant stories of loss I heard came from Bill Elkington, co-founder of the Alberta-based investment firm JV Driver

Group. After his daughter Erika died by suicide in 2015, Elkington became an outspoken advocate for mental health care and suicide prevention. He wanted no other family to experience what his had. In 2016, he formed the Erika Legacy Foundation, which was the founding partner of the WE Well-being initiative, a program to promote mental health by supplying tools, resources, and supports for young people and educators.

When I interviewed him, Elkington was remarkably emotional and open. He told me that his daughter's suicide had devastated his family, and that he had quickly descended into depression and even considered ending his own life. "What happens with suicide is that often one leads to another," he said. "And you meet lots of families where it's not just one person who died by suicide in the family. It hits multiple people. And I almost died by suicide." It was only when he finally came to terms with the mental health dimensions of suicide that his despair—and that of his wife, Sabrina, and their other children—transformed into a drive to help others. "My generation? We're not going to change our thinking," Elkington told me. "But if we get enough youth to become this army of advocates on their own mental health as well as [that of] their family and friends, we will make a huge impact on changing the well-being of our society going forward. And so that was how we got connected with WE."

While the project will live on through the Wellbeing Foundation, its capacity and impact will be diminished. Without WE Schools bringing resources directly to students, the reach of the project is curtailed. And, Elkington told me, without WE Charity actively "teaching the teachers" how to deal with mental health issues and suicide prevention, the loss is "just absolutely huge." He said that kids used to come up to him and his wife after they told their daughter's story at WE Days and say, "Thank you. I sometimes feel that way, and I don't know who to talk to." In those moments, he felt the charity made clear to young people that "even if you don't fit in elsewhere, there's a spot for you in WE." Elkington believes that the impact of the charity's mental health programming was especially important for LGBTQ and Indigenous youth, who often feel marginalized and are a focus of the Wellbeing Foundation's outreach efforts. "What we lost is the ability to distribute knowledge and compassion and explain what's actually going on in your minds to a whole generation of youth," he said. "[WE Schools] was a delivery mechanism that had the ear of so many youth that we don't have otherwise. And when you get four million youth a year touched by some aspect of WE for ten years, that's forty million people, and we [had] an opportunity to change the outcomes for so many people, to tell them, 'You're not alone.' And now that is lost."

And what of those millions of young students? Loss of access to potentially life-saving tools and resources in the midst of a well-documented pandemic-related mental health crisis is just the tip of the iceberg. Where were the news reports about the impact of discontinuing WE Schools programming across the country, including campaigns to address homelessness and develop environmentally friendly schools? What did the media think would replace WE's teaching resources for bullying, or the hundreds of WE staff dedicated to mentoring youth groups and supporting educators? What would happen to kids who wanted to develop leadership skills or effect positive change in the world? What would be the fate of Indigenous young people who could have participated in Sacred Circle programs focused on building non-profits or social enterprises?

Craig told me that his greatest fear was that two decades of progress in youth activism would be undone. "When we started in 1995, young people were the least likely demographic to volunteer in Canada. By our twenty-fifth anniversary, they were among the most likely to volunteer. What happened was hard on us, but it also was hard on a lot of students and teachers involved in our work."

Craig's comment made me think about twins Ashleigh and Emma Dzis. They were inspired by WE to work for their community in so many ways, from collecting canned goods for the food bank to knitting hats for the homeless. Over the years, they'd run countless awareness campaigns on local and global issues and had cajoled a host of area businesses into supporting their work. Did anyone ask them what they had lost? They told me they had no intention of stopping what they'd started, but without the support of WE, they knew it would be more difficult going forward. "Our WE group is continuing," Ashleigh confirmed. "But it's been really hard because certain resources, like the WE GLC and certain online campaigns, have stopped."

Perhaps the Dzis sisters, who are full of energy and drive, would have become involved in volunteering even if WE had never existed. But millions of other children would not have been motivated to serve others. The twins told me that WE had made them feel empowered and had inspired them to keep giving back year after year. "There was something so compelling about WE and the resources that it gave you," Ashleigh explained. "And it wasn't only to raise money—it was the awareness piece as well. They made you want to come back and do the same campaigns every year."

It's clear that some things really haven't changed since Craig started out all those years ago. Most non-profits still have no idea how to really engage kids like Ashleigh and Emma or take them seriously. They don't know how to help them get started or inspire them to keep going. "You can't just put a . . . young person in a room and say, 'Okay, go and raise five hundred dollars.' You have to give them help," Ashleigh noted. "A lot of campaigns we did before we were with WE, you give some money to a charity or you do a fundraiser and we never got a single letter back or anything . . . We're like, 'Oh, okay. Well, hopefully that went somewhere and helped someone.' But WE always wrote you something, showing you every day what the impact was. It kept you wanting to come back." This kind of engagement also had a multiplier effect that I haven't seen replicated by other charities. "[Our WE Club] started off as the four of us, just doing a couple of campaigns and meeting at our house," Emma said. "The next year, we came back and we had about seven members, and then this year we have around eleven members. It just keeps growing."

I remembered that Aiza Abid had also talked about the inspiration she felt as her school's WE Club grew. Every week, she and her classmates would organize fundraisers and come up with new ways to help out in the community. She told me that she was just one of countless young people who were profoundly impacted by WE. "For children who are immersed in environments like this, they can begin to adopt inclusiveness, empathy, and compassion during such formative years of their lives," she observed. The WE Clubs provided a level of social-emotional learning that kids don't necessarily get from the school football team or chess club. "WE really encouraged you to look within your community to identify needs there," and then, she explained, the organization offered the support necessary to get projects off the ground. Aiza thinks it is the broader community that has lost out with WE's closure. "Now more than ever, we need young people stepping up and supporting their communities."

Kathleen Murray is a seventeen-year-old who started studying education at Queen's University this past fall. She was a high school student when she participated in a ME to WE service trip to Tanzania, which she said was one of the highlights of her life. "It was amazing—the warmth, all the people. It was fantastic. We were so welcomed into the community." She said the experience taught her to respect the people of those communities and feel gratitude for what she has. It also inspired a desire to translate that gratitude into action to help others. "You get so much out of it. It provides you with a greater appreciation for what you have, and you really understand how other people live. Definitely bringing the lessons home to implement with your own families and your own communities is really important."

She said she was disappointed that other students would no longer be able to have the experience she did. "I think a lot of people don't get this kind of exposure here living in Canada," she noted. "It's hard for me to really tell people and my friends here at home what it was like without them actually being there and knowing. I can try, but they won't have the same appreciation or experience that I had."

One thing I wonder about is how many of these students might have gone on to start their own non-profits, as Aiza did, or take part in the organization's programs to encourage social entrepreneurship. Those opportunities have been squandered too. As WE Incubate and WE ScaleUp got off the ground in 2020, they quickly showed how passionate young people are about social innovation and how support from WE could help bring their ideas to fruition. In one early success story, Luke Vigeant scaled his growing business, an online mental health service called Inkblot, allowing him to provide affordable, barrier-free care to more people at the height of the pandemic. In another case, sixteen-year-old Avishka Gautham from Nobleton, Ontario, founded VEGETABL, a company dedicated to teaching elementary school students how to divert organic food waste otherwise destined for landfills through vermicomposting (using worms to compost and create high-quality fertilizer). But Jon Worren, the head of WE's social enterprise programs and the former lead executive of venture and corporate programs at MaRS, fears that future Luke Vigeants and Avishka Gauthams will have nowhere to go.

"Craig and Marc Kielburger . . . created a supportive environment, and we had talented people coming to us because of what they had done," he explained. "It's going to set Canada back, the loss of that leadership. There are other [social innovation] programs around. But the environment that WE represented was unique. It will take decades for something else to really replace it." Worren also said that the media's negative portrayal of ME to WE's business model had put a damper on entrepreneurial innovation across the non-profit sector. "It's brought an enormous chill into the whole charitable sector . . . Social entrepreneurs are looking at [what happened to WE and are] scared of the same thing happening to them."

Of course, this wasn't a story you were going to read in your local paper. As far as I know, journalists never sought out Worren and asked for his views, just as they never sought out Aiza Abid or Kathleen Murray or Luke Vigeant. But what rankles maybe most of all is that they paid almost no attention to teachers and the losses they would suffer. I have spoken to many of them—from current and former board members like Greg Rogers, Gerry Connelly, and Mary-Eileen Donovan; to Donna Cansfield, the former president of the Canadian School Boards Association; to younger educators who are just starting out and drawing on what they learned from WE programming as students. Every educator I spoke to saw the value in WE and keenly understood the loss.

Ruben Borba, who was involved in WE Charity programs as a student and then became a teacher himself, spoke about the clear positive impact of engaging his kids through WE. "It gives students such a self-esteem boost," he noted, "and the power to finally say, 'Hey, look! I'm not just a student, you know. I'm a vessel of change.' Being able to have that power, to have that voice, to have that advocacy not just for themselves but for [their] communities. You see the enthusiasm, you see the students, you see the light spark in them. That realization, like, 'Hey, I can change the world. If I put myself into this—if I set my goals, if I set my passion—I can do anything that I set my mind to.'" It is "a huge loss," he said, for his students to no longer have the same opportunities to grow and realize their own capacity to create positive change.

Some educators I spoke to expressed frustration and even anxiety at the prospect of a future without WE. "Anybody that I've talked to that's an educator is . . . overwhelmed. They're burnt out and they're scared," said Massimo Mercuri, a newly minted eighth-grade teacher in the Halton Catholic District School Board, just west of Toronto. "They're scared not for themselves but . . . for the kids [who] are growing up year after year lacking the motivation that they should be having. They are lacking the experiences."

Mercuri first got involved with WE when he was studying to become a teacher and participated in a ME to WE trip to Tanzania. His own experiences with the organization then became a part of his teaching. "I'm able to . . . use my experiences in a social studies lesson and help these students understand [that] there's more [to service learning] than just cleaning up litter outside your home in Oakville or . . . donating money." He said WE Charity was providing support that no one else could, at a time when the education system has become more difficult for teachers to work in and students to learn in. "[People] don't realize the impact that it has, closing the doors to WE Charity. They don't realize that these programs exist to provide that extra support to teachers so they can then make the classroom a better experience for the kids," Mercuri said. "It's worrisome. If WE Charity isn't present, that's a loss for the generations after us."

Mercuri's concerns were shared by Tania McPhee, a teacher at the Milton, Ontario, school named for Craig Kielburger. "I'll admit that I'm not sure how we'll proceed moving forward without access to the same resources," she said, noting that she routinely used WE Schools materials in her teaching. "The organization's work really frames the entire civics unit at our school because the idea behind the WE Movement is that we have a responsibility to be engaged, to be informed, and to *care*. And we're able to rely on WE programming and resources because they don't promote any specific cause or interest; instead, the cause has always been youth empowerment."

That's why it's a particular source of frustration to her that young people were all but ignored by journalists writing about WE. "I know many students wanted their voices to be heard so Canadians could better understand how much this organization mattered to them. After all, this is the organization that gave them the leadership skills to advocate for themselves and what they believe in. It taught them that . . . their voices are powerful." It is worth noting here that current and former students involved with WE were not scarce or hard to track down. Many raised their hands—they had answers to questions that reporters should have been asking. In chapter 7, I recounted how Ashleigh and Emma shared their positive experiences with the CBC's *Fifth Estate*, and the hurt they felt upon learning that the hour-long program excluded not just their voices but the voices of all young people. The stark truth is that the media was only interested in hearing negative views—those who had something good to say weren't what the story was about. So even though WE Charity was founded to serve young people, we barely heard from them at all.

WE Charity Canada board chair Greg Rogers echoed the same frustrations. He knew many students and teachers who wanted to be heard but could not find a forum—he referred some of them to me, and I interviewed them for this book. "Throughout this entire year, I don't think I ever heard the voice of a student or the voice of a teacher," he noted, "which is sad because they were the ones who were truly impacted by this." Greg had been a teacher himself—a career he was inspired to take up when he and his wife spent time living and working in Zambia in their twenties, making him acutely aware of the value of youth service and cross-cultural experiences. It was a life event he had hoped to share with his grandson, who was supposed to have gone on his first WE trip in August 2020. "I'm so disappointed and so sad, you know . . . that he may not have this experience that he was looking so forward to."

TESTIMONIAL: TANIA McPHEE

Tania McPhee teaches Canadian and international law, world issues, and civics at Craig Kielburger Secondary School in Milton, Ontario. She has been teaching for more than twenty years and has travelled the world with her students, helping them increase their cultural awareness and gain a broader perspective on global issues and sustainable development.

I was extremely disappointed when I saw how some media sources that I have trusted for a long time covered the so-called WE Charity Scandal. Little was done to take stock of all the good that came from the organization, and worse still, no attention was paid to all the damage that has resulted from the unfair coverage. This damage has impacted not just WE Charity itself and its sustainable development work but also the legacy of the hundreds of thousands of young people who have been inspired by WE programming. Where are the first-hand accounts of the educators who have witnessed their students' growth, activism, and community leadership? Why are our experiences and those of our students being left out of the media's coverage?

Good things happened at every school that took part in WE Schools programming. Teachers and students were provided with access to meaningful leadership development tools, service-learning modules, and youth engagement events. Through their participation in the WE movement, generations of Canadian students found ways to look beyond themselves and become agents of change. Much of the work that WE Charity inspired has taken place in our local communities. Hundreds of Canadian non-profit organizations have benefited from these initiatives. All the negative and unbalanced media coverage has been devastatingly damaging to the legacy of the young people who have devoted countless hours to volunteering with non-profits, spearheading initiatives, and fundraising in their schools and communities to combat issues like food insecurity, the Indigenous water crisis, and cyberbullying. This was authentic and meaningful work that contributed to a better, more equitable world for us all. One of the real tragedies—perhaps the biggest in all this—is that the youth of today and the future will no longer have access to this incredible programming and these life-changing opportunities. This story is missing from the media coverage, and as a result, from the consciousness of many Canadians.

To watch politicians and the media destroy all this without considering the perspectives of educators and the young people we serve has been profoundly disappointing. Canadians have a right to know what we lost.

Like Greg, who knew Marc when he was still a student at Brebeuf College School, Gerry Connelly saw WE grow from almost the beginning. She was the director of education at the Toronto District School Board when Craig and Marc asked her if she would support an event celebrating youth service. Connelly thought it would involve maybe a few hundred students and just about fell over when she realized the brothers were talking about thousands. But she backed it because she saw that the charity was making cultural change happen in schools across Canada. She believes that students and teachers will continue to be active in creating positive change in the years to come, but she worries their impact will be diminished. "I think WE made it clear that students wanted to be involved in the community, wanted to provide service, wanted to be involved in the whole issue of inclusion and equity and social justice, and that's never going to go away and nor should it," she said. "But without WE Charity, there's now a big gap in terms of the contribution that students can make, and I feel very sad about that."

CHAPTER 13

MANUFACTURED OUTRAGE

On September 23, 2020, Governor General Julie Payette, soon to be forced out of office in a scandal of her own, delivered the Throne Speech that opened the second session of the forty-third Parliament of Canada. With a masked Justin Trudeau sitting by her side, Payette laid out the Liberal government's plan for meeting the challenge of "the most serious public health crisis Canada has ever faced."[1] There was ambitious talk of supporting people and businesses for as long as was necessary, strengthening the middle class, creating jobs, and fighting discrimination of every kind. Payette touted the government's existing and proposed COVID-related measures, including the Safe Return to Class Fund, the Canada Emergency Response Benefit, the Action Plan for Women in the Economy, and the Black Entrepreneurship Program. But in all that, there was no mention of the CSSG, and the words "volunteerism," "non-profit," and "charity" were never uttered.

It was the start of fall 2020, and a lot of people seemed ready to put the tumultuous events of the summer behind them. And who could blame them? The economy was still in a shambles, a vaccine was still just a dream, and the country, as it turned out, was at the start of its worst COVID wave to date. Canadians could hardly be faulted for thinking there were bigger issues to address than the CSSG and WE Charity.

But evidently, someone forgot to tell that to the politicians. As everyone else was trying to look ahead, the opposition-dominated ETHI committee was continuing to dredge up the past.

A MATTER OF PUBLIC RECORD

By September, the ETHI committee had already been looking into the CSSG for months. "But wait!" you may be thinking. "Wasn't that the FINA committee?" In truth, it's hard, even for those of us immersed in these events, to keep straight the activities of two sometimes overlapping committees populated by many of the same politicians and tasked with examining the same basic issues. That was by design. The opposition parties wanted to keep the CSSG story alive and put as much of a dent as possible in Justin Trudeau's poll numbers, especially with popular new COVID spending on the table. To that end, they sought new angles to argue that there was more to be uncovered about the scandal, and thereby manufactured fresh controversy. And the pundits and journalists who had been relying on a steady stream of WE-related stories to generate clicks and boost revenues were only too happy to partner in the effort.

It mattered not that by this point, there really was no mystery left around the CSSG. The facts were a matter of public record, and the FINA committee had already heard from thirty-one witnesses. To certain members of the ETHI committee, though, it was as if none of that had ever happened, and through the rest of 2020 and into the spring of 2021, they decided to revisit many of the same questions that had already been put to rest.

And here, the Liberals did themselves no favours. In proroguing Parliament, the prime minister had bolstered the narrative that the government was continuing to hide something. When thousands of pages of documents were released to the public on August 18, Pierre Poilievre convened a press conference the next day so he could hold up selectively chosen pages of heavily redacted text. "This page blacked out," he complained to the press as he dramatically tossed each document aside. "This page blacked out. This page blacked out. Why don't we ask what's in those pages at a parliamentary committee? Well, I'll tell you why: Justin

Trudeau shut down those parliamentary committees."[2] (The redactions in question were not made by WE Charity. In a letter to the committee, Ian Shugart, then clerk of the Privy Council, said the redactions were made either because of cabinet confidentiality or because the content was unrelated to the CSSG.)

Prorogation even began to generate media attention beyond the country's borders. "Trudeau's Suspension of Parliament Amid Ethics Controversy Fuels Cries of 'Coverup,'" read a headline in the *Washington Post*.[3] The article quoted then Conservative leader Andrew Scheer as saying, "Justin Trudeau is walking out on Canadians in the middle of a major health and economic crisis in a disgusting attempt to make Canadians forget about his corruption." The BBC reported that Trudeau had narrowly survived a confidence vote that would have toppled his government, then noted that his controversial decision to suspend Parliament had "cut short several parliamentary committees looking into the WE Charity scandal."[4]

Andy Stillman, director of the US-based Stillman Family Foundation, a strong supporter of the charity, grew increasingly concerned with these and other reports. "I was confused, reading all the negative press about WE and its founders," Stillman said in an interview. He felt a responsibility to make an informed decision about whether to continue his foundation's financial support. "For my sake, and the sake of our family's foundation, I felt we needed to cut through the politics and get to the truth."

Stillman decided to fund two independent reviews by non-partisan experts. The first was by Dr. Al Rosen, the forensic auditor who looked at the charity's finances and was discussed in some detail in chapter 6. The second was a close examination of the CSSG and how it was awarded. For this report, Stillman tapped Matthew Torigian, the former deputy solicitor general of Ontario and currently a distinguished fellow in the Global Justice Lab at the University of Toronto's Munk School of Global Affairs and Public Policy. Torigian was eminently qualified, and importantly, he had no previous connection to or involvement in WE that could make him vulnerable to accusations of bias. When I spoke to him for this book, he told me he had laid down strict conditions to keep his work independent, telling Stillman and the charity, "I'll write what I write. You can do what you want with the report. But if you don't like it, I'm not changing it because it stings. It'll be what I report on it."

Torigian and his team examined more than five thousand pages of documents, emails, and other relevant material released by the federal government to the FINA committee and hundreds more pages of documents given to the committee by WE Charity. His findings, based on this extensive paper trail, reconfirmed the testimony of key civil servants, including Rachel Wernick and Ian Shugart, and elected officials like Bardish Chagger and, yes, Justin Trudeau.[5] Summarizing his conclusions in an op-ed in the *Toronto Star*, Torigian wrote, "The case is clear: WE Charity was not looking for a lifeline. It didn't get special treatment. It was properly approached by the bureaucracy. And neither the charity nor its co-founders stood to profit from the CSSG. But a story like that doesn't sell papers or threaten to bring down a government."[6]

Even though the facts on the ground were clear, they were largely ignored by opposition politicians and the media. In the public square, WE Charity and the Kielburgers continued to be looked upon and treated as if they themselves were the architects of the entire government process. They had lost countless donors and corporate sponsors, spent hours testifying before the FINA committee, suffered death threats, been dragged through the mud in the press, and endured irreparable reputational harm. And of course, WE Charity Canada—the product of twenty-five years of toil—was no more.

But here's the bitterest irony of it all. What if WE Charity had actually done everything it had been accused of doing in relation to the CSSG? Let's say, for example, that the Kielburgers had in fact enjoyed a cozy relationship with Trudeau and Morneau, pulled every string, leveraged every friendship, hired Margaret Trudeau and worked with Sophie Grégoire Trudeau as means of currying favour with the Liberal government, and invented the whole idea of the CSSG to get themselves a bailout. So what? The organization still would have done nothing wrong had Trudeau and Morneau recused themselves, and had the bureaucrats decided to solicit multiple bids for the program. But these were the two things that WE Charity had absolutely no control over and no opportunity to influence. Nobody ever asked for the organization's views on how the CSSG should be sourced or whether cabinet ministers should recuse themselves. And the charity never held itself out as having any expertise on these topics. The bottom line is that even if WE and the Kielburgers had done the worst things they were accused of doing as a means to secure the CSSG, it wouldn't have mattered if government actors had properly managed their own potential conflicts of interest.

None of this, of course, was of any relevance to ETHI committee members who did not want the music to stop. They decided to keep throwing mud and see what would stick, with little regard for anyone who might get hurt in the process.

POLITICAL PAWNS

When Parliament got back to business on September 23, all parliamentary committees also resumed their work. It took a while for ETHI to get back up to speed, though. In fact, the wheels of government being what they are, the members debated process for months and didn't get around to calling their first witness until November 27. It was December before things really got rolling.

On December 7, the committee heard from Martin Perelmuter, the president and co-founder of Speakers' Spotlight, a company that books speakers for conferences, meetings, and events. Speakers' Spotlight represents such well-known Canadians as astronaut Chris Hadfield, author Neil Pasricha, Olympian and mental health advocate Clara Hughes, and Margaret and Alexandre Trudeau. The Trudeaus, of course, were the reason the committee was interested in the agency. What's less clear is why Perelmuter himself needed to appear. As he noted in his opening statement, he had "no knowledge pertaining to the operations of WE Charity, the Liberal government or the Canada Student Service Grant program."[7] Once again, here was a witness with nothing to offer, and the session should have ended right there.

In fact, Perelmuter, his wife and co-founder, and various employees of Speakers' Spotlight had been dealing with the committee in the background since before Parliament was prorogued. On July 24, the company had received a letter from the committee clerk, asking for records pertaining to *all* Trudeau family speaking engagements for the past thirteen years. The Perelmuters were given just three days to comply—an impossible deadline complicated by the fact that all the agency's employees were working from home. "Consequently," Perelmuter told the committee, "we asked for an extension to address the order, which was granted to us." But before the revised deadline arrived, Parliament was suspended, and the clerk contacted them again to explain that the committee could not receive the documents until it had resumed its work. Seems straightforward enough. Which is why Perelmuter was surprised when, just a week later, he got a letter from Conservative MP Michael Barrett, urging Speakers' Spotlight to do "the right thing"[8] and immediately release the documents to the public. Barrett presumably understood that the committee on which he served—the Standing Committee on Access to Information, *Privacy* and Ethics (italics added)—was not able to receive the documents, and that Perelmuter would be violating the privacy rights of his clients if he unilaterally released the information Barrett was demanding. In other words, Barrett's version of doing "the right thing" involved breaking the law. He apparently didn't care.

This was all performative—the first shot in what rapidly turned into an all-out public relations war. Barrett wasn't interested in the minutiae of people's contracts—he wanted Canadians to think that the Perelmuters were stonewalling at the behest of the Liberals. Before his letter had even hit Martin Perelmuter's inbox, it was already in the hands of a reporter for the Canadian Press, who then contacted the agency looking for comment. At the same time, Barrett released the letter on social media, hoping to stoke outrage among his followers.[9]

His fellow Conservative MP Candice Bergen also got in on the act, posting the business phone number for Speakers' Spotlight on her own social media channels and encouraging people to harass the Perelmuters and their staff.[10] "A series of events that happened after that put us in a really difficult situation," Perelmuter explained to the committee members, "something I've never experienced before . . . For the first time in my 25-year career I was in a situation where I didn't feel that I could properly protect [employees] from what was going on. We had to get the police involved. It was a really nasty situation." Threats were received.

Staff members were concerned for their personal safety. Someone discovered Farah Perelmuter's private cellphone number and, her husband said, "posted it on some Facebook group with a photo of her, calling her disgusting and derogatory things. Her phone started ringing day and night, with all kinds of people calling." She was terrified and didn't want to leave the house. All pleas to the Conservatives to call off their attacks fell on deaf ears.

The Kafkaesque situation continued into November, when the committee clerk got back in touch and asked for records relating to speeches made by Justin Trudeau and Sophie Grégoire Trudeau going back to 2008. The Perelmuters advised the clerk that, consistent with Canadian privacy regulations, they held on to paper records for seven years. The company had some electronic records and would produce them, but anything on paper had been discarded before the committee requested the materials. Once again, Barrett saw a chance to make something out of nothing and set off a firestorm by falsely accusing the Perelmuters of destroying evidence.[11] The *Globe and Mail*, for its part, amplified this manufactured controversy with the headline "Speakers' Agency Purged Some Records of Trudeau Family Events Related to WE Charity Controversy."[12]

When I spoke to Martin Perelmuter in mid-2021, it was clear that the stress of those moments had stayed with him. He knew nothing about the cssg and had no affiliation with WE Charity or any political party, yet he felt like he was caught in the middle of a hurricane. "The scary part was, you wake up every morning and the first thing you do is you look at trashiness on social media accusing us of all kinds of crazy things," he told me. "You wonder what crazy stuff is going to be written today." He lamented that the consequences of this fiasco would likely haunt his agency for years to come. "When you're using private citizens or small business to accomplish what you see as a political game—that, to me, should never happen."

When Perelmuter told his story to the committee, various members offered their apologies for what he, his wife, and their employees had been through. Liberal MP Brenda Shanahan likened it to McCarthyism, "where many innocent people were dragged in front of committees and aspersions were made." Even Charlie Angus had some heartfelt words, telling him, "I don't think that should have happened. I appreciate the fact that you've come here and given us clear answers. That's what we've asked of you and you've delivered." But there were no words of contrition from Michael Barrett or any of the other Conservatives on the videoconference that day. In contributing to the narrative that the Liberals were using their supposed friends to obstruct the committee's investigation, the Perelmuters and Speakers' Spotlight had served their purpose, and the opposition members didn't appear to care about the damage done in pursuing that goal. Nor, for that matter, did the Liberals. They had managed to successfully shift the public's attention away from the prime minister's family members and his own alleged ethical lapses.

In some ways, though, Martin Perelmuter got the last word when he reminded all members that as people in a public role, their words and actions have particular consequences. "I believe in this process. I believe in this committee," he said. "That's why we're here. That's why we've co-operated through the whole process. That's why it's doubly disturbing, because if the work was done here at the committee, I would have no issue with answering questions and providing the information or documentation that was requested . . . [But] it was taken outside of the committee and thrown into the public sphere . . . and we were just held out to dry."

You might think people would have been shamed into better behaviour by this whole embarrassing episode, but of course that wasn't the case. In fact, the same day that Martin Perelmuter appeared, the committee had also asked to hear from Victor Li, WE Charity's CFO. This set off another series of events that demeaned everyone concerned.

Victor grew up in China and studied economics at one of the country's most prestigious universities before immigrating to Canada in 1999. Once he'd qualified as a chartered professional accountant, he wanted to give back to the country that had welcomed him. He found his perfect fit at WE, where he became CFO of both WE Charity and ME to WE. He'd been with the organization for more than twenty years.

Unfortunately, Victor went on medical leave early in 2020, when he was diagnosed with a cerebral aneurysm—a bulging artery in the brain that, if it ruptured, could cause paralysis or death. When he was called to testify, his legal counsel, Megan Savard, wrote to the committee to make it clear that the stress of live testimony would put his health at risk.[13] Savard offered two options: Victor could provide written responses to questions, or the committee could reschedule his appearance when his condition was stable.

This was the first in a series of escalating exchanges between the committee and Savard as hostile MPs ignored her repeated warnings about Victor's health and tried to frame him as a shady character evading their questions. "Seven months in, we have had obstruction, refusals and denials to participate," complained Charlie Angus in one committee meeting.[14] He was one of the most vicious in his attacks on Victor, downplaying his condition as "feeling sick" and accusing the whole organization of having "a sense of entitlement."[15] Not surprisingly, pundits like Charity Intelligence's Kate Bahen jumped on the bandwagon, tweeting, "WE CFO declines invitation to answer Ethics Committee questions. This is outrageous unaccountability and shames Canada's charity sector. Enough. Parliament should revoke all charities that Victor Li oversees."[16]

Marc and Craig couldn't believe it. Marc remembers thinking that the demands for Victor to testify could literally kill him. "The committee members knew that," he told me. "And they simply didn't care." Craig had a similar reaction. "There was no thought to him as a person, to his wife or his daughter," he said. "Watching the committee meetings and seeing the media and social media attack his reputation—the lack of human decency and compassion made me furious."

Even when the committee finally agreed to make some accommodations, MPs handed over almost two hundred highly detailed and involved questions and gave Victor just one week to answer them.[17] Many of the questions fell entirely outside his knowledge and responsibilities as CFO. He was asked, for instance, to provide data showing that 79 percent of young people involved with the charity voted in the 2011 Canadian election. Even legitimate questions sought a volume of material impossible to compile in a week's time. Victor was asked to provide a list of all schools the charity had built, "along with the country, addresses/location, and what donor funds went into its construction." There were literally tens of thousands of donors who had supported programs around the world over the twenty-five years the charity had been in existence. Committee members even demanded that Victor provide information on the personal finances and holdings of WE staff members (not only the Kielburgers).

Scott Baker had endured his own interrogation before FINA. But that was nothing compared to what he saw with his long-time colleague and friend. "When Victor said he needed help answering some of the questions, I expected that he was looking for access to files he didn't have at home. He had been off for months by this point," Scott recalled. "When I saw the questions, it was so overwhelming, the sheer volume. There was nothing logical or fair about them. I can only imagine the stress this caused Victor."

On March 15, just a few days after the initial deadline, Victor delivered his answers to one hundred questions, while continuing to work on the rest. But this was deemed unsatisfactory. At the March 22 meeting, Angus ranted that Victor had undermined "the trust" of the committee by not responding to the entire list within the given time frame. That evening, Canadaland posted Victor's written answers to the committee, including the cover letter from his lawyer, and reported that he risked a contempt charge if he didn't respond to the remaining questions within five days.[18] Canadaland's scoop meant that a member of the government committee charged with addressing privacy issues had decided to violate Victor's privacy by leaking confidential correspondence to the media. I can't tell you for certain which MP was responsible, but Charlie Angus was the only one quoted in the Canadaland article, and a posted list of thirteen questions that Victor allegedly failed to answer was identical to a list Angus read out in the committee meeting. (In 2018, Angus had also been sanctioned by the ethics commissioner for violating confidentiality requirements in connection with calls for other parliamentarians to be investigated.)[19]

With her client facing a barrage of false statements by MPs and resulting negative media coverage, Megan Savard felt she had no choice but to disclose Victor's medical condition to the public. "According to his doctor," she wrote in a letter she sent to the committee and also posted to social media, "a return to full-time work, or other exposure to stress, could cause a rupture of the brain aneurysm, permanent disability or death."[20] Committee members had known about the aneurysm for more than a month, but they could no longer pretend that wasn't the case. The feigned outrage had to end before ordinary Canadians became offended at the treatment of an ill man. At their next meeting, Angus said he was "hopeful" for Victor's health and not interested in "creating undue stress," but he also said he was "surprised" by Savard's letter (despite her four earlier communications about Victor's medical condition) and suggested he still could not take Victor and his lawyer at their word.[21]

Marc was, and still is, appalled by the committee's behaviour towards his friend and colleague. "Out of everything from the past year, it stands out as one of the most despicable moments I could have imagined from [people] in a position of power." I could only interview Victor briefly—fifteen minutes, and only in the morning, was all the energy he could muster. The effect of all this on both his health and his belief in Canada was distressing to see. "One of the reasons I gave up Chinese citizenship is because of my faith in democracy," he told me. But now, he told me, he felt betrayed. "I couldn't believe it. I couldn't sleep because this seemed like a nightmare. I thought it was not real. It was not the Canada I came to know. My trust and dreams have been broken."

Although the year-long affair had already been marked by plenty of low points, the treatment of both Perelmuter and Li underscored for me just how low some politicians were willing to go. ETHI committee members damaged a small business, subjected innocent people to threats and abuse, and compromised the health of a well-meaning WE employee who had absolutely nothing to offer on the topic of whether the Liberal government had violated ethics laws. All to create the impression that there were unanswered questions, although there were none. Elected representatives have more influence and bigger platforms than ordinary citizens, and in my view, they also have a corresponding obligation to think about the impact of their words and actions on private citizens. Making a game of scoring political points at all costs, as happened here, debases us all.

CALLING THE COPS

Although Marc and Craig had already testified before the FINA committee for four hours—a nearly unprecedented amount of time—it came as no surprise that certain members of the ETHI committee wanted to haul them in again. If it was possible to keep a whiff of controversy alive, opposition politicians were going to go for it. Craig and Marc, in equal parts exhausted and exasperated, agreed to voluntarily appear and were booked for March 8.[22]

Just a few days before their appearance, however, Charlie Angus dropped a bomb by essentially calling the cops on WE. He sent letters of referral on his parliamentary letterhead to the RCMP and the CRA demanding investigations into the charity's operations and publicly announced that he had done so.[23] This was a significant escalation. At this point, politicians had insisted that WE Charity and the Kielburgers be investigated by two parliamentary committees, four federal commissioners (the ethics commissioner, privacy commissioner, lobbying commissioner, and languages commissioner), and now criminal and tax authorities.

As a board member, I felt confident that neither the organization nor the brothers had engaged in any criminal activity, but things seemed to be spiralling out of control, and the organization's exposure seemed to be increasing. After consulting with counsel, the board and WE Charity management decided that the Kielburgers should no longer testify—at least not without the organization's lawyer being present. The brothers might take a reputational hit for backing out—and expressed a lot of anxiety over doing so—but it didn't make sense to appear before the ETHI committee under these circumstances. If politicians like Angus wanted the RCMP to ask questions, then he could not have the privilege of asking the very same questions himself in a parliamentary forum.

Appearing on CBC's political talk show *Power & Politics*, Guy Giorno, former chief of staff to Stephen Harper and a lawyer for WE, concurred with this view. "If you've got an allegation about you, which is with the police, you talk to the police about it," he said. "If you've got a matter or allegation about you with Canada Revenue Agency, you talk to Canada Revenue Agency. No Canadian is expected to talk to the police and also answer questions to your Conservative, Liberal, New Democrat member of Parliament about the same things the police are already investigating. That's just . . . not how we do things in Canada."[24]

Predictably, this resistance brought the opposition members to a full boil. Charlie Angus declared that he was "very, very perplexed" by the Kielburgers' stance and said he wanted to confer with his committee colleagues to decide how to respond.[25] Michael Barrett wasn't willing to wait—he tweeted that the brothers would be issued a summons to appear "in the interest of accountability to Canadians."[26] The next day, Pierre Poilievre tweeted a threat to have them both arrested. "I've got news for the Kielburgers: you will testify," he wrote. "If not, Parliament can have the Sergeant[-at-Arms] pay you a visit—and you don't want that."[27] The fact that Poilievre didn't even sit on the ETHI committee didn't seem to matter to him.[28]

Even though they had never been issued a summons—they had voluntarily agreed to testify when initially asked—Craig and Marc were soon staring at newspaper articles that amazingly implied their arrest was imminent. The *National Post* devoted many column inches to enumerating all the things that could happen to them if they stonewalled.[29] "At this point, the committees could issue a summons, compelling the Kielburgers to attend," the paper reported. "If they continue to refuse, according to the House of Commons Procedure and Practice, the committee can report it to the House of Commons . . . and they will be 'called to the Bar'—a literal brass bar across the House of Commons— to explain themselves. The House has the power, similar to a court, to compel someone's presence." *Post* columnist Rex Murphy, meanwhile, fulminated about the brothers' refusal to appear. "These two wannabe Gandhi's," he wrote, "are laying down conditions for Canada's Parliament. Two glib salesmen of western do-gooderism are telling Parliament what it may or may not expect from them!"[30] And of course, the *Toronto Sun*'s Brian Lilley also weighed in. "They built their charity, their wealth and their business by courting the spotlight, celebrity and the company of politicians," he said. "Now, Craig and Marc Kielburger are shying away from taking centre stage."[31]

"We had to ensure that our eldest daughter did not see the newspapers or any form of news over those two weeks," Marc told me, looking back months later. "I always thought that the hardest conversation with my daughter would be about dating or career choices. I never imagined having to explain why members of Parliament were threatening to arrest her father."

Craig was listening to talk radio in his car when he heard Poilievre suggest the sergeant-at-arms might turn up at their door, and he had to pull to the side of the road and compose himself. "It was reminiscent of the Hillary chants in the US: 'Lock her up. Lock her up,'" he noted. "But they were talking about me and my brother. It was surreal."

It was almost exactly a year after Rachel Wernick had called on the charity to help, and for Scott, it felt like a nightmare he couldn't wake up from. "There we were, one of Canada's top charities, being called on by the government to help deliver one of the most important pandemic support programs," he said. "Less than a year later, we've lost everything. Our organization is closing, the media is tearing us apart, and politicians are threatening to arrest our founders for crimes they didn't commit."

"COME ON, GUYS"

The brinksmanship carried on for weeks. until finally the ETHI members agreed that WE Charity's lawyer, Will McDowell, could be there alongside the Kielburgers—so long as he didn't speak so much as a word to the committee. Craig and Marc appeared on March 15. By this point, the media had reached such a frenzied pitch that the hearing was broadcast live on CBC News Network (most committee meetings are lucky to be picked up by CPAC).

When they'd testified before the FINA committee the previous July, Craig and Marc had opted not to push back on or be baited by hostile and provocative attacks, trying instead for a conciliatory approach. But this appearance would be different. After enduring months of sustained abuse and the collapse of the charity to which they had dedicated their lives, the Kielburgers had had enough. From Marc's opening statement, they made it clear that they weren't going to continue turning the other cheek.

"This forum doesn't give WE Charity, or us, the legal protections guaranteed to Canadians," Marc said. "Politicians are not impartial. Without recognizing our right to present our own evidence, this committee is trying WE Charity in the courts of public opinion and forcing testimony."[32] He also called out the lies and misinformation that had been spread—even by MPs logged into the videoconference at that very moment—and pointed out that because of parliamentary privilege, Canadians were powerless to hold unscrupulous politicians accountable. "If today is anything like our committee appearance nine months ago, you will make your speeches, denounce us, ask your questions, answer them yourself and then ignore our answers," he concluded, accurately predicting the mudslinging that was to follow.

For the next three hours, Canadians were treated to a rehash of the FINA committee testimony, with barely a new detail added. It was a political circus, and once again, Pierre Poilievre (who had inserted himself into the proceedings of a committee he did not even sit on)[33] was the ringmaster. He demanded that Craig and Marc total up the fees and expenses paid to members of the Trudeau family. The figures had been made public almost a year before, but Poilievre insisted, for the sake of theatre, that the brothers calculate the sums live. "You're going to get this number on the record," he barked, "and you're going to testify it into the record under oath because I want the total." Since those numbers were already a matter of public record, I can only assume he wanted them to repeat them on camera as a sound bite for later use in Conservative political attack ads.

Throughout the session, Angus and Poilievre constantly peppered their remarks with snide and disrespectful asides. "Come on, guys!" and "Nobody is buying this," said Angus. Poilievre persistently called Craig "my friend," as though Craig were his opponent in an academic debate rather a citizen whose integrity was being challenged on national television. At one point, Poilievre even bluntly accused Craig of perjury. "You're in a lot of trouble here, my friend," he said. "You're under oath. Perjury is a crime." This clip was replayed constantly in the media, especially by Canadaland. Of course—leaving aside that in Canada, a false statement before a parliamentary committee is not prosecuted as criminal perjury—the Kielburgers *had not lied about anything*.

Marc later told me that he was thinking about his time as a page in the House of Commons—about his idealistic belief that democracy was happening in that place, and he was helping it. But that March afternoon's theatrics crushed any idealism that remained. "The verbal shoving and shouting over each other, the lying, the sensationalist posturing for the sake of a video clip to play on their Twitter account or a sound bite for the evening news—it was like nothing I ever witnessed as a page, even in the worst moments of Question Period."

Craig said it took every ounce of control he could muster not to shout at these people whose actions had destroyed his and Marc's life's work, taken opportunities away from countless young people in Canada and around the world, and ruined the livelihoods of so many. "And here these MPs were, still at it for nothing more than political gain," he told me. From my perspective, there was not even the slightest pretence of trying to get to the truth. Even the *National Post*'s Matt Gurney—no friend to WE—said as much in his column the next day. "It's important to note that, in a way, brothers Craig and Marc Kielburger are right to claim that their organizations have been brought low by politics," he wrote, while noting how little of this latest session had to do with Trudeau and the Liberals. "If you've closely followed the whole sad saga to date, you didn't learn much on Monday. And if you came into it knowing nothing, you wouldn't have come out of it knowing much more than you started with."[34]

But as usual, other journalists were less dispassionate. *Globe and Mail* columnist Konrad Yakabuski, for example, published an opinion piece titled "The Kielburgers Need to Grow Up," in which he referred to them as "petulant spoiled children" and said "the self-pity they oozed on Monday smacked of immaturity."[35] And on a media panel on CTV's *Power Play*, Robert Fife, the *Globe and Mail*'s Ottawa bureau chief, called the Kielburgers "slimy grifters." (Some months later, in what amounted to a huge breach of journalistic ethics, Fife laughingly admitted in an interview that there were "lots of times where I think I probably was unfair, or I torqued the story too much." It was a moment captured by journalist Amy MacPherson and posted to her Twitter page.[36] And a good thing too because Fife's confession was later cut from the rebroadcast of the show.)

THE VERDICT COMES IN

On May 12, two months after the Kielburgers' turn at the ETHI committee and more than a year since WE Charity took on the CSSG, Ethics Commissioner Mario Dion issued the long-awaited report on his investigation into the government's handling of the program. It was a vindication—although one that arrived far too late to save WE Charity.

Unlike the highly partisan MPs on the ETHI committee, the ethics commissioner is a non-partisan and independent officer of Parliament. So Dion's findings stood in a stark contrast to the past year of politically charged accusations and posturing. His report was unbiased, factual, and clear.[37] On the CSSG itself, he concluded that "the creation and eventual ratification of the CSSG was not done improperly."[38] The commissioner cleared Trudeau of wrongdoing and found that the evidence showed he was not involved in the recommendation to appoint WE Charity as administrator of the CSSG. Dion stated unequivocally that the prime minister "did not give preferential treatment to WE."[39] As for former finance minister Bill Morneau, Dion found that he did have a conflict of interest and should have recused himself from the cabinet decision to appoint WE. This was because Morneau and Craig Kielburger could, in Dion's interpretation of the relevant statute, reasonably be thought of as friends. But even here, Dion made clear that nothing untoward came of this conflict. "I found no evidence," he wrote, "that Mr. Morneau was directly involved in the development of the CSSG's delivery model, including [Employment and Social Development Canada's] decision to propose WE as its administrator."[40]

In short, Dion confirmed what the organization had been shouting into the wind for so long—the government needed a third party to oversee and manage the CSSG; non-partisan bureaucrats at ESDC had recommended WE for that role; departures from normal practices were reasonable because of how quickly the CSSG program needed to be rolled out; and the prime minister and finance minister had not tipped the scales in favour of the organization.

For Marc and Craig, the reports brought both relief and anger. "I wanted to lean out a window and scream, 'You mocked us, called us liars, bullied and harassed our staff, and tore apart a charity built over twenty-five years,'" Marc recalled. "But there it was in black and white, from the mouth of an impartial and unimpeachable parliamentary officer."

"To be honest, I still can't entirely wrap my head around it," Craig told me. "They demolished decades of work by thousands of staff and countless others. Hurt so many innocent people. Wasted who knows how much taxpayer money on how many redundant overlapping inquiries. For what? For nothing. For political gamesmanship."

After Dion released his report, letters of support began to pour into the charity, with many people asking if there was any chance that WE Schools programming would one day resume. One school board superintendent in Manitoba even wrote to Dana Rudy, the province's deputy minister of education, forwarding Dion's report and noting the positive impact of WE programs on students. He mentioned, as examples, an Indigenous leadership and earth stewardship retreat and WE's "collaboration with numerous school divisions in developing a ground-breaking mental health well-being and well-becoming curriculum initiative." The ship had sailed with WE Charity's closure in Canada, but this educator wanted to make his voice heard. "It will be challenging to fill in these gaps in a post-COVID world without the partnership of organizations like WE," he said. "I am sharing this report below in an effort to help set the record straight."[41]

"Maybe we were naïve," said Scott Baker, "but when the commissioner delivered his report and the letters of support started to roll in, we really thought this might be it, our moment of vindication. Finally the politicians and the media might step back and take a sober look at everything that had happened, admit there had never been a WE Charity Scandal, and apologize for the false allegations and for letting this get so far off the rails."

But there would be no apologies, and no reflection. The same opposition politicians who had once praised the ethics commissioner for his work were less complimentary now that he hadn't said what they wanted to hear. In a video response, for example, Charlie Angus cherry-picked passages and quoted them out of context, then continued to push allegations of an improper relationship between the charity and government officials. Many news outlets gave his partisan position equal coverage to Dion's non-partisan report. The Canadian Press even reposted his video almost unedited with the headline "Angus Cries Foul Over Findings in WE Charity Report."[42] The *Globe and Mail* also reposted the video, then reported on Dion's findings with a headline that seemed to take pains to avoid saying the prime minister had been cleared ("Trudeau in Apparent Conflict on WE but Not Formal Ethics Breach, Commissioner Finds").[43]

At this point, journalists were tired of the story they'd kept alive for so long, and Dion's assessment attracted far less coverage than other events throughout the cssg affair. The news story that had started with a bang went out with a whimper. And Canadians were left with only muddy water. Indeed, it is telling that more than six months later, many people I speak to—even supporters of WE—still believe the ethics commissioner found serious lapses because of how the press reported on the findings.

"I think what stunned me was how quickly the story of our vindication was buried," Dalal told me. "After a year of accusations, the news that they were false was barely a blip. It was a one-day story, and in many outlets it didn't even make the front page. The media who had made sure that everyone would think us guilty also made sure that no one heard we were innocent."

CHAPTER 14

AN INTERNATIONAL AFFAIR

As the dust started to settle on the CSSG, the media's attention shifted to WE's international work. I can't say the pivot was surprising—there was insatiable demand for commentary on WE, and critics of the organization and the Kielburgers were bound to leave no stone unturned. A political scandal at home naturally caused some people to question whether the charity's work abroad was as impactful as the fundraising materials suggested. Critics of development work generally—there are many, for example, who believe all foreign aid is an extension of colonialism—were sure to raise questions regarding the merits of encouraging foreigners to donate to clean water campaigns or volunteer in the developing world. For those people, WE Charity was an obvious poster child for such debate. All this was expected and understandable.

But what happened next blew my mind.

Very quickly, the charity's handling of a case of employee misconduct in Kenya morphed into front-page news in Canada that hinted at international corruption. Then came a non-stop series of wild claims, ranging from corporal punishment to mismanagement of projects to deception of donors. It was an all-out attack—with journalists at highly influential outlets like Bloomberg and the CBC leading the charge, and politicians jumping on the bandwagon. Some of the most negative reporting relied heavily on accusations from a former donor whose behaviour was dubious, to put it very mildly.

In this chapter and the next, I will lay out the facts and let you be the judge, but in my view, the conduct of these journalists was highly suspect and should give every Canadian pause. They assailed the transparency and honour of the charity using tactics that were anything but transparent or honourable. Did they create the story *and then* report on it? Have they been truthful about what happened behind the scenes? Are tales of donor deception by WE Charity based on deception of donors by the storyteller?

I was not alone in my reaction. This latest onslaught provoked many donors and educators who had previously watched in silence as the WE Charity Scandal unfolded to find their voices and say, "Enough." It was the proverbial straw that broke the camel's back. Those who had devoted their time, money, and reputations to work with WE Charity in the international development sphere, as well as those who had tried to speak up but were ignored, now refused to stay on mute.

FROM BACKGROUND TO FRONT PAGE

The fracas over WE's international programs began in the summer of 2020. Ironically, it was rooted in a situation that was actually a remarkable profile in courage on the part of the WE executive team and, in particular, co-founder Marc Kielburger. In 2017, a financial spot check of Kenya operations by WE Charity in Canada revealed that the former director of the Kenyan team, Peter Ruhiu, had misappropriated funds and falsified financial records. Alarm bells went off. A special committee of the charity's board was formed to oversee the matter, and board members Michelle Douglas and Eric Morrison travelled to Kenya to personally help sort out the mess. WE Charity engaged external experts to lead an investigation, including fraud specialists Compol[1] and global accounting firm Deloitte. They examined financial and digital records and interviewed staff. The Kenyan authorities were engaged, including the local police, and the charity informed the Canadian High Commission.

The Kenyan police enlisted Marc and other senior WE staff to help with the investigation and to obtain evidence of Ruhiu's crimes by recording phone conversations with him.[2] (As proof that no good deed goes unpunished, these calls were later broadcast by Canadaland in an attempt to suggest that Marc himself was involved in a corrupt plot.) Ruhiu initially accepted responsibility and agreed to repay the misappropriated funds. But as the pressure to make restitution mounted, he changed his mind and told the Kenyan police that Marc and a group of others (WE employees, contractors, and their lawyer) had kidnapped him and forced him to confess at gunpoint. Ruhiu was subsequently charged with filing a false police report.[3] He pleaded guilty, repaid the funds, signed a written confession, and was ordered to pay a fine and serve a one-year prison term.[4]

While this situation was unfolding, Marc stayed in Kenya for months without seeing his family. To leave risked the possibility that Ruhiu would escape justice and a criminal case would never be brought. Marc's life was repeatedly threatened—when I visited Kenya in July 2018, I had to meet with him at a secret location because he was being moved every few days so that his whereabouts would remain unknown. It was apparent that he was not sleeping. He looked exhausted and was visibly shaken. He had also become aware that Ruhiu's wife (herself an employee of the charity at the time) and children were at risk of domestic violence. Marc had promised that he would help them relocate to safety in Canada. He would not leave Kenya until this outcome was certain, and he put himself at considerable risk in the process.[5] It had all the drama of a spy movie, but it was real life—and it was scary.

And then a second employee was also caught attempting to misappropriate funds from the organization. Santai Kimakeke had been hired by Ruhiu and served as a senior staffer in the Nairobi office. He had attempted to extort money from the organization and also forged signatures on cheques and bank documents to inappropriately obtain personal loans. As it had with Ruhiu, the charity investigated, collected a great deal of evidence, and turned it all over to the Kenyan police, who then charged Kimakeke with fraud, forgery, and related crimes.[6]

Through it all, the Kielburgers, the WE executive leadership team, and the board members remained focused on one thing: ensuring that any stolen funds were recovered so no donor dollars were lost. That mission was accomplished. In the end, all misappropriated funds were returned to the charity. After months of tense board meetings, fears for people's safety, and anxiety over the future of the charity's work in Kenya, we all collectively exhaled.

In its twenty-five-year history operating around the world with thousands of employees, WE had experienced only these two incidents of significant employee malfeasance. In both cases, the charity caught the misconduct, addressed it, and strengthened its controls. From my vantage point as a board member, it was all handled in an exemplary manner, and board members were full of praise for the resilience and commitment of the WE Charity team.

But it turned out that WE just couldn't catch a break.

Rather than going away quietly, Kimakeke saw an opportunity as the controversy around the CSSG grew. In July 2020, he launched a blog called *Odd Truths About WE Charity*. This was a place for him to air often bizarre claims against the organization (and to raise money—every page of the site featured a donation button and a plea for people to send him cash). In the opening post, Kimakeke declared that he was innocent of the fraud and extortion charges and had been coerced into making his confession. He then made a series of false accusations about WE. For example, he claimed that charity assets—including title deeds for two high schools, Baraka Hospital, and WE College—had been transferred to a private company belonging to the Kielburgers. (Putting aside the fact that these institutions provide free humanitarian programs and have no commercial value, the assets were in fact owned by WE Charity Canada.) And his most serious allegation was the already debunked claim that WE Charity had kidnapped Ruhiu.

The blog was live for five days until Kimakeke voluntarily shut it down and said he had made it all up. Yes, all of it. In a later sworn statement, he said he wanted to "set the record straight" and acknowledged that the claims he'd made "were simply not true."[7] Unfortunately, some of the allegations had already been shared on social media, and Kimakeke had also been in touch with none other than Jesse Brown at

Canadaland, asking him to promote the blog. Brown was only too happy to oblige—in fact, he went a step further and posted an article and a podcast episode built around his new friend's claims.[8] Once Kimakeke had recanted, he contacted Brown to clear the record, even posting on Canadaland's Twitter feed that the information he'd published was "incorrect."[9] Nevertheless, Canadaland continued to promote the false claims, publishing a second article and podcast episode in October.[10]

Things soon started to spiral. In that second article, Jesse Brown included an interview with Nicolas Moyer, then CEO of Cooperation Canada, an umbrella group for non-profits in international development.[11] As context, Brown wrote that a Canadaland investigation had revealed "a sprawling tale of money, alleged crime, espionage, and betrayal, played out across a network of entities that mirrors the WE organization's corporate structure in Canada." He asserted that a government authority had accused the charity of violating local law, and that the brothers were up to their eyeballs in some shady land transfers. "If proven true," Moyer was quoted as saying in response, "some of the allegations made in this investigation suggest the real potential for the misuse of charitable funds and the potential for the violation of either or both Canadian and Kenyan laws." Three days later, Cooperation Canada released a statement calling Canadaland's investigation "deeply concerning."[12]

As it turned out, Canadaland's allegations were not proven true. In fact, it was Brown's usual mix of inaccurate and inflammatory claims, most of which were clearly addressed in comments the charity had provided to him before publication. Scott Baker told me Moyer later confirmed in a phone call that he took Brown, a journalist, at his word and did not independently verify his reporting or seek additional information from WE Charity or Kenyan government officials.

Apparently, fact-checking also did not matter to the *Globe and Mail*'s Africa correspondent, Geoffrey York. Relying heavily on information gleaned from Canadaland, he promptly filed a story alleging that authorities were "examining governance and regulatory matters related to WE Charity's activities in Kenya, including 'assets and officials' at the Kenyan affiliate of the charity."[13] He then reported on Cooperation Canada's statement—apparently without speaking to Moyer[14]—in a front-page story headlined "Charity Coalition Says It Has Concerns About Secrecy at WE Charity."[15] "A coalition of more than 90 Canadian charities and international development agencies says it is concerned about a pattern of opaque behaviour at WE Charity," the article began.

In a subsequent email to WE, Moyer rejected York's characterization, saying that the article "attributed to Cooperation Canada a concern that we did not express," and that "our concern is with respect to the impact of stories involving the WE organizations on sector reputation and we do not pass judgment on [WE's] activities."[16] Too little, too late—the die was cast. The story had gone from Kimakeke's completely unfounded and fully retracted allegations of corruption, to the relatively obscure Canadaland podcast and posts, to the front page of the country's most widely read newspaper.

Fearing yet another firestorm, the charity opened up its books again and commissioned two independent reviews by experts who had already looked at the charity's domestic activities and the CSSG affair. The first, by forensic accountant Al Rosen, involved a detailed examination of the charity's financial and real estate transactions in Kenya. Rosen concluded that he "did not locate transactions or examples of where the Kielburger family directly benefitted financially from the various WE arrangements in Kenya."[17] The second, by Matt Torigian, former Ontario deputy solicitor general, looked at WE Charity's handling of the Ruhiu and Kimakeke incidents. "In keeping with Canadian standards," he wrote, "WE Charity and in particular Mr. Marc Kielburger addressed these matters appropriately . . . They took every reasonable step consistent with expectations in Canada and most developing countries." He went on to say, "Importantly, the delicate balance of protecting the mission of the charity, the welfare of innocent victims and witnesses, and the integrity of the criminal justice system is an accomplishment not often realized in environments such as Kenya yet was certainly accomplished in this case."[18]

If any journalists or politicians in Canada read these reports, they certainly weren't telling.

THE FIVE PILLARS

Before we go any further, it's important to explain how WE's international development model worked. Pretty much every major international charity has its roots in a simple story of people trying to address a specific problem. Oxfam got its start when Britons wanted to get food to starving women and children in enemy-occupied Greece in 1942. CARE was created as a way for Americans to send relief packages to people living in the rubble of post-war Europe. A twelve-year-old Craig Kielburger wanted to end child labour, and from that came Free the Children.

In every case, the philanthropic journey revealed that to address the problem at hand, people had to take on the underlying challenges of global poverty. It was a hard lesson for the tweens who had started Free the Children by fundraising for a rescue home for child slaves in India. "We learned that many of the freed children were later sold again," Craig explained. "Their families couldn't afford to take care of them. We had to work with the families as partners—empowering them, providing alternative income sources and education opportunities for kids, and creating resources for the villages to escape poverty."

This led WE Charity to devise a development model that was unlike those of many of its peers in the sector. Instead of appealing to donors to support programs that address just one or two specific needs—providing water, for example, or schoolbooks—the charity evolved to embrace a holistic community-based approach. This was the foundation for the WE Villages model and is the heart of what the organization refers to as its five-pillar approach. WE works with an individual community to assess all its needs and then designs interlocking interventions to meet those needs, while also respecting the cultural and environmental context. The five pillars are education, water, health, food, and opportunity. Each pillar has three components: infrastructure, operations, and capacity building. Infrastructure includes things like building schoolrooms, drilling boreholes for wells, and establishing medical clinics and hospitals. Operations includes tasks such as ensuring that those schools have teacher training programs, the boreholes have fuel and funds for repairs, and the clinics have medical supplies. Capacity building includes initiatives such as financial literacy courses, water management committees, and health education led by trained community members. The idea is to empower communities by enabling members to carry on their own uplifting. In most cases, the charity could withdraw in five to seven years, having given a community the tools it needed to maintain and build upon the gains made with limited outside intervention.

What most impressed me about the WE Villages model is the thoughtfulness behind its approach. It was born of trial and error—this was no wide-eyed, self-righteous experiment in international development that could easily backfire. In the late 1990s and early 2000s, the charity's international work became focused on building schools. This was seen as a better way to combat child labour than building rescue homes. Education, after all, is often regarded as the ticket out of poverty. But it quickly became clear that even this was an overly simplistic approach that did not address the barriers to education that exist within a particular community. It turns out that if you build it, they still may not come. The organization learned, for example, that while many communities in Kenya do value girls' education, the real barrier to girls attending school is that they are expected to spend their days gathering water from rivers some distance away. So if you want girls to be educated, you need not just schoolrooms but also easy access to clean water. You also need healthcare to make sure children are well enough to go to school. And then you need an economic system to ensure that the community will not be dependent on charitable giving in perpetuity. In other words, you need to identify sources of income so that people can continue to send their kids to school. Ultimately, WE's approach to sustainable development was to remove or at least lessen the obstacles to education.

To support a sustainable model like this, you need money and you need people working together. Here, too, WE Charity's approach evolved over time. In its early years, when the organization's overseas mission was just to build schools, donors often made targeted contributions to build a certain number of schools or schoolrooms in a particular community. But when the charity moved to its holistic, pillar-based development model more than a decade ago, it also transitioned to a fundraising model that pooled donations to allow it to address everything that was needed for a community to reach self-sustainability. This was never an exact science.

Every large project and individual community was different, and community needs changed over time. That is why the organization worked with local leaders to identify infrastructure and programming needs and decide how best to meet them. This ensured that WE Charity was not building schoolrooms that would sit empty.

As the director of WE Villages in East Africa and the former principal of WE Charity's Kisaruni high schools, Carol Moraa knows a thing or two about creating education programs. "A school is just a box made of bricks until you add students and teachers and education supplies and maintenance staff and community governance and stable funding for all those things," she explained. "A school is . . . an ecosystem that only happens through hard work, capacity building, and community mobilization."

By 2020, WE Charity was active in nine countries: China, Ecuador, Ethiopia, Haiti, India, Kenya, Nicaragua, Sierra Leone, and Tanzania. But Kenya became the laboratory to test new ideas and the flagship of the organization's global development work. It was here that ME to WE, the social enterprise, really began, establishing co-operatives to create economic opportunities for Maasai women. It was here that the organization began to explore how to take the WE Villages model to the next level, with advanced infrastructure such as a hospital with a surgery ward, a large-scale agricultural farm, and a college offering free multi-year degrees in business, agriculture, clinical medicine, and more.

"I can give so many examples of communities that we have partnered with," said Justus Mwendwa, who now heads up WE Charity Foundation's projects in Kenya. "[I have] seen young girls who studied in our primary classrooms now applying for teaching positions at Kisaruni. They have gone through Kisaruni High School, then WE College, and now they are coming back to teach the next generation. If that is not sustainability, then I don't know what sustainability would be."

Sustainability was also a guiding principle when generating funds to fuel community development. The focus was on helping people earn income so the community wouldn't have to rely solely on donations from abroad. ME to WE Artisans and ME to WE Trips both created hundreds of jobs in partner communities.[19] The trips also gave donors the opportunity to see exactly how the funding model worked—a central element of WE's thinking.

For decades, the organization welcomed Kenyan experts to shape the design of programs, third-party measurement experts to interview local communities and assess impact, and cultural experts like former Assembly of First Nations chief Shawn Atleo. Atleo travelled to Kenya to meet with leaders from the charity's partner communities and advise international staff on how to build cultural protection into development work. Like Rotary International, the organization worked to promote cross-cultural exchange and global citizenship.

Amid the CSSG coverage, WE's programs were disparaged by some and have since become the focus of "white saviourism" accusations by certain media outlets. Questions were raised as to whether the organization focused on the appeal of helping the less fortunate without addressing the underlying privilege that allowed benefactors to do so. I read those criticisms with keen interest, both as a board member and as someone who is focused on making sure that my own charitable pursuits do not inadvertently perpetuate oppression. In my view, many of the criticisms levelled at WE—including labelling ME to WE Trips as "voluntourism"—are more properly directed at the concept of international development generally. They raise interesting academic questions about whether developed countries are at some level responsible for global poverty, and as such, whether development efforts only obscure the problem. None of this, however, is unique to WE, and efforts to characterize a broad policy debate as a "problem" with a single organization served only to mislead. Suffice it to say that WE Charity was in the development field, and its work ought to be judged and measured on what it accomplished in that space.

I believed the charity worked hard to avoid engaging in voluntourism and white saviourism and to forge genuine partnerships. But I didn't want to base that belief solely on slide decks that laid out its sustainable development model and video testimonials from beneficiaries. Seeing is believing. So in July 2018, I visited WE Charity's projects in Kenya, joined by my then seven-year-old son. This was not my first trip to an impoverished region. As a nineteen-year-old, I spent a summer travelling across Mexico with eleven others, sleeping in a school bus and accepting the hospitality of the underprivileged who opened their doors to us. It was an exercise in what we called "immersion living," based on the idea that you can't think your way into new ways of living—you must live your way into new ways of thinking. That experience, coupled with extensive travels later in life, made me sensitive to how easy it is to think you are helping when you are really hurting.

So with the skepticism of a lawyer, I arrived in Kenya on high alert for signs of inauthenticity. I found none. During conversations with community members and those who worked for WE, I heard only of partnerships influenced not by the priorities of affluent Westerners but by what Kenyans wanted and needed to build their own communities. It was clear that visitors were there to learn from community members, not teach them. Outsiders were not even allowed to give gifts, lest it upset the equal partnership policy, or take pictures without knowing the individual and asking permission. "Protecting the dignity, privacy, and security of community members was of utmost importance," said Robin Wiszowaty, head of Kenyan operations and now a director of WE Charity Foundation.

My son and I met many Kenyans, learned from them, and understood them. Not perfectly, but a little better. In theory, we helped build WE College, but in truth, we made a very modest bricks-and-mortar contribution. What we gained was a sense of proximity and connection—a feeling that non-profit consultant Noah Manduke captured for me in an interview when he called WE the "antidote to nationalism."

Meanwhile, the donors who accompanied us in Kenya were not passive bystanders—they asked loads of hard questions and wanted details. I still recall Robin rolling out a giant map on a table so the donor group could see every village WE supported, track every project in progress, and understand the timeline for both development and the charity's eventual withdrawal. Donors fired off questions and she answered all of them, even translating Swahili words on maps so there could be no confusion.

For this book and during my tenure as a WE Charity board member, I have spoken to hundreds of donors, volunteers, employees, fellow directors, and most importantly, women and children in partner communities. Not once have I heard any suggestion that there was something disingenuous or self-serving about the charity's work in Kenya or elsewhere. Not once did anyone tell me that they were confused about how charitable donations were applied to support the five pillars.

In the end, of course, only two things ought to matter: the extent of WE's impact and the views of the beneficiaries. Sadly, you will find nothing about either topic in the dozens of articles and television programs that called WE Charity's international work into question. But the numbers speak for themselves. The charity's records show that over the lifetime of the WE Villages program, an estimated thirty thousand women achieved economic self-sufficiency through livelihood and entrepreneurship initiatives, more than two hundred thousand children gained the opportunity to go to school, and more than a million community members got improved access to healthcare, clean water, or sanitation facilities. The ME to WE Artisans program alone resulted in a 200 to 300 percent increase in the rate of women's income throughout the Maasai Mara region.[20]

And behind those numbers are real human beings whose voices were ignored by Canadian journalists and politicians. Voices like that of Esther Kamande, a fifteen-year-old student at WE's Kisaruni Girls Boarding High School. "Without Kisaruni, right now I'd be married and would have some kids, and not making the plans I now have because girls never finished school," she said in an interview for this book. With infectious energy and a big smile, she proclaimed, "I want to become a neurosurgeon." Esther was joined by her friends and fellow Kisaruni students Nancy Kilusu and Joy Mueni. Nancy was raised by a single mother who now operates a small farm through assistance from WE. "She has a small garden and a flock of sheep and fifteen cattle, which she didn't have before." Nancy's plans include university and perhaps law school. But she has more immediate ambitions as well. "My favourite teacher—my history teacher—I aspire to be like him because he told me when he was in school, he was the best in history. I now want to do even better than him. I know it's ambitious." Not to be outdone, Joy offered that she also wants to become a doctor and hopes to study at Kenyatta University in Nairobi because "it's the best university in Kenya."

WE also changed the life of Mama Evelyn, whose story, too, was left untold. Before the pandemic put her daily routine on hold, she worked at the Women's Empowerment Centre in the village of Enelerai. The centre—a core part of WE Charity's opportunity pillar—was designed to provide women in the Maasai Mara region with a safe place to pursue income-generating opportunities, participate in training workshops, and develop financial literacy. In 2013, Mama Evelyn became one of the first in her community to create intricate versions of traditional beadwork that could be sold abroad. ME to WE developed markets in North America through stores such as Holt Renfrew and Indigo for women like Mama Evelyn to sell their products. Six years later, she had become a trainer of other mamas and was also in charge of maintaining the centre's quality control. Mama Evelyn was also part of a group called the Village Savings and Loan Association, which provided microfinancing for small businesses in a local and sustainable way. The group's members were trained in financial literacy by WE staff. "WE has transformed the lives of mamas," she said. "This job has been able to support me as a single mother. I have been able to buy my own land and take my two children to school. I did not believe it was possible."

Other Kenyans familiar with the work of WE Charity spoke of the transformative power of its healthcare initiatives, including Baraka Hospital and its many mobile health clinics. Erik Rono is one of them. He works as a supervisor of security guards at WE properties such as Kisaruni, Baraka Hospital, and WE College. Born and raised in Narok County, Rono sent his three children to WE schools in the village of Enelerai. "Before WE, people would have to travel many kilometres to reach doctors, and roads were bad and [we] would carry people in a wheelbarrow to a hospital," he explained. "Now with WE, we have an ambulance and hospital in the community. This has especially helped in terms of maternal health."

I found it particularly interesting that all these people also mentioned how much they had benefited from visits from foreign donors and volunteers. There was no suggestion that they had engaged in any performative acts, or that benefits accrued solely to the visitors, as some commentators have suggested. "I enjoy it when visitors come to school—they teach us new things, new values, and we have a great time. We teach them what we do in our community, our language, and about our culture," Joy explained. Nancy said she enjoyed meeting new people and hearing about their "experiences and interactions" and appreciated their advice "on how to cope with high school education and the university process," and she felt that visitors in turn learned "about life here in Kenya, my language, my traditions." Erik Rono lamented that the absence of visitors to the communities was one of the hardest parts of COVID, and Mama Evelyn echoed the same thought. "When they came," she said, "we were really happy because we [could] learn new skills and how to [make] change in the community."

It has been hard to wrap my head around how the media managed to get away with critiquing WE Charity's work in Kenya without, for the most part, talking to Kenyans impacted by that work. Yet that's just what happened. The CBC's *Fifth Estate*, for example, travelled all the way to Africa, ostensibly to get to the bottom of things, and still managed to air an hour-long show that included the views of no Kenyan beneficiaries of WE programming. It seemed the height of irony, as nothing screams colonialism more than forming judgments about developing nations without talking to those who live there and acknowledging their perspectives. "There is a lot of talk condemning 'white saviourism' these days," Carol Moraa noted. "As a proud Kenyan woman, it is not lost on me that the conversationalists on the topic are often from North America—and frankly are often white. Critics are ignoring the reality that WE Charity Kenya isn't a bunch of white people in Canada but is instead a Kenyan-registered non-governmental organization operated by a team comprised of 98 percent Kenyans."

All this context is needed to understand just how misinformed reporting by outlets such Bloomberg and the CBC was, and the extent to which key voices always seemed to be left on the cutting-room floor.

TESTIMONIAL: JUSTUS MWENDWA

Justus Mwendwa has worked for WE Charity in Kenya since 2010. Focused on community development and mobilization, he started as a Community Coordinator and is now the co-executive director of WE Charity Foundation, overseeing the ongoing operations of key projects like Baraka Hospital and WE College.

Every single day I spend with WE feels like a kind of miracle. When you see someone whose child was made well because they had access to healthcare or a young boy or girl who is excited to go to school each day, it means something. I look around and I see only good things happening in the communities where WE has been. In the past two years, that's what has kept me going. I keep going because I have seen the real change in the communities around me. I keep going because I have seen the hope in the eyes of the people who live there.

This might be hard for people in Canada and other faraway places to understand, but it means a lot for a community to gain access to clean water. It's actually a matter of life and death. With no access to clean water and limited access to schools, communities cannot thrive. The quality of life in these communities is poor. People struggle to provide just the basics for their families, and there's no strength left to build for the future. It's hard to explain what that really means. WE Charity has saved lives and made better lives possible. I don't say that because I read some study or because of what donors might want to hear. I say it as a Kenyan on behalf of Kenyans. Our thoughts and voices matter too.

When I think about communities like Tarakwet, which was next on the list to receive help from WE but now won't, I think there is no reason for what happened. This organization was taken down. Why? Just because of politics? It isn't right.

We had promised these people that WE would help, and now we have to tell them that what we promised will not happen. And we have no explanation that makes sense to anyone on the ground. So much has been lost—so many lives that will not be touched. Knowing that young girls and boys have lost an opportunity to access education, knowing that parents have lost an opportunity to learn new skills or start new businesses—it's a big deal.

OF CANINGS AND KITCHENS

In August 2020, Natalie Obiko Pearson, a reporter for Bloomberg Canada, emailed WE Charity asking for information about the organization's international development projects.[21] No issue at first. Someone from WE's media relations team replied that they would be happy to assist but needed more details. What specifically was Obiko Pearson interested in knowing? What would be the focus of the article? What was the deadline?[22] They got no response.

The team followed up in September when they got word that Obiko Pearson had been contacting supporters of the organization. This time, she replied two days later. "We'll be in touch as soon as our reporting warrants it," she wrote, "with plenty of time for you to respond to any questions we may have before publication."[23]

Things went silent for months, and then, late on a Friday afternoon in mid-December, another email arrived. The article, Obiko Pearson explained, would cover "the 25-year rise of Craig and Marc Kielburger, how they built a unique charitable/for-profit organization whose influence stretched across the world, and the sudden demise of WE Charity amid a Canadian political controversy."[24] Her email included dozens of detailed questions covering everything from WE real estate holdings in Kenya to allegations of corporal punishment at the Kisaruni Girls Boarding High School. Queries about very serious allegations often began with the vague preface "Some have criticized . . ." and then invited reaction. This is a tactic often described as spaghetti journalism—throw everything at the wall and see what sticks. The charity was given five business days to respond—apparently Obiko Pearson's version of "plenty of time."

The Bloomberg questions were loaded with inaccurate information, including claims that boarding students were not allowed to go home on school holidays if paying guests were visiting, and that donor plaques were so frequently switched that staff joked they should be made of Velcro. WE Charity answered the questions as fully as possible, corrected the inaccuracies, and provided hundreds of pages of supporting documentation. The organization also offered to arrange interviews with the head of its Kenyan programs, other senior staff, and local community members, and urged the reporter to set up her own interviews with Kenyan government officials who could provide her with accurate first-hand information. All these offers were rebuffed.

On December 29, *Bloomberg Businessweek* published "How a Charity Superstar Innovated Its Way to Political Scandal," a 6,200-word feature article that heaped scorn on everything the charity had ever done, from school programming to engagement with celebrities and corporations to the relationship with ME to WE.[25] It noted in an almost dismissive manner that the organization had provided a seventy-one-page reply to questions with four hundred pages of supporting material, as though the information overload made the content less worthy of careful consideration. Without sober reflection, it replayed all the debunked myths perpetuated by the likes of Kate Bahen, Jesse Brown, and the opposition politicians who had attacked the CSSG process. And to my mind, it denigrated the efforts and accomplishments of generations of students, educators, and staff members.

But the harshest criticisms were levelled at WE's international work. The story said, for example, that the organization had slowed and duplicated construction work on major projects "to ensure a steady supply of feel-good tasks for donor groups." I found this to be a head-scratcher because there is sadly no shortage of poverty for donor groups to address. WE Charity operated in countries with thousands of communities in need of assistance—new projects began all the time, and there was no need to slow anything down or manufacture opportunities to pitch in. The article also claimed that after partnering with Chip Wilson's imagine1day charity in Ethiopia, WE had effectively sabotaged its work by cutting staff and funding. In fact, Wilson had praised the partnership in an article he published in *Maclean's* magazine just a month earlier. "We appreciated their forward-looking perspective," he wrote of WE Charity. "They helped communities build and operate businesses of their own, setting them up for success without foreign aid."[26] And in an interview for this book, he said he had no regrets about the merger and still supported the organization and its mission. "We did our due diligence. We saw first-hand the work they were doing. Our family's collective experiences made it more than apparent that WE was a first-rate operation."

Some of the allegations raised by the Bloomberg reporters were downright absurd. The article recounted one colourful story about a kitchen that Craig allegedly insisted be jury-rigged the night before a major donor was to arrive to open the Women's Empowerment Centre. The donor, the article claimed, expected a kitchen and one had to be created out of thin air. "Mayhem ensued," according to Bloomberg. "Employees were instructed to cobble together a makeshift kitchen with equipment from a nearby high school. Photographs of the result show pots and pans hanging neatly on the wall and tidy shelves stacked with cups and plates. When the donors left, it all went back to the school." But I looked into the situation and it turns out the supposedly fake kitchen was very real—built over months, with chiselled stone walls, cement floors, and piped water. After talking to Craig, Carol, and others on the ground on Kenya, I learned that Craig had simply suggested the kitchen be better decorated in advance of a ceremony to open the centre. I also confirmed that the donor in question had seen the kitchen before and after decorations were added, understood that Bloomberg's allegations were inaccurate, and continued to work with the charity long after the article was published.

The most troubling assertion in the article, though, was that WE Charity allowed corporal punishment—specifically, caning—to take place at Kisaruni Girls Boarding High School and other schools it operated in the country. A student named Branice Koshal claimed "she was thrashed for not doing well enough on exams." Two others—who, Bloomberg said, had asked not to be named "for fear of retribution"— alleged they were caned "on the back, the legs, the buttocks, the hands." One of the three said her whole class was caned after some students were caught using a phone to study for their exams.

These accusations were a bolt from the blue. I know my heart sank. If this were true, my tenure as a WE Charity director was over—I wanted no part in an organization that condoned such practices. In the moment and again in writing this book, I've asked hard questions of Robin, Carol, Marc, Craig, Dalal, and everyone in between to assess whether there is any merit to the allegations. And I'm satisfied there is not.

So where did this incendiary claim come from?

"I was horrified," said Carol, who was responsible for WE Charity's schools in Kenya. "Bloomberg wrote only generalities in their initial questions, so we were only able to say that we had never heard of any such incidents, and that corporal punishment was forbidden in WE schools, where teachers are trained in non-physical discipline." But once the article had been published, she explained, the details helped with a full investigation. Carol spoke to school principals, teachers, students, government officials, and local elders to make sure no such thing had occurred or could occur. She had a representative of Kisaruni try to reach Branice Koshal directly to find out what had happened, but Koshal declined to speak about the matter. Carol then managed to track down former students who had attended the school in 2015, when, according to Bloomberg, that entire class was caned, as well as some classmates of Koshal's. The students all denied the allegations and provided written statements to this effect so that WE Charity could be confident that nothing improper was happening under its watch. Carol also reached out to Mary Milo, then principal of Kisaruni's main campus, and discovered that she had a very concerning story to tell.

In early January 2021, Milo said, she was contacted by a former Kisaruni teacher named Geoffrey Kikenye Wambua. He told Milo that he'd received a phone call from a man named David, who identified himself as a journalist. (This was Bloomberg's Kenyan correspondent, David Herbling.) David said he had been given Kikenye's name and contact information by Branice Koshal. He asked if Kikenye had ever seen corporal punishment used during his time at Kisaruni. Kikenye said that he had not.[27] After the call, he reached out to Koshal to ask who had started the caning rumours. "The journalist," she replied. Kikenye asked why, and Koshal responded, "I don't really know." To make sure Milo had things straight, Justus Mwendwa also reached out to Kikenye and confirmed it all, including that Kikenye himself had never witnessed any form of corporal punishment at WE Charity schools.

Soon, other students came forward to say that they had been approached by the same reporter, and that he had tried to coax them into saying there was corporal punishment at Kisaruni. One young woman (I will call her Ann) said that a journalist named David had called her cousin in mid-January and offered her money. David then called Ann and asserted that an entire class had been caned during examinations in 2015 because some students had phones. Ann told him that she had heard of no such incident. The reporter continued to push. "Which kind of cane did teachers use in school?" he asked. "Do they use a pipe or a branch to beat you? If you make a mistake at school, do they chase you home?" Ann kept insisting she had never been beaten, and David kept refusing to back down. The conversation wrapped up with the Bloomberg journalist offering Ann money to take a phone to school and put him in contact with other students. To get rid of him, she relented and provided the phone number of a friend (I'll call her Jane).

On January 14, David Herbling phoned Jane, but she didn't pick up because she was in class. At lunchtime, she met with Carol Moraa to explain the situation, and together they tried to call David back. He eventually phoned again while the two women were still together. Jane put the call on speakerphone, and Carol recorded the conversation using her own phone. I reviewed an English transcription of the recording (the conversation was primarily in Swahili). It was very brief. The journalist initially refused to identify himself and then gave only his first name, David from Bloomberg. Immediately, he pressed Jane with a blunt leading question: "Which punishment incident do you remember?" When she said, "There was no punishment in Kisaruni," the reporter abruptly hung up.

This story is alarming for many reasons, not least because the reporter seemed to pressure students into saying what he wanted them to, and because of the allegations that he offered them money.[28] Also concerning is that when he got answers that didn't line up with the story he wanted to tell, he simply hung up rather than making those answers part of his reporting. Although the published article does include a statement from Carol Moraa, denying the caning allegations, it gives no room to the many students who also refuted those claims. But the most troubling thing, in my view, is that all these interactions took place in January—which is *after* the Bloomberg article had already been published. Despite having printed serious allegations, the reporters appeared to be checking their claims or seeking corroboration after the fact. Even after WE Charity's lawyers submitted a letter to Bloomberg detailing all of Herbling's conduct, with written statements from multiple students who denied ever being caned, there were no retractions, and the story remains in the public space.[29]

THE REED COWAN EPISODE

As it turned out, the Bloomberg article set off perhaps the most disturbing turn in WE's parade of horribles. The claim that the organization frequently switched out donor plaques caught the eye of a Las Vegas news anchor named Reed Cowan and unleashed a furor. I don't use the word "disturbing" lightly. Cowan's allegations were troubling and painful to hear, and left me feeling numb. His subsequent behaviour, however, was awful and left me enraged, and it has been covered by absolutely no one in the Canadian public space. Until now.

In 2006, Reed Cowan had lost a young son, Wesley, in a tragic accident. After seeing Craig on *The Oprah Winfrey Show*, he was inspired to raise money for WE Charity to support the construction of schoolhouses in Kenya. Cowan contributed roughly $20,000 himself, and his friends and family contributed another $50,000. These generous donations helped support four schoolrooms. Two of those had plaques honouring Wesley. The plaques were not something that Cowan paid for or even requested—they were presented to him by the charity as a gesture of thanks.[30]

When Natalie Obiko Pearson was researching the *Bloomberg Businessweek* article, she asked about this rumour that donor recognition plaques were frequently switched. The WE media relations team told her that no such thing had ever happened. But it later became apparent that two plaques mounted almost fifteen years ago—one for Cowan and the second for another donor to the same village—had indeed been removed. Contrary to what was reported in the Bloomberg article, though, plaque switching was not a common occurrence; a months-long investigation by a third party identified only these two occurrences.[31] In fact, the practice of placing plaques on primary schools had largely ceased a decade ago, at the request of the communities the schools served. As a result, the concept of *switching* plaques to allow more donors to be recognized made little sense, since there were hundreds of buildings with no plaques on them. Also, as noted, WE Charity had long ago moved away from a model that tied specific donations to particular pieces of infrastructure in favour of its pillar-based approach.

What happened with Cowan's plaque was that a large foundation wanted to take over sponsorship of the entire school campus and expand it because the surrounding community had grown. The charity reached out to donor groups that had sponsored individual buildings—one of those groups, for example, was Oprah's Angel Network—and got their permission to take over the buildings and replace their plaques. But somehow, Reed Cowan was overlooked, and a plaque dedicated to his son was replaced without his knowledge or consent. Cowan presumably realized this when, after reading the Bloomberg piece, he did some research and found that the plaque placed on the schoolroom dedicated to Wesley had been removed and the room now bore a different name.

Cowan was understandably devastated, and he contacted the charity and exchanged several emails and phone calls with Craig, who apologized profusely for the error. "I called him to apologize because I was horrified when I found out what had happened with the plaque," Craig explained. "We wanted to do our best to make things right for him." The organization found a photo of the original plaque and made a replica that was restored to the schoolroom. A board member also reached out, as did Robin Wiszowaty, who had met Cowan on his trips to Kenya, but these entreaties were not well received.

The removal of Cowan's plaque was a terrible mistake that should never have happened. It is important, however, to put the mistake in context. Any business or charity that has operated for twenty-five years is bound to have some dissatisfied customers or donors. Mistakes happen—even at the most reputable places. When they do, the appropriate thing to do is to apologize, own it, and try to make things right. If that doesn't work, in a worst-case scenario, an incident might lead to a lawsuit. It was unthinkable, however, that an issue relating to a charity's recognition of a particular donor fifteen years ago would land atop the agenda of a parliamentary ethics committee. Yet that is precisely what happened here.

Although Cowan later said that as a journalist himself, he had "not wanted to participate in the process of selling papers or helping bloggers get web clicks for outlets or boosting ratings on the back of my beautiful son,"[32] he apparently began to reach out to reporters on social media (or so I am told, as all of that content has since been deleted). Unsurprisingly, this caught the attention of opposition politicians, and just like that, Cowan was booked to appear before the ETHI committee on February 26, 2021. A star witness ready to tell his story.

"I'm here today to speak for and on behalf of this little guy right here. This is Wesley Cowan," he said in his opening statement to the committee, tearfully holding a photo of his son. It was heartbreaking and moving, and in that moment, I admit to feeling a sense of shame as a board member.

But then things got shameful in ways I could never have imagined.

Until this public appearance, the only issue Cowan had raised with the charity was the removal of the plaque. But now, goaded on by certain MPs, he went much further. He told the members, "I believe I am connected to what I presume are millions of dollars raised [for the charity]," and then insinuated that WE had possibly misused donations and failed to deliver on projects. When asked by Charlie Angus whether he could verify if all the schools he had funded had actually been built, Reed replied: "I can't." And when Angus suggested that WE Charity might have a "pattern" of deceiving donors, Cowan agreed that perhaps there was a "pattern of duplicitous relations with donors, " and then declared, "I feel as though my son has been the victim of fraud."

I was shell-shocked. Somehow, the charity had gone from being blamed for an error with a gifted plaque on a schoolroom in Kenya to being publicly accused of defrauding donors! All without a shred of evidence. Cowan himself never alleged that his donation did not fulfill its purpose of supporting schools. As for the "millions of dollars" Cowan took credit for—as opposed to the $70,000 he and his friends and family had actually contributed—he later confirmed that he was referring to sums he assumed had been raised over the years by Spencer West, a motivational speaker who was a paid employee of WE Charity and had been introduced to the organization by Cowan.

Following his testimony, Cowan took to Twitter, releasing a series of videos full of increasingly bizarre statements.[33] He again claimed responsibility for millions of dollars in donations to WE, seemingly in an attempt to inflate the significance of both his generosity and his grievance. He then demanded the Kielburgers resign, release all employees from any confidentiality agreements, and disclose confidential donor records. And although he had offered no evidence to support his claims of fraud—indeed, they were demonstrably false—he called for the CRA and the IRS to investigate the charity.

The allegations of double-dealing and the pleas for the tax authorities to get involved were duly picked up and extensively repeated by Canadian newspapers. "'Horrifying' stories of WE Charity's alleged plaque-swapping and other dubious practices [have] prompted calls for investigations by the RCMP, the Canada Revenue Agency and the U.S. Internal Revenue Service," declared a *National Post* piece.[34] Under the headline "Donor Asks IRS to Open Fraud Investigation into WE Charity," Bloomberg provided a summary of events that was grossly misleading.[35] "Group admitted removing plaque honoring donor's dead child," read the first bullet point. "Canadian parliament already probing group's work in Kenya," said the second. BNN Bloomberg followed up a few days later with an article (co-authored by David Herbling, the Kenyan reporter accused of offering money to students) alleging that WE Charity had left behind "a trail of enraged, grieving donors."[36] But of course, there was no such trail. Other than Cowan—whose experience was understandably painful—there remains no evidence of widespread concern among donors.

Opposition MPs were only too happy to join the fray, once again casting the Kielburgers as villains. As you may recall from the previous chapter, Charlie Angus, for one, seized on Cowan's call for an official investigation and sent letters to the RCMP and the CRA, formally demanding investigations of the charity. Meanwhile, Cowan seemed to be sinking under the weight of his decision to throw himself into the middle of a political firestorm. In a series of emails to Robin Wiszowaty on March 4, he pleaded with the organization not to use its "narrative shapers" to "downplay [his] involvement" in raising funds for the charity, lamented that "having to testify thrust me into something larger than I ever expected," said he wished her and Craig "no harm as human beings," and professed to be seeking help for a "near nervous breakdown."[37] Robin tried to provide comfort by assuring him that the board was looking into donor transparency issues as a result of his experience, and by confirming that his contributions had benefited the many children who were educated over fifteen years in the schoolhouses he'd helped support. It was to no avail.

In late March, WE Charity received a demand letter from Cowan's legal counsel.[38] When I read it, I didn't know whether to laugh or cry. He and his lawyers insisted that the organization pay him a staggering sum—$20 million in damages and another $20 million if Wesley's name wasn't immediately removed from all WE buildings (plus $250,000 to repay Cowan and others for donations and another $150,000 to reimburse his travel to Africa). It was nearly two thousand times the amount he had personally donated to WE Charity in all the years he was involved with the organization. According to the demand letter, a portion of the money ($250,000) would go to Cowan's new Reed Cowan Philanthropy Fund. The $20 million in damages would be for his personal benefit, although he could choose to share it with his fund if he wished.

And here's the kicker: if WE Charity paid up, Cowan agreed to remove all his social media posts and decline additional press interviews. In other words, the organization could buy his silence. If the demands were not met or his letter was made public, however, Cowan said he would use his media connections to expose the charity to "additional heights of public infamy." To back up his threat, he listed his current and previous media employers, which included affiliates of Fox and the Sinclair Broadcast Group. The evening the charity received his letter, the *New York Post*—which was one of the outlets Cowan said he could use to punish the organization if it failed to meet his demands—reached out about a potential story.[39] The *Post* had never reported on WE Charity before.

There was much hand-wringing within WE as to how to handle the already delicate situation. Paying was of course a non-starter, but people debated whether to make the letter public. I voiced my strong view that the letter *had to be made public*. A journalist was demanding an astronomical sum of money in exchange for silence and threatening to make a public spectacle of the charity if he was not paid off. In the end, everyone agreed.

When WE told the *Post* about Cowan's demand for millions of dollars, the paper dropped its story. Meanwhile, the organization's counsel responded to Cowan's lawyers, calling out the letter for what it was: attempted extortion. "We are attorneys; we understand the hard-nosed tactics that are part of U.S. litigation," wrote Joseph Kroetsch. "But you have demanded that a children's charity bankrupt itself to pay your client tens of millions of dollars he does not claim to have lost. You have backed that demand by threatening to report our client to law enforcement if WE Charity does not pay. You have threatened to escalate a public relations assault against WE Charity, including through your client's own media employer."[40]

Of course, Cowan never launched his threatened media assault, he never made any legal claim, and his lawyers never responded to Kroetsch's letter. Instead, Cowan went silent and, to my knowledge, never made any further public statement on the matter.

Meanwhile, the *Washington Post* advised WE Charity that it planned to write about Cowan's story, and the organization decided to give the paper a copy of Cowan's demand letter and the response from Kroetsch. So Cowan got his story, but it was probably not the one he was hoping for. In his April 2, 2021, column, the *Post*'s media critic, Erik Wemple, wrote, "The case underscores the importance of journalists maintaining a bulwark between their professional pursuits and their private crusades . . . Members of the media should be mighty careful about ever whipping out scary language about 'public infamy,' given their role in facilitating such an outcome."[41] A news story in Cowan's hometown paper, the *Las Vegas Review-Journal*, quoted Mary Hausch, a former managing editor and professor of media ethics, as saying the case "cruises some ethical lines" and is in breach of professional standards, which require journalists to "avoid conflicts of interest, real or perceived."[42]

North of the border? A deafening silence. Having amplified Cowan's allegations of fraud and donor deception through numerous articles and front-page headlines, the Canadian media now had nothing to say about the attempted extortion. It was not for a lack of newsworthiness—members of Parliament had provided Cowan with a national forum to make incendiary allegations about a charity, and Cowan then privately threatened to bankrupt that charity. Yet not a single outlet reported on the $20 million demand or explained to Canadians that his fraud accusations and his claims of having raised millions for the charity were entirely false.

"What I found mind-boggling," said Robin, "was that not one single reporter bothered to ask Carol or me or anyone here in Kenya the status of the schools that Reed helped fund. I could have told them the schools are still there, accomplishing the goal he intended. They're filled with students and teachers every day for the past fifteen years. Students are getting an education, vaccinations, access to clean water and school gardens for lunches."

When US newspapers began reporting negatively on Cowan's demands, he deleted all his social media posts about WE Charity and refused to speak publicly on the matter. But he did reach out privately to the organization once again—this time to express regret for all that had transpired in an email filled with agony, introspection, and a request to call off the US media attack dogs. "I am sorry for all pain on all sides," Cowan wrote to Marc and Craig on April 11.[43] He said he wished he could go back and told the brothers he did "not wish you both or anyone in your family harm." Most startlingly, he said, "I regret to the depths my attorney's words in the demand letter," which, he insisted, "doesn't speak for my intentions that I've held all along."

This disavowal and *mea culpa*—like almost everything else in the WE Charity Scandal—came too late, and the genie would not fit back in the bottle. I cannot claim to understand the pain Cowan felt when he learned the plaque bearing his son's name had been removed. That he had a right to be angry is beyond dispute. But to then spin that into unfounded allegations of fraud and an attempt to enrich himself is inexcusable. Whatever the plaque said, the school built in Wesley's memory was still there, as Robin noted, creating a brighter future for students.

Meanwhile, because the Canadian media never reported the extortion attempt, in the public eye Cowan remained a grief-stricken father whose trust was betrayed, rather than someone whose broader agenda smacks of opportunism. And to this day, no politicians or journalists have owned up to, let alone apologized for, their misplaced reliance on Cowan's allegations.

Still, I presumed that going forward, no Canadian journalist would have the temerity to continue to use Cowan as a source for anything relating to WE.

How wrong I was.

CHAPTER 15

THE FIFTH ESTATE

Just before Christmas 2020, Marc and Craig spent four hours answering questions from journalist Mark Kelley for an episode of *The Fifth Estate* that Kelley said would tell the entire twenty-five-year story of WE Charity. There was a measure of trust on the part of the Kielburgers—after all, the CBC is a public broadcaster, financed largely by taxpayer dollars, and it touts its commitment to journalistic principles of accuracy, balance, and fairness. The brothers understood there would be tough questions, but they were told by the CBC that this would also be an opportunity to remind viewers of all the good the organization had done and to put a period at the end of the sentence as it wound down its Canadian operations.

But it quickly became clear that Kelley had other plans.

Throughout the interview, his focus was squarely on the negative and sometimes even the absurd. For example, he said an organizer for WE Day LA had told him that Marc Kielburger "freaked out" when he saw that the lineup of speakers included a transgender activist because he thought it would be problematic for Republican donors. (Marc had already approved the lineup and the speech, and WE Days routinely included speakers from the LGBTQ community.) Kelley also asked if the organization monitored staff emails after that idea was put to him by Matthew Cimone, a former employee who'd worked at WE fifteen years earlier. ("I can say with absolute certainty that we do not, have not, nor do we ever 'monitor' the emails of staff," Dan Kuzmicki, WE's director of enterprise services, confirmed in a statement.)[1]

Most concerning to me was how little Kelley and his team—including *Fifth Estate* producer Harvey Cashore—understood about the cultures and communities in which WE Charity operated and the work the organization did on the ground. For instance, Kelley brought up the supposedly fake kitchen that Bloomberg reporter Natalie Obiko Pearson had asked about in her emails and later described in her lengthy article. He was told there was no truth to that rumour, but Harvey Cashore raised it again in a conversation with Marc and Craig in early January. This time, he was shown a picture of a substantial kitchen built of chiselled stone, with a cement floor and piped clean water—proof that nothing had been slapped together to fool a donor—but he continued to protest. If it was a kitchen, he asked, why was there no refrigerator? The organization had to explain that rural Kenyans do not typically have refrigerators because homes often do not have electricity.[2] Many people would have felt embarrassed about making such an error, but apparently Cashore did not. The CBC went ahead and alleged in its February documentary that the charity "manufactured" a kitchen overnight to deceive a donor.

I've written elsewhere in the book about this echo-chamber activity, but Cashore and Kelley's approach highlights once again the dangers when journalists repackage their competitors' work. In their rush to produce a constant stream of content and be first out with a new story or a fresh angle on an old one, too many journalists report as fact things they haven't taken the time to verify for themselves. No matter what you think about the Kielburgers or the WE organization, you should question the way the media told this story, starting with allegations about the CSSG that were later shown to be false and continuing right up to the present moment. Along the way, too many reporters set their professional skepticism and sometimes even their ethics aside.

THE PRICE WE PAID

This was the backdrop against which members of WE Charity's executive and senior leadership teams gathered together on a videoconference to watch "The Price WE Paid: An Investigation into WE Charity's Rise and Fall from Grace" in February 2021.[3] They all understood there was a lot at stake. Marc recalled, "We were all holding out the vague hope that the program would be a more even-handed presentation of how things had gotten so out of control, but deep down we knew it wouldn't be good."

Alarm bells went off when the face of Jesse Brown filled the screen. That Mark Kelley was presenting him as a reliable source of information was almost comical because at roughly the same time, the CBC's top brass was accusing Brown of being a purveyor of fake news. On December 14, 2020, the network had issued a press release to refute a Canadaland article alleging that the president of the Canadian broadcaster lived in Brooklyn.[4] "This assertion [by Canadaland]," the release said, "has been repeated by other media, including *The National Post* and *Le Devoir*, and spread on websites, such as The Post Millennial, Canada Proud, and True North. It is false." The statement went on to say that despite receiving clarification, Brown refused to issue a correction (a situation well known to WE Charity).

Nevertheless, he was a cornerstone of the *Fifth Estate* episode, which started out by recycling well-trodden issues with the prime minister, WE Day speakers, corporate partners, and the funding model. But the show soon veered off in an unexpected direction. At about the halfway point, while the screen filled with footage of Craig in front of a massive machine digging deep into the ground, Kelley began to talk about the importance of clean water projects to the charity's Kenya mission. "But," he asked, "was it always clear where the donors' money went?" This was the first indication to the public that the CBC had a new theory to float—one that would eventually span three programs and several corresponding articles stretching through almost the entirety of 2021.

The theory was that the charity was tricking its donors into funding the same project many times over, a practice known as double pledging. The CBC was implying fraud—a very serious charge that would soon be asserted even more directly by the *Fifth Estate* team. For now, Kelley offered as evidence several social media and online posts that he said showed different organizations "appear[ing] to take credit for funding the same borehole in [the] same Kenyan village." He singled out a group from Whistler and a student group from UBC, saying both "said they paid for a clean drinking water project in [the Kenyan village of] Kipsongol."

When she heard this latest allegation, Dalal knew it didn't look good. "I remember thinking, 'People are going to believe what is being said. Because of who they are—*The Fifth Estate*—people are going to think they have done their research. They're going to think that their sources are legitimate. People aren't going to give us the benefit of the doubt. What are we going to do?'"

But the CBC *hadn't* done its research. Kelley provided a voice-over that painted a picture of upset donors, but not a single donor was featured on camera. And the very people Kelley claimed were duped later said he was wrong—in lawyer-speak, the purported victims said the crime never happened. The group from Whistler, for example, had donated money raised through an event called the Whistler Water One Climb. The brainchild of Stuart and Della McLaughlin, owners of Whistler Water, this event inspired almost two thousand people to scale Grouse Mountain, overlooking Vancouver, and raised more than $100,000 for WE Villages water projects in Kenya. The McLaughlins—who described themselves as "heartbroken" about what happened to WE Charity—told me they are skeptical by nature and had travelled to Kenya to see WE's impact for themselves. "I wanted to see whether WE was living up to its commitment around creating sustainable projects, understanding what it is really doing, seeing first-hand," Stuart explained. "It was important for me to see the sustainability and to know that what had been built wouldn't fall apart after five years." The McLaughlins later publicly criticized *The Fifth Estate*'s reporting and said they weren't the least bit confused about how their donations were used. They understood that a water project is much more complex than simply drilling a borehole, and they supported the idea of pooling resources to create the greatest impact for a community.

So what about that student group from the University of British Columbia? Mark Kelley specifically said he had talked to James Cohen, the head of that group, and Cohen said he'd been told the UBC donation "paid for the entire borehole in Kipsongol." There was just one problem: Cohen knew and understood that his group's $5,000 contribution was in fact funding a water kiosk connected to a six-figure infrastructure project. There were several unequivocally clear email exchanges from years earlier between the charity and Cohen discussing how his group's donation was one part of a much larger water project. In one email from 2015, for example, a WE Charity team member wrote, "You are correct, a borehole does cost a lot more than $5,000. On average the general cost of a borehole is $250,000."[5] The larger infrastructure project is a substantial undertaking that involves drilling, piping, distribution points, pump machinery, and years of fuel, repairs, and community water education. What's disturbing is that the CBC was told about the comprehensive water projects prior to the broadcast and went ahead with the allegation anyway.[6] Despite also receiving the email exchanges between Cohen and WE Charity, *The Fifth Estate* never admitted its mistake, and the original broadcast was re-aired on at least four occasions. It still remains uncorrected online to this day.

Other donors who were not explicitly referenced in the program also came forward to reject the CBC's claims. One older gentleman whose church had donated generously to WE Charity many years earlier spoke with Harvey Cashore and then later relayed that conversation to Scott Baker. "After speaking with Mr. Cashore," Scott told me, "he thought that he had been deceived by the charity. He became convinced that he had been told by the charity that he was the only donor to fund a specific water project. But when I searched our email records, I was able to send him exchanges from years ago telling him that he was one of many contributors to the water project. The man apologized for jumping to conclusions. Mr. Cashore had put an idea in his head, and he misremembered the events."

None of this was surprising to me. The CBC has a reputation for accurate and responsible reporting, and most people would assume that its journalists have done the legwork and are sure of what they're saying when they put forward a set of supposed facts. It's little wonder that some people began to question their own recollections, especially when trying to recall events from years ago.

To make matters worse, Cashore and Kelley doubled down on their original claims in a segment broadcast on CBC's *The National* in March.[7] And their "donor deception" theory increasingly began to rest on allegations by Reed Cowan, whose outrageous claims before Parliament were the fuel that helped this fire take hold. Harvey Cashore later told many interviewees that Cowan's testimony had sparked his interest in the story. But as we saw in the last chapter, Cowan had acted with unclean hands and should never have been trusted as a source by anyone who calls himself an investigative journalist.[8]

The *National* segment accused the organization of deliberately raising more money than needed for a water project in the village of Osenetoi. One of the supposedly deceived donors featured was Donna McFarlane, a retired teacher from Mount Forest, Ontario. She was the first and only donor to be shown on camera in either this segment or the first *Fifth Estate* episode. Donna was an active WE fundraiser who had been to Kenya three times to see the programs with her own eyes. She told me in an interview that she understood the model and the work and was so disappointed with the CBC's portrayal of her views that she wrote a letter to the editor of her local newspaper to try to set the record straight. "Unfortunately CBC reporting took parts of my answers to certain questions and tacked the words onto answers to other questions in order to make it seem that I agreed with an attack on WE Charity . . . When I told them that our experience had been completely positive and that WE Charity had always sent us regular updates about the work our money was helping to finance, they kept repeating, 'But surely you were upset to learn that other groups also were fundraising for the deep bore well at Osenetoi, just as you were!' In actual fact we always knew other groups were raising funds for this community."[9]

McFarlane also wrote to the CBC ombudsman, Jack Nagler, describing the questionable practices that had been used in her interview.[10] "It would be very important to watch the entire raw footage of the interview and to listen to the voice not on camera," she said. "This voice belongs to Harvey Cashore as he periodically heckles me in an attempt to unsettle or fluster me into agreeing with the negative statements he was putting forward. At one point, he even shoved printed material in front of me and asked me to comment on it immediately . . . Mark [Kelley] and Harvey both guaranteed me that my very positive experience with WE Charity would be the focus of my interview, but in actual fact edited my words to serve their own purposes."[11]

McFarlane's version of events was confirmed by Barb Cowan, also a retired teacher and a member of the same fundraising group. She was present for McFarlane's interview and subsequently complained to a high-ranking executive at the CBC.[12] In her email, she described one troubling moment when both Kelley and Cashore were pressuring McFarlane to watch a video of Reed Cowan.[13] When she refused, Cashore took what Barb Cowan described as "great liberties" to summarize Reed Cowan's allegations. "He clearly wanted to prove Reed Cowan's claim that WE Charity essentially tricks donors into believing they are raising funds for one thing and then uses the money elsewhere," Barb Cowan wrote. She said she was shocked by the journalists' "extremely biased" conduct, which she called "dishonest and deceptive."

Other donors cited in an article on the CBC News website also came forward, writing an open letter to the CBC to object to what they described as "misinformation."[14] They said that the article "did not fairly represent our responses to [Kelley and Cashore's] questions," and they voiced their "frustration and disappointment in the CBC's reporting."[15] Stuart McLaughlin was among those who signed the open letter, and on the day *The National* piece aired, he also emailed Mark Kelley to complain that the CBC continued to misrepresent where the money from his Grouse Mountain fundraiser had gone. "I would have thought the journalistic standards of our national media outlet and the *National* specifically would be much higher than this," he wrote.[16]

Meanwhile, several former WE employees were also pushing back. Faith Bachlow, who'd worked on the donor relations team but had left the organization five years earlier, wrote to Harvey Cashore to express concerns after doing an interview with him.[17] She told him that she knew personally of many former staffers who had elected not to speak with him because they felt he was not open to reporting information that disagreed with the narrative he'd decided on. "I never encountered a donor who was confused about where their money was going, how it was spent, or what it was doing," she wrote. "Not one." She implored Cashore to be transparent and tell viewers that there are many long-serving former employees who have said on the record that they don't agree with his donor deception theory. "I hope you do your job and give the audience what it deserves," she concluded, "which is all sides and the truth, not just your version of [it]." Of course, that never happened.

Given the political and media climate, it took courage for these people to speak out, both publicly and behind the scenes, against a story that Canadians had been led to believe was true. Despite this, the allegations continued to be recycled in other news outlets. The *National Post* repeated the CBC's already disproven—but not properly corrected—story about James Cohen, declaring, "[Reed] Cowan isn't the first donor to express frustration regarding allegedly dubious WE Charity donor recognition practices."[18] Bloomberg combined Cowan's story with the allegations *The Fifth Estate* had whipped up for its own article about the supposed trail of grieving donors.[19] The CBC returned the favour by picking up on Bloomberg's reporting on Cowan's story. Back and forth it went, with everyone reporting the same story and trying to construct an overarching narrative of a legion of angry donors who felt duped.

But after nine months of negative reports about donor concerns, there were no hordes of grieving supporters confirming the allegations and adding more. By September 2021, out of tens of thousands of total donors, just two had come forward with complaints: Reed Cowan and another donor to the same village. Both grievances concerned donor plaque recognition from approximately fifteen years earlier and not the quality of WE Charity's work or the impact of the funding on the ground. "We were stunned, confused, and utterly demoralized," said Robin Wiszowaty, referring to herself and other Kenya staff members. "These are people of very high personal integrity. We were being accused of horrible things when all we wanted to do was help people."

Justus Mwendwa felt much the same way. "This was taking a real toll on our team here in Kenya," he explained. "They had already been through so much and had done so much for the communities during the pandemic. Many had dedicated their lives for over a decade or longer to

WE Charity, fighting to end the extreme poverty in the communities of their homeland. It was so demoralizing to hear journalists half a world away trashing all our hard work."

LEADING THE WITNESS

By the spring of 2021, Mark Kelley, Harvey Cashore, and the *Fifth Estate* team had advanced their narrative about donor deception in two national broadcasts and multiple online articles. But big and embarrassing holes had been poked in that storyline. The only donor featured on camera, Donna McFarlane, publicly complained about her words being manipulated, and a witness to her interview—also a retired schoolteacher—wrote to the CBC to say Kelley and Cashore were selective with the truth. Eight donors who were presented as purported victims of deception wrote an open letter saying they had not been victimized. And evidence provided by WE Charity directly refuted what the CBC put on the air about James Cohen and his group at UBC.

To my mind, the story was dead. But Kelley and Cashore were undeterred and continued to hunt for disgruntled donors to corroborate the tale they'd already told Canadians.

The question I've been asked by many people is why *The Fifth Estate* barrelled forward. My answer is unsatisfying—I don't know. Maybe Kelley and Cashore thought they would eventually find deceived donors if they just kept looking. Maybe they had invested too much time and professional capital in the story and had to salvage it even though it had fallen apart. Maybe someone in a corner office pressured them to keep pursuing a high-profile story that would attract viewers and boost ratings. It wouldn't be the first time that happened. In 2019, the *Globe and Mail* wrote about a staff revolt that took place when *Fifth Estate* producers proposed a series of episodes about a notorious killer.[20] The idea, according to the *Globe*, was "part of a bid to shore up the program's failing ratings," which had dropped by 16 percent from the previous season. An internal CBC strategy document shared with the *Globe* described a three-step process to build viewership, including targeting viewers "who are already deep in [the] conversation," offering "a cluster of stories from different angles," and creating "social buzz." Sounds like a step-by-step recipe for what happened with WE Charity.

And WE's experience was not isolated. In January 2022, a former Calgary medical examiner named Evan Matshes launched a $15 million lawsuit against the CBC, as well as Mark Kelley and Harvey Cashore, alleging that *The Fifth Estate* had defamed him in a January 2020 two-part episode called "The Autopsy: What If Justice Got It Wrong?"[21] The episodes "foster[ed] false allegations that Dr. Matshes had caused or contributed to miscarriages of justice and wrongful convictions," the suit charged. It called the story "deliberately dramatic" and "misleading," and said it was "the result of selective and incomplete presentation of opinion, conjecture, and facts calculated to present . . . a distorted, inaccurate, incomplete and wrongful picture of the circumstances."

Even some of the CBC's own employees have raised concerns about how the broadcaster has been operating. In a widely shared Substack post published in January 2022, journalist Tara Henley said that she had resigned from the CBC over concerns about journalistic integrity.[22] "When I started at the national public broadcaster in 2013," Henley wrote, "the network produced some of the best journalism in the country. By the time I resigned last month, it embodied some of the worst trends in mainstream media. In a short period of time, the CBC went from being a trusted source of news to churning out clickbait that reads like a parody of the student press."

Whatever Cashore and Kelley's reason for refusing to let go, their efforts were relentless. According to reports to WE Charity, one donor group received forty-three calls or emails from the CBC and felt they were being harassed. The *Fifth Estate* team also called one supporter's local church and another's ex-husband's workplace.

John Knapp, a retired teacher who was involved with WE for more than twenty years, was one of the donors the CBC approached. Before retiring, Knapp had overseen a large and thriving WE Club at his school, and he'd taken part in eleven trips to WE projects by himself, with students, and with other educators. "It's the only program I've ever been involved in in thirty-five-plus years in education that I would consider 100 percent successful for every participant," he said. "And that's astounding." But this wasn't what Harvey Cashore wanted to hear when he set up an interview with Knapp. Every time the former teacher said something positive about the organization, Cashore tried to steer the conversation back to the donor deception theory. Knapp was so concerned that he wrote to Brodie Fenlon, the CBC's editor-in-chief, to complain that Cashore's approach was "at best manipulative, and at worst highly unethical."[23] Other donors said their assertions were dismissed or their words twisted.

So if Cashore and his team weren't listening to anyone who had good things to say, who were they listening to? It turned out that since at least August 2020, they'd been scouring social media to try to find posts where two or more donors appeared to be funding the same WE Charity project.[24] Kelley and Cashore had been offered the opportunity to speak with Kenyan government officials, local community leaders, WE Charity staff and donors, and independent auditors and investigators, but instead they went with a keyword search on Twitter.

Where was the due diligence? Did they cross-reference emails or other documents to determine whether these donors were fully funding a project or had ever been told they were by the organization? If so, they never showed any of those documents on their broadcasts. Did they consider the possibility that they *themselves* might have misunderstood something when trying to interpret a donor's intentions in the Twittersphere? Was the CBC the one telling donors they had fully funded a project when the donors had no such view to begin with? That seemed to be exactly what had happened with James Cohen and eventually others.

After Donna McFarlane's vocal statements about unethical editing by *The Fifth Estate*, some donors and former staff became so concerned about being misrepresented that they started to record their interviews with the CBC, and they later shared those recordings with WE Charity.[25] Once again, a pattern is evident. Harvey Cashore persistently kicks things off by presenting Reed Cowan as an example of donor fraud, elevating his credibility by explaining that Cowan testified in front of a parliamentary committee on this subject, then stating falsely that "no one knows where the money went." He also fails to mention Cowan's extortion attempt.

In these recordings, Cashore sounds less like an unbiased journalist and more like a prosecutor trying to persuade a jury to see a case his way. "I think about every village that's part of the Free the Children system on my spreadsheets," he told one interviewee, referring to a tracking system he'd cobbled together. "So on the left-hand column is everybody I could find on social media or Twitter or a blog or whatever that stated they funded a school, you know, or a well or whatever. And so, you know, what I can say factually right now is I'm getting way more groups and individuals saying they funded a school, for example, in Irkaat, let's say, or Mwangaza than schools exist." But this was hardly the smoking gun Cashore seemed to think it was. One donor emailed the CBC to explain that her friends had posted individually about a fundraising effort they undertook as a group. "All of us collectively donated to the same project," she wrote. "The pictures can be the same school or project because we were part of the same fundraiser."[26] In other words, ten individual Twitter posts about a donation was not proof that WE Charity had funded the same project ten times over. But that's exactly what Cashore appeared to believe, and that's the scenario he put to the people he was interviewing.

This theory that donors had been duped became the cornerstone of the CBC's efforts over the next few months and eventually was the basis of a second full episode of *The Fifth Estate*, "Finding School No. 4," broadcast on November 18, 2021.[27] (I'll come back to this episode later in the chapter.) As they worked on this second story, Cashore and his team sent hundreds of emails to WE Charity donors, seeking anyone who might be confused about the organization's model. In one introductory email to a donor, a CBC staffer named Matthew Pierce wrote, "Research we have done indicates that there is a discrepancy between how many schools were built and how many donors believe they funded a school. To that end, we're hoping to speak with donors in an effort to help us understand the discrepancy."[28]

In this way, Cashore and his team were not simply suggesting that they believed there *may* be a discrepancy—they were starting outreach by telling donors there *was* a discrepancy and asking them to react to it as though it were established fact. For example, in another message shared with me, Pierce, copying Harvey Cashore, asked a donor for "any documents or emails which explain how WE came to choose the school in Esinoni as one of those that you fully funded?"[29] Note that he didn't ask the donor—Mark Quattrocchi, a motivational speaker who had cycled around the world to raise money for education[30]—if he had fully funded a school. He just put those words in Quattrocchi's mouth. The claim that donors were told they alone had "fully funded" a school, a water project, or some other program was essential to the CBC's narrative. But Quattrocchi went back through his public communications and determined that he had never claimed or even implied he had fully funded a school in Esinoni. "You ask how WE chose the schools that I had 'fully funded,'" he replied to Pierce. "I think you may have the wrong idea (did I say I fully funded them? I don't believe I said that—can you please show me where I said that? If not, why would you attribute those specific words to me?). My donations helped to fund those schools. I don't think the schools could have been built without those donations, but I don't think that no one else helped too."[31]

As I read these emails, it occurred to me that the public broadcaster seemed to lack even a basic understanding of WE Charity's five-pillar model of international development. When someone is "fundraising for a school," that does not necessarily mean they are giving money to construct a new school building. As any parent who has participated in a PTA bake sale or Bingo night knows, schools require constant fundraising. When the organization was trying to meet the education needs of a community overseas, the actual school building was only one small piece of the puzzle. Those schools also needed teachers and books and chalk and paper. They needed security and maintenance. At the high school level, the students were boarded, so they needed places to live and meals to eat. The teachers also needed living accommodations and professional development opportunities. Money donated to the education pillar supported health and environmental clubs, inter-school competitions, and initiatives to improve enrolment, attendance, and performance. In most cases, the cost of building and maintaining schools and then supporting the education pillar for five to seven years was in the hundreds of thousands of dollars. And as surrounding communities grew, it wasn't unusual for the organization to go back to add additional educational infrastructure. The financial commitment didn't end when a single schoolroom was built—in fact, that was just the beginning.

Also seemingly lost on the *Fifth Estate* team was the representative model of fundraising used by countless charities, including WE. Donors to PLAN International may receive a photo of a specific child, but their funds are "pooled with those from other generous Canadians" to help an entire village.[32] World Vision explains that when someone donates for a schoolhouse, the charity "pools donations to provide schools in as many communities as possible."[33]

These charities encourage donations by highlighting concrete rather than abstract contributions. Similarly, WE Charity talked about what it costs to build a school or a borehole as a way of expressing the value of meeting specific fundraising targets. This also created a visual that people could relate to. On social media—which the CBC relied on as a primary source of information—things sometimes get fuzzy because people might use shorthand terms like "raising money for a school" as a way to talk about fundraising for education in a community. This did not mean that a donor "owned" a piece of infrastructure or had some exclusive claim to it. In my view, the CBC's suggestion that people like Donna McFarlane should be offended to learn that others had contributed to the same project reflects a particularly cynical take on charitable giving—the idea that donors should be dissatisfied if they had no exclusive claim to a particular school or well in the developing world.

In August 2021, when WE Charity Foundation was relaunched as the entity that would manage projects in Kenya going forward, its website featured pictures and maps of the 852 schoolrooms—including support structures such as libraries and administrative offices—that the charity had built or repaired in the country over the years.[34] Even today, anyone can look at the site and click on, say, Irkaat, a community featured prominently in *The Fifth Estate*'s second broadcast. Irkaat's page shows photos of each of the village's sixty-six schoolrooms, which include classrooms, a kitchen, teacher accommodations, and a laboratory for the high school students.[35] There's also detailed information about the community itself and the real-life impact of each of the five pillars. At the bottom of the page is a map showing the location of all sixty-six structures. This same information is available for the twenty-nine other Kenyan communities where WE is active.

Dalal Al-Waheidi provided all this information—including the complete list of 852 newly built and renovated schoolrooms—to Harvey Cashore on August 16, 2021. In her accompanying email, she implored him to stop misinforming donors by circulating lower figures that were "inconsistent with the data we have provided," and to contact the organization if he believed the data was incorrect or incomplete.[36] Cashore never replied to the message or gave the charity an opportunity to comment on his research and allegations. When he and Mark Kelley later went to Kenya to film footage for their broadcast, they visited Irkaat for themselves and declared that only twenty-eight "schools" had been built. But they didn't count many individual classrooms or any of the support buildings, and they visited only one of four spots around the village where classrooms could be found. "It was painful when they put up this screen of Irkaat and said, 'We think that there's been this many schools fully funded, and there's this many schools that we saw there,'" Robin later told me. "And I was thinking, 'We sent you a map that had sixty-six structures on it, and you chose to go to only one location within Irkaat and then presented that as though it was a whole.'"

A DIPLOMATIC INCIDENT

On September 3, 2021, a year after he'd started reporting on WE Charity, Cashore wrote to Robin to tell her that he was making his first trip to Kenya to see the organization's work for himself. He would be there the following week, he said, and wanted her help to set up interviews and arrange visits to schools.[37] Robin welcomed the news and said she was happy to facilitate the trip, but she also had some advice for Cashore. "I sincerely hope that you are coming with an open mind," she wrote, "and will truly take the time to consider and understand how our development model works, hear from the people whose lives have been directly affected by the changes in their communities, and appreciate that while you seem to be focused on counting buildings, the sustainable change that is at the heart of what we do is about a lot more than structures."[38]

But that's not what happened.

Cashore told Robin that he had received an invitation to visit from the office of Narok County governor Samuel Tunai in August.[39] (Narok County is home to WE College, Baraka Hospital, and many of WE's partner communities.) The governor has since confirmed to WE Charity that as far as he is aware, no such invitation was issued. Also concerning was that when a self-described "local handler for the Canadian Broadcasting Corporation" got in touch with Tunai to set up an interview for Kelley and Cashore, the overture was anything but transparent. The handler, John Njiru, omitted any mention of WE and reframed the interview request as "an opportunity and platform to market the County of Narok." He said the governor would be able to showcase the county "as an Investment Haven for the wealthy, and the go-to investment destination for those that want to be in the Tourism Sector."[40] Njiru then asked the governor to get in touch with him so he could help "swing the interview" in his favour.

It was an inauspicious start, and perhaps no surprise, then, that when Tunai eventually sat down with Kelley, the governor's staff recorded the whole interaction. (His office later shared the recording with WE Charity.) *The Fifth Estate*, however, painted these actions as evidence that the governor was hostile to the journalists and wanted to thwart their investigation. Had Canadian viewers known how the governor was approached—he was essentially lied to in the context of a show about whether WE Charity told lies—they might have seen his actions in quite a different light.

As the interview began, Tunai spoke about the challenges faced by communities in his region. He talked specifically about female genital mutilation and explained how the charity had had a noticeable impact on that issue through its Kisaruni Girls Boarding High School, which not only gave girls a chance at an education but also helped many avoid becoming child brides. "This is why I can stand up and say WE Charity has done a good job," he told Kelley, calling himself "a great promoter and supporter of WE."[41]

But most of this part of the conversation ended up on the cutting-room floor. Kelley had other things he wanted to talk about. "What would you say—and I'm asking you just to think about this for a second—if more money was raised for Kenya and Narok County than was actually spent in Narok County?" He phrased this as a hypothetical—just an interesting question for the governor to ponder—but he was in fact levelling a very serious charge without a shred of evidence to support it. When Tunai did not take the bait the first time, Kelley repeated the question toward the end of the interview, in a moment that did make it to air. The governor promptly halted the conversation.

It was another in a long line of jaw-dropping developments for the people at WE. "Without ever [putting] this question [to the] charity and providing an opportunity for clarification," Scott Baker said, "the CBC was raising a very serious allegation about a Canadian charity in front of a foreign government official who could shut down the charity's humanitarian programs in the country." Carol Moraa told me that the moment sadly didn't surprise her. "I felt like they were not sincere in coming to Kenya. They already had a preconceived show. They already knew what they wanted on the show and coming to Kenya was just a smokescreen."

Unfortunately, things would get worse from there, with the CBC crew almost provoking a diplomatic incident.

In the days leading up to Cashore and Kelley's September 9 arrival, Robin had twice explained to them that because of the pandemic, access to government-run primary schools was severely restricted and Cashore would need to get written permission to enter any school grounds.[42] (Although WE Charity helps to fund primary schools, they are legally owned and operated by local governments.) Robin wanted to ensure that the CBC team had what they needed because her slight hope was that once they saw the projects in action, their perceptions of the charity's work might finally begin to shift. Cashore assured her, in writing, that he had secured the necessary permission,[43] so she began discussing plans for them to visit some schools a few days after their arrival.

But on September 10, Robin received another message from Cashore, who had already tried to go to a school and take photos of it, only to be turned away. "After getting permission a week ago to film the exterior of school rooms at Motony," Cashore wrote, "we were told 'calls were made' and the permission was retracted."[44] Robin took this as a thinly veiled accusation that she or someone else at WE was trying to block the visit. It didn't make any sense. "This is what we wanted all along. Why would we 'make calls' to block his reporting?"

She offered to help him fix the problem but said she would need a copy of the written permission he told her he'd been given. She asked multiple times, but he never produced anything. In the meantime, Carol phoned local ministry of education officials and also sent an urgent letter asking them to reach out to the ministry's headquarters in Nairobi to get the CBC journalists special permission to enter schools.[45]

Robin told me that a few days later, she learned from staff at the Motony school that when the CBC crew had shown up, the local handler (John Njiru again) claimed he, Kelley, and Cashore were representatives of WE Charity. The deputy head teacher didn't believe him and wouldn't let them onto school grounds. Imagine the outcry if reporters from another country had come to Canada at the height of the pandemic and tried to make their way onto school grounds with a film crew, all without permission. And Cashore and his crew didn't do this just once. Over the weekend of September 11–12, even though the ministry of education still had not given the permission needed, the *Fifth Estate* team went from community to community, trying to bluff their way into each location, just as they had at Motony. Locals told Robin that at some schools, the journalists claimed to be working with WE Charity. At others, they suggested they were guests of Kenyan ministry of education officials. And in at least one instance, they brought a drone and flew it over schoolrooms to take aerial photos until they were asked to leave.

This was not simply a case of someone cutting through unnecessary red tape. "These government rules exist for a reason," Carol explained. "There was a dire shortage in Kenya of vaccines, ventilators, and medical supplies. The CBC journalists had travelled in multiple airports, on several international flights, were in hotels and taxis in the big cities. They arrived in Kenya and the next day were running around, going village to village in the rural regions, where people have not been vaccinated and have very limited healthcare if they got sick. All without following rules or taking precautions." (In September 2021, only about 1 percent of rural Kenyans had been vaccinated, according to publicly available information.)[46]

Herickson Ngeno, a representative from the ministry of interior and a prominent local leader, told the WE team that the authorities were flooded with complaints from the schools and surrounding communities. The ministry of education also confirmed that the CBC crew had never secured the needed authorization to begin with. "They say they have permission from the government. They say they are donors to WE," complained Ngeno. "They do not respect us. They lied to us to gain entry to our schools . . . We have never felt more insulted."

The government wouldn't let the matter go without sanction. On September 13, a regional representative of the office of the president of Kenya issued a harsh reprimand to Canada's national broadcaster, citing its employees' "misconduct and illegal actions," which included the criminal offences of misrepresenting government officials, trespassing on government land, and flying a drone without a licence.[47] Governor Tunai similarly expressed his disappointment to the CBC. In a letter to Brodie Fenlon, editor-in-chief of CBC News, he wrote: "In view of the activities that ensued after the interview and in particular the unethical conduct of the said CBC reporters, I am of the reasonable view that Mr. Njiru's request to me was in bad faith and entailed an ulterior motive and purpose."[48]

In time, *The Fifth Estate*'s November 2021 documentary would suggest that all this drama was part of an attempt by WE Charity to impede its investigation. This made no sense, of course, because the charity had been begging the CBC to visit and wanted Kelley and Cashore to see it all. Carol even pleaded with them to visit the purportedly fake kitchen! But to be sure that I was not missing any subtle form of heavy-handedness or some working of Kenyan connections, I asked each of Marc, Craig, Robin, and Carol a point-blank question: "Did you do anything or learn of anyone doing anything to interfere with Mark Kelley and Harvey Cashore when they visited Kenya?" Each said no.

TESTIMONIAL: GOVERNOR SAMUEL TUNAI

Samuel Kuntai Ole Tunai is the governor of Narok County, Kenya. He studied public administration and international relations at the University of Nairobi and is a prominent businessperson, active in livestock farming, agriculture, tourism, and real estate. He was born and raised in Narok County and is the proud father to four daughters.

I fondly remember my first meeting with Marc Kielburger many, many years ago, when he was a young man working to set up schools and community projects around the Maasai Mara, which was an area of greatest need, with challenges of illiteracy and female genital mutilation, as well as no job opportunities. I want to say that what WE Charity is doing today is exactly what Marc said he wanted to do more than twenty years ago, except on a much greater scale, with an impact I couldn't imagine.

They've changed the lives of young people who could have been murdered or fallen victim to early marriage and female genital mutilation, which still exists to some extent. Those girls and boys have an opportunity to go to school now; their lives completely changed, and they get the best lives for themselves and for their community.

Before I became governor of Narok, I joined the board of the not-for-profit Mara Conservancy and I worked more closely with WE Charity. I know their work well, and I believe no other organization in Kenya has made the impact that WE has for young people.

In Narok, 65 percent of the population is made up of young people, but they face many challenges. Most of them are school dropouts with no future, but thanks to WE, these young people have a chance, and they'll be able to acquire the skills they need to become self-employed or seek work elsewhere.

Because of Kisaruni Girls Boarding High School, our young girls have an opportunity to go to school. Thousands of girls would not have had this future because the government does not have these resources. And if you combine all other non-governmental organizations in Narok County today, they aren't doing 5 percent of what WE has.

To see the negative publicity in the Canadian media makes me emotional because those people are doing a disservice and injustice to our boys and girls who today have a future because of WE Charity.

The vision that WE had was really big. It was changing lives and changing communities.

1. Before the CSSG affair, WE Charity had many positive and long-standing relationships with media partners. David Walmsley, editor-in-chief of the *Globe and Mail,* even appeared on the WE Day stage to tell the young audience about the importance of media literacy.

2. An entire wall of the WE GLC was taken up with glowing headlines and admiring profiles.

3. Marc and Craig wrote a regular column that appeared in the *Globe and Mail,* the *Toronto Star,* and some Postmedia dailies.

4. Prime Minister Justin Trudeau testified before the Standing Committee on Finance, or FINA committee, on July 20, 2020.

5. Marc and Craig also appeared before the FINA committee and were grilled for an unprecedented four hours.

6. In its dozen-year history, WE Day welcomed to the stage people of all political stripes. Here, former prime minister Stephen Harper greets participants, although he declined his invitation to appear at the event each year he was in office.

7. In 2013, Harper's wife, Laureen, hosted a WE Day after-party at 24 Sussex Drive. Future Conservative leader Erin O'Toole was there and posted this photo to Twitter.

REED COWAN
As an individual | À titre personnel

The Washington Post

Opinion: Sinclair anchor demands $20 million from charity over fraud allegations

WE

A WE Charity office in Toronto on Sept. 9. (Cole Burston/Bloomberg)

Opinion by Erik Wemple
Media critic

8. Las Vegas journalist Reed Cowan stirred up a hornet's nest when he went before the ETHI committee and offered emotional testimony that suggested the charity may have deceived donors.

9. Cowan's testimony was the foundation of the CBC's suggestion that WE Charity misled donors about development projects in Kenya—including the number of schoolrooms built.

10. Later, WE Charity accused Cowan of trying to extort millions of dollars from the charity—a story picked up by American media outlets but ignored by their Canadian counterparts.

11

12

11. Robin Wiszowaty was the head of WE Charity's Kenyan operations and is now the co-executive director of WE Charity Foundation. She learned Swahili through immersive living with a rural Maasai family.

12. WE Charity partnered with local communities on a five-pillar model of international development. The pillars were water, health, food, opportunity, and of course, education.

13. Carol Moraa is one of the Kenyans leading WE programs in her country. A respected educator, she was the founding principal of WE's Kisaruni group of schools. Here she's celebrating the first graduating class from the girls' high school.

13

14. The endless bad press and resulting collapse in donations took an unbelievable toll. In September 2020, the charity announced it was closing, and soon after, the treasured WE GLC was put on the market.

15. Charlie Angus of the NDP was relentless in his criticism of the charity, even though his own children had been involved in the WE Schools program and had participated in ME to WE Trips.

16. Conservative Pierre Poilievre was a more predictable opponent of WE, given his long-standing hostility toward anything he viewed as a government handout and his penchant for courting controversy.

OFFICE OF THE PRESIDENT
MINISTRY OF INTERIOR
AND
CO-ORDINATION OF NATIONAL GOVERNMENT

ASSISTANT COUNTY COMMISSIONER
MULOT DIVISION
P O BOX 92-20503
OLOLULUNGA
13/09/2021

Dear Sirs,

RE: VISIT BY JOURNALISTS FROM CANADA TO SCHOOLS IN NAROK WEST

We wish to expresses our condemnation of the misconduct and illegal actions of representatives of the Canadian Broadcasting Corporation.

We wish to bring to your attention that the following actions are criminal offenses in Kenya:

- Misrepresenting government officials is a criminal offense.
- Trespassing on government land is a criminal offense.
- Flying a drone in Kenya without a license is a criminal offense.

There is no record of the Ministry of Education issuing permission to the Canadian Broadcasting Corporation to film in schools in September 2021. Please be politely advised that permission is always required to visit or film at Ministry of Education schools.

We have received multiple reports from school officials that representatives of the Canadian Broadcast Corporation trespassed and filmed at multiple schools on September 11, 2021. Trespassing on government land is a criminal offense.

We have received multiple reports from school officials that representatives of the Canadian Broadcast Corporation actively misrepresented themselves as "being representatives from the Ministry of Education", to visit and film at schools. Misrepresenting a government official is a serious criminal offense.

School officials informed us that representatives of the Canadian Broadcast Corporation have used a drone multiple times. Use of a drone in Kenya without a license is a criminal offense.

We object in the strongest terms the actions of the Canadian Broadcasting Corporation. We reserve the right to take additional action.

Cease your activities as described above immediately.

JAMES NDERITU NDUNGU

13 SEP 2021

J.N.N

ASSISTANT COUNTY COMMISSIONER
MULOT DIVISION

CC

1. GOVERNOR -NAROK COUNTY
2. DEPUTY COUNTY COMMISSIONER- NAROK WEST
3. WE CHARITY COLLEGE COORDINATORS

17. The CBC ran into trouble in Kenya when the Office of the President issued a stern warning that its journalists had engaged in misconduct and illegal acts by misrepresenting government officials, trespassing on government land (by filming in schools without permission), and flying a drone without a licence.

We stand with WE Charity

An open letter from donors to CBC's editor-in-chief

Dear Mr. Fenlon,

Together we represent the donors who have made the most substantive financial contributions to the WE Villages program in Kenya.

We are proud to have helped support a development model that has created meaningful and sustainable change and has saved and empowered tens of thousands of lives.

WE Charity's development model is holistic. It takes funding from multiple donors to ensure schools and school rooms are built and can deliver education to children over the long term, or for a borehole to be drilled and succeed as part of a full community water system.

This multi-faceted approach often requires multiple supporters to contribute to a community development initiative. For example, WE Charity's "education pillar" not only builds, repairs and renovates primary and secondary school rooms, including classrooms, libraries, teacher accommodations and teacher administration spaces, it also delivers multi-year programming that includes student lunches, teacher training and community education initiatives.

As you know, WE Charity has been the subject of media scrutiny over the past year, including three features by the Fifth Estate. Following initial stories, several featured donors published a letter expressing serious concerns about how they were represented, pointing to inaccuracies in the reporting. Since then, many other significant donors have expressed their concerns and pointed to their on-going and continued support of WE Charity and its model.

Nonetheless, the CBC has continued down an ill-informed path. The Fifth Estate has repeatedly reached out to many of us and/or to members of our organizations over the last few months. We do not agree with their thesis that we, as donors, were misled about the projects in Kenya. We supported WE Charity precisely because of its holistic model that welcomes many supporters. We have all been to Kenya and have witnessed first-hand the impact our donations have made in the country.

We do not see any public interest in this kind of journalism. We are requesting your personal assurance that our voices, as major donors of the projects, will be appropriately reflected and considered.

We are asking you, as Editor in Chief, to prevent further damage to the work and to the communities in Kenya that we have tried so hard to help.

Sincerely,

18. This open letter to the CBC was signed by many high-profile Canadians who represented the majority of donations made to WE Charity programs in Kenya. It was published in newspapers across Canada.

WE DEMAND ANSWERS

Questions that must be asked of the Kielburgers at committee

BRIAN LILLEY — Opinion

Co-founders Craig, left, and Marc Kielburger, far right, with Sophie Grégoire-Trudeau as they appear at the WE Day celebrations in Ottawa in 2015.

Cancelled contract prompts questions

NEWS 9

Charity likened to a 'cult'

BRIAN LILLEY

Probed reporters' personal lives, publisher tells committee

Did Kielburgers hire Trudeau's family after Liberals ramped up WE funding, and other burning questions for today's testimony

QUID BRO QUO?

» LILLEY, PAGE 3

THE GLOBE AND MAIL

ONTARIO EDITION • FRIDAY, JULY 10, 2020 • GLOBEANDMAIL.COM

PM's family members paid by WE to speak

Trudeau's mother, brother and wife received more than $280,000 combined for speeches at charity's events

Boys of summer are finally back

FINANCIAL POST
U.S. ECONOMY'S COVID-CRISIS A GLOBAL WORR

NATIONAL POST

THE PROPERTY BROTHERS

KIELBURGERS FACING SCRUTINY FOR $50 MILLION WE REAL ESTATE EMPIRE

Vaccine challenge: high risk, high reward

Infecting the healthy, in bid to cure the sick

There is no circumstance under (which) a civilian aircraft can be downed just by human error

NP
nationalpost.com

Bureaucrats felt 'pressure' to pick WE

BRIAN PLATT AND CHRISTOPHER NARDI

OTTAWA • Newly published govern

of the $543.5 million agreement with WE to administer the Canada Student Service Grant. The program promised to pay up to $5,000 to eligible students

Stude
sent w
partici
testing
be offe
in-sch
cinatio
schools
see a su

Albe
Hinsha
90,000
staff to
before

---

19. The press was relentless in its efforts to bring down the charity. The almost fanatical hunger for negative WE content didn't let up even when the charity shut its doors.

Kielburger brothers up against the wall

Despite this terrible start, Robin continued to try to ensure that the *Fifth Estate* crew would get an accurate picture of WE's activities because she understood that they had the power to negatively influence the charity's fundraising efforts and its programs in Kenya. Carol even took the team on tours of Baraka Hospital, WE College, and the Kisaruni and Nglot high schools. She told me she was disappointed, however, when the camera crews seemed primarily interested in shooting any plaques they happened to spot, indicating an ongoing obsession with donor recognition.

Following the tours, the CBC team did do a sit-down interview with Carol, but once again, things did not go the way the organization had hoped. Although she tried to describe the complexity of real development work, Mark Kelley kept repeating the same questions about money spent on bricks and mortar. The interview lasted just sixteen minutes and then Kelley thanked her for her time. But before they wrapped up, Cashore jumped in to ask about multiple donors for a schoolroom. The questions seemed more combative, and Carol told me she felt both defeated and deflated. "He flew all the way to Kenya and asked one question," she said of Cashore. "I explained over and over, but it did not seem like the answer he wanted. I am not even sure if he wanted to talk to me at all . . . I told Mark [Kelley], 'Can you please talk to beneficiaries around here? Talk to patients at Baraka. Let's go to the high school. You can talk to some learners there. Pick any that you want to talk to.' But of course, he wouldn't . . . From what we understand, the journalists didn't make any effort to speak to any students, any teachers, or any community members. I do not know how to make them understand something they do not want to understand." Months later, she told me that the experience still rankled. "I felt like the interview of me was just a way of showing [they] talked to an African on the ground." In the actual hour-long broadcast, Carol appears on screen for just under three minutes, with Kelley speaking over her for a good portion of this time. Her entire interview is boiled down to 246 words.

Given Carol's experience and the negative reports coming from Kenya, the WE team back in Canada had few illusions about what *The Fifth Estate* would say when the show eventually aired. But they weren't expecting what happened when producer Harvey Cashore finally reached out for comment.[49] After explaining that the program had been "taking a look at the primary schoolhouses that the charity has constructed over a period of more than 15 years and comparing that to the number of donations that were stated to have funded primary schoolhouses in Kenya," Cashore said he had just two questions to put to the organization: Did WE Charity pay performers for their appearances on stage at WE Days? And were expenses related to Craig Kielburger's wedding paid for by an entity called WE Education Inc.? (The answer to the first question is no and the answer to the second question is yes, except that WE Education Inc. was the personal company of Craig and Marc Kielburger. Its name was changed when Free the Children became WE Charity to avoid any confusion.)[50]

Marc, for one, told me he was dumbfounded. What did either of these questions have to do with Kenya, and how could Cashore *still* be asking about WE Days after all this time? But an even greater concern was that he appeared to be reneging on a promise to interview Robin and give her the opportunity to respond on camera to the CBC's allegations as the person responsible for financial matters in Kenya. "You have concluded that you do not need to include WE Charity's perspective on financial matters, budgets, WE Charity's decision-making process or its allocation of funding," Marc wrote in his reply, "given that you agreed (in writing) that . . . these topics would be raised in Robin's interview."[51] He also pointed out that in failing to provide questions or spell out allegations, the show was, in his opinion, not adhering to the CBC's own journalistic standards and practices.[52] "You have not provided us the fair opportunity to respond and counter what appears to be the very flawed fundamental premise of your story."

Marc also questioned why Cashore would rush to broadcast when he knew that forensic accountant Ken Froese—whom Cashore himself regularly used as a source—was in the middle of reviewing the charity's Kenya financials, project allocations, and related expenses. The organization had retained Froese to conduct this review after hearing that the CBC's reporters had suggested to Governor Tunai that millions of dollars earmarked for Kenya had never made it to that country. And the charity had kept the CBC informed about the timeline for Froese's work—the review would be complete long before the conclusion of *The Fifth Estate*'s season.

"We are prepared and willing to share the results of his independent findings with you," Marc wrote. "If you are going to suggest impropriety (as you have countless times to our donors who have, in turn, rejected the premise) you must share with us the details and basis for that assumption. If you are indeed seeking the truth . . . we assume you will consider [Froese's] findings before you continue your reporting."[53] Cashore responded by repeating his two original questions and ignoring the rest of Marc's concerns.

Meanwhile, Robin was flummoxed by the CBC's decision not to interview her on financial topics that she was expressly told she would be given a chance to address—especially since those topics were at the core of the planned coverage and were issues she (and not Carol) was best positioned to speak to. Instead, the CBC told her, after already airing promotions for the show that revealed its conclusions, she would be limited to correcting anything that Carol had said. "I had been waiting for weeks for Mr. Cashore to arrange a time for my interview so I could answer questions and ensure the truth came forward," Robin said. "His earlier email was clear: 'We would want to interview you as country director.' He lied to me. How could I not be given the opportunity to respond to any allegations about our work in Kenya?" Later she told me that the whole experience was like a nightmare. "You have those dreams . . . where you are shouting and shouting and nobody can hear you, and you don't know why nobody can hear you because you're shouting really hard with all your might. I felt like they had taken the microphone away . . . They tease you with the microphone, but then they take it away. I'm shouting, 'I have things to say. This is my personal integrity. This is our life's work. And who are you to silence me?'"

THE SHOW WENT ON

When the show finally aired, Robin was not the only one who felt like she was living in a nightmare. It took less than a minute for Reed

Cowan's face to appear—a clear signal to me, as well as the WE team, that the program was not going to be above board. In fact, before he'd even said his own name, Mark Kelley was asking, "Where did all that money go?" This was apparently the CBC's new theory: that donations made to support WE's projects in Kenya had never even got to the people they were intended to help.

Kelley's case rested on a review of online posts and the stories of two donors: Watson Jordan and Rukshan de Silva. Jordan is a former North Carolina teacher who in 2015 raised money for WE Charity in memory of his infant son, William. De Silva was in his final year at Iroquois Ridge High School, in a suburb outside Toronto, when he raised money for the organization in 2008. He and his classmates, he told Kelley, wanted to build a schoolhouse as their grad-year fundraising initiative. Both men spoke on the broadcast of the deep personal connection they felt to the projects. "Man, how impactful would that be for those kids to go from having no school to a school?" Jordan remembered thinking when he first heard about WE's Adopt-a-Village program. Kelley described the excitement Jordan felt when he got a package of materials telling him that his village would be Irkaat and, the show claimed, his school would be school no. 4—the one referenced in the episode's title.

De Silva also remembers the excitement when his class reached its fundraising goal. "We went to actually donate the money in person at [WE Charity's] office in Toronto," he told *The Fifth Estate*. "We wanted it to be an ongoing partnership. We didn't want it to be a one-time donation." Five years later, when he was in Kenya on his own, he reached out to WE Charity and asked if he could visit Pimbiniet, the village his school had donated to. There were no available staff members from the Toronto headquarters or the Nairobi office, but the organization helped him hire a driver and arranged for locals in the village to show him around. "I met with the teacher," de Silva recalled, "and he kind of gave me a tour of the old school. And then they showed me the new school as well that was constructed with the funds that we donated. And I was really proud to see everything that we had spent four years fundraising for. Just to see the fruits of that labour was incredible."

For so many donors, Kelley told viewers, "it was that connection to the bricks-and-mortar schoolhouse . . . that mattered most." And that got *The Fifth Estate* wondering what they would find if they went to visit these villages for themselves. "So we decided to go to Kenya and look for Watson Jordan's schoolhouse and Rukshan de Silva's and others."

In Pimbiniet, Kelley said, the villagers flew a WE Charity flag, a sign of the gratitude they felt toward the organization. But Kelley was on a particular mission and apparently not focused on what the locals thought. He reported that "we counted twenty schoolhouses, [but] our spreadsheet shows WE Charity had received donations to fully fund forty-eight." And with that spreadsheet in hand, he went looking for what he called "the classroom that was funded by Rukshan de Silva." Did the young man know, Kelley wondered, that his schoolhouse was paid for by others? "Back in Nairobi, we called [him] to ask."

In fact, he did a lot more than ask. He *told* de Silva that the letters "MPCF," clearly visible on a photograph de Silva had taken when he was in Pimbiniet back in 2013, stood for the Michael Pinball Clemons Foundation, and that this was proof the former CFL star had "already funded that school." A dejected-looking de Silva replied, "If what you're saying is true, that's really disappointing."

But here's the problem: the things Kelley said about both the number of schoolrooms in Pimbiniet and the school de Silva thought he had helped fund *weren't* true. There were fifty-six schoolrooms in Pimbiniet—far more than the CBC's own count showed. And Clemons and de Silva did not fund the same schoolroom—in fact, there was no evidence that the classroom de Silva took a picture of was associated in any way with his high school class.

How, then, did de Silva come to believe he'd funded that particular room? Remember what he said to Mark Kelley—while he was being shown around by a community paid teacher, the man had pointed to the schoolroom de Silva later photographed and told him that was his school. It is possible that there was a simple miscommunication between the local teacher and de Silva. In Pimbiniet (and elsewhere in the region), schoolrooms are typically stand-alone structures, similar to the one-room rural schoolhouses historically found in Canada. All the individual primary schoolrooms are collectively referred to as Pimbiniet Primary School. From the perspective of a local teacher who is asked, "Is this the school my high school in Canada helped support?" the answer would be yes, regardless of which of the dozens of individual schoolrooms the donor was focused on. This local teacher would never have heard of Iroquois Ridge High School and would have had no way of knowing how fundraising allocations worked. This confusion could have been easily avoided had *The Fifth Estate* followed standard journalistic practices and allowed the charity to react to claims prior to broadcasting them. WE would have told the CBC that the picture de Silva took was not of a schoolroom connected with his high school. Better yet, the organization could have spoken directly to de Silva and cleared up any misunderstanding before things escalated.

All this focus on de Silva's photograph, though, made me wonder what else he might have captured that day. So I went to his Facebook page to have a look.[54] There, anyone who's interested can scroll through the fifty-three photographs he's posted in a folder helpfully labelled "Pimbiniet Primary School." His beautiful shots document the scope of the work that was still taking place in the village years after de Silva's high school fundraising campaign. He shows derelict schoolrooms under renovation and bright new rooms packed with students. Desks are piled with books and papers, and blackboards are covered with diagrams and math equations. Outside, new bricks wait to be laid and the soccer field waits to host the next game. Children are shown collecting water from a pump and lining up for lunch between classes. It was a story of a village transformed by the collective efforts of many, many people. I had to wonder how someone could look around at all that and not think to himself, "I'm proud to have been a part of this."

I felt sorry for Rukshan de Silva. He had a wonderful—and real—achievement that he now seemed to view as a sham. But I also felt angry at Kelley and Cashore for taking that sense of pride away from him. What proof did they offer him that he'd been deceived? Did they seek out the teacher who'd toured him around to ask why he said that particular school was de Silva's? Did they produce internal WE documents showing that the schoolhouse had been funded three or four or more times over? Did they ask de Silva for proof that he was told his money was going to that specific schoolhouse, and that his high school would be the only contributor to that building? Did they even take the time to look through his photographs, as I had done, to appreciate all the positive change WE had brought to Pimbiniet, thanks to people like him? In fact, a single smart question would have caused the whole story to unravel: "Did anyone *from WE Charity* tell you this was *your* schoolhouse?" But then there would have been no outrage, no emotion, and no show.

"Well, okay," you may be saying, "perhaps de Silva had simply misunderstood or was told the wrong thing by someone who was trying to be helpful. But that doesn't explain what happened to Watson Jordan. He apparently had a document proving that he was told he'd fully funded schoolhouse no. 4 in Irkaat—they even showed it on the broadcast." I thought the same thing, so I tracked down the exact document Jordan was sent and read it for myself.

The first thing I realized was that it was a marketing piece—like a newsletter that would be sent to multiple donors.[55] It had been personalized, but only in the vaguest ways, with a header reading "In Loving Memory of William Peter Jordan" and two passing references to "the Jordan Family." The rest of the document—more than a thousand words—is the exact same text that would have been sent to numerous other donors who contributed money to support one of the five pillars in Irkaat. Still, I went through it with a fine-tooth comb. If this was *The Fifth Estate*'s smoking gun, I thought, it must say somewhere that Jordan had "fully funded" schoolhouse no. 4 or indicate in some other way that the school was his.

But of course, it didn't. "The education pillar in Irkaat is growing!" the document read. "We are so excited to report that the fourth new classroom at Irkaat Primary School is now complete . . . This classroom will join the other three completed classrooms and will provide generations of students with the chance to learn and build a brighter future for themselves, their families and their entire community." Next to the paragraph is a photograph of the long-sought school no. 4 with the most benign of captions: "Classroom 4 completed." Nowhere does it say, "This is your schoolhouse," or "You have fully funded this." Not even close.

I can't blame Watson Jordan for misreading a document or misremembering what he might have been told years earlier. That happens. But it is fair to question *The Fifth Estate*'s sincerity in reporting that Jordan was told he'd "fully funded" a school based on a document that says nothing of the sort. In fact, the report covers a range of other projects taking place in the same village—agribusiness training, clean water initiatives, and mobile health clinics, to name a few. The document does not suggest that Jordan funded any of these projects—it simply reports on them in general terms, just as it did the schoolhouse.

But that did not stop Mark Kelley from making the claim that somewhere along the way, WE Charity had told Jordan that he'd fully funded schoolhouse no. 4. Later, when promoting the episode on the CBC podcast *Front Burner*, Kelley told host Angela Sterritt that WE Charity had deceived Jordan.[56] Seeming to quote the charity, he said, "He was sent a picture: 'This is your schoolhouse, schoolhouse no. 4, in the village of Irkaat.'" But Kelley had made up this quote, plain and simple. To accuse WE Charity of deceiving a donor, the CBC had to invent a deceptive statement.

Once again, I felt sorry for Watson Jordan, as I had for Rukshan de Silva. I very much hope that the CBC did not exploit the Jordan family's loss of a child, given that Cashore often told potential interviewees that this story was inspired by Reed Cowan, who had himself lost a child. "In the end, I've been deceived," Jordan said. "Lying to people who have lost children about doing something good on their behalf—that doesn't seem like an awesome group of people to lie to." I agree, but who did the lying?

I accept that after their encounter with Mark Kelley and the *Fifth Estate* crew, both Jordan and de Silva felt deceived—because they were told they'd been deceived. But there is a difference between *feeling* deceived and *being* deceived, and in both cases, the CBC produced no evidence to suggest that the men's money did not go exactly where they were told it would go. The vision they'd wanted to support—of educating children in Kenya—is a reality thanks to them and so many others like them. Watson Jordan's dream of going to Kenya and reading kids some of the books he never got to read to his son could come true tomorrow. The kids are there, the books are there, the schoolrooms are there. As Carol Moraa said on the broadcast, "It's about the impact, the lives that are touched every single day." Even Mark Kelley acknowledged this when he was promoting the show on CBC Radio's *The Current.* "WE Charity has been [in the Maasai Mara region] for two decades making a difference," he told host Matt Galloway.[57] When Galloway asked about the charity's impact on the ground, Kelley said it was "significant." "They've built a girls' high school. They've built a boys' high school . . . They've built a hospital that's a critical lifeline for people in this impoverished region. The impact is real."

Despite this admission, it seemed there was no information WE Charity could provide that *The Fifth Estate* wasn't prepared to ignore or misconstrue. Even hard evidence. For example, although the organization supplied Harvey Cashore with pictures of all 852 schoolrooms it had built or renovated in Kenya, *The Fifth Estate* insisted on saying the definitive count was 360—a number WE had given to Parliament months earlier for a very different purpose. That figure was expressly described in the submission to Parliament as "not exhaustive," as it did not include a wide range of structures and facilities and was offered solely to demonstrate that the charity had made a tangible impact on the ground in Kenya. Once it had an exhaustive count, WE Charity updated Parliament, providing the 852 number, along with images and maps. But because Kelley and Cashore's thesis was that they had identified social media posts suggesting 900 schools had been funded, they could not live with the charity's count. It would be too close. So what did they do? They pretended that the update to Parliament never occurred, omitted the "not exhaustive" language from the initial submission when presenting the charity's count to viewers, and cut the portion of Carol Moraa's interview where she explains that the 360 figure did not include many educational structures and was not comprehensive.[58]

The CBC then went one step further. On television and radio, Mark Kelley said that the charity's count of 852 schools and schoolrooms was inflated because it deemed latrines to be schoolrooms. Of course that sounds suspect. But here's the problem: it's false. WE Charity specifically told the CBC that latrines were *not included* in the counts. Multiple times. In a September 22 email, for example, Carol told the CBC: "Please note that latrines . . . are not included in these numbers (you had shared you were unsure of that in our interview, and I want to be clear on this fact)."[59] And after hearing Kelley mention latrines on the radio on the morning of November 18, Robin sent an urgent message to the CBC: "During the interview on *The Current*, Mark [Kelley] said that we included latrines in the counting of the structures. We have made it clear in all of our communications with you that is not the case and Carol further confirmed that with you when you met in Kenya. If that is mentioned in the broadcast we ask that you please remove it."[60]

But when I watched the show that night, there was Kelley, talking about latrines.

In another brazen example, WE Charity provided the CBC with a preliminary report from forensic auditor Ken Froese that addressed the organization's expenditures in Kenya.[61] It had to be preliminary because the CBC would not wait for the final report before going to air. Even so, Froese had already reached a clear conclusion: all money WE Charity raised in Canada and the US for Kenya was used in Kenya. Case closed, right? Not so fast. Despite receiving the report prior to broadcast, Kelley *still* opened the episode by asking, "Where did all that money go?" Worse still, the CBC then went on to misquote Froese's report in an article discussing their investigation so that it appeared he said the opposite of what he actually did.[62]

Froese's report states that funds raised in Canada and the US for Kenya over an eight-year period ending August 2020 totalled approximately $74 million, and that WE Charity actually spent $83.8 million on Kenya during the same period. In other words, all the money designated for Kenya was spent on Kenya—and then some. In breaking it down, Froese explained that some costs for programming, "including payments to third party suppliers to support Kenyan operations and a share of administrative costs," were recorded in Canada because they were paid for by WE Charity Canada.[63] The CBC article, however, omitted this key information and instead said only "costs for WE Canada, including administration, were $29 million." This may sound like nothing to some people, but it was a huge omission because it suggested that $29 million went to bloated WE administrative costs and operations in Canada rather than being directed to Kenyan programs. The misleading edit by the CBC painted a picture of exactly the kind of bad behaviour the charity was being accused of.

The CBC's response to the organization's immediate demand for a correction still baffles me. Diana Swain, executive producer of *The Fifth Estate*, said, "I've reviewed the paragraph, and I'm confident that we make appropriate reference to Kenya. In fact, the story as a whole is about money raised for and spent in Kenya. The country is referenced in each of the three lines in the paragraph you cited."[64]

You have to wonder, why misstate the record and then refuse to correct it? But the article remains uncorrected online at the time of writing.

FINDING THEIR VOICES

For over eighteen months, it often felt like WE Charity stood alone. There were private messages of support, of course, and the occasional op-ed or letter to the editor, but for the most part, the public space was dominated by fierce critics. *The Fifth Estate*'s ongoing reporting changed the dynamic. Those who knew the charity's work best became, well, sick of it all. Donors began to revolt against the false media narrative.

When I sat down in July 2021 with Dave Richardson—a member of one of Canada's most prominent philanthropic families—he told me he was going to be blunt. And he was. He said that in his view, the politicians' conduct had been "deplorable and despicable," and the decimation of the charity represented "a part of political Canada I never wanted to see." On the Kielburgers, Richardson was adamant: "They have never let me down. They have done great things to make the world better, and continue to do so. The world still needs people like Craig and Marc, maybe now more than ever."

By September, Richardson had clearly lost patience with the media as well—the CBC, in particular. After observing how the views of donors were misrepresented in the initial *Fifth Estate* broadcast, and knowing there was more to come, he spearheaded an effort to organize those prepared to speak out publicly and push back. This resulted in an open letter to the CBC, signed by seventy-seven donors who collectively represented the majority of donations made to WE Villages programs in Kenya. It was a who's who of Canadian business and philanthropy, including the Right Honorable Kim Campbell, Michael "Pinball" Clemons, Gail Asper, Chip Wilson, Heather Skoll, Jennifer Tory, Danielle Saputo, and John Peller. Signatories also included grassroots community organizers who had been fundraising for WE Charity for years. They strongly rejected the suggestion that they had been misled about how their money was used. "WE Charity's development model is holistic," read the letter. "It takes funding from multiple donors to ensure schools and school rooms are built and can deliver education to children over the long term, or for a borehole to be drilled and succeed as part of a full community water system."[65] The letter asked for assurance "that our voices, as major donors of the projects, will be appropriately reflected and considered." In his cover email, Richardson noted that he was "extremely concerned about continued inaccurate and unsubstantiated reporting by the *Fifth Estate* that is misrepresenting how WE Charity works."[66] And on behalf of signatories, he said, "We have stayed out of the fray until now, but we will no longer allow false reporting by the CBC to harm our reputations, or more importantly, harm the projects and the children in Kenya."

"It was a very emotional moment when Dave told me what he wanted to organize. He called it 'ME *for* WE,' and that made me smile," Craig recounted. "We spent a lot of time feeling alone. So now, seeing so many who never lost faith and are willing to stand by us—I had no words."

Educators followed suit. On September 22, Mark Burke, a retired teacher formerly with the Toronto Catholic District School Board, submitted a letter signed by fifty current and former educators, including directors of education, school board administrators, trustees, and teachers, representing hundreds of schools and tens of thousands of students.[67] "As WE Charity winds down its Canadian operations, we are struck by the impact that politics and media coverage has had on an organization that has created so much good," the letter read. "We want to speak up in the hopes of preventing any further misleading reporting on WE Charity's development projects."

To my mind, this letter filled a vacuum—so little had been heard from educators throughout the CSSG affair and the subsequent critiques of the charity's international work. You would think that the CBC would be excited to feature this new perspective. These educators—all donors as well—told the broadcaster that "what always appealed to us was that our support was not just about building empty schoolrooms; it was about ensuring that the schools and educators had the resources to ensure children can thrive." They understood, they said, "that multiple donors may support the same school or school room."

In total, I am aware of more than 125 WE Charity donors and supporters who wrote, individually or collectively, to the CBC. Many of those donors had been approached by the CBC over the previous months and felt their voices or experiences were not accurately represented. They shared their emails and letters with the charity and authorized the charity to share them with me. In them, donors big and small sounded similar themes. People wrote about their personal experiences with the charity and what they had observed when visiting WE Villages sites. Every letter I read also explained, substantively and thoughtfully, how their money was spent, and how the development pillars worked. And the letters were highly critical of the CBC's donor deception theory. The messages I reviewed typically ended with a plea that the broadcaster include the donor's perspective in any future reporting.

One letter was penned by Ross Hynes, the former Canadian High Commissioner to Kenya, Uganda, and Pakistan; a former ambassador to Rwanda, Burundi, Eritrea, and Somalia; and Canada's representative for the UN Environment Programme, UN-Habitat, and the UN Commission on Human Rights. "As Canada's High Commissioner to Kenya from 2006 to 2010," he wrote to Catherine Tait, the president of the CBC, "I and my wife, Vanessa, gained extensive exposure to WE's work and remarkable impact on communities—both the physical infrastructure built (hospitals, school rooms, boreholes, etc.) and local capacity created . . . Indeed, in my 35 years as a Canadian public servant, government executive and representative in some of the world's most challenging developmental environments, I can't say I've encountered any more dedicated or effective ambassadors for our country and its values."[68]

Rosanne Leddy, a registered respiratory therapist from Hamilton, Ontario, is the chair of MAD4Maddie, a community group that raised funds for WE Charity for approximately twelve years. In a pointed letter to Cashore and Diana Swain, Leddy recounted travelling to Kenya to see WE's work first-hand and assured the CBC that "WE Charity was always clear and up-front with [us]. We, along with I would assume, all donors to WE Village programs, know that our fundraising is meant to support systems, not simply the initial infrastructure, but on-going operating expenses . . . As a donor to and supporter of WE Charity, their model always made sense to me. I believe that every major charity in Canada operates this way. I know for certain that the M4M committee was aware of where our fundraising dollars went."[69] She expressed dismay with the CBC's coverage of WE because it "consistently excluded any voices supporting the charity," and she made clear that she was writing because she was worried about the consequences of what she perceived as the network's misleading reporting. "The charity's ability to fundraise and the future of those humanitarian projects will be forever altered by your choices. I witnessed how kids in Canada began to think outside of themselves because of the work that WE did in Canadian schools . . . I hope that you carefully consider the consequences of your actions, and what impact you are having on the lives of people in some of the most impoverished regions of the world." Finally, she made a simple request: "If you choose to pursue your negativity towards WE Charity, I hope that you will take at least a few moments to reflect on my words in your reporting."

Her request was denied.

Jon Levy, the former CEO of Mastermind Toys, wrote Brodie Fenlon to express his concern "about the nature of CBC's coverage of the charity and the resulting harm on our young people, both here in Canada, and within WE-supported communities in the developing world."[70] Having visited WE Villages sites and conducted his own due diligence, Levy said he knew *The Fifth Estate* was "simply wrong" when it asserted that donors had been deceived by the charity. "If the CBC found a few people who were confused about how donations work," he said, "this does not represent the majority of us, who provided the most funds towards the

WE Villages program." Like the others, Levy asked that his position be "clearly and sufficiently represented" in any future reporting. "I seek your personal commitment that if CBC continues to report on WE Charity that the perspective of the 75+ donors is given equal weight and equal broadcast time."

All these people were putting themselves out there because they felt the charity was being maligned. They were showing courage and sticking up for what they believed in. And all they asked in return was that their views be taken seriously and be given equal weight.

None of it seemed to matter.

THE REAL SCANDAL

Even though all this correspondence arrived at the CBC before *The Fifth Estate's* "Finding School No. 4" was aired, these voices received only the amount of airtime the CBC evidently thought they deserved—*eighty-three seconds* of the one-hour broadcast.[71] And many of those seconds were taken up by Mark Kelley stating that the donor comments were part of "an aggressive campaign to stop our investigation." He then flagged that at least one donor had previewed a letter to the president of the CBC with Craig Kielburger. "A clue," Kelley called it, "as to who was involved in the campaign."

This was a clear attempt to leave viewers with the impression that the positive feedback need not be taken seriously. I'm sure it worked. But it struck me as ridiculous on two levels. First, there is nothing untoward in WE and the Kielburgers engaging in dialogue with donors who wrote to the CBC. How could it be otherwise? Wouldn't it have been strange if Craig Kielburger was *not* involved in the effort to set the record straight? And second, what difference did it make? Whether coordinated or not, 125 Canadian donors from all walks of life had told the CBC what they thought about the idea that they were confused about where their dollars went. These people asked their national broadcaster to tell their side of the story too. To *include* them. And every one of them had deeper familiarity with the work of the charity than Mark Kelley's key witnesses: Watson Jordan, Rukshan De Silva, and Reed Cowan. It is absurd to suggest, as the CBC implicitly did, that a slew of Canadian billionaires, business leaders, athletes, politicians, community organizers, and teachers were all so beholden to the Kielburgers that they sent on-the-record letters to the CBC that didn't really reflect how they felt.

It was, to my mind, a convenient way to discount their voices and avoid disrupting the storyline. To offer an analogy, it was as though the CBC aired a documentary touting the perspective of a few climate change deniers, and then mentioned, in a dismissive tone, that hundreds of climate scientists had offered a different take as part of an orchestrated campaign by environmentalists. Then cue the credits.

Nevertheless, Brodie Fenlon felt compelled to offer a defence of the CBC's journalism. In an article published two days after "Finding School No. 4" aired, Fenlon argued the public interest case for the story, insisted that the CBC adheres to "some of the highest journalistic standards in the industry," and noted the challenges faced by the investigating team.[72] He then said that the letters to the CBC from donors were similar in ways that "suggested a coordinated campaign." No mention of teachers, no mention of substance, and nothing about whether any effort had been made to figure out what was true and what was false. Fenlon concluded by asserting that the CBC's journalists had acted as expected and had lived up to "the five principles of our journalistic standards: accuracy, fairness, balance, impartiality and integrity."

This probably seemed like an unremarkable response to most readers. To me, however, it was profound because of what it didn't say. Could Fenlon have taken the same position, I wondered, if he'd told Canadians about the lie the CBC's handler had told the Kenyan governor, or if he'd volunteered that the journalists tried to take pictures at Kenyan schools during a global pandemic without securing permission? Would he have been able to say what he said if he'd revealed that the CBC produced no evidence that anyone had been told they "fully funded" a school or borehole? Or that the CBC misrepresented the number of schoolrooms on the ground in Kenya? Could he have claimed journalistic integrity if he'd acknowledged that purported victims—people like Donna McFarlane and Stuart McLaughlin—had rejected the CBC's claims and were standing with WE?

I couldn't help contrasting Fenlon's defiant stance with the attitude displayed by ABC 7, an ABC affiliate in San Francisco. On April 8, 2021, the network's evening news broadcast included a nine-minute story called "WE Charity Under Investigation." The report featured Charlie Angus and Pierre Poilievre—each of whom provided their standard (and now disproven) negative commentary regarding the charity—and played back all the worst coverage from Bloomberg, Reed Cowan, *The Fifth Estate*, and others. But unlike the CBC and most other Canadian media outlets, ABC 7 made three rounds of corrections when presented with evidence that the claims made on its show were false or misleading. The station also agreed to delete the story from its web archive, and the journalist responsible deleted her social media posts about WE Charity.[73]

In the end, though, the fact that the CBC has never corrected its mistakes is less troubling to me than its decision to leave out the most worthy story of all by ignoring the voices of the thousands of children who attend WE schools in Kenya and around the world. They could have told a marvellous and inspirational tale. But to my knowledge, the *Fifth Estate* team did not speak with even one student or teacher when they visited Kenya. They did not talk to any of the hundreds of thousands of patients treated at Baraka Hospital, or any of the recipients of millions of meals distributed as part of WE's COVID relief programs. No interviews with Mama Evelyn or other women entrepreneurs.

All of this, it seems, was irrelevant.

For me, reflecting back, it was sadly emblematic of the past two years and the whole sordid affair. Of a persistent refusal to take stock of the human cost of the political and media-driven hysteria surrounding WE Charity. Of a tragic fixation with bringing down the high-flying Kielburgers and no consideration of the collateral consequences for so many who had always had their feet planted firmly on the ground. Of amplifying every misstep of WE so that, very quickly, people forgot to reflect with pride on all the good this homegrown institution had done and all the good it was positioned to do. Of putting partisan gain and media clicks ahead of service to society. And most shamefully, of peddling falsehoods and stoking outrage when, in the end, there was simply nothing there.

Isn't that the *real* WE Charity Scandal?

EPILOGUE

THE ROAD AHEAD

In October 2021, a brief article on the CTV News website caught my eye. "An organization that received $5.8 million from the federal government to help job seekers from under-represented communities," the article began, "is refusing to say if it paid the prime minister's mother, Margaret Trudeau, to speak at an event it held this month."[1]

The organization in question was Elevate, a Toronto-based non-profit with a mission to bring together "entrepreneurs, corporate innovators, policymakers and students to help solve complex social problems."[2] It had hired Trudeau to speak about mental health issues and the pandemic at Think 2030, an initiative to explore how best to accomplish the United Nations' Sustainable Development Goals. Other prominent speakers included Chris Hadfield, Jane Goodall, and Emmanuel Acho.[3] Among the event's partners were MasterCard, RBC, Interac, and the *Globe and Mail*.

In addition to pursuing corporate partnerships, Elevate, the article explained, also lobbied the government for funding through the Federal Economic Development Agency for Southern Ontario, more commonly known as FedDev Ontario, and had at one time been registered to lobby the Prime Minister's Office as well. The $5.8 million in funding from FedDev was to help marginalized Canadians find work in the tech sector and creative industries.

So a non-profit agency got money from the federal government to facilitate job opportunities for members of the BIPOC and LGBTQ communities. And this same agency had also paid money to the prime minister's mother to appear at an event to speak about mental health.

Where had I heard all this before?

I could only imagine the outrage that Charlie Angus and Pierre Poilievre had to be feeling. All those months they'd spent sounding the alarm about the CSSG and Trudeau's cozy backroom deals, and here he was, right back at it again. What would Kate Bahen have to say? Or Mark Blumberg? Or Jesse Brown? How soon would it be before hot headlines about the "Elevate Scandal" hit the press?

Instead . . . crickets. Of all the critics who'd pounced on WE Charity during the CSSG controversy, Conservative MP Michael Barrett was the only one to comment on the Elevate situation, and even that was just a single post on social media.[4] And other than the CTV story I'd stumbled upon, news outlets were completely silent. In fact, the only other coverage I could find was a positive story the *Globe and Mail* had published about the $5.8 million funding announcement back in June. The paper failed to disclose to readers that it was also Elevate's media partner,[5] and when Margaret Trudeau was hired to speak just months later, the *Globe* never published a follow-up article about the apparent quid pro quo involved in hiring the prime minister's mother soon after scoring millions in taxpayer money.

WINNERS AND LOSERS

The reappearance of Margaret Trudeau, back speaking at conferences and corporate events and advocating for mental health awareness—as she had done so eloquently and passionately on the WE Day stage and at fundraising events for the charity—made me realize that while the world had been turned upside down for everyone who worked at or benefited from WE Charity, the rest of the characters in this story came out just fine.

Justin Trudeau wriggled free of the opposition's ethics complaints, was exonerated by Mario Dion, shrugged off the RCMP referrals, and then carried on with business as usual. In September, he even managed to retain power, despite having forced a pandemic election no one wanted. But the $610 million trip to the polls—the most expensive election in Canadian history[6]—didn't give him the majority government he so desired. When all the votes were counted, the Liberals added only five seats to their total. In other words, Trudeau landed right back where he started. And on the campaign trail, after two years of pearl-clutching and hand-wringing by opposition politicians, the WE Charity Scandal wasn't even a blip on the radar screen.

Pierre Poilievre and Charlie Angus easily held their seats in Parliament—although Justin Trudeau outperformed them both, garnering an impressive 50.3 percent of the votes in his Montreal riding. Today, they remain two of the highest-profile members of their respective parties. Poilievre has announced that he's running to replace Erin O'Toole as the leader of the Conservative Party, and he is considered an early favourite to win—in no small part, I think, because of the profile boost he received over the past two years at the expense of WE Charity and the children and teachers it served. Angus, too, is well placed for a leadership bid when that job becomes available again. He was even voted Best Mentor by his fellow MPs for *Maclean's* annual Parliamentarians of the Year Awards.[7]

Kate Bahen of Charity Intelligence rode the WE Charity Scandal to bigger and better things. Her organization is now actively working with media outlets like the *Globe and Mail* to assist in investigative reports.[8] Lawyer Mark Blumberg is also still going strong and has solidified his position as a go-to guy for media commentary on the charitable sector.

Jesse Brown's Canadaland website continues to thrive,[9] and his interest in WE Charity shows little sign of abating. In 2020, he was named one of *Toronto Life's* fifty most influential Torontonians.[10] Coming in at number 45, he just squeezed out Matt Galloway, host of CBC Radio's *The Current*, and Sally Catto, the broadcaster's general manager of entertainment, factual, and sports. "He and his team ignited a firestorm with their long-term reporting on the WE Charity and its cozy relationship with the Liberals," gushed *Toronto Life*. "When the dust settled, a finance minister was gone, $30 million in funding was withdrawn, WE's Canadian operation was wrapped up and Trudeau's eternal sheen was tarnished." And the *Globe and Mail* named Canadaland's *White Saviours* one of the top podcasts of 2021, praising it for "exposing crimes, lies and a penchant for profit," even though the podcast had offered no real evidence of any of these things.[11]

Other journalists and media outlets were also flourishing in the wake of the scandal. Bloomberg was recognized for its coverage of WE Charity by the Society for Advancing Business Editing and Writing, and reporter Natalie Obiko Pearson won the Columbia Journalism School's prestigious Christopher J. Welles Memorial Prize. In their citation for the award, the judges specifically called out Obiko Pearson's work on WE Charity, which, they said, "read like a financial thriller."[12]

The *Globe and Mail* was also lauded for its coverage of WE Charity. In 2020, fellow journalists awarded the daily a National Newspaper Award for political writing for its "in-depth look at the public policy questions raised by the WE scandal, and at the WE organization itself."[13] The award was shared by Geoffrey York, Paul Waldie, Bill Curry, Marieke Walsh—and yes, Jaren Kerr, Jesse Brown's protégé from Canadaland, who'd landed himself a plum job at the country's leading newspaper.

No awards for the *Toronto Star*, as far as I'm aware, but the paper did just miss out on one coveted prize. After reporting several times about WE Charity's supposedly suspicious real estate holdings, the *Star* put in a below-market-value offer to buy the WE GLC, the charity's crown jewel. Apparently the paper could see the benefit in owning a state-of-the-art, technologically advanced building right in the downtown core of Canada's largest city. But in the end, they were outbid by a group of investors who paid more than the independent valuation for the property. And then—in the "you can't make this stuff up" category—*Star* journalist Marco Chown Oved began investigating the new owners of the property and questioning whether WE Charity sold it on the cheap in some form of sweetheart deal. If it wasn't all so tragic, there would be comic irony in a *Star* reporter suggesting that buyers might have underpaid when *Star* executives appear to have concluded that they overpaid. And there is irony, too, in the *Toronto Star* attacking the way the charity wound down when it had published the article on Iqbal Masih that inspired Free the Children in the first place.

As predicted, Oved's eventual piece implied that the WE GLC was sold for less than it should have been. No amount of information could convince him otherwise. He even left out an on-the-record statement from JLL, the global real estate firm that conducted the independent valuation, confirming that the building had not been undersold. Telling readers that simple truth just wouldn't sell papers, I guess. (As a member of the board subcommittee handling real estate sales before I left the organization, I can assure you that the process was as buttoned-up and wrapped in external expert advice as anything I've seen.)[14]

And what about Mark Kelley, Harvey Cashore, and the rest of the team at *The Fifth Estate*? As I write this, there are rumours that they're still pursuing leads, hunting down sources, and trying to unearth more on the organization. I know that no matter how much they dig, they're not going to find what they're looking for. Audit after audit has proven that WE Charity spent donors' money exactly how they said they would—on the ground, in impoverished communities in Kenya and elsewhere, by bringing people clean water and healthcare and schools for their children. But if they don't want to believe the numbers, Kelley and Cashore can trust the evidence they saw with their own eyes as they travelled throughout the Maasai Mara region. As Kelley told the CBC's Matt Galloway in a radio interview, "The impact is real."

Looking back, it is easy to understand why these people did what they did and said what they said. For politicians like Angus and Poilievre, it was a political gambit that ultimately didn't pay off. Journalists needed clicks and headlines—particularly to stay relevant in the age of social media and alternative news sources—and those weren't going to come from a sober separation of fact from fiction. And pundits needed to claim their moment in the spotlight when opportunity knocked. None of which is to say that WE Charity was blameless. The organization made its fair share of gaffes and missteps along the way, and I take a measure of responsibility for that.

But the answer to why Canadians swallowed it all is more elusive. Why were people so quick to accept that WE and the Kielburgers were up to no good when they were presented with no actual evidence that laws were broken, ethical standards were breached, or money was missing? Why were supporters of the charity so quick to go into hiding when their own contributions were called into question? Why did no one produce a scathing documentary about how students were robbed of the CSSG in the middle of a pandemic? Why did no journalists write about the relationship between WE and opposition politicians, call out Charlie Angus for demanding an RCMP investigation off the back of testimony from an extortionist, or ponder how the CBC could claim that multiple donors had "fully funded" the same international projects when no piece of paper said any such thing? Worst of all, why did almost no one talk to students, teachers, and project beneficiaries to get their perspective and assess whether the losses were worth it? Maybe it is because, as businessman Bill Elkington suggested to me, "whenever Canadians have done something successful on the world stage, we have to tear it down, say we did it wrong, or say if somebody got ahead, that person must have cheated." Or maybe we have become too accepting of what I have called the Americanization of politics. Or perhaps we are simply too trusting of the media to tell us what to think. I don't have the answers, but I know these questions merit some soul-searching.

In the end, even if you dislike WE Charity or the Kielburgers, you should have concerns about the way their main critics behaved. And Canadians should ask themselves whether there was value in destroying a homegrown children's charity that inspired generations of young people to serve others. The losses are staggering. Millions of students will go without programming that focused on mental health and wellness. There will be no more WE Day celebrations of local and international acts of service. No more Halloween food drives, walks for clean water, or campaigns to support Indigenous communities. No more galvanizing young people to volunteer for thousands of other non-profits. And in impoverished communities around the world, there will be no new wells, community gardens, clinics, hospitals, schools, or entrepreneurial programs for women.[15] These are things we have all lost.

ARISING FROM THE ASHES

For the organization, meanwhile, the fallout continues. Backed into a corner by ongoing misleading media coverage, the charity felt it had no choice but to explore legal options. As I write this, WE Charity has just filed a lawsuit against the CBC for its "false and defamatory" reports, which include *The Fifth Estate*'s claim that the charity deceived donors about its work in Kenya. "The complaint cites extensive evidence showing that the CBC knowingly or recklessly disregarded the truth in its reporting," said the charity's lawyer, Joseph Kroetsch, in a press release. "In this lawsuit, WE Charity will demonstrate how at every step, the

CBC pursued a false, preconceived narrative despite clear evidence that it was wrong."[16] Several WE donors are helping to financially support the lawsuit. And Theresa Kielburger, mother of Marc and Craig, is suing Canadaland, Jesse Brown, Jaren Kerr, and others for "disseminating and propagating . . . defamatory statements."[17] This suit is in response to Canadaland's *White Saviours* podcast, where Brown recited journalist Isabel Vincent's charge, made in 1996, that the Kielburgers' mother had "deposited hundreds of thousands of dollars in donations directly into the family's personal bank account" in the early days of Free the Children. These were the exact same claims at the heart of the decades-old *Saturday Night* libel suit, which ended when the magazine and the journalists consented to a judgment by the court—none of which Brown got around to telling his listeners.

I understand why WE Charity and the Kielburgers feel it is important to set the record straight and seek redress for harms the charity and its beneficiaries have suffered. But at this point in our story, I'd like to look forward, not back. I take that cue from the interviews I conducted with numerous WE Charity staff members. Despite everything that has happened, these remarkable people had little appetite for dwelling too long on the negative, and their feelings of bitterness and frustration almost always gave way to talk of hope and a need to get back to doing good. For them, WE was always more than just a place to work—it was a mission and a movement that was bigger than the charity itself, and that needed to live on even if the organization did not. WE Charity got caught up in a wildfire—that is beyond dispute. But even after the most devastating blaze, something survives. New life arises from the ashes.

"Over the past couple of years there has been so much that left me stunned in a negative way," Marc told me. "But if there is one thing that has floored me in a positive way, it is the dedication and strength of the WE team. Every day they had to wade through a torrent of abuse. That's demoralizing when all you're trying to do is help others. And yet through it all—Robin continuing in Kenya, Scott in Ecuador, Dalal in the office, and so many others—they continued to believe in the mission and were there to support each other. I don't have the words to say how much I love all these people."

Dalal shared Marc's feelings of gratitude and awe. "I had staff telling me that they were getting called out over the holiday dinner table," she said. "Parents and siblings were pressing them to leave WE because it would . . . look better for their CV. How many people could resist that kind of pressure? But so many did. And to them, I am forever grateful."

I too have deep admiration for the resilience and courage of the team at WE Charity. It would have been completely understandable for people to walk away in the face of so much unrelenting criticism. But most did not flinch. I hope people take notice of that. The same is true of the hundreds of donors and educators who wrote to the CBC to express their concerns with *The Fifth Estate*'s reporting. I had expected that some might retreat after a second incendiary documentary aired in November 2021, but instead they stood firm and said they continued to support WE in a letter that was published in national newspapers across Canada.

All these people refused to back down because they saw that amid the political sound bites and daily headlines, the organization never lost sight of its priorities. It delivered over a million emergency meals to families overseas and provided COVID education and relief to more than a hundred thousand people in Kenya. Baraka Hospital was transformed into a vaccine distribution centre, and millions of dollars in medical supplies were shipped to the region. In Haiti, the team helped outfit a hospital with solar power. In Sierra Leone, work continued on a new high school. And at home in Canada, the WE Schools team digitized 100 percent of its resources, including lesson plans, classroom activities, and self-care programming, ensuring that students would have access to these after WE Charity Canada was no longer in existence. In addition, hundreds of thousands of students and teachers were supported through the pandemic with virtual WE Well-being mental health resources.

I would be remiss if I did not also give credit to my fellow WE Charity board members, who steered the ship through the storm both before and after I stepped down to write this book. The directors brought a degree of commitment and seriousness to their work that was truly inspiring. Governing an organization in the midst of an unparalleled crisis—particularly one that had people questioning that very governance—was thankless work. It would have been easy for people to say it was too much, but instead they stayed the course, asked hard questions of the Kielburgers and WE management, took nothing for granted or on faith, and kept their sights firmly on protecting those who needed the organization most. On those days when I felt demoralized or wondered if the hits would ever stop, my fellow board members were there to boost me up and remind me of the reasons we all signed on with WE in the first place. Many of them still have their sleeves rolled up, ready for whatever comes next.

So what will that new life from the ashes look like? Now that WE Charity Canada is no more, what does the future hold? Unfortunately, some of the international projects started by the organization before COVID and the CSSG were not completed by the time the charity started to shut down. As I explained earlier in the book, the WE Villages model involved bringing a partner community to sustainability in five to seven years. The organization launched those projects expecting to have ongoing funding to see them through. But when the money dried up and the charity shut down, a new way forward had to be found. The solution was the sale of WE Charity's real estate holdings, which had always served as a kind of large-scale rainy day fund that could be used if the worst happened. Even though those assets had been the source of considerable controversy and finger-pointing, they saved the day in the end in terms of delivering for impoverished people. The buildings owned by WE Charity have now been sold, and the revenue generated has been allocated to two foundations, each with a distinct focus and purpose.

WE Charity Foundation will support operations in Kenya, completing half-finished work in many communities. The vast majority of projects were closed out by the end of 2021, with only a few left to complete over the next year or two. The foundation will also sustain key projects that are beyond the core five pillars and require ongoing financial support, including Baraka Hospital, the boarding high schools, the Women's Empowerment Centre, and WE College. It is vitally important to continue this work for the sake of the children who need an education, the patients who need healthcare, the women who need earning opportunities, and the students who want to be trained as nurses, farmers, or entrepreneurs and then use those valuable skills to benefit their communities.

It's important to note that WE Charity Foundation, although based in Canada, is largely governed *by* Kenyans *for* Kenyans. Dr. Steve Mainda, a respected local economist and healthcare expert, is the foundation's co-chair, alongside former WE Charity board member Gerry Connelly. And Kenyans make up 99 percent of the staff managing the projects on the ground. Carol Moraa is still there, bruised but not broken, her passion for empowering the women and girls of her region undiminished. Justus Mwendwa has taken up a new role as co-executive director of WE Charity Foundation, working with Robin Wiszowaty, who has been "commuting" from the US to Kenya while waiting for her young children to be fully vaccinated. Craig and Marc, meanwhile, have stepped back so WE Charity Foundation can have a fresh start.

But the rest of the infrastructure funded by donors and built by WE—the wells and pipelines and water kiosks and primary schools—will be independently maintained by the communities they serve, exactly as the charity always intended. It's devastating to think that there will be no new projects in Kenya, Ethiopia, India, and the many other countries where WE Charity was active, but it's comforting to me that the five-pillar model left a meaningful legacy that anyone who worked for or supported WE can be proud of.

The second of the legacy entities, the Wellbeing Foundation, will continue to support youth mental health initiatives. Certain donors who funded the purchase and construction of the WE GLC asked that, upon its sale, a portion of proceeds be directed to this important mission. The WE Well-being team had already made great strides in creating a national K–12 curriculum in the belief that all children should have access to evidence-based mental health education in schools, including resources to teach brain health, resilience, and self-care. Now the program will continue to grow, adding new resources for students and educators, such as an online portal full of classroom tools and activities for all ages.

Dalal is overseeing the next phase of WE Charity, including its continuing operations as the organization winds down in Canada and carries on its efforts in the US. Under her leadership, WE Charity US is moving forward with the support of donors who have remained loyal. In fact, in the wake of the CSSG fiasco, several US corporate donors conducted their own independent reviews of WE Charity and then decided to double down on their involvement with the organization. Microsoft was one. When its review was complete, the corporation not only renewed its support but increased funding in this time of great need. Microsoft has also made a commitment to help scale WE's educational programs and make them available in more countries worldwide.[18] And even as Canada's public broadcaster, the CBC, has focused on tearing down WE Charity, a new partnership has been forged with the flagship US Public Broadcasting Service (PBS) station in Washington, DC, to deliver WE Well-being resources to students across the US. The broadcaster adapted existing WE Well-being materials into an award-winning animated series to support social-emotional health and promoted the program to benefit schools and families.[19]

Thanks to supporters like these, WE Charity US will continue its work with teachers, students, and social entrepreneurs through virtual programming such as podcasts, videos, motivational talks, and curriculum kits. And the WE Schools and WE Well-being resources will remain available to educators around the world, including in Canada, through the power of digital technology. While it does not address or compensate for the huge loss that will be faced in Canadian classrooms because of the closure of WE Charity in Canada, it is at least a small comfort that young people from Vancouver Island to St. John's are not—through choices made for them by politicians and the media—deprived of programming offered to kids in Seattle and Boston.

WE Charity US is also playing a key role in fundraising for projects in Ecuador—the one country where the organization's development work is not just continuing but growing. As a caretaker of part of the Amazon rainforest and one of just seventeen megadiverse countries in the world, Ecuador has incredible global importance. WE Charity US and its American donors have always felt a personal connection to the Ecuadorian Indigenous peoples who were a focus of much of WE's work there. With Kenya as a template, the goal is to build the same five pillars of sustainable development in regions like Chimborazo and Napo.

This effort is taking place under the leadership of Scott Baker, who has returned to Ecuador from his COVID exile (reuniting with the dog he had to leave behind with family in 2020). Working once again with the local team and living among the small remote communities he's supporting, Scott is rediscovering the passion he had as a young volunteer, camping out in the Kielburgers' backyard in the early days of Free the Children.

As for ME to WE, it is too soon to tell. It has been a parade of non-stop crises over the past two years, and Craig told me that because all efforts have been focused on saving the charity, the social enterprise was put into hibernation. Also, so much of ME to WE's model—the trips and retail sales—is still broken because of COVID. But the hope is that the company can eventually be revived to continue creating employment for marginalized people and channelling funds to WE Charity US and its global mission.

I asked Craig where his head is at, nearly two years after the nightmare began. He told me that he's worked harder than he ever has in his life just to ensure that all the impacts of a quarter century are not lost beyond recovery. There is a sense of responsibility, something he has felt since he was a young boy, that he very clearly carries with him. He admitted that he's feeling drained, but like Marc, he quickly pivots from focusing on his feelings to expressing deep gratitude to Dalal, Scott, Robin, Carol, Justus, and so many others who stayed on through the storm and fought to keep the mission alive.

In a way, Craig is going back to where it all began, taking counsel from those who advised him in the early days, like Jeff Skoll. He has never wavered in his conviction that social enterprise is the key to tackling the world's most pressing environmental and social issues. That conviction, he said, was only strengthened when he saw how quickly donor dollars can evaporate—a phenomenon he called the "fragility of good." For that reason, he and Marc are still thinking about innovative ways to use social entrepreneurship to solve the sometimes insurmountable challenges facing our world. They know it will take time to come to terms with all that has happened and to truly take stock of the consequences. And they know that a lot of self-reflection is in order. But their defining and seemingly insatiable drive to do more is ever-present. The same idealistic ethic that Marc shared with me when we were fourteen—good enough is simply not good enough—still animates the way the brothers think about the years ahead.

Where will those plans end up? That remains to be seen, but this much I can say: the doors of WE Charity Canada may have closed, but the passion and idealism that drove the organization cannot be so easily locked away.

ACKNOWLEDGMENTS

This is a book I felt compelled to write—the story just had to be told, and it seemed I was uniquely positioned to tell it. But that didn't make the task any less daunting. As a first-time author tackling a controversial political scandal, I felt plenty of apprehension. I found my way through it by leaning on a large group of people to whom I am deeply indebted. Without them, this book would not exist and many important voices would remain unheard.

On the production side, I was supported by an all-star team. Dean Baxendale, head of Optimum Publishing, was the driving force behind it all. He shared my sense that the media and politicians had let Canadians down and was not prepared to leave things that way. I'm especially grateful for his patience as the project perpetually grew in scope and the timeline kept getting pushed.

Janice Weaver, my editor, is the unsung hero behind this project. I previously had only a passing appreciation for the work that an editor does, and now I have a profound respect for the craft. But the word "editor" does not capture the depth of Janice's contribution. She was a true partner in the writing process and the person whose counsel I relied on most. I also had two incredibly hard-working and talented research assistants, Yvonne Mazurak and Sean Deasy. They tirelessly gathered and distilled the information necessary to bring this story to life. I'm also grateful for the cooperation and support I received from WE Charity staff, who provided reams of material and tracked down anything I asked for.

I must extend special thanks to former prime minister Kim Campbell, both for her thoughtful foreword and for the insights she provided in a series of interviews. She was exceedingly generous with her time and advice, and she brought to bear decades of experience inside and outside public life. Her perspectives on how Canadians perceive themselves, how they are perceived around the world, and how they ought to strive to be perceived helped frame a lot of my research and thinking.

I was also blessed to be able to call upon a long list of "thought partners"—in Canada and the US—who allowed me to bounce ideas off them, reviewed portions of the manuscript, and didn't hesitate to challenge me on controversial topics. They include dozens of friends, family members, colleagues, subject matter experts in areas like charity law, the philanthropic sector, and the media, and supporters and detractors of WE Charity and the Kielburgers. There are too many names to list, but all those who chatted and debated with me about this book—whether on Zoom calls, around cottage firepits, or while taking socially distant walks—helped make it stronger.

And I would be remiss if I did not express my gratitude to all those who served with me on the WE Charity board, particularly as the scandal unfolded. We were all passionate about the charity's mission and scarred deeply by how little attention was paid to that mission when WE came under attack. My many conversations and commiserations with that group were an important source of motivation and inspiration. Greg Rogers, Gerry Connelly, and Kannan Arasaratnam stand out for going above and beyond in offering insights and identifying the right people to talk to. Almost a dozen other current and former board members sat for interviews, shared their candid takes on what went right and what went wrong, and provided important historical perspective on the charity's twenty-five-year legacy.

As it does with most things in my life, the support of family meant everything. My wife, Rippi, strongly encouraged me to write this book—even when I was initially hesitant—despite knowing that virtually every other responsibility in our already hectic life was going to land on her plate. She read every word of the manuscript and offered sage advice, while at the same time making huge sacrifices by picking up all the slack while I typed away. My eleven-year-old son was also a key contributor. We had visited WE Villages in Kenya together, and that experience left an indelible impression that allowed him to offer perspective and reminded me of just what has been lost through the closure of WE

Charity in Canada. And with his customary patience and good nature, he bore with me when this book put constraints on our time together. My parents, brother, sister-in-law, and extended family all humoured me as I droned on about this book for months, while offering encouragement that made it easier to keep barrelling forward when the going got tough.

This book also would not have been possible without the support of my professional family at my law firm, Milbank LLP. When I first considered writing this book, I broached the idea with some of my partners—including the chairman of our firm (Scott Edelman), the chair of our litigation practice (George Canellos), and the then head of our risk management committee (Thomas Arena)—with a degree of trepidation. They could have expressed reservations for any number of reasons. If they had done so, the project would never have gotten off the ground. But they were supportive and encouraging, and graciously helped make room for me to pursue this project amid a busy practice. I also owe a debt to Anthony Cassino, who leads Milbank's pro bono practice and read drafts of every chapter. He told me in plain words what worked, what didn't, and how the content made him feel. That feedback was invaluable. The views expressed in this book are of course completely my own and do not represent the views of anyone at Milbank or any of our clients.

Finally, I am extremely grateful to the dozens of teachers, students, Kenyan community members, donors, and former WE staff who sat for interviews and shared their feelings and experiences. Speaking to them was the most enriching part of this journey, and providing a space for their voices to be heard is the most satisfying part of having written this book. I hope they feel well served. Special credit goes to Aiza Abid, Gerry Connelly, Tania McPhee, Justus Mwendwa, Martin Sheen, Jennifer Tory, Governor Samuel Tunai, and Chip Wilson, who graciously authored the first-person testimonials that are a key part of this work.

If you find this book does a good job of setting the record straight or changes the way you perceive the WE Charity Scandal and the forces that shaped it, it is in large part because of the contributions of the above people and groups. Any shortcomings, of course, are entirely my own.

NOTES

Additional information and supporting documents can be found at the publisher's website, www.WhatWELost.com.

CHAPTER 1: BAD OMENS

1.   "#MyFreedomDay," CNN online, March 16, 2020, http://cnn.com/specials/world/myfreedomday/.

2.   Staff, "Sophie Grégoire Trudeau Experiencing Flu-like Symptoms, Being Tested for COVID-19," *Ottawa Citizen*, March 12, 2020, https://ottawacitizen.com/news/national/sophie-gregoire-trudeau-experiencing-flu-like-symptoms-being-tested-for-covid-19.

3.   Michael Fraiman. "The Coronavirus Knows No Borders. Just Ask Sophie Grégoire Trudeau," *Maclean's*, March 13, 2020, http://macleans.ca/news/canada/the-coronavirus-knows-no-borders-just-ask-sophie-gregoire-trudeau/.

4.   Sophie Durocher, "Le dangereux voyage de Sophie Grégoire Trudeau," *Journal de Montréal*, March 18, 2020, https://www.journaldemontreal.com/2020/03/18/le-dangereux-voyage-de-sophie-gregoire-trudeau/.

5.   Sarah Laing, "Has Prince Harry Been Exposed to Coronavirus? From Idris Elba to Sophie Trudeau: Harry's Possible Chain of Infection," *The Kit*, March 18, 2020, https://thekit.ca/life/royal-report/prince-harry-coronavirus-lewis-hamilton/.

6.   Chris Selley, Twitter, March 17, 2020, 9:21 p.m., https://twitter.com/cselley/status/1240085957006831621.

7.   CTV *News with Sandie Rinaldo*, CTV News, March 21, 2020, https://www.ctvnews.ca/ctv-national-news/video?clipId=1920419/.

CHAPTER 2: GOOD ENOUGH IS NOT GOOD ENOUGH

1.   Scott Gilmore, "In Defence of WE," *Maclean's*, July 21, 2020, https://www.macleans.ca/opinion/in-defence-of-we/.

2. Mark Bourrie, "The Attempted Murder of the Kielburgers," *Fairpress* (blog), October 12, 2020, https://fairpress.ca/the-attempted-murder-of-the-kielburgers/.

3. Tracy Rysavy, "Free the Children: The Story of Craig Kielburger," YES! magazine, October 1, 1999, https://www.yesmagazine.org/issue/issues-power-of-one/1999/10/01/free-the-children-the-story-of-craig-kielburger.

4. Glenda Bartosh, "Fork in the Road: Quit Cherry-Pickin' Those Cherries," *Pique News Magazine*, July 4, 2020, https://www.piquenewsmagazine.com/food/quit-cherry-pickin-those-cherries-2537570.

5. Brenda Spiering, "Two Teachers Who Helped Their Kids Start a Movement," *Canadian Living*, March 22, 2019, https://www.canadianliving.com/life-and-relationships/community-and-current-events/article/two-teachers-who-helped-their-kids-start-a-movement.

6. Spiering, "Two Teachers."

7. This issue was examined by the Honourable Stephen Goudge, who wrote, "Like many parents who have the means to do so, Fred and Theresa Kielburger have provided financial support for their children; in this case, they have financially supported their children's work. I do not believe that the business arrangements used to effect this generosity are inappropriate or indicative of any untoward dealings between Fred and Theresa and WE." Hon. Stephen Goudge, QC, "Independent Assessment of WE's Co-Founders' Compensation, WE's Reporting Protocols, and Relationship with Theresa and Fred Kielburger," May 23, 2019.

8. Rysavy, "Free the Children."

9. Rysavy, "Free the Children."

10. "WE Charity," Charity Navigator, 2019, https://www.charitynavigator.org/ein/161533544.

11. See, for example, "Legal Structures for Social Ventures: Social Enterprise, Social Business and Cooperatives in Canada," MaRS Startup Toolkit, MaRS, https://learn.marsdd.com/article/legal-structures-for-social-ventures-social-enterprise-social-business-and-cooperatives-in-canada/; Susan Manwaring and Andrew Valentine, "Social Enterprise in Canada," Miller Thomson LLP, https://www.millerthomson.com/assets/files/article_attachments2/S-Manwaring_A-Valentine_Social-Enterprise-in-Canada_Miller-Thomson.pdf; Mark Blumberg, "Social Enterprise and Canadian Charities: Are Recent Changes to DQ + Charitable Gift Acts Enough?" *Canadian Charity Law* (blog), March 22, 2010, https://www.canadiancharitylaw.ca/blog/social_enterprise_and_canadian_charities_-_are_recent_changes_to_dq_charita/.

12. CRA Policy Statement CPS-019.

13. *Income Tax Act*, s. 149.1(2)(a).

14. "Our data shows that 7 out of 10 charities we've evaluated spend at least 75% of their budget on the programs and services they exist to provide. And 9 out of 10 spend at least 65%," Charity Navigator, "Financial Score Conversions and Tables," accessed September 30, 2021, https://www.charitynavigator.org/index.cfm?bay=content.view&cpid=48#PerformanceMetricTwo/.

15. The Honourable Peter Cory, "Governance Structure of Free the Children," Toronto, April 14, 2010.

16. The Honourable Peter Cory, "Independent Review of Free the Children Governance and Real Estate Purchases from 2006–2011," Toronto, March 8, 2011.

17. The Honourable Stephen T. Goudge, "Independent Assessment of WE Charity's Real Estate Holdings and Practices," Toronto, November 13, 2019.

18. Goudge, "Independent Assessment."

19. Scott McCallum, "WE Charity and ME to WE Relationship," December 12, 2018.

CHAPTER 3: A CALL TO SERVE

1. Rachel Wernick, email message to Craig Kielburger, April 19, 2020.

2. David Lasby, *Imagine Canada's Sector Monitor: Charities & the* COVID-*19 Pandemic*, Imagine Canada, May 2020, https://imaginecanada.ca/sites/default/files/COVID-19%20Sector%20Monitor%20Report%20ENGLISH_0.pdf.

3. Parliament of Canada, House of Commons, Standing Committee on Finance (FINA): Hearing before FINA, 43rd Parl., 1st sess., July 28, 2020, https://www.ourcommons.ca/DocumentViewer/en/43-1/FINA/meeting-45/evidence.

4. This number is cumulative over the lifetime of WE Charity, and it is based on the charity's records of educator-verified reporting of volunteer hours.

5. Prince Harry, "WE Day UK 2014" (speech, Wembley Arena, London, March 7, 2014), https://www.royal.uk/speech-prince-harry-we-day-wembley-arena-london/.

6. Gord Downie, "WE Day Canada" (speech, Parliament Hill, Ottawa, July 2, 2017).

7. Lieutenant-General (ret.) Roméo Dallaire, "WE Day Canada" (speech, Parliament Hill, Ottawa, July 2, 2017).

8. Governor General David Johnston, "WE Day Canada" (speech, Parliament Hill, Ottawa, July 2, 2017).

9.   Charlie Angus, Twitter, September 9, 2020, 7:00 p.m., https://twitter.com/charlieangusndp/status/1303830767097839616.

10.   Charlie Angus, Twitter, July 2, 2020, 7:20 a.m., https://twitter.com/CharlieAngusNDP/status/1278649715840737281.

11.   Pierre Poilievre, Twitter, July 16, 2020, 5:44 p.m., https://twitter.com/pierrepoilievre/status/1283880322954932226.

12.   Alex Boutilier, "How WE Charity's Youth Pitch Worked Its Way Through Trudeau's Government," *Toronto Star*, July 17, 2020, https://www.thestar.com/politics/federal/2020/07/17/how-we-charitys-youth-pitch-worked-its-way-through-trudeaus-government.html.

13.   Marieke Walsh and Bill Curry, "WE Charity Pitch to Morneau's Office Prior to Trudeau Announcement Included Student Service," *Globe and Mail*, July 22, 2020, https://www.theglobeandmail.com/politics/article-top-civil-servant-pledges-expansive-public-document-release-on-we/.

14.   WE Charity tracked information on the delivery of meals from the start of the pandemic. The information was correct at the time of printing.

CHAPTER 4: MISSION CREEP

1.   Mario Dion, *Trudeau III Report* (Ottawa: Office of the Conflict of Interest and Ethics Commissioner, May 2021), https://ciec-ccie.parl.gc.ca/en/investigations-enquetes/Pages/Trudeau3Report.aspx.

2.   Prime Minister Justin Trudeau, "Prime Minister's Remarks on Support for Students and New Grads Affected by COVID-19" (speech, Ottawa, April 22, 2020), https://pm.gc.ca/en/news/speeches/2020/04/22/prime-ministers-remarks-support-students-and-new-grads-affected-covid-19.

3.   Dion, *Trudeau III Report*.

4.   Trudeau, "Support for Students."

5.   "Government Spending, WE Charity and the Canada Student Service Grant—July 21, 2020," Government of Canada, December 21, 2020, https://www.canada.ca/en/privy-council/corporate/transparency/briefing-documents/parliamentary-committees/standing-committee-finance/government-spending-we-charity-canada-student-service-grant-july-21-2020.html.

6.   Parliament of Canada, House of Commons, Standing Committee on Access to Information, Privacy and Ethics: Hearing before ETHI, 43rd Parl., 2nd sess., December 4, 2020, https://www.ourcommons.ca/DocumentViewer/en/43-2/ETHI/meeting-14/minutes.

7.   Parliament of Canada, House of Commons, Standing Committee on Finance (FINA): Hearing before FINA, 43rd Parl., 1st sess., August 13, 2020,

https://www.ourcommons.ca/DocumentViewer/en/43-1/FINA/meeting-51/evidence.

8. Parliament of Canada, House of Commons, Standing Committee on Access to Information, Privacy and Ethics (ETHI): Hearing before ETHI, 43rd Parl., 1st sess., August 11, 2020, https://www.ourcommons.ca/DocumentViewer/en/43-1/ETHI/meeting-12/evidence.

9. In her testimony, Speevak noted that "the issues that Volunteer Canada has raised about the Canada Student Service Grant program were about the elements, scope and timing of the program, and not the process for selecting WE Charity or WE Charity itself." Parliament of Canada, House of Commons, Standing Committee on Finance (FINA): Hearing before FINA, 43rd Parl., 1st sess., July 16, 2020, https://www.ourcommons.ca/DocumentViewer/en/43-1/FINA/meeting-41/evidence.

10. Dion, *Trudeau III Report*.

11. "On April 28, ESDC submitted a proposed design and implementation plan for the CSSG. It recommended WE as the administrator of the program. Approved in principle by the Cabinet Committee on the federal response to the coronavirus disease (COVID-19) on May 5, the proposal was to be presented to the full Cabinet for ratification on May 8." Dion, *Trudeau III Report*, p. 2.

12. Commissioner Dion was appointed to a seven-year term as conflict of interest and ethics commissioner of Canada in January 2018. He is supported by the Office of the Conflict of Interest and Ethics Commissioner. The commissioner is independent from the government because he reports only to Parliament and is selected in consultation with every party that has a seat in the House of Commons.

13. Dion, *Trudeau III Report*, p. 22.

14. Dion, *Trudeau III Report*, p. 33.

15. Catherine Cullen and Janyce McGregor, "Teachers to Be Paid $12K to Recruit and Manage Students Under Government Program with WE Charity," CBC News, June 30, 2020, https://www.cbc.ca/news/politics/pandemic-student-we-charity-trudeau-1.5633674.

16. See, for example, Parliament of Canada, House of Commons, Standing Committee on Access to Information, Privacy and Ethics (ETHI): Hearing before ETHI, 43rd Parl., 2nd sess., November 30, 2020, https://www.ourcommons.ca/DocumentViewer/en/43-2/ETHI/meeting-13/evidence#Int-11047964; Parliament of Canada, House of Commons, Standing Committee on Access to Information, Privacy and Ethics (ETHI): Hearing before ETHI, 43rd Parl., 1st sess., July 22, 2020, https://www.ourcommons.ca/DocumentViewer/en/43-1/FINA/meeting-43/evidence; Charlie Angus, Twitter, July 22, 2020, 8:07 p.m., https://twitter.com/CharlieAngusNDP/

status/1286090495085748225.

17.   Vanmala Subramaniam, "Government's $912M Contract for Student Volunteer Program Was Awarded to a WE Shell Company," *National Post*, July 22, 2020, https://nationalpost.com/news/na-foundation.

CHAPTER 5: THE STORM AFTER THE CALM

1.   Alex Ballingall, "Ottawa Outsources Student-Grant Program to a Toronto Charity That Works with Justin Trudeau's Wife," *Toronto Star*, June 25, 2020, https://www.thestar.com/politics/federal/2020/06/25/ottawa-outsources-student-grant-program-to-a-toronto-charity-that-works-with-justin-trudeaus-wife.html.

2.   Bill Curry, "Trudeau Accused of Cronyism Over Giving WE Charity a Contract to Run $912-Million Student Volunteer Program," *Globe and Mail*, June 26, 2020, https://www.theglobeandmail.com/politics/article-trudeau-accused-of-cronyism-over-giving-we-charity-a-contract-to-run/.

3.   Dion, *Trudeau III Report*.

4. Éric Grenier, "Poll Tracker: Pandemic Boosts Liberals Back into Majority Territory," CBC News, June 26, 2020, https://www.cbc.ca/news/politics/grenier-polltracker-26june2020-1.5627260.

5.   See, for example, Anthony Furey, "Let's Hope the Election Distracts from Canada's COVID Mania," *Toronto Sun*, August 7, 2021, https://torontosun.com/opinion/columnists/furey-lets-hope-the-election-distracts-from-canadas-covid-mania/. "Say what you want about the whole affair," Furey wrote, "But it was a nice change of subject matter from the pandemic. The WE scandal elbowed out of the way our at times hour-by-hour obsession with all things COVID."

6.   Pierre Poilievre campaign website, accessed September 3, 2021, https://www.withpierre.ca/.

7.   "Conservative MP Apologizes for 'Hurtful' Comments on Aboriginal People," CBC News, June 12, 2008, https://www.cbc.ca/news/canada/conservative-mp-apologizes-for-hurtful-comments-on-aboriginal-people-1.712106.

8.   Alice Chen, "Poilievre Sweeps a Suite of Categories in the 27th Annual Politically Savvy Survey," *Hill Times*, June 23, 2021, https://www.hilltimes.com/2021/06/23/poilievre-sweeps-a-suite-of-categories-in-the-27th-annual-politically-savvy-survey/303013.

9.   Charlie Angus campaign website, accessed September 3, 2021, https://www.charlieangus.ca/.

10.   Charlie Angus, Twitter, June 30, 2020, 7:54 p.m., https://twitter.com/

CharlieAngusNDP/status/1278114749868380161.

11.   Charlie Angus, Twitter, August 15, 2019, 7:57 p.m., https://twitter.com/
CharlieAngusNDP/status/1162151461939294209.

12.   Charlie Angus, Twitter, March 28, 2019, 6:50 a.m., https://twitter.com/
CharlieAngusNDP/status/1111219112687095814.

13.   Charlie Angus, Twitter, November 21, 2020, 10:20 a.m., https://twitter.
com/CharlieAngusNDP/status/1330169182957211654.

14.   Parliament of Canada, House of Commons, Standing Committee on
Finance (FINA): Hearing before FINA, 43rd Parl., 1st sess., July 28, 2020,
https://www.ourcommons.ca/DocumentViewer/en/43-1/FINA/meeting-45/
evidence.

15.   Charlie Angus, Twitter, June 29, 2020, 8:48 p.m., https://twitter.com/
CharlieAngusNDP/status/1277765886565326848/.

16.   Pierre Poilievre, Twitter, October 6, 2020, 4:19 p.m., https://twitter.com/
PierrePoilievre/status/1313574667689644032/.

17.   Pierre Poilievre, Twitter, June 28, 2020, 1:08 p.m., https://twitter.com/
PierrePoilievre/status/1277287855715422210.

18.   Charlie Angus, Twitter, July 3, 2020, 9:51 a.m., https:// twitter.com/
CharlieAngusNDP/status/1279050057283764224.

19.   Mary Dawson, *The Trudeau Report* (Ottawa: Office of the Conflict of
Interest and Ethics Commissioner, 2017), https://ciec-ccie.parl.gc.ca/en/
publications/Documents/InvestigationReports/The%20Trudeau%20Report.
pdf, p. 2.

20.   Mario Dion, *Trudeau II Report* (Ottawa: Office of the Conflict of
Interest and Ethics Commissioner, Parliament of Canada, 2019), https://ciec-
ccie.parl.gc.ca/en/publications/Documents/InvestigationReports/Trudeau%20
II%20Report.pdf, p. 44.

21.   John Paul Tasker, "'I Take Responsibility,' Trudeau Says in Wake of
Damning Report on SNC-Lavalin Ethics Violation," CBC News, August 14,
2019, https://www.cbc.ca/news/politics/trudeau-snc-ethics-commissioner-
violated-code-1.5246551.

22.   Tyler Dawson, "Critics Denounce WE Charity Campaign-Style Ad
for Justin Trudeau Amid PM's Scandal Over Charity Links," *National* Post,
July 10, 2020, https://nationalpost.com/news/critics-denounce-we-charity-
campaign-style-ad-for-justin-trudeau-amid-pms-scandal-over-charity-links.

23.   Even as Grégoire Trudeau was supporting youth mental health through
WE, her official bio claimed she was working as "an official spokesperson for
Plan Canada's 'Because I Am a Girl' initiative and the FitSpirit Foundation."
Both organizations also receive government funding. See https://liberal.ca/

meet-sophie-gregoire-trudeau/.

24. Parliament of Canada, House of Commons, Standing Committee on Finance (FINA): Hearing before FINA, 43rd Parl., 1st sess., July 22, 2020, https://www.ourcommons.ca/DocumentViewer/en/43-1/FINA/meeting-43/evidence.

25. Dion, Mario, *Morneau II Report* (Ottawa: Office of the Conflict of Interest and Ethics Commissioner, 2019), https://ciec-ccie.parl.gc.ca/en/publications/Documents/InvestigationReports/Morneau%20II%20Report.pdf, p. 11.

26. Right to Play is a non-profit organization engaging vulnerable children around the world through sports, games, creativity, and free play. Right to Play, *Won't Stop Us: 2020 Annual Report*, https://righttoplaydiag107.blob.core.windows.net/rtp-media/documents/Right_To_Play_Annual_Report_-_CNO.pdf.

27. Plan International Canada is a general international development charity, with gender equality as a foundational objective. "Where Your Money Goes," Plan International Canada, accessed September 27, 2021, https://plancanada.ca/where-your-money-goes.

28. Erin O'Toole, email message to Marc Kielburger, November 7, 2016.

29. Erin O'Toole, email message to Marc Kielburger, November 10, 2016.

30. Erin O'Toole, email message to Marc Kielburger, March 21, 2017.

31. Erin O'Toole, email message to Marc Kielburger, March 7, 2018.

32. Erin O'Toole, email message to Marc Kielburger, March 24, 2019.

33. "231 School Project," Pinball Clemons Foundation, accessed September 3, 2021, https://www.pinballfoundation.ca/123214fdkfdf4.

34. Erin O'Toole, Twitter, April 29, 2013, 6:17 p.m., https://twitter.com/erinotoole/status/328996530570817536.

35. Nico Johnson, "Peter MacKay Deletes Tweet Praising WE Charity After Wife Spoke at Event," *Post Millennial,* July 10, 2020, https://thepostmillennial.com/breaking-peter-mackay-deletes-tweet-praising-we-charity-after-wife-spoke-at-event.

36. Arthur White-Crummey, "Premier Scott Moe Spends Winter Vacation in Kenya with WE Charity," *Regina Leader-Post,* January 13, 2020, https://leaderpost.com/news/saskatchewan/premier-scott-moe-spends-winter-vacation-in-kenya-with-we-charity.

37. Curry, "Trudeau Accused of Cronyism."

38. Parliament of Canada, House of Commons, Standing Committee on Finance (FINA): Hearing before FINA, 43rd Parl., 1st sess., July 28, 2020, https://www.ourcommons.ca/DocumentViewer/en/43-1/FINA/meeting-45/

evidence.

39. "Federal Ministers and Health Officials Province COVID-19 Update," CPAC, June 25, 2020, https://www.cpac.ca/episode?id=8db5c2d9-53f0-4102-9718-4f0fc6cdce1f.

40. "Support for Students and Recent Graduates Impacted by COVID-19," Finance Canada, accessed September 3, 2021, https://www.canada.ca/en/department-finance/news/2020/04/support-for-students-and-recent-graduates-impacted-by-covid-19.html.

41. Janyce McGregor. "PM's Mother Margaret and Brother Alexandre Were Both Paid to Speak at WE Charity Events," CBC News, July 9, 2020, https://www.cbc.ca/news/politics/margaret-justin-trudeau-we-charity-1.5643586.

42. Parliament of Canada, House of Commons, Standing Committee on Access to Information, Privacy and Ethics (ETHI): Hearing before ETHI, 43rd Parl., 1st sess., July 17, 2020, https://www.ourcommons.ca/DocumentViewer/en/43-1/ETHI/meeting-6/evidence. See also Angus's Twitter feed: "I am just someone concerned that nearly a billion dollars of emergency funding was privatized to the Kielburger group in the middle of a pandemic" (July 30, 2020, 7:38 p.m., https://twitter.com/CharlieAngusNDP/status/1288982269261225984) and "Having run out of means to distract attention from @JustinTrudeau's billion dollar Kielburger meltdown [supporters] are calling for the arrest of journalists who bother Liberal ministers" (August 3, 2020, 8:18 p.m., https://twitter.com/charlieangusndp/status/1290442048013848579). In all, Angus used this $900 million figure in public statements more than twenty-five times.

43. Ryan Patrick Jones, "Trudeau Defends Decision to Have Charity with Ties to Family Administer Student Volunteer Program," CBC News, June 26, 2020, www.cbc.ca/news/politics/we-charity-student-volunteer-program-1.5628610.

44. Bill Curry, "Volunteer Canada Declined to Work for WE Charities Over Wage Concerns with Student Grant Program," *Globe and Mail*, June 28, 2020, www.theglobeandmail.com/politics/article-volunteer-canada-declined-to-work-for-we-charities-over-wage-concerns/.

45. Christopher Nardi, "Records Show Charity Closely Tied to PM Received Multiple Sole-Source Contracts," *National Post*, June 29, 2020, nationalpost.com/news/politics/records-show-charity-closely-linked-to-trudeau-has-received-multiple-sole-source-contracts-from-liberal-government.

46. Eddie Chau, "#WeHaveAProblem: Canadians Upset Over We Charity Controversy," *Toronto Sun*, June 30, 2020, torontosun.com/news/national/wehaveaproblem-canadians-dont-agree-with-trudeau-awarding-900m-to-charity.

47. "PM Trudeau Provides Update on Federal Response to COVID-19,"

CPAC, June 26, 2020, https://www.cpac.ca/episode?id=4caf7d2a-3b53-404c-9181-81407934cb7a.

48. Curry, "Trudeau Accused of Cronyism."

49. Ballingall, "Ottawa Outsources Student-Grant Program."

50. Lee Berthiaume, "Marc Kielburger Backtracks After Saying PMO Contacted WE About $900M Program," *Toronto Star,* June 30, 2020, https://www.thestar.com/politics/federal/2020/06/30/marc-kielburger-backtracks-after-saying-pmo-contacted-we-about-900m-program.html.

51. Berthiaume, "Marc Kielburger Backtracks."

52. John Paul Tasker, "Federal Government, WE Charity Agree to Part Ways on Summer Student Grant Program," CBC News, July 3, 2020, https://www.cbc.ca/news/politics/we-charity-student-grant-program-1.5636332.

53. "Media Statement—WE Charity," Canada Newswire, July 3, 2020, https://www.newswire.ca/news-releases/media-statement-we-charity-853384204.html.

54. Tasker, "Federal Government, WE Charity Agree to Part Ways."

55. Emerald Bensadoun, "Trudeau Admits He Did Not Recuse Himself from WE Contract Vote," Global News, July 8, 2020, https://globalnews.ca/news/7153106/trudeau-we-charity-recuse/.

56. Janyce McGregor, "Bill Morneau Has Family Ties to WE Charity, Did Not Steer Clear of Cabinet Discussion of Contract," CBC News, July 10, 2020, https://www.cbc.ca/news/politics/we-charity-contract-morneau-1.5644839.

57. Bill Morneau, "My Statement on the Administration of the Canada Student Service Grant," Twitter, July 13, 2020, 3:54 p.m., https://twitter.com/Bill_Morneau/status/1282765267307843587.

58. Brian Lilley, "Liberal Connections to WE Continue to Pile Up," *Toronto Sun,* July 11, 2020, https://torontosun.com/opinion/columnists/lilley-liberal-connections-to-we-continue-to-pile-up.

59. "Margaret Trudeau," Harry Walker Agency, accessed September 3, 2021, https://www.harrywalker.com/speakers/margaret-trudeau.

60. McGregor, "PM's Mother Margaret."

61. Christopher Nardi, "Trudeau Government Arranged $1.18 Million for WE Day Event Featuring Margaret Trudeau," *National Post,* July 15, 2020, https://nationalpost.com/news/politics/trudeau-government-contributed-1-18-million-to-we-day-event-in-2017-during-which-pms-mother-was-likely-paid-to-speak.

62. "A Message from WE Charity and Its Co-Founders," *Toronto*

Star, July 13, 2020, https://www.pressreader.com/canada/toronto-star/20200713/281711206947727.

CHAPTER 6: PILING ON

1.   Charity Intelligence Canada website, accessed October 22, 2021, https://www.charityintelligence.ca/charity-details/261-charity-intelligence.

2.   Parliament of Canada, House of Commons, Standing Committee on Finance (FINA): Hearing before FINA, 43rd Parl., 1st sess., August 6, 2020, https://www.ourcommons.ca/DocumentViewer/en/43-1/FINA/meeting-49/evidence.

3.   Charity Intelligence Canada, T3010 Registered Charity Information Return Section B—Directors/Trustees and Like Officials, July 1, 2019, to June 30, 2020, Canada Revenue Agency, https://apps.cra-arc.gc.ca/ebci/hacc/srch/pub/t3010/v25/t3010ovrvw.

4.   Raveena Aulakh and Amy Dempsey, "Audit of Charities Encounters Resistance," *Toronto Star*, November 15, 2011, https://www.thestar.com/news/gta/2011/11/15/audit_of_charities_encounters_resistance.html.

5.   Andy Levy-Ajzenkopf, "Charity Intelligence: Transparent on Transparency?" *Charity Village*, November 21, 2011, https://charityvillage.com/charity_intelligence_transparent_on_transparency_/.

6.   Jesse Brown, "WE Charity Moved Millions to Private Kielburger Company," Canadaland, July 18, 2020, https://www.canadaland.com/we-charity-was-in-financial-trouble-before-covid-says-charity-watchdog/.

7.   WE Charity's auditor noted the waiver in the 2018 audit report. "Under the terms of the facilities agreement, the organization is required to meet certain financial covenants. As of August 31, 2018, these covenants have not been met. However, the bank has provided the organization with written confirmation that the covenant requirement has been waived for the current period." Kestenberg, Rabinowicz Partners LLP Chartered Professional Accountants, "WE Charity Non-Consolidated Financial Statements for the Eight Month Period Ended August 31, 2018," August 31, 2018.

8.   Kate Bahen, Twitter, June 26, 2020, 7:42 p.m., https://twitter.com/kate_bahen/status/1276662105366765569.

9.   Kate Bahen, Twitter, March 15, 2021, 2:31 p.m., https://twitter.com/kate_bahen/status/1371529411716087810.

10.   When Rosen, along with analysts Ross Healey and Paul Sagawa, first sounded the alarm on Nortel, not many believed that the company's stock value would one day collapse. To many, the stock looked invincible at its $150-per-share rate. But Dr. Rosen's warning would prove prophetic, and

eventually Nortel shares plummeted to between $4 to $5. Simon Doyle, "Meet the Man Who Told You So," *Ottawa Citizen*, January 13, 2005.

11.   Al Rosen and Mark Rosen, *Swindlers: Cons & Cheats and How to Protect Your Investments from Them* (Toronto: Madison Press Books, 2011).

12.   The executive summary specifies that "the donors for this analysis are the Stillman Family Foundation." The Stillmans are long-standing donors to WE Charity who have contributed heavily to development efforts in Kenya, among other things. See: Rosen & Associates Limited, "Executive Summary," *Report for WE Charity* (Toronto: Rosen & Associates Limited, 2020), p. 2.

13.   Rosen, *Report for WE Charity*, p. 8.

14.   Rosen, *Report for WE Charity*, p. 4.

15.   Rosen, *Report for WE Charity*, p. 7.

16.   Kate Bahen, interview by Nahlah Ayed, *The Current*, CBC Radio, July 13, 2020, https://www.cbc.ca/radio/thecurrent/the-current-for-july-13-2020-1.5647242/july-13-2020-episode-transcript-1.5647817.

17.   Parliament of Canada, House of Commons, Standing Committee on Finance (FINA): Hearing before FINA, 43rd Parl., 1st sess., August 6, 2020, https://www.ourcommons.ca/DocumentViewer/en/43-1/FINA/meeting-49/evidence.

18.   Kieran Leavitt, "Pandemic-Battered Charities Seek a Lifeline by Running For-Profit Businesses," *Toronto Star*, September 10, 2020, https://www.thestar.com/politics/federal/2020/09/10/pandemic-battered-charities-seek-a-lifeline-by-running-for-profit-businesses.html/.

19.   See, for example, "Political Scandal Sheds Light on Long-Standing Questions About WE Charity's Complex Operations," CBC Radio, July 31, 2020, https://www.cbc.ca/radio/day6/we-charity-siberian-wildfires-getting-lost-in-the-woods-covid-19-and-nostalgia-and-more-1.5669027/political-scandal-sheds-light-on-long-standing-questions-about-we-charity-s-complex-operations-1.5669043, and Stewart Bell and Andrew Russell, "Trudeau Gov. Contract for $912M Student Program Was with WE Charity's Real Estate Holding Foundation," Global News, July 22, 2020, https://globalnews.ca/news/7203337/trudeau-we-charity-foundation-real-estate-holding-company/.

20.   Leavitt, "Pandemic-Battered Charities."

21.   Parliament of Canada, House of Commons, Standing Committee on Access to Information, Privacy and Ethics (ETHI): Hearing before ETHI, 43rd Parl., 2nd sess., December 4, 2020, https://www.ourcommons.ca/DocumentViewer/en/43-2/ETHI/meeting-16/evidence.

22.   At the time that ME to WE was established, charities in Ontario were subject to the Charitable Gifts Act (Ontario), R.S.O. 1990, c. C.8, s. 2(1),

which included a provision commonly interpreted as prohibiting charities from owning greater than a 10 percent interest in any business. The Charitable Gifts Act was repealed in 2009.

23.   Under the Income Tax Act (ITA), s. 149.1(2)(a), charitable organizations such as WE Charity can have their charitable registration revoked if they are found to have carried on a business that is not a related business of that charity. "Related business" is defined in the ITA, s. 149.1(1) to include a business that is run substantially by volunteers. The Canada Revenue Agency's approach to related business activities is otherwise set out in published guidance statements. In particular, Policy Statement CPS-019.3 CRA states that for a business conducted by a charity to be "related," it must meet two requirements: it must be "linked" to the charity's charitable purposes, and it must be "subordinate" to those purposes. CRA elaborates of each of these requirements in CPS-019.

24.   See, for example, Mark Blumberg, Twitter, October 9, 2020: "At Blumberg's Canadian Charity Law Institute we will be covering CRA Charities Directorate, State of the Sector, ONCA updates, CNCA updates, WE Charity scandal, Race and Racism in the NPO sector, Charity transparency, and charity political activities." The tweet has since been deleted. See also, Mark Blumberg, Twitter, October 20, 7:30 p.m.: "Today is the last day to register for our Charity Law Institute covering CRA Charities Directorate, State of the Sector, ONCA, CNCA updates, WE Charity scandal, Race and Racism in the NPO sector, Charity transparency, and charity political activities," https://twitter.com/canadiancharity/status/1318696094138773512/

25.   Frustrated that attempts to correct the record were being ignored, Baker and Al-Waheidi sent a letter to Charity Intelligence, listing specific quotes from Bahen containing false statements, and addressing each in turn. Scott Baker and Dalal Al-Waheidi, letter to Kate Bahen at Charity Intelligence, July 21, 2020, https://staticsb.we.org/f/52095/x/cdabb9319a/charity-intellegence-letter-july-21.pdf. WE Charity then followed up on August 6, 2020, with a statement to correct the record on additional comments made on social media and in Bahen and Thomson's testimony at the Standing Committee on Finance. "WE Charity's Statement in Response to Testimony by Charity Intelligence before the Standing Committee on Finance," August 6, 2020, https://www.newswire.ca/news-releases/we-charity-s-statement-in-response-to-testimony-by-charity-intelligence-before-the-standing-committee-on-finance-818451226.html.

26.   Parliament of Canada, House of Commons, Standing Committee on Finance (FINA): Hearing before FINA, 43rd Parl., 1st sess., August 6, 2020, https://www.ourcommons.ca/DocumentViewer/en/43-1/FINA/meeting-49/evidence.

27.   Katie Nicholson and Jacques Marcoux, "Pro Sports Foundations Get Poor Marks from Charity Watchdog," CBC News, May 15, 2019, https://www.

cbc.ca/news/canada/manitoba/sports-foundations-charity-1.4884705.

28.   Kate Bahen (Charity Intelligence Canada), letter to True North Youth Foundation, May 1, 2019, "Latest News," True North Youth Foundation, accessed September 2, 2021, https://www.truenorthyouthfoundation.com/news/charity-intelligence-canada-issues-apology-to-the-true-north-youth-foundation/.

29.   Jesse Brown, "The Time I 'Faked' a CBC Scene," Canadaland, January 16, 2015, https://www.canadaland.com/time-i-faked-cbc-scene/.

30.   "Kevin Donovan Reveals the Journalism Behind the Jian Ghomeshi Scandal," CBC Radio, October 7, 2016, https://www.cbc.ca/radio/day6/episode-306-syrian-doctors-under-siege-investigating-ghomeshi-arctic-climate-change-luke-cage-and-more-1.3792840/kevin-donovan-reveals-the-journalism-behind-the-jian-ghomeshi-scandal-1.3792891.

31.   Simon Houpt, "Journalist Jesse Brown Is Quick to Expose the Failures of Canadian Media. What About His Own?," Globe and Mail, January 17, 2015, https://www.theglobeandmail.com/arts/books-and-media/journalist-jesse-brown-is-quick-to-expose-the-failures-of-canadian-media-but-what-about-his-own/article22488107/.

32.   "Canadaland 2020 Transparency Report," Canadaland.com, July 15, 2021, https://www.canadaland.com/2020-transparency-report/; "The Globe and Mail Remains Canada's Top Publisher Brand," Globe and Mail Corporate News statement, October 21, 2020, https://pr.theglobeandmail.com/oct-21-2020/.

33.   Jaren Kerr, "Craig Kielburger Founded WE to Fight Child Labour. Now the WE Brand Promotes Products Made by Children," Canadaland, October 15, 2018, https://www.canadaland.com/craig-kielburger-founded-we-to-fight-child-labour-now-the-we-brand-promotes-products-made-by-children/.

34.   Jesse Brown and Jaren Kerr, "The Canadaland Investigation of the Kielburgers' WE Movement," October 15, 2018, in Canadaland (podcast), https://www.canadaland.com/podcast/the-canadaland-investigation-of-the-kielburgers-we-movement/.

35.   Jaren Kerr, "WE Charity versus Canadaland," panel discussion at the Investigative Reporters and Editors conference, Toronto, May 4, 2019.

36.   Canadaland claimed in both the article and the podcast that WE had raised "$47 million in revenue from corporate partners alone." The outlet was informed prior to publication that the figure was not correct but published it anyway. Additionally, an image entitled "keyfindings-top-20-partners" and embedded in the article was selectively altered. Either Canadaland or its unnamed source removed half the content from a PowerPoint slide and failed to disclose this to the public. The unaltered list of partners would have contradicted the article's narrative regarding corporate partnerships, as well as the incorrect revenue figure. Kerr, "Child Labour."

37. Goudge, "Real Estate Holdings and Practices."

38. John Chapman, Miller Thomson LLP, letter to Jesse Brown, October 10, 2018.

39. Jaren Kerr, "How the Kielburgers Handle the Press," Canadaland, November 19, 2018, https://www.canadaland.com/how-the-kielburgers-handle-the-press/.

40. *The Fifth Estate*, season 46, episode 5, "The Price WE Paid: An Investigation into WE Charity's Rise and Fall from Grace," directed by Harvey Cashore, written by Mark Kelley, aired February 4, 2021, https://www.cbc.ca/player/play/1853832771651.

41. Jesse Brown, "A Former WE Employee Speaks Out," *Canadaland* (podcast), June 30, 2019, https://www.canadaland.com/podcast/284-a-former-we-employee-speaks-out/.

42. Jesse Brown, Twitter, July 2, 2020, 8:52 p.m., https://twitter.com/JesseBrown/status/1278854037748801536/.

43. Jesse Brown, Twitter, July 20, 2020, 3:13 p.m., https://twitter.com/JesseBrown/status/1285291768695660547.

44. David Akin, Twitter, July 20, 2020, 3:24 p.m., https://twitter.com/davidakin/status/1285294630771265538.

45. James McLeod (@jamespmcleod) in a since-deleted tweet.

46. Marieke Walsh, Paul Waldie, and David Milstead, "Lobbying Commissioner Launches Review of WE Charity," *Globe and Mail*, September 11, 2020, https://www.theglobeandmail.com/politics/article-lobbying-commissioner-launches-review-of-we-charity/.

47. Paul Waldie, "WE Charity Spent More Than $600,000 on U.S. Political Consultants, IRS Filings Show," *Globe and Mail*, July 29, 2020, https://www.theglobeandmail.com/politics/article-we-charity-spent-hundreds-of-thousands-on-us-political-consultants/.

48. Brandi Proctor, "Thousands Headed to Baltimore for WE Day," Fox 45 News, March 27, 2018, https://foxbaltimore.com/news/local/thousands-headed-to-baltimore-for-we-day.

49. Paul Waldie, "Big Names Continue to Donate to WE Charities in the U.S., Despite Recent controversy," *Globe and Mail*, August 3, 2020, https://www.theglobeandmail.com/world/article-big-names-continue-to-donate-to-we-charities-in-the-us-despite/.

50. Sylvia Stead, email message to Scott Baker, October 28, 2020.

51. Brian Lilley, "Maybe We Should Have Been Looking at WE Charity Earlier," *Toronto Sun*, July 7, 2020, https://torontosun.com/opinion/columnists/lilley-maybe-we-should-have-been-looking-at-we-charity-earlier.

52. Brian Lilley, "WE Flips for Real Estate," *Toronto Sun*, July 20, 2020, https://torontosun.com/opinion/columnists/lilley-we-flips-for-real-estate. The online version of the article has since been corrected.

53. Brian Lilley, "Real Estate Is Central to the WE/Kielburger story," *Toronto Sun*, July 29, 2020, https://torontosun.com/opinion/columnists/lilley-real-estate-is-central-to-the-we-kielburger-story.

54. Vanmala Subramaniam, "Property Brothers: Kielburgers Facing Scrutiny Over WE Organization's $50M Real Estate Empire", *National Post*, July 20, 2020, https://nationalpost.com/news/property-brothers-kielburgers-facing-scrutiny-over-we-organizations-50m-real-estate-empire.

55. Mark Blumberg, "The WE Charity Scandal and Its Impact on the Canadian Charity Sector," *Foundation* (September/October 2020), https://foundationmag.ca/the-we-charity-scandal-and-its-impact-on-the-canadian-charity-sector/.

56. Goudge, "Real Estate Holdings and Practices."

57. Scott McCallum, "WE Charity Real Estate Report," October 19, 2019.

58. Michelle Douglas, Toronto, October 1, 2019.

59. Travis Dhanraj, Twitter, August 2, 2020, https://mobile.twitter.com/Travisdhanraj/status/1290039536001507329.

60. Randall Mang, "The Real Scandal? Canadians Unwittingly Allowed WE Charity to Be Assailed," *Medium*, September 22, 2020, https://medium.com/@randallanthonycommunications/the-real-scandal-4949865f1cc8.

61. Elizabeth Grieco, "Fast Facts About the Newspaper Industry's Financial Struggles as McClatchy Files for Bankruptcy," Pew Research Centre, February 14, 2020, https://www.pewresearch.org/fact-tank/2020/02/14/fast-facts-about-the-newspaper-industrys-financial-struggles/.

62. "Ottawa Bolsters Struggling Media with $600M in Tax Measures," CTV News, November 21, 2018, https://www.ctvnews.ca/politics/ottawa-bolsters-struggling-media-with-600m-in-tax-measures-1.4186881.

63. Frank Bruni, "Ted Cruz, I'm Sorry," *New York Times*, June 17, 2021, https://www.nytimes.com/2021/06/17/opinion/frank-bruni-final-times-column.html.

CHAPTER 7: OPEN FLOODGATES

1. *The Fifth Estate*, "The Price WE Paid."

2. *The Fifth Estate*, "The Price WE Paid."

3. Kerr, "Child Labour."

4. Oliver Balch, "Mars, Nestlé and Hershey to Face Child Slavery Lawsuit in US," *Guardian*, February 12, 2021, https://www.theguardian.com/global-development/2021/feb/12/mars-nestle-and-hershey-to-face-landmark-child-slavery-lawsuit-in-us.

5. June Findlay, "Yes, #WeHaveAProblem—and Not Just Because of Trudeau," *Flare*, July 21, 2020, https://fashionmagazine.com/flare/we-charity-corruption-trudeau-kielburger/. See also https://about.me/junefind.

6. Wency Leung, "Looking for Future Change-Makers," *Globe and Mail*, September 21, 2017, https://www.theglobeandmail.com/life/we-day-un-speakers-on-how-to-empower-women-andgirls/article36338674/.

7. "Celebrities," Oxfam International website, accessed October 3, 2021, https://www.oxfam.org/en/tags/celebrities/; "Partners," Care International website, accessed October 3, 2021, https://www.care-international.org/who-we-are-1/partners; "News & Stories, Celebrity Ambassador," World Vision International website, accessed October 3, 2021, https://www.worldvision.org/tags/celebrity-ambassador/.

8. "Meet Jason Saul, Founder and CEO of Mission Measurement," WE.org, accessed October 3, 2021, https://www.we.org/en-CA/about-we/we-charity/governance/mission-measurement/.

CHAPTER 8: BIPOC RECKONING

1. Amanda Maitland, "Racism in Canada: My Story at WE," Instagram, June 16, 2020, https://www.instagram.com/tv/CBhDviFDfG6/?utm_source=ig_embed&ig_rid=55cb797f-71b7-43ef-be40-a7dcdb6164ee.

2. Jacqueline Sanderlin and Dalal Al-Waheidi, "WE's Commitment to Ending Racism and Empowering Communities," June 18, 2020, https://www.we.org/en-CA/transparency-reporting/anti-racism/we-commitment-to-ending-racism/.

3. Raia Carey (@coach.carey), Instagram comment, June 13, 2020, https://www.instagram.com/p/CA7-k6uBt0x/.

4. John Vennavalley-Rao and Ben Cousins, "Racialized Former WE Employees Accused Charity of Oppressive Incidents," CTV News, July 8, 2020, https://www.ctvnews.ca/canada/racialized-former-we-employees-accused-charity-of-oppressive-incidents-1.5016789.

5. Farrah Merali, "Former WE Charity Employee Says Staff Tried to Silence Her by Rewriting Anti-racism Speech," CBC News, July 7, 2020, https://www.cbc.ca/news/canada/toronto/we-charity-amanda-maitland-1.5639716.

6. Anon Yimity, email to WE Charity board of directors, July 1, 2020.

7. Dr. Jacqueline Sanderlin and Greg Rogers, email to Anon Yimity, July 3,

2020.

8.   Marc Kielburger and Craig Kielburger, "An Update on WE's Commitment to Anti-racism and to Take Action," July 2, 2020, https://www.we.org/en-CA/transparency-reporting/anti-racism/update-on-commitment-to-ending-racism/.

9.   Marc Kielburger, "A Statement from WE Charity Co-Founders, Marc Kielburger and Craig Kielburger," Instagram, July 4, 2020, https://www.instagram.com/p/CCNZuwUAZER/.

10.   Marc Kielburger, Craig Kielburger, Dalal Al-Waheidi, and Russ McLeod, "Welcoming Ideas on Taking Action on Anti-racism," July 6, 2020, https://www.we.org/en-CA/transparency-reporting/anti-racism/welcoming-ideas-on-taking-action-on-anti-racism/.

11.   Anon Yimity, email to WE Charity board of directors, July 6, 2020.

12.   Anon Yimity, email to WE Charity board of directors, July 7, 2020.

13.   WE Charity Canadian and US Board of Directors, "Open Letter from the Canadian and US Board of Directors," July 23, 2020, https://www.we.org/en-CA/transparency-reporting/anti-racism/open-letter-from-the-board/.

14.   "Diversity & Inclusion Report: Findings and Recommendations," December 16, 2020, https://www.we.org/en-CA/transparency-reporting/anti-racism/final-diversity-and-inclusion-report/.

15.   "Diversity & Inclusion Report."

16.   Maitland, "Racism in Canada."

CHAPTER 9: HIGH AND DRY

1.   Parliament of Canada, House of Commons, Standing Committee on Finance (FINA): Hearing before FINA, 43rd Parl., 1st sess., July 28, 2020, https://www.ourcommons.ca/DocumentViewer/en/43-1/FINA/meeting-45/evidence.

2.   Parliament of Canada, House of Commons, Standing Committee on Access to Information, Privacy and Ethics (ETHI): Hearing before ETHI, 43rd Parl., 1st sess., August 11, 2020, https://www.ourcommons.ca/DocumentViewer/en/43-1/ETHI/meeting-12/evidence.

3.   Tonda MacCharles, "WE Charity Says It Will Pay Back Remaining Money for Student Volunteer Program as Soon as Ottawa Can Take It," *Toronto Star*, August 12, 2020, https://www.thestar.com/politics/federal/2020/08/12/we-charity-says-it-will-pay-back-remaining-money-for-student-volunteer-program-as-soon-as-ottawa-can-take-it.html.

4.   Government conflicts of interest were addressed in section 24.1 of the contribution agreement, which states: "No current or former public servant

or public office holder to whom the Conflict of Interest Act (S.C.2006, c. 9, s. 2), the Policy on Conflict of Interest and Post-Employment or the Values and Ethics Code for the Public Sector applies shall derive a direct benefit from the Agreement unless the provision or receipt of such benefit is in compliance with the said legislation or codes." Section 24.2 states: "No member of the Senate or the House of Commons shall be admitted to any share or part of the Agreement or to any benefit arising from it that is not otherwise available to the general public." "Canada's Covid-19 Economic Response Plan: Support for Students and Recent Graduates, Contribution Agreement Between Her Majesty the Queen in Right of Canada Represented by the Minister of State (Diversity, Inclusion and Youth) and WE Charity Foundation Canada," signed June 23, 2020.

5. Parliament of Canada, House of Commons, Standing Committee on Finance (FINA): Hearing before FINA, 43rd Parl., 1st sess., August 13, 2020, https://www.ourcommons.ca/DocumentViewer/en/43-1/FINA/meeting-51/evidence.

6. Christopher Nardi, "Federal Minister in Charge of Student Volunteer Grant Program Can't Say How Much of $30 million Paid to WE Has Been Reimbursed," *National Post*, August 11, 2020, https://nationalpost.com/news/politics/federal-minister-in-charge-of-student-volunteer-grant-program-cant-say-how-much-of-30-million-paid-to-we-has-been-reimbursed.

7. "PM Trudeau on COVID-19 Exposure App, WE Charity Controversy," CPAC, July 31, 2020, https://www.cpac.ca/episode?id=cfd310f3-39da-4265-b14c-f1209a6fe40b.

8. Parliament of Canada, House of Commons, Standing Committee on Finance (FINA): Hearing before FINA, 43rd Parl., 1st sess., July 16, 2020, https://www.ourcommons.ca/DocumentViewer/en/43-1/FINA/meeting-41/evidence.

9. Parliament of Canada, House of Commons, Standing Committee on Finance (FINA): Hearing before FINA, 43rd Parl., 1st sess., July 21, 2020, https://www.ourcommons.ca/DocumentViewer/en/43-1/FINA/meeting-42/evidence.

10. "Emergency Community Support Fund," Community Foundations of Canada, accessed September 4, 2021, https://communityfoundations.ca/initiatives/emergency-community-support-fund/.

11. Parliament of Canada, House of Commons, Standing Committee on Finance (FINA): Hearing before FINA, 43rd Parl., 1st sess., July 16, 2020, https://www.ourcommons.ca/DocumentViewer/en/43-1/FINA/meeting-41/evidence.

12. Parliament of Canada, House of Commons, Standing Committee on Finance (FINA): Hearing before FINA, 43rd Parl., 1st sess., July 21, 2020,

https://www.ourcommons.ca/DocumentViewer/en/43-1/FINA/meeting-42/
evidence.

13. Christopher Nardi, "Federal Government Won't Say Which Organizations
Other Than WE Charity It Considered to Run $900 Million Student Volunteer
Grant Program," *National Post*, July 6, 2020, https://nationalpost.com/news/
politics/federal-government-wont-say-which-organizations-other-than-we-
charity-it-considered-to-run-900-million-student-volunteer-grant-program.

14. Rachel Gilmore, "Feds Considered Other Groups Before WE Deal but
Most Were Never Told About Program," CTV News, July 27, 2020, https://
www.ctvnews.ca/politics/feds-considered-other-groups-before-we-deal-but-
most-were-never-told-about-program-1.5040923.

15. Dion, *Trudeau III Report*, p. 2.

16. Krause describes herself as a one-time constituency representative for
John Duncan, the former member of Parliament for Vancouver Island North.
Vivian Krause, résumé, accessed September 20, 2021, fairquestions.typepad.
com/files/vivian-krause-resume-3.pdf.

17. Parliament of Canada, House of Commons, Standing Committee on
Finance (FINA): Hearing before FINA, 43rd Parl., 1st sess., July 22, 2020,
https://www.ourcommons.ca/DocumentViewer/en/43-1/FINA/meeting-43/
evidence.

18. Rachel Aiello, "Morneau Reveals He's Paid Back More Than $41K in
Travel Expenses to WE, Faces Calls to Resign," CTV News, July 22, 2020,
https://www.ctvnews.ca/canada/morneau-reveals-he-s-paid-back-more-
than-41k-in-travel-expenses-to-we-faces-calls-to-resign-1.5033933; Mélanie
Marquis, "*Affaire unis: Les frères Kielburger se font malmener par l'opposition
en comité*," *La Presse*, July 28, 2020, https://www.lapresse.ca/actualites/
politique/2020-07-28/affaire-unis-les-freres-kielburger-se-font-malmener-
par-l-opposition-en-comite.php; Brian Lilley, "WE Denies Selling User
Data," July 22, 2020, https://torontosun.com/news/national/we-denies-
selling-user-data/.

19. Robert Fife and Steven Chase, "Federal Elections Watchdog Looking
into WE Charity, Researcher Says," *Globe and Mail*, April 8, 2021, https://
www.theglobeandmail.com/politics/article-federal-elections-watchdog-
looking-into-we-charity-researcher-says/.

20. The deputy commissioner of compliance, Brent Homan, confirmed that
any personal information collected for the CSSG was "used to administer it
for the short time it was in operation and was not used or disclosed for other
purposes." He concluded that no one else had access to the data. "Therefore,
we are of the view," he said, "that there are no indications that personal
information collected in the course of the CSSG was collected, used, stored or
disclosed in a manner that contravenes the PIPEDA [Personal Information

Protection and Electronic Documents] Act." Brent Homan, Office of the Privacy Commissioner of Canada, letter to William C. McDowell, counsel to WE Charity, July 5, 2021.

CHAPTER 10: A QUESTION OF GOVERNANCE

1. Parliament of Canada, House of Commons, Standing Committee on Finance (FINA): Hearing before FINA, 43rd Parl., 1st sess., July 28, 2020, https://www.ourcommons.ca/DocumentViewer/en/43-1/FINA/meeting-45/evidence.

2. John Ibbitson, "How Michelle Douglas Broke Down the Canadian Military's LGBT Walls," *Globe and Mail,* October 23, 2017, https://www.theglobeandmail.com/news/politics/interrogation-dismissal-and-now-an-apology-to-michelle-douglas/article36700166/.

3. Emily Gwiazda, "Michelle Douglas," *Canadian Encyclopedia*, October 19, 2018, https://www.thecanadianencyclopedia.ca/en/article/michelle-douglas.

4. Michelle Douglas, statement to media on WE's real estate philosophy, October 1, 2019.

5. Michelle Douglas, statement to the media.

6. During my tenure as a board member, I was not charged with providing legal advice to the board as counsel for the board or WE Charity. My involvement in legal issues was limited to helping analyze and explain matters for the benefit of other board members.

7. Michelle Douglas, email message to WE Charity board of directors, US and Canada, March 16, 2020.

8. Parliament of Canada, House of Commons, Standing Committee on Finance (FINA): Hearing before FINA, 43rd Parl., 1st sess., July 28, 2020, https://www.ourcommons.ca/DocumentViewer/en/43-1/FINA/meeting-45/evidence.

9. Michelle Douglas, letter to Canadaland, May 22, 2019.

10. Michelle Douglas, letter to Canadaland, April 15, 2019.

11. Parliament of Canada, House of Commons, Standing Committee on Finance (FINA): Hearing before FINA, 43rd Parl., 1st sess., July 28, 2020, https://www.ourcommons.ca/DocumentViewer/en/43-1/FINA/meeting-45/evidence.

12. Michelle Douglas, Twitter, June 28, 2020, 10:37 p.m., https://twitter.com/MDouglas_YOW/status/1277430955427483648.

13. Michelle Douglas, Twitter, June 28, 2020, 10:47 p.m., https://twitter.com/MDouglas_YOW/status/1277433356888821760.

14.   Catherine Cullen, "WE Charity Saw Resignations, Departures from Senior Ranks Before Landing Government Contract," CBC News, July 2, 2020, https://www.cbc.ca/news/politics/we-charity-pandemic-covid-coronavirus-trudeau-1.5635379.

15.   Greg Rogers and Dr. Jacqueline L. Sanderlin, open letter posted in response to media reports on WE Charity's board overhaul, July 26, 2020.

16.   Jesse Brown, "WE Charity Moved Millions to Private Kielburger Company," Canadaland, July 18, 2020, https://www.canadaland.com/we-charity-was-in-financial-trouble-before-covid-says-charity-watchdog/.

17.   Marieke Walsh and Greg McArthur, "Former WE Charity Chair Says She Resigned Over 'Concerning Developments' at the Organization," *Globe and Mail*, July 27, 2020, https://www.theglobeandmail.com/canada/article-former-we-charity-chair-says-she-resigned-over-concerning/.

18.   Parliament of Canada, House of Commons, Standing Committee on Finance (FINA): Hearing before FINA, 43rd Parl., 1st sess., July 28, 2020, https://www.ourcommons.ca/DocumentViewer/en/43-1/FINA/meeting-45/evidence.

19.   Parliament of Canada, House of Commons, Standing Committee on Access to Information, Privacy and Ethics (ETHI): Hearing before ETHI, 43rd Parl., 2nd sess., November 30, 2020, https://www.ourcommons.ca/DocumentViewer/en/43-2/ETHI/meeting-13/evidence/.

20.   Parliament of Canada, House of Commons, Standing Committee on Finance (FINA): Hearing before FINA, 43rd Parl., 1st sess., July 21, 2020, https://www.ourcommons.ca/DocumentViewer/en/43-1/FINA/meeting-42/evidence.

21.   "WE Charity Hearings Reveal Troubling Governance Structure," BNN Bloomberg, July 28, 2020, https://www.bnnbloomberg.ca/canada/video/we-charity-hearings-reveal-troubling-governance-structure-watchdog~2003521.

22.   Marie-Danielle Smith, Aaron Hutchins, Jason Markusoff, and Claire Brownell, "The Rise and Fall of WE," *Maclean's*, September 9, 2020, https://www.macleans.ca/longforms/we-charity-kielburgers-scandal/.

23.   Chris Selley, "It's Time to Disentangle WE from the Canadian State," *National Post*, July 28, 2020, https://nationalpost.com/opinion/chris-selley-its-time-to-disentangle-we-from-the-canadian-state. For full disclosure, I went to McGill University with Selley, we lived in the same residence in our first year, and we have friends in common.

24.   Licia Corbella, "Trying to Profit from the Trudeau Name May Sink WE Charity," *Calgary Herald*, July 29, 2020, https://calgaryherald.com/opinion/columnists/corbella-trying-to-profit-from-the-trudeau-name-may-sink-we-charity/.

CHAPTER 11: POLITICAL ROADKILL

1.   ickstr@hotmail.com, email message to WE Charity Public Relations, July 31, 2020, 2:01 p.m.

2.   billcollins22@mail.com, email message to WE Charity Public Relations, July 28, 2020, 10:46 p.m.

3.   Derrick Snowdy (@jdsnowdy), Twitter, July 28, 2020, Snowdy's account has since been shut down.

4.   Brian Lilley, "WE Flips for Real Estate."

5.   Quentin Mitchell (real estate broker for Property Link Africa), email message to Sylvia Stead at the *Globe and Mail*, August 21, 2020, and accompanying account of interaction with Winne Kamau. For the record, Stead disputed Mitchell's account and told WE Charity that Kamau had said she did not pose as a buyer when she arranged to see the property. Stead did not offer any explanation for why a *Globe* reporter would then have needed to be shown the property by a real estate agent.

6.   Jody Wilson-Raybould testified for approximately three and a half hours. Parliament of Canada, House of Commons, Standing Committee on Justice and Human Rights (JUST): Hearing before JUST, 42nd Parl., 1st sess., February 27, 2019, https://www.ourcommons.ca/DocumentViewer/en/42-1/JUST/meeting-135/evidence/.

7.   Parliament of Canada, House of Commons, Standing Committee on Finance (FINA): Hearing before FINA, 43rd Parl., 1st sess., July 28, 2020, https://www.ourcommons.ca/DocumentViewer/en/43-1/FINA/meeting-45/evidence.

8.   Parliament of Canada, Senate of Canada, Proceedings of the Special Senate Committee on the Charitable Sector, Issue No. 7, September 24, 2018, https://sencanada.ca/en/Content/Sen/Committee/421/CSSB/07ev-54228-e/.

9.   Parliament of Canada, House of Commons, Standing Committee on Finance (FINA): Hearing before FINA, 43rd Parl., 1st sess., July 28, 2020, https://www.ourcommons.ca/DocumentViewer/en/43-1/FINA/meeting-45/evidence/.

10.   Under the bylaws of WE Charity Foundation, WE Charity (as founding member) has the exclusive right to vote on any changes to the foundation's governing documents (articles and bylaws), as well as on the admission of any additional founding members and the removal of ordinary members. The founding member also has the sole right to appoint and remove a minority of the board of directors. All this was put in place so that WE Charity could ensure that WE Charity Foundation remains aligned with the overall charitable mission of WE.

11.   Judith Timson, "Too Polite or Too Rude? Summer's Dog Days Provide

a Uniquely Canadian Crisis," *Toronto Star*, July 30, 2020, https://www.thestar. com/life/opinion/2020/07/30/too-polite-or-too-rude-summers-dog-days-provide-a-uniquely-canadian-crisis.html.

12.   Lobbying rules state that the threshold after which lobbying represents a significant part of one's duties is 20 percent or more. Office of the Commissioner of Lobbying Canada, "A Significant Part of Duties ('The 20% Rule')," lobbycanada.gc.ca, accessed September 12, 2021, https://lobbycanada. gc.ca/en/rules/the-lobbying-act/advice-and-interpretation-lobbying-act/a-significant-part-of-duties-the-20-rule/.

13.   The Lobbying Act requires those who are paid by an organization to be formally registered as lobbyists on the Registry of Lobbyists. Once a person is registered, his or her interactions with government officials are tracked on the registry. The act and the registry create transparency so that Canadians are aware who the government is talking to and who is trying to influence our leaders. But the act does not require volunteers to be registered—something plainly stated on the front page of the Lobbying Commissioner's website: "The Act applies to individuals who are paid to lobby. People who lobby on a voluntary basis are not required to register."

14.   Mark Blumberg, "Which Charities Received the Most Money from the Federal Government in 2019?," *Canadian Charity Law* (blog), September 6, 2021, https://www.canadiancharitylaw.ca/blog/which-charities-received-the-most-money-from-the-federal-government-in-2019/.

15.   Jody Wilson-Raybould, Twitter, July 8, 2021, 9:30 a.m., https://twitter. com/Puglaas/status/1413128438592933898/.

16.   Gary Mason, "Campaign Hatred Is a Frightening Sign of Our COVID Times," *Globe and Mail*, August 31, 2021, https://www.theglobeandmail.com/opinion/article-campaign-hatred-is-a-frightening-sign-of-our-covid-times/.

17.   Parliament of Canada, House of Commons, Standing Committee on Finance (FINA): Hearing before FINA, 43rd Parl., 1st sess., July 30, 2020, https://www.ourcommons.ca/DocumentViewer/en/43-1/FINA/meeting-47/evidence.

18.   "PM Trudeau on COVID-19 Exposure App, WE Charity Controversy," CPAC, July 31, 2020, https://www.cpac.ca/episode?id=cfd310f3-39da-4265-b14c-f1209a6fe40b.

CHAPTER 12: CLOSING DOORS

1.   See, for example, Rachel Emmanuel, "WE Charity's Financial Problems Were Well-Known: Assessors," iPolitics, August 6, 2020, https://ipolitics. ca/2020/08/06/we-charitys-financial-problems-were-well-known-assessors/; Kathleen Harris, "Government 'Dropped the Ball' on WE Charity Deal,

Qualtrough Says," CBC News, August 11, 2020, https://www.cbc.ca/news/politics/liberal-we-charity-student-program-chagger-qualtrough-1.5681995; Rachel Aiello, "Resignation Calls Revived Over WE Affair, as PM Skips Special House Sitting," CTV News, August 12, 2020, https://www.ctvnews.ca/politics/resignation-calls-revived-over-we-affair-as-pm-skips-special-house-sitting-1.5060755; James Anthony, "Trudeau Denies CFL $30 Million Loan, but Could Afford $900 Million Gift to WE Charity," *Post Millennial*, August 17, 2020, https://thepostmillennial.com/trudeau-denies-cfl-30-million-loan-but-could-afford-900-million-gift-to-we-charity; Teresa Wright, "WE Charity Laying Off Dozens in Canada and U.K., Looks to Sell Real Estate," Global News, August 13, 2020, https://globalnews.ca/news/7271884/we-charity-layoffs-real-estate/; Joan Bryden and Teresa Wright, "WE Charity Registers as Lobbyist, Lays Off Staff, Looking to Sell Real Estate," *Toronto Star*, August 13, 2020, https://www.thestar.com/news/canada/2020/08/13/we-charity-laying-off-staff-looking-to-sell-real-estate-in-toronto.html.

2.   Brian Lilley, "Kielburgers and WE Fall to Earth After Getting Burned by Trudeau," *Toronto Sun*, August 13, 2020, https://torontosun.com/opinion/columnists/lilley-kielburgers-and-we-fall-to-earth-after-getting-burned-by-trudeau.

3.   David Moscrop, "Opinion: Misplaced Lack of Trust in the State Is at the Heart of Canada's WE Charity Scandal," *Washington Post*, August 6, 2020, https://www.washingtonpost.com/opinions/2020/08/06/misplaced-lack-trust-state-is-heart-canadas-we-charity-scandal/.

4.   Andrew Scheer, Twitter, August 17, 2020, 8:01 p.m., https://twitter.com/AndrewScheer/status/1295511165615972352.

5.   Jagmeet Singh, Twitter, August 17, 2020, 7:55 p.m., https://twitter.com/theJagmeetSingh/status/1295509633751224322.

6.   Justin Trudeau, "Remarks on Changes to the Ministry and an Upcoming Speech from the Throne," (Ottawa, August 18, 2020), https://pm.gc.ca/en/videos/2020/08/18/remarks-changes-ministry-and-upcoming-speech-throne.

7.   Keg Spirit Foundation, "The Keg Spirit Foundation Takes a Pause Along with We Charity, But Remains Committed to Evaluating WE Programs Going Forward," media statement, July 29, 2020.

8.   Tara Deschamps, "Sponsors, WE Charity 'Mutually' Agreed to Part Ways, According to WE," CTV News, July 28, 2020, https://www.ctvnews.ca/business/sponsors-we-charity-mutually-agreed-to-part-ways-according-to-we-1.5041972.

9.   Paul Waldie, "Virgin Suspends WE Charity Donations, Telus Drops Partnership, as Sponsors Review Ties," *Globe and Mail*, July 23, 2020, https://www.theglobeandmail.com/politics/article-major-sponsors-review-ties-to-we-charity-telus-drops-multiyear/.

10.   Bryann Aguilar, "Ontario Government Cuts Ties with WE Charity Amid Controversy," CTV News, July 31, 2020, https://toronto.ctvnews.ca/ontario-government-cuts-ties-with-we-charity-amid-controversy-1.5047733.

11.   Brian Lilley, "Ontario Government Bows Out of Relationship with WE," *Toronto Sun*, July 31, 2020, https://torontosun.com/opinion/columnists/lilley-ontario-government-bows-out-of-relationship-with-we/.

12.   Staff, "Province Backing Away from $260K Contract with WE Charity," CBC News, August 5, 2020, https://www.cbc.ca/news/canada/saskatoon/province-backing-away-from-contract-with-we-charity-1.5674850.

13.   SickKids Hospital, "SickKids Releases New Research on How COVID-19 Pandemic Has Impacted Child and Youth Mental, Physical Health," July 8, 2021, https://www.sickkids.ca/en/news/archive/2021/research-covid-19-pandemic-impact-child-youth-mental-physical-health/. See also Statistics Canada, "Survey on COVID-19 and Mental Health, September to December 2020," March 18, 2021, https://www150.statcan.gc.ca/n1/daily-quotidien/210318/dq210318a-eng.htm.

14.   "WE Speaks: With Martin Luther King III," January 23, 2018, https://www.facebook.com/WEmovement/videos/we-speaks-with-martin-luther-king-iii/1804857026251456/.

15.   Lisa LaFlamme, "Interview with Craig and Marc Kielburger," CTV News, September 9, 2020, https://www.youtube.com/watch?app=desktop&v=m_p5PRLy2os&ab_channel=CTVNews.

16.   CTV News, September 9, 2020, https://www.youtube.com/watch?v=ktE1Srd-nHs.

17.   Pierre Poilievre, Twitter, September 10, 2020, 9:57 a.m., https://twitter.com/PierrePoilievre/status/1304056303002808321.

18.   Douglas Quan, "Keep Watching the Money as WE Charity Shuts Its Canadian Operations, Observers Say," *Toronto Star*, September 10, 2020, https://www.thestar.com/news/canada/2020/09/10/keep-watching-the-money-as-we-charity-shuts-its-canadian-operations-observers-say.html.

CHAPTER 13: MANUFACTURED OUTRAGE

1.   Julie Payette, "A Stronger and More Resilient Canada" (Speech from the Throne, Ottawa, September 23, 2020), https://www.canada.ca/en/privy-council/campaigns/speech-throne/2020/speech-from-the-throne.html.

2.   Lee Berthiaume, Jim Bronskill, and Joan Bryden, "Opposition Parties Decry Redacted WE Documents, Allege Continuing Coverup," *Toronto Star*, August 19, 2020, https://www.thestar.com/business/2020/08/19/opposition-parties-decry-black-ink-in-we-documents-allege-continuing-coverup.html.

3.   Amanda Coletta, "Trudeau's Suspension of Parliament Amid Ethics Controversy Fuels Cries of 'Coverup,'" *Washington Post,* August 19, 2020, www.washingtonpost.com/world/the_americas/trudeaus-suspension-of-parliament-amid-ethics-controversy-fuels-cries-of-coverup/2020/08/19/4d6708f6-e1a6-11ea-82d8-5e55d47e90ca_story.html.

4.   "Canada's Trudeau Survives Latest Confidence Vote," BBC News, October 21, 2020, www.bbc.com/news/world-us-canada-54635712.

5.   Matthew A. Torigian, *Independent Review (Final Report): WE Charity Canada and Canada Student Service Grant* (October 2020), https://staticsb.we.org/f/52095/x/ee39895aa0/mt_independent-review-we-charity-canada-cssg-final-report.pdf?_ga=2.251215750.1035348662.1604022514-996026327.1592157803.

6.   Matthew Torigian, "Forensic Analysis Exonerates WE Charity and the Canadian Government," *Toronto Star,* November 3, 2020, www.thestar.com/opinion/contributors/2020/11/03/forensic-analysis-exonerates-we-charity-and-the-canadian-government.html.

7.   Parliament of Canada, House of Commons, Standing Committee on Access to Information, Privacy and Ethics (ETHI): Hearing before ETHI, 43rd Parl., 2nd sess., December 7, 2020, https://www.ourcommons.ca/DocumentViewer/en/43-2/ETHI/meeting-15/evidence.

8.   Lee Berthiaume, "Conservatives Ask Speaking Agency to Release Records of WE Charity Payments to Trudeau Family," *Globe and Mail*, August 27, 2020, https://www.theglobeandmail.com/politics/article-conservatives-ask-speaking-agency-to-release-records-on-we-charitys/.

9.   Michael Barrett, Twitter, August 27, 2020, 10:30 a.m., https://twitter.com/MikeBarrettON/status/1298991302713815040.

10.   Candice Bergen, "Producing these documents sooner rather than later would set Speakers' Spotlight apart from other organizations caught up in Trudeau's web of scandal and corruption. I hope they understand the important role they can play in uncovering the truth. Please call them and encourage them to release these documents: 1-800-[redacted]," Facebook, August 27, 2020, https://www.facebook.com/CandiceBergenMp/.

11.   Michael Barrett, Twitter: "breaking at Ethics Committee we learn that legally ordered WE documents have been destroyed," November 9, 2020, 2:56 p.m., https://twitter.com/MikeBarrettON/status/1325890007022891010/.

12.   Marieke Walsh, "Speakers' Agency Purged Some Records of Trudeau Family Events Related to WE Charity Controversy," *Globe and Mail*, November 10, 2020, https://www.theglobeandmail.com/politics/article-speakers-agency-purged-some-records-of-trudeau-family-events-related/.

13.   Megan Savard, email message to Miriam Burke and ETHI@parl.gc.ca,

November 30, 2020.

14.   Parliament of Canada, House of Commons, Standing Committee on Access to Information, Privacy and Ethics (ETHI): Hearing before ETHI, 43rd Parl., 2nd sess., February 19, 2021, https://www.ourcommons.ca/DocumentViewer/en/43-2/ETHI/meeting-20/evidence/.

15.   Parliament of Canada, House of Commons, Standing Committee on Access to Information, Privacy and Ethics (ETHI): Hearing before ETHI, 43rd Parl., 2nd sess., March 22, 2021, https://www.ourcommons.ca/DocumentViewer/en/43-2/ETHI/meeting-25/evidence.

16.   Kate Bahen, Twitter, February 21, 2021, 10:23 a.m., https://twitter.com/kate_bahen/status/1363509558866546688/.

17.   A witness appearing before the committee in person could expect to face fifteen to twenty questions or thereabouts.

18.   Danielle Paradis, "WE CFO Risks Contempt with Unanswered Questions," Canadaland, March 22, 2021, https://www.canadaland.com/we-cfo-risks-contempt-with-unanswered-questions/.

19.   Mario Dion, *Angus Report I* (Ottawa: Office of the Conflict of Interest and Ethics Commissioner, 2018), https://ciec-ccie.parl.gc.ca/en/publications/Documents/InvestigationReports/Angus%20Report%20I.pdf and *Angus Report II* (Ottawa: Office of the Conflict of Interest and Ethics Commissioner, 2018), https://ciec-ccie.parl.gc.ca/en/publications/Documents/InvestigationReports/Angus%20Report%20II.pdf.

20.   Megan Savard, Twitter, March 24, 2021, 5:12 p.m., https://twitter.com/megan__savard/status/1374831474873139201/.

21.   Parliament of Canada, House of Commons, Standing Committee on Access to Information, Privacy and Ethics (ETHI): Hearing before ETHI, 43rd Parl., 2nd sess., March 29, 2021, https://www.ourcommons.ca/DocumentViewer/en/43-2/ETHI/meeting-26/evidence/.

22.   Miriam Burke, email message to William C. McDowell, February 15, 2020.

23.   In a since-deleted tweet, Angus wrote, "Reed Cowan is a major fundraiser and advisory board member for WE Charity. His allegations of donor misrepresentation are shocking. He is calling for an IRS and @RCMP investigation of WE. Today I wrote to CRA and RCMP to support an investigation." Twitter, February 28, 2021. See also Kate McKenna and Harvey Cashore, "MP Joins Former Donor in Calling for RCMP Investigation into WE Charity Following Testimony," CBC News, February 28, 2021, https://www.cbc.ca/news/canada/rcmp-investigation-we-charity-1.5931253/.

24.   Guy Giorno, interview with Vassy Kapelos, *Power & Politics,* CBC News, March 8, 2021.

25.   Joan Bryden, "Kielburger Brothers Say They Won't Testify Before 'Partisan' Commons Committee," CBC News, March 3, 2021, https://www.cbc.ca/news/politics/kielburger-brothers-committee-we-charity-1.5935533.

26.   Michael Barrett, Twitter, March 3, 4:32 p.m., https://twitter.com/mikebarretton/status/1367226316085411840?lang=en.

27.   Pierre Poilievre, Twitter, March 4, 2021, 6:03 p.m., https://twitter.com/pierrepoilievre/status/1367611763076845575.

28.   The ETHI committee had not summoned Craig and Marc at that point (the committee voted on March 8, 2021, to issue a summons), so there was in fact no obligation to enforce. Furthermore, the authority to take people into custody is exercised by a vote of entire 338-member House of Commons. The parliamentary power to confine someone has not been used for 108 years and, according to some legal experts, is likely no longer consistent with the Canadian Charter of Rights and Freedoms.

29.   Tyler Dawson, "Here's What Can Happen If the Kielburger Brothers Refuse to Testify Before Parliament," *National Post*, March 5, 2021, https://nationalpost.com/news/politics/heres-what-can-happen-if-the-kielburger-brothers-refuse-to-testify-before-parliament.

30.   Rex Murphy, "The Kielburgers Have Conditions for Parliament? Who Do They Think They Are?" *National Post,* March 12, 2021, https://nationalpost.com/opinion/rex-murphy-the-kielburgers-have-conditions-for-parliament-who-the-hell-do-they-think-they-are.

31.   Brian Lilley, "Investigations into WE Police and Tax Officials Is Exactly What Is Needed," *Toronto Sun*, March 6, 2021, https://torontosun.com/opinion/columnists/lilley-investigations-into-we-police-and-tax-officials-is-exactly-what-is-needed.

32.   Parliament of Canada, House of Commons, Standing Committee on Access to Information, Privacy and Ethics (ETHI): Hearing before ETHI, 43rd Parl., 2nd sess., March 15, 2021, https://www.ourcommons.ca/DocumentViewer/en/43-2/ETHI/meeting-24/evidence/.

33.   Parliament of Canada, House of Commons, Standing Committee on Access to Information, Privacy and Ethics (ETHI): Hearing before ETHI, 43rd Parl., 2nd sess., March 15, 2021, https://www.ourcommons.ca/DocumentViewer/en/43-2/ETHI/meeting-24/minutes.

34.   Matt Gurney, "Kielburgers Torpedo Relationship with Liberals—'We Never Prorogued Parliament,'" *National Post*, March 15, 2021, nationalpost.com/opinion/matt-gurney-evasive-kielburgers-torpedo-relationship-with-liberals-we-never-prorogued-parliament.

35.   Konrad Yakabuski, "The Kielburgers Need to Grow Up," *Globe and Mail*, March 17, 2021, www.theglobeandmail.com/opinion/article-the-kielburgers-need-to-grow-up/.

36. Amy MacPherson, Twitter: "20/26 #CAF #DND #CDNpoli In the case of Robert Fife, he admitted to a career filled with 'torquing' his stories too much It was an incredible confession that was later scrubbed from re-broadcast of Power n Politics when someone realized the implications. This is original copy," June 26, 2021, twitter.com/MsAmyMacPherson/status/1408806511321694216/.

37. Members of the ETHI committee eventually issued three competing reports: a majority report from the opposition, an addendum paper from the Conservative members, and a dissenting report from the Liberals. The majority report included some entirely sensible recommendations for strengthening government procurement processes to prevent potential conflicts of interest. But it also put forward several highly politicized recommendations, including one that the government make no contracts with shell companies—a continued attempt to mischaracterize WE Charity Foundation.

38. Dion, *Trudeau III*, p. 36.

39. Dion, *Trudeau III*, p. 2.

40. Dion, *Morneau II*, p. 43.

41. Manitoba school superintendent, email message to Dana Rudy, deputy minister of education, May 17, 2021.

42. "NDP Ethics Critic Charlie Angus Cries Foul Over Findings in WE Charity Report," Canadian Press, YouTube video, May 14, 2021, https://www.youtube.com/watch?v=fU9WbiTpW8o.

43. Bill Curry and Marieke Walsh, "Trudeau in Apparent Conflict on WE but Not Formal Ethics Breach, Commissioner Finds, Moreau's Action Declared a Clear Violation," *Globe and Mail*, May 13, 2021, https://www.theglobeandmail.com/politics/article-trudeau-cleared-in-we-charity-controversy-but-ethics-commissioner/.

CHAPTER 14: AN INTERNATIONAL AFFAIR

1. Compol Associates Ltd. (Compol), which has expertise in assisting leading foreign entities, multinationals, governments, and NGOs in carrying out sensitive and complex investigations, was retained by WE Charity in 2017 to look into suspected misconduct and fraudulent activities by Peter Ruhiu. Compol's year-long inquiry was supported by local investigators, forensic experts, and legal advisers. Compol found that Ruhiu did misappropriate funds, and all the money was eventually recovered. "Independent analysis confirmed that despite the temporary misuse of funds, there were no physical impacts or undue delays related to the projects Mr. Ruhiu was responsible for overseeing. All projects formerly under his purview were inspected by certified engineers to verify they were sound and constructed in accordance

with relevant requirements." Ellis de Bruijn, CEO Compol, letter, September 29, 2021.

2.   A police file (OB. No. 7/13/11/2017) indicates that when Marc Kielburger made the original complaint to police at the Girigi police station in 2017, he was advised by Constable Kelli to "continue to collect evidence to allow for police action."

3.   On September 7, 2018, Ruhiu was charged with giving false information to a person employed in the public service contrary to section 129(b) of the penal code (police charge sheet OB. No. 17/06/07/2018). He was ordered to pay a fine and was sentenced to a one-year prison term; see also *Republic of Kenya v. Ruhiu Mbugua Peter*, in the Chief Magistrates Court at Kiambu before Hon. P. Gichohi, March 4, 2021.

4.   Peter Ruhiu, letter, October 26, 2018. He was also separately charged with theft, although all funds were recovered (police charge sheet OB. No. 34/06/08/2018).

5.   Ruhiu's wife and children are still living safely in Canada today.

6.   The Kenyan police charge sheet (Case No. CR 161/18/2020) states that Santai Punyua Kimakeke was charged with demanding property by written threats contrary to section 299 of the penal code, forgery contrary to section 345 as read with section 349 of the penal code, and uttering a false document contrary to section 353 of the penal code.

7.   Santai Kimakeke, sworn statement witnessed by Kenyan solicitor Francis Munyororo, July 6, 2020.

8.   Jesse Brown, "Crime and Fraud at WE Charity in Kenya," Canadaland, July 3, 2020, www.canadaland.com/crime-and-fraud-at-we-charity-in-kenya/. See also Jesse Brown, "WE Charity: Lawyers, Guns and Money," *Canadaland* (podcast), July 6, 2020, https://www.canadaland.com/podcast/332-we-charity-lawyers-guns-and-money/.

9.   Santai Kimakeke, Twitter, October 17, 2020: "Disappointed that @ JesseBrown @Canadaland continues to publish inaccurate information about WE Charity Kenya. I contacted him BEFORE his initial July 6th report sharing that I had provided incorrect information to him." See also Santai Kimakeke, sworn statement witnessed by Kenyan solicitor Francis Munyororo, October 7, 2020.

10.   Jesse Brown, "'Regulatory Mischief': WE Charity in Kenya," Canadaland, October 16, 2020, https://www.canadaland.com/we-charity-in-kenya/. See also Jesse Brown, "WE Charity: In Desperation There Is Opportunity," *Canadaland* (podcast), October 19, 2020, www.canadaland.com/podcast/344-we-charity-in-desperation-there-is-opportunity/. The false allegations were repeated again in a Canadaland podcast series titled *The White Saviours*. The fact that Kimakeke had recanted his allegations and tried

to contact Canadaland to clear the air was noted in fine print on the podcast webpage, under the heading "Official Responses from the WE Organization."

11.   Brown, "Regulatory Mischief."

12.   Cooperation Canada, "Statement on Allegations Concerning WE Charity Operations in Kenya," Cooperation Canada website, October 19, 2020, https://cooperation.ca/we-charity-kenya/.

13.   Geoffrey York, "WE Charity Affiliate Under Scrutiny in Kenya Over 'Regulatory and Governance' Issues," *Globe and Mail*, October 16, 2020, https://www.theglobeandmail.com/world/article-we-charity-affiliate-under-scrutiny-in-kenya-over-regulatory-and/.

14.   Nicolas Moyer, email message to Scott Baker, October 28, 2020.

15.   Geoffrey York, "Charity Coalition Says It Has Concerns About Secrecy at WE Charity," *Globe and Mail*, October 19, 2020, https://www.theglobeandmail.com/world/article-canadian-charity-coalition-says-it-has-concerns-about-secrecy-at-we/.

16.   Nicolas Moyer, email message to Scott Baker, October 28, 2020.

17.   Rosen & Associates Limited, *Report for WE Charity—Kenyan Entities*, December 17, 2020.

18.   Matthew Torigian, *Independent Review: WE Charity Canada and Free the Children Kenya Response to Allegations of Staff Malfeasance*, October 2020.

19.   In 2018, Mission Measurement confirmed this: "The travel operations required to fulfill trip experiences create three hundred and fifty jobs annually in partner communities." Mission Measurement also found that donor visits by doctors and nurses created mutual learning opportunities between Western and Kenyan healthcare workers. Global travel has been recognized by the United Nations as one of the keys to creating empowerment in developing countries. Mission Measurement, *ME to WE Social Enterprises, Inc. Impact Report: A Summary of Evaluation Results of ME to WE's Social Enterprise Model*, November 2018.

20.   ME to WE calculated this figure based on women who were working and earning a minimum wage of 296 KSh (approximately CAD$3.33) per day in 2015. Women's income varied, but based on data maintained by WE from October 2015, ME to WE artisans were earning an average of 969.855 KSh (CAD$10.92) per day.

21.   Natalie Obiko Pearson, email message to WE Charity Public Relations, August 12, 2020.

22.   WE Charity Public Relations, email message to Natalie Obiko Pearson, August 14, 2020.

23.   Natalie Obiko Pearson, email message to WE Charity Public Relations, September 21, 2020.

24.   Natalie Obiko Pearson, email message to WE Charity Public Relations, December 11, 2020.

25.   Natalie Obiko Pearson, Danielle Bochove, and David Herbling, "How a Charity Superstar Innovated Its Way to Political Scandal," *Bloomberg Businessweek,* December 29, 2020, https://www.bloomberg.com/news/features/2020-12-29/oprah-trudeau-and-covid-we-charity-innovated-its-way-to-political-scandal.

26.   Chip Wilson, "The Attack on WE Led to an Immense Loss," *Maclean's,* November 18, 2020, https://www.macleans.ca/opinion/the-attack-on-we-led-to-an-immense-loss/.

27.   Geoffrey Kikenye Wambua, statement regarding Bloomberg article, January 12, 2021.

28.   WE Charity later learned that David Herbling had in recent years been named in two defamation lawsuits. In one, a woman he accused of corruption was awarded the equivalent of approximately US$18,000 in damages. See Mary M'Mukindia v. National Media Group Limited and David Herbling, High Court of Kenya at Nairobi (civil case no. 5 of 2016), and also Peter Nyabuti v. Nation Media Group and David Herbling, High Court of Kenya at Nairobi (civil case no. 431 of 2015).

29.   See Joseph Kroetsch, counsel for WE Charity, letter to Katherine Kriegman Graham, Esq., attorney for Bloomberg, L.P., January 18, 2021. Graham responded in an email, dated March 4, 2021, in which she stated that "we are confident that our reporter acted entirely appropriately," and suggested that differing stories told to WE or others by those who had submitted written statements may be a product of coercion or intimidation.

30.   "Reed, I will also ask our country director to create a plaque at one school and stone base with carving in the other school compound you helped to support. I would like to offer this in honour of your son. Reed, you do not need to pay for the plaques. This is a small token of our appreciation." Dalal Al-Waheidi, email message to Reed Cowan, December 4, 2006. Cowan responded, "Thank you for the picture of the school sign and the GENEROUS GENEROUS OFFERING of the sign and the stone base and carving. You have made my night." Reed Cowan, email message to Dalal Al-Waheidi, December 4, 2006.

31.   Joseph M. Kamau, former director of Kenya's Directorate of Criminal Investigations (CID), conducted an independent assessment of the allegations regarding issues with donor plaques. "I conclude that the alleged issues with the two donor plaques referenced in the Bloomberg News articles, based on the information I have collected in my review, were isolated incidents and is not endemic of a larger issue, but rather an isolated error." Joseph M. Kamau, *Report from Joseph M. Kamau, former director of Kenya's Directorate of Criminal Investigations (CID), Re: Free The Children Kenya,* June 25, 2021.

32. Parliament of Canada, House of Commons, Standing Committee on Access to Information, Privacy and Ethics (ETHI): Hearing before ETHI, 43rd Parl., 2nd sess., February 26, 2021, https://www.ourcommons.ca/DocumentViewer/en/43-2/ETHI/meeting-22/evidence.

33. All posts by Reed Cowan related to WE Charity have since been deleted.

34. Christopher Nardi, "'Shocked, Astonished, Horrified': WE's Alleged Dubious Fundraising Methods Could Have Negative Impact on Other Charities," *National Post,* March 1, 2021, https://nationalpost.com/news/canada/shocked-astonished-horrified-wes-dubious-fundraising-methods-could-have-negative-impact-on-other-charities.

35. Danielle Bochove and Natalie Obiko Pearson, "Donor Asks IRS to Open Fraud Investigation into WE Charity," Bloomberg, March 1, 2021, https://www.bloomberg.com/news/articles/2021-03-01/donor-asks-irs-to-open-fraud-investigation-into-we-charity.

36. Natalie Obiko Pearson, Danielle Bochove, and David Herbling, "WE Charity's Actions Leave a Trail of Enraged, Grieving Donors," BNN Bloomberg, March 5, 2021, https://www.bnnbloomberg.ca/we-charity-s-actions-leave-a-trail-of-enraged-grieving-donors-1.1572805.

37. Reed Cowan, email message to Robin Wiszowaty, March 4, 2021.

38. I. Scott Bogatz, letter to WE Charity, March 26, 2021.

39. Melissa Klein, email message to WE Charity public relations, March 26, 2021.

40. Joseph Kroetsch, counsel for WE Charity, letter to I. Scott Bogatz, attorney for Reed Cowan, April 1, 2021.

41. Erik Wemple, "Sinclair Anchor Demands $20 Million from Charity Over Fraud Allegations," *Washington Post*, April 2, 2021, https://www.washingtonpost.com/opinions/2021/04/02/sinclair-broadcast-group-reed-cowan-we-charity/.

42. Brianna Erickson, "Las Vegas News Anchor Demands $20M Amid Fraud Allegations," *Las Vegas Review-Journal*, April 7, 2021, https://www.reviewjournal.com/entertainment/tv/las-vegas-news-anchor-demands-20m-amid-fraud-allegations-2324392/.

43. Reed Cowan, email message to Marc Kielburger and Craig Kielburger, April 11, 2021.

CHAPTER 15: THE FIFTH ESTATE

1. Dan Kuzmicki, undated statement, provided to Harvey Cashore on January 7, 2021.

2. See, for example, Carol Moraa, letter to CBC, January 19, 2021. I later learned that WE Charity had also explained the circumstances surrounding the kitchen to Harvey Cashore at other points in time.

3. *The Fifth Estate*, "The Price WE Paid."

4. "Get the Facts: No, CBC/Radio-Canada's President Does Not Live in the United States," December 14, 2020, https://cbc.radio-canada.ca/en/media-centre/catherine-tait-does-not-live-in-the-united-states.

5. WE Charity, email message to James Cohen, September 23, 2015.

6. Scott Baker, email message to Harvey Cashore, January 18, 2021.

7. "Multiple Donors Raised Money for the Same WE Charity Project," *National*, March 7, 2021, https://www.cbc.ca/player/play/1870120003643.

8. Harvey Cashore biography, International Consortium of Investigative Journalists, accessed November 28, 2021, https://www.icij.org/journalists/harvey-cashore/.

9. Donna McFarlane, letter to the editor, *Wellington Advertiser*, March 24, 2021, https://www.wellingtonadvertiser.com/letter/what-about-balance/.

10. Donna McFarlane first wrote to Jack Nagler, the CBC ombudsman, on March 9, 2021. She followed up on April 22 and again on September 4.

11. Donna McFarlane, email message to Jack Nagler, September 4, 2021.

12. Barb Cowan, email message to Barbara Williams, CBC's executive vice-president of English services, September 29, 2021.

13. Barb Cowan is no relation to Reed Cowan.

14. Harvey Cashore, Kate McKenna, and Mark Kelley, "Multiple WE Charity Donors Raised Money for Same Borehole Well in Kenyan Village," CBC News, March 8, 2021, https://www.cbc.ca/news/canada/we-charity-free-the-children-donations-borehole-well-osenetoi-kenya-1.5938928.

15. Barb Cowan, Tom Cowan, Dr. Aubrey Kassirer, Koren Kassirer, Bob McFarlane, Donna McFarlane, Della McLaughlin, and Stuart McLaughlin, "An Open Letter from Our Donors in Response to CBC," posted to we.org (https://www.we.org/en-CA/our-donors-response-to-cbc-misrepresentation) and delivered by email from Donna McFarlane to Jack Nagler, March 9, 2021.

16. Stuart McLaughlin, email message to Mark Kelley, March 7, 2021.

17. Faith Bachlow, email message to Harvey Cashore, October 24, 2021.

18. Nardi, "'Shocked, Astonished, Horrified.'"

19. Pearson, Bochove, and Herbling, "Enraged, Grieving Donors."

20. Simon Houpt, "CBC's Plan to Boost the Fifth Estate Ratings with a Series About Paul Bernardo Divides Staff and Angers Activists," *Globe*

and Mail, July 17, 2019, https://www.theglobeandmail.com/arts/article-as-viewership-drops-cbcs-the-fifth-estate-eyes-a-series-about-paul/.

21.   Kevin Martin, "Former Calgary Medical Examiner Files $15-Million Defamation Lawsuit Against the CBC Over Two-Part Episode of The Fifth Estate," *Calgary Herald,* January 17, 2022, https://calgaryherald.com/news/local-news/former-calgary-medical-examiner-files-15-million-defamation-lawsuit-against-the-cbc-over-two-part-episode-of-the-fifth-estate.

22.   Tara Henley, "Speaking Freely: Why I Resigned from the Canadian Broadcasting Corporation," Substack, January 3, 2022, https://tarahenley.substack.com/p/speaking-freely.

23.   John Knapp, email message to Brodie Fenlon, CBC News editor-in-chief and executive director of daily news, September 8, 2021.

24.   *The Fifth Estate,* "The Price WE Paid."

25.   These recordings were shared with me with the consent of the original interviewees.

26.   Anonymized WE Charity donor, email message to Harvey Cashore, August 30, 2021.

27.   *The Fifth Estate,* season 47, episode 6, "Finding School No. 4: WE Charity's Donor Deception in Kenya," directed by Harvey Cashore, written by Mark Kelley, aired November 18, 2021, https://gem.cbc.ca/media/the-fifth-estate/s47e06.

28.   Matthew Pierce, email message to WE Charity corporate donor, September 20, 2021.

29.   Matthew Pierce, email message to Mark Quattrocchi, September 24, 2021.

30.   After his world tour was completed, Quattrocchi worked for WE Charity for a time as a motivational speaker.

31.   Mark Quattrocchi, email message to Matthew Pierce, September 26, 2021.

32.   "FAQs," PLAN International, accessed January 23, 2022, https://plancanada.ca/faqs.

33.   "Build a School," World Vision, accessed January 23, 2022, https://donate.worldvision.org/give/build-a-school.

34.   "Our Work in Kenya," WE Charity Foundation, accessed November 28, 2021, https://www.wecharity.org/kenya.

35.   "Irkaat," WE Charity Foundation, accessed November 28, 2021, https://www.wecharity.org/irkaat.

36.   Dalal Al-Waheidi, email message to Harvey Cashore, August 16, 2021.

37. Harvey Cashore, email message to Robin Wiszowaty, September 3, 2021.

38. Robin Wiszowaty, email message to Harvey Cashore, September 6, 2021.

39. "Governor Tunai's office kindly offered an invitation to us in August, and we are in the process of lining up a specific time for that interview as well." Harvey Cashore, email message to Robin Wiszowaty, September 3, 2021.

40. John Njiru, email message to Samuel Tunai, governor of Narok County, September 8, 2021.

41. Staff recording of Samuel Tunai's interview with Mark Kelley, September 10, 2021.

42. Robin Wiszowaty, email message to Harvey Cashore, September 9, 2021.

43. Harvey Cashore, email message to Robin Wiszowaty, September 9, 2021.

44. Harvey Cashore, email message to Robin Wiszowaty, September 10, 2021.

45. Carol Moraa, letter to Stephen Ochieng, sub county director of education, Narok West, September 10, 2021.

46. "Share of population fully vaccinated against the coronavirus (COVID-19) in Kenya as of September 29, 2021, by county," Statista, accessed October 1, 2021, www.statista.com/statistics/1252641/share-of-population-fully-vaccinated-against-covid-19-in-kenyan-counties/.

47. Office of the President of Kenya, Ministry of Interior and Co-Ordination of National Government, letter to the Canadian Broadcasting Corporation, September 13, 2021.

48. Samuel Tunai, letter to Brodie Fenlon, September 24, 2021.

49. Harvey Cashore, email message to Marc Kielburger, November 4, 2021.

50. The charity explained to the CBC that WE Education Inc. was renamed Global Impact Fund Inc. in 2017. Global Impact Fund was founded in 2003 as Kiel Projects Inc. and is personally owned by Craig and Marc Kielburger. It is unrelated to WE Charity, ME to WE, or any charitable or business activities of either entity. Global Impact Fund received revenues earned through the Kielburgers' consulting work, their compensation for serving on boards of directors, and their non-WE-related speaking engagements. This private entity paid for some expenses related to Craig Kielburger's wedding. WE Education Inc. is unrelated to WE Education for Children Ltd. in Kenya.

51. Marc Kielburger, email message to Harvey Cashore, November 9, 2021.

52. "Journalistic Standards and Practices," CBC News, accessed November 28, 2021, https://cbc.radio-canada.ca/en/vision/governance/journalistic-standards-and-practices.

53. Marc Kielburger, email message to Harvey Cashore, November 5, 2021.

54. Wandering Feet Photography (Rukshan de Silva), Facebook, January 21, 2014, https://www.facebook.com/wanderingfeetphotography/photos/.

55. "Creating Sustainable Change," we.org, *2017 Irkaat Report* for annual donor communication.

56. Angela Sterritt, "WE Charity Misled Donors About Building Schools in Kenya," *Front Burner* (podcast), November 24, 2021, https://www.cbc.ca/listen/cbc-podcasts/209-front-burner.

57. "The Fifth Estate Investigates WE Charity Schools," *Current*, November 18, 2021, https://www.cbc.ca/listen/live-radio/1-63-the-current/clip/15879195-the-fifth-estate-investigates-we-charity-schools.

58. "The photo list is not exhaustive but provides hundreds of sample programs." WE Charity Submission to the Standing Committee on Access to Information, Privacy and Ethics, April 16, 2021.

59. Carol Moraa, email message to Harvey Cashore and Mark Kelley, September 22, 2021.

60. Robin Wiszowaty, email message to Harvey Cashore and Mark Kelley, with Diana Swain in copy, November 18, 2021.

61. Marc Kielburger, email message to Harvey Cashore, with Diana Swain in copy, November 8, 2021.

62. Matthew Pierce, Harvey Cashore, Mark Kelley, and Kate McKenna, "WE Charity Misled Donors About Building Schools in Kenya, Records Show," CBC News, November 18, 2021, https://www.cbc.ca/news/canada/we-charity-misled-donors-records-show-1.6251985.

63. Ken Froese, *Re: Forensic Accounting Review—WE Charity (Canada and* USA*)*, November 17, 2021.

64. Diana Swain, email message to Robin Wiszowaty, November 18, 2021.

65. Undated letter to Brodie Fenlon, editor-in-chief and executive director of daily news at CBC, emailed by Dave Richardson, September 16, 2021.

66. Dave Richardson, email message to Brodie Fenlon, September 16, 2021.

67. Undated letter signed by fifty current and retired educators, emailed as an attachment to a message from Mark Burke to Brodie Fenlon, September 21, 2021.

68. Ross Hynes, email message to Catharine Tait, with Barbara Williams in copy, September 26, 2021.

69. Rosanne Leddy, email message to Harvey Cashore, with Diana Swain in copy, November 11, 2021.

70. Jon Levy, email message to Brodie Fenlon, September 23, 2021.

71.   *The Fifth Estate*, "Finding School No. 4."

72.   Brodie Fenlon, "What Happened Behind the Scenes of Our WE Charity Investigation," CBC News, November 20, 2021, https://www.cbc.ca/news/editorsblog/editors-blog-we-charity-investigation-behind-the-scenes-1.6256936.

73.   WE Charity and KGO Television, Inc. signed a settlement agreement in December 2021.

EPILOGUE: THE ROAD AHEAD

1.   Glen McGregor, "Prime Minister's Mother Spoke at Event Hosted by Organization That Received Federal Funding for Jobs Program," CTV News, October 25, 2021, https://www.ctvnews.ca/politics/prime-minister-s-mother-spoke-at-event-hosted-by-organization-that-received-federal-funding-for-jobs-program-1.5637616/.

2.   "Our Story," Elevate, accessed December 7, 2021, https://elevate.ca/our-story/.

3.   "Elevate Launches Think 2030, a National Initiative to Advance Critical Issues of Equality, Sustainability and Well-being in Canada," Elevate, August 17, 2021, https://elevate.ca/2021/08/17/elevate-launches-think-2030-a-national-initiative-to-advance-critical-issues-of-equality-sustainability-well-being-in-canada/.

4.   Michael Barrett, Twitter, October 25, 2021, 9:06 p.m., https://twitter.com/MikeBarrettON/status/1452803746157801480/.

5.   The Canadian Press, "Ottawa Gives $5.8-million to Elevate for New Program Helping Job Seekers from Under-represented Communities," *Globe and Mail,* June 3, 2021, https://www.theglobeandmail.com/business/article-ottawa-gives-58-million-to-elevate-for-new-program-helping-job-seekers/.

6.   Roxanna Woloshyn, "This Is Canada's Most Expensive Election," CBC News, September 6, 2021, https://www.cbc.ca/news/politics/canada-election-expensive-cost-1.6164267.

7.   Staff, "The Winners of the *Maclean's* Parliamentarians of the Year Awards," *Maclean's,* January 12, h2021, https://www.macleans.ca/politics/ottawa/the-winners-of-the-macleans-parliamentarians-of-the-year-awards/.

8.   "*The Globe*'s initial analysis focused on summarizing Canada-wide revenue, property and net assets. But as the analysis became more detailed, it became clear we needed the help of experts in charity finance. We turned to Charity Intelligence Canada, a charity that provides analysis and ratings on the finances and transparency of the charitable sector. Charity Intelligence reanalyzed *The Globe*'s data to arrive at a picture of the Roman Catholic

Church's finances in Canada." Tom Cardoso and Tavia Grant, "How Much Canadian Wealth Does the Catholic Church Have? Inside *The Globe* Investigation," *Globe and Mail*, August 7, 2021, https://www.theglobeandmail.com/canada/article-catholic-church-canadian-assets-methodology/.

9.   "Canadaland's 2020 Transparency Report," Canadaland, July 15, 2021, https://www.canadaland.com/2020-transparency-report/.

10.   Staff, "The Influentials 2020," *Toronto Life*, November 18, 2020, https://torontolife.com/city/the-50-most-influential-torontonians-of-2020/.

11.   Gabrielle Drolet, "The Five Best Canadian Podcasts from 2021 Were Binge-Worthy True Stories of Greed, Crime and Corruption," Globe and Mail, December 14, 2021, https://www.theglobeandmail.com/arts/article-the-five-best-canadian-podcasts-from-2021-were-binge-worthy-true/.

12.   "Announcing the Winners of the 2021 Christopher J. Welles Memorial Prize and WERT Prize for Outstanding Global Business Journalism by a Female Journalist," Columbia Journalism School, October 20, 2021, https://journalism.columbia.edu/announcing-winners-2021-christopher-j-welles-memorial-prize-and-wert-prize-outstanding-global.

13.   "Finalists Announced for 2020 National Newspaper Awards," Newswire, March 18, 2021, https://www.newswire.ca/news-releases/finalists-announced-for-2020-national-newspaper-awards-811746916.html.

14.   On September 16, 2020, WE Charity's directors passed a motion appointing a special board advisory committee to support and guide the management team throughout the process of selling WE's charitable real estate in Canada. The board selected Colliers International to act as WE Charity's realtors. The charity also engaged global real estate firm JLL to perform an independent valuation and assessment of the properties. WE Charity received multiple bids for the WE GLC, and in August 2021, the building was sold to Generation Capital for $1.15 million higher than its assessed value. Generation Capital is an investment firm lead by Geoff Beatty, the former president and deputy chairman of the Woodbridge Company, a privately held investment holding firm for the Thomson family. The Thomsons are primarily known for the many newspapers they own. Marco Chown Oved, "Before Selling Properties for an Apparent Loss, WE Charity Shut Down Another Bidder Before He Could Offer a Higher Price," *Toronto Star*, February 11, 2022, https://www.thestar.com/news/investigations/2022/02/11/why-we-charitys-sale-of-downtown-toronto-property-left-one-bidder-baffled.html.

15.   Before the pandemic, WE Charity had committed to expanding its WE Villages program to Bomet County, which is adjacent to Narok County in Kenya. Twenty communities had been identified for partnership. Projects in two, Kabolwo and Lugumek, had started and will continue. But the rest of the work has now been shelved, and the remaining eighteen communities will

not get approximately 180 schoolrooms, a mobile health clinic, 18 boreholes, 36 water kiosks, 18 community farms, and a women's empowerment centre. The women's centre, which would have been similar to those built in Narok County, Ecuador, and India, would have delivered alternative income and financial literacy programs to female entrepreneurs. Robin Wiszowaty reminded me of what that loss meant in real terms: "[In Bomet] they are now losing the path of possibility that expands [from the women's centre] so that a woman knows her own potential and power for her family and community. And then Bomet will be missing all of the collateral effects from that. What happens to the balance of gender? The volume of the voice of the women? The example that gives to their daughters?"

16.   "WE Charity Sues the Canadian Broadcasting Corporation for Defamation in Lawsuit Citing Mountain of Evidence," Newswire, February 9, 2022, https://www.newswire.ca/news-releases/we-charity-sues-the-canadian-broadcasting-corporation-for-defamation-in-lawsuit-citing-mountain-of-evidence-840188570.html.

17.   "Craig Kielburger's Mom Launched a $3 Million Lawsuit Accusing Canadaland of Being 'Fake News,'" Press Progress, November 15, 2021, https://pressprogress.ca/craig-kielburgers-mom-launched-a-3-million-lawsuit-accusing-canadaland-of-being-fake-news/.

18.   At the end of 2021, educators in more than 130 countries had access to the charity's educational resources.

19.   "Little Actions Make a Big Difference" was created in partnership with Well Beings, a national service of WETA-TV, the flagship PBS station in Washington, DC. The program offers easy-to-use, science-based tools and actions to support social-emotional health. Based on the *WE Well-being Playbook*, the animated series was the winner of the 2021 W3 Gold Award for Social Content & Marketing: Health & Wellness and the Davey Silver Award for Online Health & Fitness Video, both presented by the Academy of Interactive and Visual Arts, https://wellbeings.org/series/little-actions-make-a-big-difference/.

INDEX

TAWFIQ S. RANGWALA was born and grew up in Toronto and earned degrees at McGill University and Osgoode Hall. Now based in New York City, he is a partner in the Litigation and Arbitration group at Milbank LLP, one of America's premier international law firms. He specializes in conducting sensitive internal investigations, defending white-collar criminal and regulatory proceedings, and litigating a wide range of commercial disputes. Rangwala also devotes a significant portion of his practice to pro bono matters addressing systemic discrimination, and he has been widely recognized for his work fighting racism and injustice in both criminal and civil cases. In 2021, he was named Pro Bono Lawyer of the Year by Chambers Diversity & Inclusion. Rangwala sits on the board of Legal Services NYC, a non-profit group providing legal aid to low-income New Yorkers, and was on the board of WE Charity until he stepped down in 2021 to write *What WE Lost*.